OXFORD WORLD'S CLASSICS

THE CANTERBURY TALES

GEOFFREY CHAUCER (*c*.1343–1400), the son of a well-to-do London wine-merchant with court connections, began his career as a page in the household of Elizabeth, Countess of Ulster, wife of Edward III's son Lionel, Duke of Clarence. As a squire serving in Edward III's army when the king invaded France in 1359, he was captured at the siege of Rheims, and subsequently ransomed. A few years later he married Philippa de Roet, a lady-in-waiting to Constance of Castile, the second wife of John of Gaunt, Duke of Lancaster. It was to commemorate John of Gaunt's first wife, Blanche, that Chaucer composed in 1368 *The Book of the Duchess*, the earliest work that can confidently be attributed to him. He served in various campaigns in France and Spain, and twice visited Italy as a negotiator on important diplomatic missions. By the age of 31 he had been appointed Controller of Customs and Subsidy of Wools, Skins, and Hides in the port of London, a very responsible post which he held for twelve years. During this period he found time to write such major and innovatory works as *The House of Fame*, *The Parliament of Fowls*, and *Troilus and Cressida*. In 1386 he became a Justice of the Peace and Knight of the Shire to represent Kent in Parliament. Soon afterwards his wife died, and he devoted the rest of his life to composing the *Canterbury Tales*, a project that was never completed. He died in 1400 and was buried in Westminster Abbey.

DAVID WRIGHT was Gregory Fellow in Poetry at the University of Leeds. Besides his collected poems, *To the Gods the Shades*, he has published an autobiography, *Deafness*, edited the poems of Hardy and Edward Thomas, and translated *Beowulf* into modern English prose. He died in 1994.

OXFORD WORLD'S CLASSICS

For over 100 years Oxford World's Classics have brought
readers closer to the world's great literature. Now with over 700
titles—from the 4,000-year-old myths of Mesopotamia to the
twentieth century's greatest novels—the series makes available
lesser-known as well as celebrated writing.

The pocket-sized hardbacks of the early years contained
introductions by Virginia Woolf, T. S. Eliot, Graham Greene,
and other literary figures which enriched the experience of reading.
Today the series is recognized for its fine scholarship and
reliability in texts that span world literature, drama and poetry,
religion, philosophy and politics. Each edition includes perceptive
commentary and essential background information to meet the
changing needs of readers.

OXFORD WORLD'S CLASSICS

═══

GEOFFREY CHAUCER

The Canterbury Tales

═══

A verse translation
with an Introduction and Notes by
DAVID WRIGHT

[handwritten notes:]

Contest of Skill
- most amusing & instructive (21)
  ↓   ↓
 carnal   spiritval
- meritocracy
- election of judge
  • every one votes

OXFORD
UNIVERSITY PRESS

28-30

OXFORD
UNIVERSITY PRESS

Great Clarendon Street, Oxford OX2 6DP

Oxford University Press is a department of the University of Oxford.
It furthers the University's objective of excellence in research, scholarship,
and education by publishing worldwide in

Oxford New York

Athens Auckland Bangkok Bogotá Buenos Aires Calcutta
Cape Town Chennai Dar es Salaam Delhi Florence Hong Kong Istanbul
Karachi Kuala Lumpur Madrid Melbourne Mexico City Mumbai
Nairobi Paris São Paulo Singapore Taipei Tokyo Toronto Warsaw

with associated companies in Berlin Ibadan

Published in the United States
by Oxford University Press Inc., New York

Translation, Introduction, Chronology and Notes
© David Wright 1985
Select Bibliography © Geoffrey Ivy 1985

The moral rights of the author have been asserted

Database right Oxford University Press (maker)

First published as a World's Classics paperback 1986
First published as an Oxford World's Classics paperback 1998
Reissued 2008

British Library Cataloguing in Publication Data

Data available

Library of Congress Cataloging in Publication Data

Data available

9780199535620

1

Printed in Great Britain by
Clays Ltd, St Ives plc

For
Will Sulkin: instigator
and
C. H. Sisson: grant translateur

CONTENTS

INTRODUCTION

There is nothing quite like Chaucer's *Canterbury Tales* in conception and execution. It is not just the range and variety of the poetry and of the tales themselves, or of their themes and subject-matter, but the realism of the portraits of the people who tell the stories, and the interplay between the tales and the characters of the tellers, that is completely original. In conceiving the idea of a pilgrimage to Canterbury in which the travellers amuse themselves by competing to tell the best story they know, Chaucer hit on a device by which he was able to hold up a mirror, not only to the England of his times, but the world we live in. As William Blake said,

The characters of Chaucer's pilgrims are the characters which compose all ages and nations: as one age falls, another rises, different to mortal sight, but to immortals only the same; for we see the same characters repeated again and again, in animals, in vegetables, minerals, and in men; nothing new occurs in identical existence; Accident ever varies, Substance can never change or decay. Of Chaucer's characters, as described in his Canterbury Tales, some of the names or titles are altered by time, but the characters themselves for ever remain unaltered, and consequently they are the physiognomies or lineaments of universal human life, beyond which Nature never steps. Names alter, things never alter. I have known multitudes of those who could have been monks in the age of monkery, who in this deistical age are deists. As Newton numbered the stars, and as Linneus numbered the plants, so Chaucer numbered the classes of men ... Every age is a Canterbury pilgrimage; we all pass on, each sustaining one or other of these characters.

Geoffrey Chaucer was born to an eventful age. He began life in the reign of Edward III, some time between 1340 and 1345, and died in 1400, a few weeks after Richard II was deposed and Henry IV crowned king. The Hundred Years War had broken out a few years before Chaucer's birth. The great naval victory of Sluys took place in his lifetime, as did the battles of Crécy and Poitiers, in which English bowmen destroyed the chivalry of France, and in so doing helped to end the feudal system (though here the deciding event was probably the Black Death of 1349, and a series of further plagues which ultimately reduced the population of England by as much as a third). It was an age of religious schism exacerbated by two rival and warring popes, one in Rome and another in Avignon; of Wyclif, the church reformer and, according to tradition, first translator of the Bible into English; an age, too, of social unrest and uprisings, culminating in the peasants' revolts in France and England, when Wat Tyler and his followers sacked London, murdered the Archbishop of Canterbury, and almost became masters of England. It was an age of transition (though every age is that) when chivalry was at its zenith—the Order of the Garter was founded in 1349—while at the same time the feudal structure was starting to crumble and the mercantile class (to which Chaucer belonged) beginning to flex its muscle. French, as the language of court and Parliament, was on its way out; in 1363 Parliament was first summoned in English, which by the time of Chaucer's birth was well on the road to domination.

Though Chaucer was born over two hundred years earlier, we know a good deal more for certain about his life than we do of Shakespeare's. But then Chaucer was a public man as well as a poet: an eminent civil servant, diplomat, administrator, Justice of the Peace, and Member of Parliament; his wife was closely connected with the court and his sister-in-law married to one of the most powerful members of the royal family. Shakespeare moved in less exalted circles, so naturally fewer documentary records of his affairs survive.

The first we hear of Chaucer is, as D. S. Brewer remarks, 'a characteristic combination of vagueness and sharp outline'. It is an inventory of clothes bought for him when he was a page in the household of Elizabeth, Countess of Ulster, the wife of Edward III's son Lionel, Duke of Clarence, and the date is 4 April 1357. She paid out seven shillings—about £100 today—for a pair of shoes, a jacket, and a pair of black-and-red breeches. That Christmas she made him a further gift of clothing at Hatfield in Yorkshire, where the boy Chaucer would have met his coeval, Edward III's fourth son, John of Gaunt; and most probably his own future wife, Philippa de Roet, then in the service of the countess.

Chaucer's father was John Chaucer, a well-to-do vintner or

wholesale wine-merchant with a house in Thames Street, at that time one of the wealthiest districts in London. The family came from Ipswich and had been in the wine trade for a generation or two. John Chaucer's wife was Agnes de Copton, a rich heiress related by a former marriage to the Baron of the Exchequer and Keeper of the King's Purse. They were obviously able to afford to give their son a good education. Chaucer may have learned his ABC in an infant's school of the kind described in the *Prioress's Tale*, and gone on to St Paul's cathedral school. He would have learned Latin with the aid of a 'Cato'—an anthology of proverbs and adages supposedly collected by Dionysius Cato: Chaucer often refers to this book in *The Canterbury Tales*. Later he would have gone on to study Ovid's *Metamorphoses*, a poem which influenced him all his life. Much of the teaching would have been in French, though before he died English was to become the medium of instruction in schools. There is a possibility that he may have studied law at the Inner Temple some time between 1360 and 1366 since, according to Thomas Speght's 1598 edition of Chaucer, a certain Master Buckley saw in the records of the Inner Temple (now lost) that 'Geffrye Chaucer was fined two shillings for beatinge a Franciscan Fryer in fletestreate'. In view of what is said about friars in *The Canterbury Tales*, the incident seems not unlikely.[1]

All that is probability: but what is certainly known is that Chaucer went to France with Edward III's invading army in November 1359, and was captured by the French during the siege of Rheims. On 1 March 1360 he was ransomed by the Keeper of the King's Wardrobe for £16—about £5000 nowadays —which was a little less than the ransom paid out for Sir Robert de Clynton's war-horse. Soon afterwards he was employed as a messenger to take letters from Calais to England, and that is the last we hear of him for another six years. It has been supposed that he may have gone with Lionel, Duke of Clarence to Ireland when the latter became viceroy, but it is more probable that he

---

[1] Chaucer was again in trouble in 1380, when one Cecily Chaumpaigne released him from every sort of action 'tam de raptu meo'. 'Raptu' means rape or abduction. Nothing more is known about the case, but the word was probably used in the latter meaning. Chaucer's own father had been abducted when a boy by his aunt, in an attempt to force him to marry her daughter, and so gain control of certain family property in Ipswich that he had inherited.

was in service with the king. By 1366 he was married. In that year a certain Philippa Chaucer was given an annuity of 10 marks (about £400) for past and future services by Queen Philippa, whose lady-in-waiting she had become. She was the daughter of Sir Paon de Roet, one of the Flemish knights who had come over in the train of Philippa of Hainault when she married Edward III. Philippa Chaucer made her own career, and seems to have become a person of some consequence. After the death of the queen in 1368, she attended Constance of Castile, the second wife of John of Gaunt, Duke of Lancaster. Philippa's sister, Katharine Swynford, was the governess or duenna of Constance's two daughters, and later became the mistress, and on Constance's death the wife, of John of Gaunt. Nothing is known of Chaucer's relations with his wife, but they were probably much happier than the digs at marriage in the *Merchant's Tale* and the *Wife of Bath's Prologue* seem to imply. In the fourteenth century the institution of marriage was an accepted Aunt Sally: the domineering wife was a stock joke, like the mother-in-law joke of the Victorian music-halls.

Meanwhile Chaucer was advancing his public career. Early in 1368 he went to Spain with the Black Prince, whose victory at Najaro put Pedro the Cruel on the throne of Castile.[2] In the same year he became an Esquire of the King's Household. Apart from personal service, the duties of a squire could include going abroad on diplomatic errands, and that is how Chaucer was often employed during the next ten years. His most important journeys were those to Italy in 1372 and 1378. On the first of them he was one of the three commissioners sent to the Duke of Genoa to arrange the choice of an English port where Genoese merchants could set up their headquarters. He visited Florence, then a great place for books, where he must certainly have acquired Dante's *Divina Commedia*. His second trip, when he gave his friend the poet John Gower power of attorney to act in his absence, was with Sir Edward de Berkely to negotiate 'for certain affairs touching the expedition of the King's war' with Bernabo Visconti, Duke of Milan,[3] and his son-in-law, the great condottiere soldier of

[2] Pedro was later assassinated by his brother, and Chaucer made him the subject of one of the 'tragedies' in the *Monk's Tale*.

[3] He was murdered in 1385 and his fate is another of the Monk's 'tragedies'. See 'Of Bernardo of Lombardy' in the *Monk's Tale*.

fortune, Sir John Hawkwood. Visconti was a tyrant but a close friend of Petrarch, who was godfather to one of his sons. On this visit Chaucer became acquainted with the work of Boccaccio, notably his *Filostrato* and *Teseide*, which latter became the basis of the *Knight's Tale*. However, Chaucer seems never to have heard Boccaccio's name, and probably found his works in unsigned manuscripts.

In June 1374 Chaucer was appointed to the responsible and onerous post of Controller of the Customs of Wools, Skins, and Hides in the port of London. The wool trade was the foundation of the country's wealth, and wool customs a main source of the king's revenue. Chaucer had to keep the accounts in his own hand and oversee the collectors, who were all substantial city business men—one of them was William Walworth, the future lord mayor of London who brought the Peasants' Revolt of 1381 to an end when he stabbed Wat Tyler to death at Smithfield. This post Chaucer held for twelve years, longer than anyone else, so he must have been a success. When he was given the additional post of Controller of Petty Customs in 1382, he became the only person in Richard II's reign to hold both offices simultaneously.

While he was Controller, Chaucer and his wife lived in a house above Aldgate, one of the four original city gates. In those years he must have been very comfortably off. Besides his income as Controller, he had an annuity from the king, and the grant of a daily pitcher of wine—which he commuted to another annuity —as well as a pension from John of Gaunt. His wife also received annuities from John of Gaunt and the king. It has been calculated that their combined income was probably around £99 a year—say £30,000 in today's money. No wonder Chaucer could afford to collect a considerable library. Books were of course very scarce and expensive before the invention of printing; few households possessed more than one. Chaucer had sixty—a good deal more than many an Oxford and Cambridge college could boast.

All this while, despite so busy and full a life, Chaucer was writing poetry. In the court circles where he moved as a young man, English was spoken but the language of culture was French or Latin. His choosing to write in English was a new departure, almost as revolutionary as Dante's decision to abandon Latin for the vernacular at the beginning of the century, though when Chaucer started to write he had probably never heard of Dante.

The innovation caught on: his contemporary, John Gower, who
had begun by composing all his works in Latin or French, ended
by following Chaucer's lead. Theirs was the English of cultivated
Londoners; in the fourteenth century the vernacular was spoken
in a variety of dialects. Chaucer himself observed of his *Troilus
and Cressida*: 'ther is so grete diversite/In Englissh and in writing
of our tonge .../That thou be understonde, God I biseche!'
Eventually it was Chaucer's London dialect that evolved into
standard English, though this was due not so much to Chaucer's
literary achievement as to the political, social, and economic
importance of London, which drew to it people from all parts of
the kingdom.

Chaucer's earliest work was probably the translation of a long
love poem in French, the *Roman de la Rose*, into octosyllabic
couplets—though only the first 1700 lines can be attributed to
him with any certainty. There followed *The Book of the Duchess*,
in the same metre, a courtly and aristocratic elegy on the death
of Blanche of Lancaster, John of Gaunt's first wife, written about
1368–9. However, it was in Book II of his unfinished *House of
Fame* that Chaucer first displayed that genius for vivid characteri-
zation, bland irony, oblique humour, and mix of practicality and
imagination, rhetoric and realism, that he brought to full flower-
ing in his *Canterbury Tales* and in *Troilus and Cressida*. Chaucer
was not, of course, the only poet writing in English at that time.
Masterpieces like *Sir Gawain and the Green Knight*, *The Pearl*,
and William Langland's *Piers Plowman* were roughly contem-
poraneous with *The Canterbury Tales*. But these works are rather
the last fruits of an Anglo-Saxon metric, more suited to that
stronger, inflected language than the freer Middle English that
succeeded it: the end rather than the beginning of a tradition.
For Chaucer discarded their Anglo-Saxon alliteration—dismissing
it as 'rum, ram, ruf'—in favour of an adaptation of French
versification and rhyme-schemes 'so far but no farther than the
language allowed ... It brought a new clarity into English verse;
the language itself grew clearer.'[4] Indeed Chaucer's metrical inno-
vations alone are enough to earn him the title of 'father of
English poetry' bestowed upon him by Dryden. In one of his
earliest translations, *An A.B.C.*, he used a five-stress line, the

[4] C. H. Sisson, *Times Literary Supplement*, 12 September 1980.

pentameter, apparently for the first time in English poetry. For
The Parliament of Fowls he cut down and simplified—'since rym
in Englissh hath such scarcity'—the intricate structure of the
French ballade-form to produce a seven-line stanza called 'rhyme-
royal' which he later used with great success for long narrative
poems like *Troilus and Cressida*. He also invented that staple of
English poetry, the rhyming pentameter or heroic couplet, first
employed in his *Legend of Good Women*. It became the principal
metre for *The Canterbury Tales*. In it Chaucer found he had an
ideal vehicle, not only for either rhetoric or the plain style, but
narration, description, and conveying the rhythms of ordinary
talk.

   Chaucer's poetry was designed to be read aloud—printing was
not invented for nearly a hundred years after his death. If an
illustration in an early manuscript of *Troilus and Cressida* is to
be believed, Chaucer himself read his poems to a court audience.
That he did so seems attested by the mask or persona that he
creates for himself in *The Canterbury Tales* and in poems like
The House of Fame. There he poses as a portly, bookish, well-
meaning, rather dim-witted sort of chap, not much good at
making love or poetry, but doing the best he can; which may be
'a simple and easy way of endearing the poet to his audience and,
by implication, of winning delighted acclaim when he wrote
better than he had promised. It may also have had something to
do with Chaucer's bourgeois origins and his position as court poet
seeking to please his social superiors.'[5] And also, perhaps, to do
with disassociating himself from any dangerous or upsetting
opinions expressed in the poetry.

   The Canterbury Tales were begun about 1387, in which year,
so far as is known, Philippa Chaucer died. The poet continued
to work on them till his own death thirteen years later, when
he left them unfinished. He had given up his posts of Controller
of Customs in 1386 and moved from his lodging at Aldgate to
another in Kent, most probably in Greenwich. At any rate by
1386 Chaucer had become a Justice of the Peace, and one of the
two Knights of the Shire to represent Kent in Parliament. There
he had no easy time. In February 1388 was convened the 'Merci-
less Parliament', when the baronial party led by Richard II's

[5] S. S. Hussey, *Chaucer: An Introduction.*

uncle, the Duke of Gloucester, imprisoned or beheaded the king's friends, some of whom were Chaucer's Custom-house colleagues. However, in May 1389 the young king, having reached the age of twenty-three, successfully asserted his right to rule and re-assumed the reins. Shortly afterwards Chaucer was appointed Clerk of the King's Works, responsible for the maintenance and repair of the Palace of Westminster, the Tower of London, and other royal palaces. One of his first tasks was to put up the scaffoldings for two sets of tournaments held at Smithfield in 1390—a job which obviously furnished material for the brilliant description of the great tournament in Part IV of the *Knight's Tale*. In that year Chaucer managed to get robbed no less than three times in four days—on the second occasion twice on the same day by the same robbers! who stole not only the money he was carrying but his horse as well. It was a considerable sum, worth about £6000; however, the money was not his, but the king's. He was excused from repaying it, but not long after was replaced as Clerk of the Works and appointed deputy keeper of the royal forest of North Petherton in Somerset: which may have been some kind of sinecure. There seems to be no truth in the legend of his impoverished old age. Without going into more detail it may be said that Chaucer remained reasonably well off for the rest of his life. Both Richard II, and Henry IV who deposed him in 1399, continued to pay annuities to the poet, who in the last year of his life leased a house in the garden of Westminster Abbey. There he died and was buried in what has since come to be called 'Poet's Corner'. In his lifetime Chaucer was famous and highly regarded, so this may have been a special honour, for Westminster Abbey was then primarily a burial place of royalty. Chaucer was in fact only the second commoner to be interred there. According to the inscription on his tomb, erected more than a century and a half after his death, he died on 25 October 1400.

The late Patrick Kavanagh remarked, 'it takes a lot of living to make a poem'. A lot of living is what Chaucer put in before he sat down to write his *Canterbury Tales*. To reflect life in its variety, illuminate the humdrum and penetrate the motives and actions of men and women, requires a thorough involvement in the actual world. No one could have had a better preparation than Chaucer for a work of such scope. He had served in military campaigns, and travelled widely as a diplomat; as a courtier he was familiar with politics and high life, as an administrator with all sorts and conditions of people; moreover, he was one of the new men, a bourgeois, neither insulated in the coded world of the feudal aristocracy nor trapped in the bondage of the labouring classes. Apart from that, he was a man of exceptionally wide reading, not only by the standards of his times: he read and spoke French and Italian as well as Latin, was expert in astronomy, and had more than a smattering of physics, history, theology, philosophy, medicine, law, and even alchemy. His two visits to Italy must have been crucial—it was the Italy of the Trecento, when cities like Milan, Florence, and Pisa were built or building. Here he became acquainted with the New Learning, with the work of Petrarch, Boccaccio, and above all 'the grete poete of Ytaille/That highte Dante'.

Dante's choice of the vernacular for poetry must have confirmed Chaucer in his view that he had been right to choose English as the medium for his own. The subtle deployment of telling realistic detail in the *Divina Commedia* must also have had an influence when Chaucer came to describe the pilgrims in the *General Prologue* to his *Canterbury Tales*. The debt to Boccaccio —whose name Chaucer never mentions, but whose work he knew well—is more obvious but less profound. From him he took, and transformed, the plots and dramatis personae for *Troilus and Cressida* and the *Knight's Tale*. It is possible that Boccaccio's somewhat mechanic contrivance for hooking together the collection of stories in the *Decameron* gave Chaucer the idea for his Canterbury pilgrims. But if so, Chaucer transmuted Boccaccio's metal into gold. The story-tellers of the *Decameron* all belong to one class and, moreover, are pasteboard figures. There is nothing like the quarrelling Reeve and Miller, or Friar and Summoner scoring off one another with their scurrilous tales—and incidentally drawing some of the most realistic pictures of ordinary daily life in medieval England. There is nothing like the 'marriage debate' sparked off by the Wife of Bath's magnificent feminist monologue: the Oxford Scholar's half-ironic story of patient Griselda, the Merchant's bitter tale of January and May, and its resolution by the generous Franklin. Chaucer is the only English writer to treat marriage (as distinct from love) seriously and at length in poetry. There have been essays by George Meredith,

Coventry Patmore, and above all by Thomas Hardy, but Chaucer's treatment of this intractable theme is certainly the most balanced. Well might Gavin Douglas write of him:

> For he was evir (God wait) all womanis frend.

The Canterbury Tales were left unfinished. There were to have been a hundred and twenty of them: Chaucer was ever the man to bite off more than he could chew. He completed little more than a score of them, and the Cook's and the Squire's tales remain fragments. Not all of them are appropriate to the tellers: the *Sea-Captain's Tale*, for instance, was obviously first meant for the Wife of Bath. The Sergeant-at-Law announces that he will speak in prose, but his tale is in rhyme-royal. The Second Nun, who is listed but not described in the *General Prologue*, is given one of Chaucer's earliest essays in poetry—a versified *Life of St Cecilia* which he must have felt would be a pity to waste. The comparatively unsuccessful stories by the Manciple and the Physician are not related to their tellers and were probably composed before Chaucer conceived his scheme for *The Canterbury Tales*. But in all of them, even in the Second Nun's pietistic legend of St Cecilia, Chaucer's personality is present, reflecting a humane, modest, unassumingly ironic and unobtrusively deprecatory turn of mind; detached, yet informed with huge gusto and curiosity, and an active acceptance and enjoyment of life: Keats's 'negative capability' immensely amplified and embracing every manifestation of the world as it is.

That intimate conversational undertone remains more or less impossible to translate or counterfeit in modern English. All the same—though well aware of the foolhardiness of the venture, as my earlier prose rendering will attest—I have undertaken to translate *The Canterbury Tales* into verse. In making the attempt I have preferred to sacrifice, for the sake of the immediacy, directness, and plain speech that make up the real poetry of the original, any strict adherence to Chaucer's rhyme-schemes, whether the couplets which are the vehicle of the *General Prologue* and most of the Tales, or the rhyme-royal of the remainder. The idea has been rather to suggest them by such contemporary alternatives as half-rhymes, quarter-rhymes, or assonance real or imaginary, and so keep, as nearly as possible, to Chaucer's tone and to what he is actually saying. It is often claimed that Chaucer's language is so near modern English that only a little, if any, study is required to read him without difficulty. This, if I may say so, is a fallacy. Many of the still-extant words that Chaucer uses have shifted their meanings and nuances; some idioms and many references are now incomprehensible, quite apart from the great number of words in Chaucer's large vocabulary that have long fallen out of use and been forgotten. All the same this version is not offered as any kind of substitute—as were Dryden's magnificent renderings—but as an introductory prolusion to the real thing.

DAVID WRIGHT

6 March 1984

ACKNOWLEDGEMENTS

I would like to thank Dr Geoffrey Ivy, Senior Lecturer in English at Durham University, and Professor S. S. Hussey, Lecturer in Historical English at Lancaster University, for invaluable advice and assistance in the interpretation of crucial passages and in the revision of the final draft, and Mr Victor Watts, Senior Lecturer in English Language and Medieval Literature at Durham University, for advice on Northumbrian dialect in the *Reeve's Tale*; and last but not least C. H. Sisson, to whom I am indebted for overlooking this translation. Needless to say, for any errors the responsibility is mine. I would also like to thank Northern Arts for financial assistance enabling me to devote time to the work.

SELECT BIBLIOGRAPHY

Bibliography

Albert C. Baugh, *Chaucer*, Goldentree Bibliographies, 2nd edn. (Arlington Heights, Illinois, 1977).

Texts

The most informative and compendious edition of the poem is to be found in F. N. Robinson, ed., *The Works of Geoffrey Chaucer*, 2nd edn. (London, 1957), but the volume which contains it is cumbersome to handle. A 3rd edition is said to be 'in preparation'; see George Kane, *Chaucer*, Past Masters series (Oxford, 1984), 117–18. Robinson's text of *The Canterbury Tales* has been published separately by A. C. Cawley, revised edn. (London, 1975).

J. M. Manly and E. Rickert, eds., *The Text of the Canterbury Tales*, 8 vols. (Chicago, 1940) contains not a reading-text but a list of variants, which demonstrate that a definitive edition of the poem is not possible. The most serious problem is the ordering of the tales, which has become the subject of a continuing debate (see below under *Criticism*). Manly and Rickert describe in detail each of the eighty and more manuscripts of the poem. The study of book-production at the end of the manuscript period and of the mentality of Chaucer's original readers is a developing line of research: see A. I. Doyle and M. B. Parkes, 'The production of copies of the *Canterbury Tales* and the *Confesso Amantis* in the early fifteenth century', in M. B. Parkes and Andrew Watson, eds., *Medieval Scribes, Manuscripts & Libraries* (London, 1978), 163–210; also Janet Coleman and J. A. Burrow below, under *Background: Life and Thought*.

Sources

The texts printed by W. F. Bryan and Germaine Dempster, eds., *Sources and Analogues of Chaucer's Canterbury Tales* (Chicago, 1941) are not merely scholarly curiosities, but a necessary ingredient of any informed discussion of Chaucer's poetry, as witness the excellent critical use made of some of them by Charles Muscatine, *Chaucer and the French Tradition: a Study in Style and Meaning* (Berkeley, 1957).

Life of Chaucer

There is no accepted 'Life of Chaucer', but instead a two-way traffic between Chaucer criticism and the *Chaucer Life-Records*, edited by

Martin M. Crow and Claire C. Olson (Oxford, 1966). As critical fashions change, different aspects of the poet's domestic life and career, preserved in the records, are brought into prominence and explored. Brief summaries occur in most editions, including Robinson's. For more extensive accounts, of recent date, see: Derek S. Brewer, *Chaucer*, 3rd edn. (London, 1973); S. S. Hussey, *Chaucer: an Introduction*, 2nd edn. (London, 1981).

Background: Life and Thought

The following is a brief selection from the wide variety of titles on offer: W. C. Curry, *Chaucer and the Mediaeval Sciences*, 2nd edn. (London, 1960). D. W. Robertson, *A Preface to Chaucer* (London, 1963). R. S. Loomis, *A Mirror of Chaucer's World* (Princeton, 1965). Gervase Mathew, *The Court of Richard II* (London, 1968). Derek S. Brewer, ed., *Geoffrey Chaucer*, Writers and their Background series, G. Bell and Son (London, 1974). Beryl Rowland, ed., *Companion to Chaucer Studies*, 2nd edn. (New York, 1979). Janet Coleman, *English Literature in History 1350–1400: Medieval Readers and Writers* (London, 1981). J. A. Burrow, *Medieval Writers and their Work: Middle English Literature and its Background 1100–1500* (Oxford, 1982).

Criticism

Although critical fashions alter, the best Chaucer criticism does not go out of date. An example of this is G. L. Kittredge, *Chaucer and his Poetry* (Cambridge, Mass., 1915). It is now generally acknowledged that, contrary to what Kittredge supposed, mimetic realism was not Chaucer's primary aim in poetry. But Kittredge's comments on the individual pilgrims in *The Canterbury Tales*, and on Chaucer's attitude to life, can still enliven the reader's responses to the poem. Hence the usefulness of J. A. Burrow, ed., *Geoffrey Chaucer: A Critical Anthology* (London, 1969), with its well-chosen extracts and admirable introductions to the different periods of criticism. The first extract, from Chaucer himself, is dated ?1380 and the last 1968. Equally useful are Edward Wagenknecht, ed., *Chaucer: Modern Essays in Criticism* (New York, 1959) and Robert J. Schoeck and Jerome Taylor, eds., *Chaucer Criticism I: The Canterbury Tales* (Notre Dame, 1960). Between them, these reprint a number of influential articles. Over half of the essays in E. T. Donaldson, *Speaking of Chaucer* (London, 1970) relate to *The Canterbury Tales*. Two of them in particular, 'Chaucer the Pilgrim' and 'The Idiom of Popular Poetry in the Miller's Tale', stimulate critical thinking about, respectively, Chaucer's use of his narrator and his sensitivity to nuances of style.

As mentioned under *Texts* (above), there is no consensus of opinion to be derived from the manuscrips of *The Canterbury Tales* as to the order in which should be placed the fragmentary blocks of tales. Since Chaucer left the poem unfinished, it is probable that no arrangement of the existing tales would represent his ultimate intention, even supposing that this had been formulated by him before he died. The problem of the relationship between the pilgrimage framework and the tales themselves remains a tantalizing one. Good books have been written about different sections of the poem, e.g. Jill Mann, *Chaucer and Medieval Estates Satire* (Cambridge, 1973), on the *General Prologue*, and V. A. Kolve, *Chaucer and the Imagery of Narrative: The First Five Canterbury Tales* (Stanford, 1984), to name only two. The following is a selection from the large number of books that set out to interpret the poem as a whole: Ralph Baldwin, *The Unity of the Canterbury Tales*, Anglistica 5 (Copenhagen, 1955); Paul Ruggiers, *The Art of the Canterbury Tales* (Maidson, 1965); Robert M. Jordan, *Chaucer and the Shape of Creation* (Cambridge, Mass., 1967); Donald R. Howard, *The Idea of the Canterbury Tales* (Berkeley, 1976); Charles A. Owen, *Pilgrimage and Storytelling in the Canterbury Tales* (Norman, 1977); Helen Cooper, *The Structure of the Canterbury Tales* (London, 1983).

A CHRONOLOGY
OF GEOFFREY CHAUCER

Age

c.1343   Born in London, son of John Chaucer, vintner, and
Agnes de Copton

1357   Entered as a page in the household of Elizabeth, Coun-   14
tess of Ulster, wife of Lionel, Duke of Clarence, son of
Edward III

1359   Goes as a squire to France with Edward III's army of   16
invasion, and is captured by the French at the siege of
Rheims

1360   Ransomed on 1 March for £16 and employed as a   17
messenger carrying letters from Calais to England

c.1366   Marries Philippa de Roet, daughter of Sir Paon de Roet,   23
a lady-in-waiting to Queen Philippa of Hainault, wife of
Edward III

1368   His wife Philippa Chaucer becomes lady-in-waiting to   25
Constance of Castile, wife of Edward III's son John of
Gaunt, Duke of Lancaster. Chaucer accompanies
Edward, Prince of Wales (the Black Prince) to Spain and
is appointed an Esquire of the King's Household.
Composes *The Book of the Duchess*

1369   Campaigns in France in the service of John of Gaunt   26

1372   Visits Italy as one of three commissioners to negotiate   29
with the Duke of Genoa. Visits Florence

1374   Acquires house above Aldgate and is appointed Con-   31
troller of Customs and Subsidy of Wools, Skins, and
Hides in the port of London

1377   In France 'on the king's secret affairs'. Death of Edward   34
III; Richard II becomes king

1378   Visits Italy in the retinue of Sir Edward de Berkeley to   35
negotiate with Bernabo Visconti, Duke of Milan

c.1379   Composes *The House of Fame*   36

1381   Peasants' Revolt and death of Wat Tyler   38

1382   Appointed Controller of Petty Customs on Wines   39

Fragment I (Group A)

GENERAL PROLOGUE

When the sweet showers of April have pierced
The drought of March, and pierced it to the root,
And every vein is bathed in that moisture
Whose quickening force will engender the flower;
And when the west wind too with its sweet breath
Has given life in every wood and field
To tender shoots, and when the stripling sun
Has run his half-course in Aries, the Ram,*
And when small birds are making melodies,
That sleep all the night long with open eyes,
(Nature so prompts them, and encourages);
Then people long to go on pilgrimages,
And palmers* to take ship for foreign shores,
And distant shrines, famous in different lands;
And most especially, from all the shires
Of England, to Canterbury they come,
The holy blessed martyr* there to seek,
Who gave his help to them when they were sick.

   It happened at this season, that one day
In Southwark at the Tabard where I stayed
Ready to set out on my pilgrimage
To Canterbury, and pay devout homage,
There came at nightfall to the hostelry
Some nine-and-twenty in a company,
Folk of all kinds, met in accidental
Companionship, for they were pilgrims all;
It was to Canterbury that they rode.
The bedrooms and the stables were good-sized,
The comforts offered us were of the best.
And by the time the sun had gone to rest
I'd talked with everyone, and soon became
One of their company, and promised them
To rise at dawn next day to take the road

4/29 are purely good

For the journey I am telling you about.
   But, before I go further with this tale,
And while I can, it seems reasonable
That I should let you have a full description
Of each of them, their sort and condition,
At any rate as they appeared to me;
Tell who they were, their status and profession,
What they looked like, what kind of clothes they dressed in;
And with a knight, then, I shall first begin.
   There was a knight, a reputable man,
Who from the moment that he first began
Campaigning, had cherished the profession
Of arms; he also prized trustworthiness,
Liberality, fame, and courteousness.
In the king's service he'd fought valiantly,
And travelled far; no man as far as he
In Christian and in heathen lands as well,
And ever honoured for his ability.
He was at Alexandria when it fell,
Often he took the highest place at table
Over the other foreign knights in Prussia;
He'd raided in Lithuania and Russia,
No Christian of his rank fought there more often.
Also he'd been in Granada, at the siege
Of Algeciras; forayed in Benmarin;
At Ayas and Adalia he had been
When they were taken; and with the great hosts
Freebooting on the Mediterranean coasts;
Fought fifteen mortal combats; thrice as champion
In tournaments, he at Tramassene
Fought for our faith, and each time killed his man.
This worthy knight had also, for a time,
Taken service in Palatia for the Bey,
Against another heathen in Turkey;
And almost beyond price was his prestige.*
Though eminent, he was prudent and sage,
And in his bearing mild as any maid.
He'd never been foul-spoken in his life
To any kind of man; he was indeed
The very pattern of a noble knight.

But as for his appearance and outfit,
He had good horses, yet was far from smart.
He wore a tunic made of coarse thick stuff,
Marked by his chainmail, all begrimed with rust,
Having just returned from an expedition,
And on his pilgrimage of thanksgiving.

With him there was his son, a young squire,
A lively knight-apprentice, and a lover,
With hair as curly as if newly waved;
I took him to be twenty years of age.
In stature he was of an average length,
Wonderfully athletic, and of great strength.
He'd taken part in cavalry forays
In Flanders, in Artois, and Picardy,
With credit, though no more than a novice,
Hoping to stand well in his lady's eyes.
His clothes were all embroidered like a field
Full of the freshest flowers, white and red.
He sang, or played the flute, the livelong day,
And he was fresher than the month of May.
Short was his gown, with sleeves cut long and wide.
He'd a good seat on horseback, and could ride,
Make music too, and songs to go with it;
Could joust and dance, and also draw and write.
So burningly he loved, that come nightfall
He'd sleep no more than any nightingale.
Polite, modest, willing to serve, and able,
He carved before his father at their table.

The knight had just one servant, a yeoman,
For so he wished to ride, on this occasion.
The man was clad in coat and hood of green.
He carried under his belt, handily,
For he looked to his gear in yeoman fashion,
A sheaf of peacock arrows, sharp and shining,
Not liable to fall short from poor feathering;
And in his hand he bore a mighty bow.
He had a cropped head, and his face was brown;
Of woodcraft he knew all there was to know.
He wore a fancy leather guard, a bracer,
And by his side a sword and a rough buckler,

And on the other side a fancy dagger,
Well-mounted, sharper than the point of spear,
And on his breast a medal: St Christopher,
The woodman's patron saint, in polished silver.
He bore a horn slung from a cord of green,
And my guess is, he was a forester.

    There was also a nun, a prioress,
Whose smile was unaffected and demure;
Her greatest oath was just, 'By St Eloi!'
And she was known as Madame Eglantine.
She sang the divine service prettily,
And through the nose, becomingly intoned;
And she spoke French well and elegantly
As she'd been taught it at Stratford-at-Bow,
For French of Paris was to her unknown.
Good table manners she had learnt as well:
She never let a crumb from her mouth fall;
She never soiled her fingers, dipping deep
Into the sauce; when lifting to her lips
Some morsel, she was careful not to spill
So much as one small drop upon her breast.
Her greatest pleasure was in etiquette.
She used to wipe her upper lip so clean,
No print of grease inside her cup was seen,
Not the least speck, when she had drunk from it.
Most daintily she'd reach for what she ate.
No question, she possessed the greatest charm,
Her demeanour was so pleasant, and so warm;
Though at pains to ape the manners of the court,
And be dignified, in order to be thought
A person well deserving of esteem.
But, speaking of her sensibility,
She was so full of charity and pity
That if she saw a mouse caught in a trap,
And it was dead or bleeding, she would weep.
She kept some little dogs, and these she fed
On roast meat, or on milk and fine white bread.*
But how she'd weep if one of them were dead,
Or if somebody took a stick to it!
She was all sensitivity and tender heart.

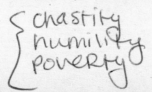

Her veil was pleated most becomingly;
Her nose well-shaped; eyes blue-grey, of great beauty;
And her mouth tender, very small, and red.
And there's no doubt she had a fine forehead,
Almost a span in breadth, I'd swear it was,
For certainly she was not undersized.
Her cloak, I noticed, was most elegant.
A coral rosary with gauds* of green
She carried on her arm; and from it hung
A brooch of shining gold; inscribed thereon
Was, first of all, a crowned 'A',
And under, *Amor vincit omnia*.*

With her were three priests, and another nun,
Who was her chaplain and companion.

There was a monk; a nonpareil was he,
Who rode, as steward of his monastery,
The country round; a lover of good sport,
A manly man, and fit to be an abbot.
He'd plenty of good horses in his stable,
And when he went out riding, you could hear
His bridle jingle in the wind, as clear
And loud as the monastery chapel-bell.
Inasmuch as he was keeper of the cell,*
The rule of St Maurus or St Benedict
Being out of date, and also somewhat strict,
This monk I speak of let old precepts slide,
And took the modern practice as his guide.
He didn't give so much as a plucked hen
For the maxim, 'Hunters are not pious men',
Or 'A monk who's heedless of his regimen
Is much the same as a fish out of water',
In other words, a monk out of his cloister.
But that's a text he thought not worth an oyster;
And I remarked his opinion was sound.
What use to study, why go round the bend
With poring over some book in a cloister,
Or drudging with his hands, to toil and labour
As Augustine bids? How shall the world go on?
You can go keep your labour, Augustine!
So he rode hard—no question about that—

Kept greyhounds swifter than a bird in flight.
Hard riding, and the hunting of the hare,
Were what he loved, and opened his purse for.
I noticed that his sleeves were edged and trimmed
With squirrel fur, the finest in the land.
For fastening his hood beneath his chin,
He wore an elaborate golden pin,
Twined with a love-knot at the larger end.
His head was bald and glistening like glass
As if anointed; and likewise his face.
A fine fat patrician, in prime condition,
His bright and restless eyes danced in his head,
And sparkled like the fire beneath a pot;
Boots of soft leather, horse in perfect trim:
No question but he was a fine prelate!
Not pale and wan like some tormented spirit.
A fat roast swan was what he loved the best.
His saddle-horse was brown as any berry.
    There was a begging friar, a genial merry
Limiter,* and a most imposing person.
In all of the four Orders there was none
So versed in small talk and in flattery:
And many was the marriage in a hurry
He'd had to improvise and even pay for.*
He was a noble pillar of his Order,
And was well in and intimate with every
Well-to-do freeman farmer of his area,
And with the well-off women in the town;
For he was qualified to hear confession,
And absolve graver sins than a curate,
Or so he said; he was a licentiate.*
How sweetly he would hear confession!
How pleasant was his absolution!
He was an easy man in giving shrift,
When sure of getting a substantial gift:
For, as he used to say, generous giving
To a poor Order is a sign you're shriven;
For if you gave, then he could vouch for it
That you were conscience-stricken and contrite;
For many are so hardened in their hearts

They cannot weep, though burning with remorse.
Therefore, instead of weeping and prayers,
They should give money to the needy friars.
The pockets of his hood were stuffed with knives
And pins to give away to pretty wives.
He had a pleasant singing voice, for sure,
Could sing and play the fiddle beautifully;
He took the biscuit as a ballad-singer,
And though his neck was whiter than a lily,
Yet he was brawny as a prize-fighter.
He knew the taverns well in every town,
And all the barmaids and the innkeepers,
Better than lepers or the street-beggars;
It wouldn't do, for one in his position,
One of his ability and distinction,
To hold acquaintance with diseased lepers.
It isn't seemly, and it gets you nowhere,
To have any dealings with that sort of trash,
Stick to provision-merchants and the rich!
And anywhere where profit might arise
He'd crawl with courteous offers of service.
You'd nowhere find an abler man than he,
Or a better beggar in his friary;
He paid a yearly fee for his district,
No brother friar trespassed on his beat.
A widow might not even own a shoe,
But so pleasant was his In principio*
He'd win her farthing in the end, then go.
He made his biggest profits on the side.
He'd frolic like a puppy. He'd give aid
As arbitrator upon settling-days,
For there he was not like some cloisterer*
With threadbare cape, like any poor scholar,
But like a Master of Arts, or the Pope!
Of the best double-worsted was his cloak,
And bulging like a bell that's newly cast.
He lisped a little, from affectation,
To make his English sweet upon his tongue;
And when he harped, as closing to a song,
His eyes would twinkle in his head just like

[handwritten margin note: If there's $ around anything he'll do (obsequious)]

The stars upon a sharp and frosty night.
This worthy limiter was called Hubert.

A merchant was there, on a high-saddled horse:
He'd a forked beard, a many-coloured dress,
And on his head a Flanders beaver hat,
Boots with expensive clasps, and buckled neatly.
He gave out his opinions pompously,
Kept talking of the profits that he'd made,
How, at all costs, the sea should be policed
From Middleburg in Holland to Harwich.
At money-changing he was an expert;
He dealt in French gold florins on the quiet.
This worthy citizen could use his head:
No one could tell whether he was in debt,
So impressive and dignified his bearing
As he went about his loans and bargaining.
He was a really estimable man,
But the fact is I never learnt his name.

There was a scholar from Oxford as well,
Not yet an MA, reading Logic still;
The horse he rode was leaner than a rake,
And he himself, believe me, none too fat,
But hollow-cheeked, and grave and serious.
Threadbare indeed was his short overcoat:
A man too unworldly for lay office,
Yet he'd not got himself a benefice.
For he'd much rather have at his bedside
A library, bound in black calf or red,
Of Aristotle and his philosophy,
Than rich apparel, fiddle, or fine psaltery.
And though he was a man of science, yet
He had but little gold in his strongbox;
But upon books and learning he would spend
All he was able to obtain from friends;
He'd pray assiduously for their souls,
Who gave him wherewith to attend the schools.
Learning was all he cared for or would heed.
He never spoke a word more than was need,
And that was said in form and decorum,
And brief and terse, and full of deepest meaning.

Moral virtue was reflected in his speech,
And gladly would he learn, and gladly teach.
   There was a wise and wary sergeant-at-law,
A well-known figure in the portico
Where lawyers meet; one of great excellence,
Judicious, worthy of reverence,
Or so he seemed, his sayings were so wise.
He'd often acted as Judge of Assize
By the king's letters patent, authorized
To hear all cases. And his great renown
And skill had won him many a fee, or gown
Given in lieu of money. There was none
To touch him as a property-buyer; all
He bought was fee-simple, without entail;*
You'd never find a flaw in the conveyance.
And nowhere would you find a busier man;
And yet he seemed much busier than he was.
From yearbooks he could quote, chapter and verse,
Each case and judgement since William the First.
And he knew how to draw up and compose
A deed; you couldn't fault a thing he wrote;
And he'd reel all the statutes off by rote.
He was dressed simply, in a coloured coat,
Girt by a silk belt with thin metal bands.
I have no more to tell of his appearance.
   A franklin—that's a country gentleman
And freeman landowner—was his companion.
White was his beard, as white as any daisy;
Sanguine his temperament; his face ruddy.
He loved his morning draught of sops-in-wine,
Since living well was ever his custom,
For he was Epicurus' own true son
And held with him that sensuality
Is where the only happiness is found.
And he kept open house so lavishly
He was St Julian to the country round,
The patron saint of hospitality.
His bread and ale were always of the best,
Like his wine-cellar, which was unsurpassed.
Cooked food was never lacking in his house,

[handwritten annotations: "not of 3 estates", "FOOD = food", "not of 3 estates b/c his mind ≠ body are out of balance. He is all body"]

Both meat and fish, and that so plenteous
That in his home it snowed with food and drink,
And all the delicacies you could think.
According to the season of the year,
He changed the dishes that were served at dinner.
He'd plenty of fat partridges in coop,
And kept his fishpond full of pike and carp.
His cook would catch it if his sauces weren't
Piquant and sharp, and all his equipment
To hand. And all day in his hall there stood
The great fixed table, with the places laid.
When the justices met, he'd take the chair;
He often served as MP for the shire.
A dagger, and a small purse made of silk,
Hung at his girdle, white as morning milk.
He'd been sheriff, and county auditor:
A model squireen, no man worthier.

    A haberdasher and a carpenter,
A weaver, dyer, tapestry-maker—
And they were in the uniform livery
Of a dignified and rich fraternity,
A parish-guild: their gear all trim and fresh,
Knives silver-mounted, none of your cheap brass;
Their belts and purses neatly stitched as well,
All finely finished to the last detail.
Each of them looked indeed like a burgess,
And fit to sit on any guildhall dais.
Each was, in knowledge and ability,
Eligible to be an alderman;
For they'd income enough and property.
What's more, their wives would certainly agree,
Or otherwise they'd surely be to blame—
It's very pleasant to be called 'Madam'
And to take precedence at church processions,
And have one's mantle carried like a queen's.

    They had a cook with them for the occasion,
To boil the chickens up with marrowbones,
Tart powdered flavouring, spiced with galingale.
No better judge than he of London ale.
And he could roast, and seethe, and boil, and fry,

Make a thick soup, and bake a proper pie;
But to my mind it was the greatest shame
He'd got an open sore upon his shin;
For he made chicken-pudding with the best.
    A sea-captain, whose home was in the west,
Was there—a Dartmouth man, for all I know.*
He rode a cob as well as he knew how,
And was dressed in a knee-length woollen gown.
From a lanyard round his neck, a dagger hung
Under his arm. Summer had tanned him brown.
As rough a diamond as you'd hope to find,
He'd tapped and lifted many a stoup of wine
From Bordeaux, when the merchant wasn't looking.
He hadn't time for scruples or fine feeling,
For if he fought, and got the upper hand,
He'd send his captives home by sea, not land.
But as for seamanship, and calculation
Of moon, tides, currents, all hazards at sea,
For harbour-lore, and skill in navigation,
From Hull to Carthage there was none to touch him.
He was shrewd adventurer, tough and hardy.
By many a tempest had his beard been shaken.
And he knew all the harbours that there were
Between the Baltic and Cape Finisterre,
And each inlet of Britanny and Spain.
The ship he sailed was called 'The Magdalen'.
    With us there was a doctor, a physician;
Nowhere in all the world was one to match him
Where medicine was concerned, or surgery;
Being well grounded in astrology
He'd watch his patient with the utmost care
Until he'd found a favourable hour,
By means of astrology, to give treatment.
Skilled to pick out the astrologic moment
For charms and talismans to aid the patient,
He knew the cause of every malady,
If it were 'hot' or 'cold' or 'moist' or 'dry',
And where it came from, and from which humour.*
He was a really fine practitioner.
Knowing the cause, and having found its root,

He'd soon give the sick man an antidote.
Ever at hand he had apothecaries
To send him syrups, drugs, and remedies,
For each put money in the other's pocket—
Theirs was no newly founded partnership.
Well-read was he in Aesculapius,
In Dioscorides, and in Rufus,
Ancient Hippocrates, Hali, and Galen,
Avicenna, Rhazes, and Serapion,
Averroës, Damascenus ,Constantine,
Bernard, and Gilbertus, and Gaddesden.*
In his own diet he was temperate,
For it was nothing if not moderate,
Though most nutritious and digestible.
He didn't do much reading in the Bible.
He was dressed all in Persian blue and scarlet
Lined with taffeta and fine sarsenet,
And yet was very chary of expense.
He put by all he earned from pestilence;
In medicine gold is the best cordial.
So it was gold that he loved best of all.

There was a business woman, from near Bath,
But, more's the pity, she was a bit deaf;
So skilled a clothmaker, that she outdistanced
Even the weavers of Ypres and Ghent.
In the whole parish there was not a woman
Who dared precede her at the almsgiving,
And if there did, so furious was she,
That she was put out of all charity.
Her headkerchiefs were of the finest weave,
Ten pounds and more they weighed, I do believe,
Those that she wore on Sundays on her head.
Her stockings were of finest scarlet red,
Very tightly laced; shoes pliable and new.
Bold was her face, and handsome; florid too.
She had been respectable all her life,
And five times married, that's to say in church,
Not counting other loves she'd had in youth,
Of whom, just now, there is no need to speak.
And she had thrice been to Jerusalem;

Had wandered over many a foreign stream;
And she had been at Rome, and at Boulogne,
St James of Compostella, and Cologne;
She knew all about wandering—and straying: → *sexval appetite*
For she was gap-toothed, if you take my meaning.*
Comfortably on an ambling horse she sat,
Well-wimpled, wearing on her head a hat
That might have been a shield in size and shape;
A riding-skirt round her enormous hips,
Also a pair of sharp spurs on her feet.
In company, how she could laugh and joke!
No doubt she knew of all the cures for love,
For at that game she was a past mistress. *abortions*

   And there was a good man, a religious.
He was the needy priest of a village,
But rich enough in saintly thought and work.
And educated, too, for he could read;   *N/A*
Would truly preach the word of Jesus Christ,
Devoutly teach the folk in his parish.
Kind was he, wonderfully diligent;
And in adversity most patient,
As many a time had been put to the test.
For unpaid tithes he'd not excommunicate, } *generosity*
For he would rather give, you may be sure,
From his own pocket to the parish poor; } *@ its finest*
Few were his needs, so frugally he lived.
Wide was his parish, with houses far asunder,
But he would not neglect, come rain or thunder,
Come sickness or adversity, to call
On the furthest of his parish, great or small;
Going on foot, and in his hand a staff.
This was the good example that he set:
He practised first what later he would teach.
Out of the gospel he took that precept;
And what's more, he would cite this saying too:
'If gold can rust, then what will iron do?'
For if a priest be rotten, whom we trust,
No wonder if a layman comes to rust.
It's shame to see (let every priest take note) } *if leaders*
A shitten shepherd and a cleanly sheep. *are corrupt what can we expect of the people*

It's the plain duty of a priest to give
Example to his sheep; how they should live.
He never let his benefice for hire
And left his sheep to flounder in the mire
While he ran off to London, to St Paul's
To seek some chantry and sing mass for souls,
Or to be kept as chaplain by a guild;*
But stayed at home, and took care of his fold,
So that no wolf might do it injury.
He was a shepherd, not a mercenary.
And although he was saintly and virtuous,
He wasn't haughty or contemptuous
To sinners, speaking to them with disdain,
But in his teaching tactful and humane.
To draw up folk to heaven by goodness
And good example, was his sole business.
But if a person turned out obstinate,
Whoever he was, of high or low estate,
He'd earn a stinging rebuke then and there.
You'll never find a better priest, I'll swear.
He never looked for pomp or deference,
Nor affected an over-nice conscience,
But taught the gospel of Christ and His twelve
Apostles; but first followed it himself.
      With him there was his brother, a ploughman,
Who'd fetched and carried many a load of dung;
A good and faithful labourer was he,
Living in peace and perfect charity.
God he loved best, and that with all his heart,
At all times, good and bad, no matter what;
And next he loved his neighbour as himself.
He'd thresh, and ditch, and also dig and delve,
And for Christ's love would do as much again
If he could manage it, for all poor men,
And ask no hire. He paid his tithes in full,
On what he earned and on his goods as well.
He wore a smock, and rode upon a mare.
      There was a reeve as well, also a miller,
A pardon-seller and a summoner,
A manciple, and myself—there were no more.

grind wheat & sell flower

The miller was a burly fellow—brawn
And muscle, big of bones as well as strong,
As was well seen—he always won the ram
At wrestling-matches up and down the land.
He was barrel-chested, rugged and thickset,
And would heave off its hinges any door
Or break it, running at it with his head.
His beard was red as any fox or sow,
And wide at that, as though it were a spade.
And on his nose, right on its tip, he had
A wart, upon which stood a tuft of hairs
Red as the bristles are in a sow's ears.
Black were his nostrils; black and squat and wide.
He bore a sword and buckler by his side.
His big mouth was as big as a furnace.
A loudmouth and a teller of blue stories
(Most of them vicious or scurrilous),
Well versed in stealing corn and trebling dues, *, cheating*
He had a golden thumb—by God he had! *ppl*
A white coat he had on, and a blue hood.
He played the bagpipes well, and blew a tune,
And to its music brought us out of town.

A worthy manciple* of the Middle Temple
Was there; he might have served as an example
To all provision-buyers for his thrift
In making purchase, whether on credit
Or for cash down: he kept an eye on prices,
So always got in first and did good business.
Now isn't it an instance of God's grace,
Such an unlettered man should so outpace
The wisdom of a pack of learned men?
He'd more than thirty masters over him,
All of them proficient experts in law,
More than a dozen of them with the power
To manage rents and land for any peer
So that—unless the man were off his head—
He could live honourably, free of debt,
Or sparingly, if that were his desire;
And able to look after a whole shire
In whatever emergency might befall;

And yet this manciple could hoodwink them all.
   There was a reeve,* a thin and bilious man;
His beard he shaved as close as a man can;
Around his ears he kept his hair cropped short,
Just like a priest's, docked in front and on top.
His legs were very long, and very lean,
And like a stick; no calf was to be seen.
His granary and bins were ably kept;
There was no auditor could trip him up.
He could foretell, by noting drought and rain,
The likely harvest from his seed and grain.
His master's cattle, dairy, cows, and sheep,
His pigs and horses, poultry and livestock,
Were wholly under this reeve's governance.
And, as was laid down in his covenant,
Of these he'd always rendered an account
Ever since his master reached his twentieth year.
No man could ever catch him in arrears.
He was up to every fiddle, every dodge
Of every herdsman, bailiff, or farm-lad.
All of them feared him as they feared the plague.
His dwelling was well placed upon a heath,
Set with green trees that overshadowed it.
At business he was better than his lord:
He'd got his nest well-feathered, on the side,
For he was cunning enough to get round
His lord by lending him what was his own,
And so earn thanks, besides a coat and hood.
As a young man he'd learned a useful trade
As a skilled artisan, a carpenter.
The reeve rode on a sturdy farmer's cob
That was called Scot: it was a dapple grey.
He had on a long blue-grey overcoat,
And carried by his side a rusty sword.
A Norfolk man was he of whom I tell,
From near a place that they call Bawdeswell.
Tucked round him like a friar's was his coat;
He always rode the hindmost of our troop.
   A summoner* was among us at the inn,
Whose face was fire-red, like the cherubim;

internal life

All covered with carbuncles; his eyes narrow;
He was as hot and randy as a sparrow.
He'd scabbed black eyebrows, and a scraggy beard,
No wonder if the children were afraid!
There was no mercury, white lead, or sulphur,
No borax, no ceruse, no cream of tartar,
Nor any other salves that cleanse and burn,
Could help with the white pustules on his skin,
Or with the knobbed carbuncles on his cheeks.
He'd a great love of garlic, onions, leeks,
Also for drinking strong wine, red as blood,
When he would roar and gabble as if mad.
And once he had got really drunk on wine,
Then he would speak no language but Latin.
He'd picked up a few tags, some two or three,
Which he'd learned from some edict or decree—
No wonder, for he heard them every day.
Also, as everybody knows, a jay
Can call out 'Wat' as well as the Pope can.
But if you tried him further with a question,
You'd find his well of learning had run dry;
'*Questio quid juris*'* was all he'd ever say.
A most engaging rascal, and a kind,
As good a fellow as you'd hope to find:
For he'd allow—given a quart of wine—
A scallywag to keep his concubine
A twelvemonth, and excuse him altogether.
He'd dip his wick, too, very much sub rosa.
And if he found some fellow with a woman,
He'd tell him not to fear excommunication
If he were caught, or the archdeacon's curse,
Unless the fellow's soul was in his purse,
For it's his purse must pay the penalty.
'Your purse is the archdeacon's Hell,' said he.
Take it from me, the man lied in his teeth:
Let sinners fear, for that curse is damnation,
Just as their souls are saved by absolution.
Let them beware, too, of a '*Significavit*'.*
Under his thumb, to deal with as he pleased,
Were the young people of his diocese;

He was their sole adviser and confidant.
Upon his head he sported a garland
As big as any hung outside a pub,*
And, for a shield, he'd a round loaf of bread.

    With him there was a peerless pardon-seller*
Of Charing Cross, his friend and his confrère,
Who'd come straight from the Vatican in Rome.
Loudly he sang, 'Come to me, love, come hither!'
The summoner sang the bass, a loud refrain;
No trumpet ever made one half the din.
This pardon-seller's hair was yellow as wax,
And sleekly hanging, like a hank of flax.
In meagre clusters hung what hair he had;
Over his shoulders a few strands were spread,
But they lay thin, in rat's tails, one by one.
As for a hood, for comfort he wore none,
For it was stowed away in his knapsack.
Save for a cap, he rode with head all bare,
Hair loose; he thought it was the *dernier cri*.
He had big bulging eyes, just like a hare.
He'd sewn a veronica* on his cap.
His knapsack lay before him, on his lap,
Chockful of pardons, all come hot from Rome.
His voice was like a goat's, plaintive and thin.
He had no beard, nor was he like to have;
Smooth was his face, as if he had just shaved.
I took him for a gelding or a mare.
As for his trade, from Berwick down to Ware
You'd not find such another pardon-seller.
For in his bag he had a pillowcase
Which had been, so he said, Our Lady's veil;
He said he had a snippet of the sail
St Peter had, that time he walked upon
The sea, and Jesus Christ caught hold of him.
And he'd a brass cross, set with pebble-stones,
And a glass reliquary of pigs' bones.
But with these relics, when he came upon
Some poor up-country priest or backwoods parson,
In just one day he'd pick up far more money
Than any parish priest was like to see

In two whole months. With double-talk and tricks
He made the people and the priest his dupes.
But to speak truth and do the fellow justice,
In church he made a splendid ecclesiastic.
He'd read a lesson, or saint's history,
But best of all he sang the offertory:
For, knowing well that when that hymn was sung,
He'd have to preach and polish smooth his tongue
To raise—as only he knew how—the wind,
The louder and the merrier he would sing.

    And now I've told you truly and concisely
The rank, and dress, and number of us all,
And why we gathered in a company
In Southwark, at that noble hostelry
Known as the Tabard, that's hard by the Bell.
But now the time has come for me to tell
What passed among us, what was said and done
The night of our arrival at the inn;
And afterwards I'll tell you how we journeyed,
And all the remainder of our pilgrimage.
But first I beg you, not to put it down
To my ill-breeding if my speech be plain
When telling what they looked like, what they said,
Or if I use the exact words they used.
For, as you all must know as well as I,
To tell a tale told by another man
You must repeat as nearly as you can
Each word, if that's the task you've undertaken,
However coarse or broad his language is;
Or, in the telling, you'll have to distort it
Or make things up, or find new words for it.
You can't hold back, even if he's your brother:
Whatever word is used, you must use also.
Christ Himself spoke out plain in Holy Writ,
And well you know there's nothing wrong with that.
Plato, as those who read him know, has said,
'The word must be related to the deed.'
Also I beg you to forgive it me
If I overlooked all standing and degree
As regards the order in which people come

Here in this tally, as I set them down:
My wits are none too bright, as you can see.
    Our host gave each and all a warm welcome,
And set us down to supper there and then.
The eatables he served were of the best;
Strong was the wine; we matched it with our thirst.
A handsome man our host, handsome indeed,
And a fit master of ceremonies.
He was a big man with protruding eyes
    —You'll find no better burgess in Cheapside—
Racy in talk, well-schooled and shrewd was he;
Also a proper man in every way.
And moreover he was a right good sort,
And after supper he began to joke,
And, when we had all paid our reckonings,
He spoke of pleasure, among other things:
'Truly,' said he, 'ladies and gentlemen,
Here you are all most heartily welcome.
Upon my word—I'm telling you no lie—
All year I've seen no jollier company
At one time in this inn, than I have now.
I'd make some fun for you, if I knew how.
And, as it happens, I have just now thought
Of something that will please you, at no cost.
    'You're off to Canterbury—so Godspeed!
The blessed martyr give you your reward!
And I'll be bound, that while you're on your way,
You'll be telling tales, and making holiday;
It makes no sense, and really it's no fun
To ride along the road dumb as a stone.
And therefore I'll devise a game for you,
To give you pleasure, as I said I'd do.
And if with one accord you all consent
To abide by my decision and judgement,
And if you'll do exactly as I say,
Tomorrow, when you're riding on your way,
Then, by my father's soul—for he is dead—
If you don't find it fun, why, here's my head!
Now not another word! Hold up your hands!'
    We were not long in making up our minds.

It seemed not worth deliberating, so
We gave our consent without more ado,
Told him to give us what commands he wished.
'Ladies and gentlemen,' began our host,
'Do yourselves a good turn, and hear me out:
But please don't turn your noses up at it.
I'll put it in a nutshell: here's the nub:
It's that you each, to shorten the long journey,
Shall tell two tales *en route* to Canterbury,
And, coming homeward, tell another two,
Stories of things that happened long ago.
Whoever best acquits himself, and tells
The most amusing and instructive tale,
Shall have a dinner, paid for by us all,
Here in this inn, and under this roof-tree,
When we come back again from Canterbury.
To make it the more fun, I'll gladly ride
With you at my own cost, and be your guide.
And anyone who disputes what I say
Must pay all our expenses on the way!
And if this plan appeals to all of you,
Tell me at once, and with no more ado,
And I'll make my arrangements here and now.'

    To this we all agreed, and gladly swore
To keep our promises; and furthermore
We asked him if he would consent to do
As he had said, and come and be our leader,
And judge our tales, and act as arbiter,
Set up our dinner too, at a fixed price;
And we'd obey whatever he might decide
In everything. And so, with one consent,
We bound ourselves to bow to his judgement.
And thereupon wine was at once brought in.
We drank; and not long after, everyone
Went off to bed, and that without delay.

    Next morning our host rose at break of day:
He was our cockcrow; so we all awoke.
He gathered us together in a flock,
And we rode, at little more than walking-pace
Till we had reached St Thomas' watering-place,

Where our host began reining in his horse.
'Ladies and gentlemen, attention please!'
Said he. 'All of you know what we agreed,
And I'm reminding you. If evensong
And matins are in harmony—that's to say,
If you are still of the same mind today—
Let's see who'll tell the first tale, and begin.
And whosoever baulks at my decision
Must pay for all we spend upon the way,
Or may I never touch a drop again!
And now let's draw lots before going on.
The one who draws the short straw must begin.
Sir Knight, my lord and master,' said our host,
'Now let's draw lots, for such is my request.
Come near,' said he, 'my lady Prioress,
And, Mister Scholar, lay by bashfulness,
Stop dreaming! Hands to drawing, everyone!'
To cut the story short, the draw began,
And, whether it was luck, or chance, or fate,
The truth is this: the lot fell to the knight,
Much to the content of the company.
Now, as was only right and proper, he
Must tell his tale, according to the bargain
Which, as you know, he'd made. What more to say?
And when the good man saw it must be so,
Being sensible, and accustomed to obey
And keep a promise he had freely given,
He said, 'Well, since I must begin the game,
Then welcome to the short straw, in God's name!
Now let's ride on, and listen to what I say.'
     And at these words we rode off on our way,
And he at once began, with cheerful face,
His tale. The way he told it was like this:

THE KNIGHT'S TALE

PART ONE

Once on a time, as old histories tell us,
There was a duke whose name was Theseus,
Who was of Athens lord and governor,
And in his day so great a conqueror
There was none mightier beneath the sun.
Many a wealthy kingdom he had won;
What with his generalship and bravery
He'd conquered all the land of Femeny,
Realm of the Amazons, once called Scythia,
And married there its Queen Hippolyta,
And brought her home with him to his country
With splendour, pomp, and solemn pageantry,
And also her young sister Emily.
And thus with music and in victory
I'll leave this noble duke, and let him ride
To Athens with his armed host at his side.

    And trust me, were it not too long to hear,
I would have told you fully the manner
In which the kingdom of Femeny
Was won by Theseus and his cavalry;
Especially the great battle fought between
The Amazons and the Athenian men;
And of the siege laid to Hippolyta,
The beautiful fierce Queen of Scythia;
And of the feast they held for the wedding,
The storm that blew up on the voyage home;
But all these things I must pass over now.
I have, the Lord knows, a large field to furrow,
Weak oxen in the team to draw my plough.
The remainder of the tale is long enough.
I'll not get in the way of anyone:
Let every fellow tell his tale in turn,
And now let's see which of us is to win
The dinner—where I left off, I'll begin.

This duke of whom I'm speaking, having come
Almost to the approaches of the town,
In the height of all his triumph and his joy
Perceived out of the corner of his eye
There kneeling in the highway, two by two,
A company of ladies in a row;
In clothes of black each one of them was clad.
But such a cry, such clamouring they made
That in this world there is no creature living
That ever heard the like of their lamenting;
Nor of their clamour would they stint, until
One of them clutched the reins of his bridle.

'Who may you be, that at my homecoming
Disturb the celebration with your crying?
Have you such jealousy', said Theseus,
'Of these my honours, that you lament thus?
And who's menaced you? or has done you hurt?
And now tell me if it may be put right,
And why you are all clad in black like this.'

Whereupon, fainting, with a deathlike face,
So it was pitiful to see and hear,
The eldest lady of the group made answer:
'My lord, you to whom Fortune has assigned
Victory and a conqueror's garland,
We grudge you neither glory nor honour,
But we beseech your mercy and succour.
Have mercy on our woe and our distress!
On us poor women, in your nobleness
Of heart, let but one drop of pity fall!
Indeed, sir, there is none amongst us all
Who was not once a duchess or a queen,
And is now destitute, as may be seen,
Since Fortune and her fickle wheel makes sure
That no prosperity can be secure.
And truly, lord, to watch your coming, we
In this the temple of Divine Pity
Have waited a whole fortnight for you here.
Now help us, sir, since it lies in your power.

'I who weep and wail in misery like this
Was once the wife of King Capaneus

Who died at Thebes—a curse upon that day!
And all of us who are dressed as you see,
We who are making all this lamentation,
Have each of us lost husbands in that town,
Killed in the siege. And now the ancient Creon
Who is, alas, the lord now of the city,
Brimful of anger and iniquity,
Out of tyrannic malice has defiled
The bodies of our husbands who were killed,
And dragged them all together in a heap;
And he will neither vouchsafe nor permit
Either their burial or burning, but
Has given them over to the dogs to eat.'

     And with these words, as soon as they were spoken,
They fell upon their faces, sadly crying
'Have some compassion on us wretched women!
And let our sorrow sink into your heart.'
With a breast filled with pity, the good duke
Leapt from his war-horse when he heard them speak.
It seemed to him as if his heart must break,
Seeing them so forlorn and desolate,
Who formerly had been of high estate;
And in his arms he raised up each of them
And tried to give them comfort; there and then
He swore upon his honour as a knight
He would put forth the utmost of his might
So to avenge them on the tyrant Creon
All Greece would talk about his overthrowing
By Theseus, and say he had been served
As one whose death had richly been deserved.
And thereupon his banner he displayed
And, delaying no longer, forth he rode
Toward the town of Thebes with his host.
He would not go near Athens, nor would rest
And take his ease for even half a day,
But pushed on, lodging that night on the way,
Having sent, with Hippolyta the queen,
Her sister Emily, so fair and young,
On to the town of Athens, there to stay
While he rode on; there is no more to say.

The red image of Mars with spear and shield
Gleams in his broad white standard till the fields
Seem lit on all sides with its glittering.
And borne next to his banner is his pennon
Of richest gold, embroidered with a great
Head of the Minotaur which he killed in Crete.
Thus rode this conquering duke; among the flower
Of chivalry he rode, in his armed power
To Thebes; where in splendour he drew up
Upon a field where he purposed to fight.
But, not to make too long a tale of this,
He fought with Creon, who was King of Thebes,
And killed him, as befits a valiant knight,
In fair combat, and put his men to flight;
And after that he took the town by storm,
And wall and beam and rafter he tore down,
And to the ladies he restored again
The bodies of their husbands who were slain
For funeral rites, as was the custom then.
But to describe it would take all too long—
The lamentation and the din of mourning
That went up from the ladies at the burning
Of the dead bodies, and the great honour
Duke Theseus, that noble conqueror,
Paid to the ladies when they took their leave—
For it is my intention to be brief.

And now this noble duke, this Theseus,
With Creon slain, and Thebes taken thus,
Quietly rested in the field all night,
All Creon's kingdom lying at his feet.
The pillagers went busily to work
After the battle and the Theban rout,
To rummage in the pile of slaughtered men
And strip the armour and the clothes from them.
Among the heap of corpses there they found
Pierced through and through with many a deep wound,
Two young knights lying bleeding side by side,
Both in the same expensive armour clad;
One of the two was Arcita by name,
The other knight was known as Palamon.

They were not quite alive nor wholly dead;
Seeing their coat-of-arms, the heralds said
That they were cousins of the royal blood
Of Thebes: that two sisters gave them birth.
Out of the heap of dead they were dragged forth.
Gently the looters bore them to the tent
Of Theseus; who thereupon had them sent
At once to Athens, to remain in prison
For ever, for he would not hear of ransom.
Then the great duke, so soon as this was done,
Gathered his host together and rode home
Crowned with the laurel of a conqueror,
And there lives on in happiness and honour
For ever after; what more need I say?
And Palamon and his friend Arcita
Are in a tower, in misery and grief
For evermore; no gold can buy release.

    So time passed, year by year and day by day,
Till it so happened, in the month of May,
That Emily, lovelier to look upon
Than is the lily on its stalk of green,
And fresher than the May with flowers new—
For with the rose's colour strove her hue,
Nor can I tell the lovelier of the two—
Well before day, as she was wont to do,
Was risen and dressed and ready to go out,
For, as you know, the nights are not for sleep
In May. The season stirs in every heart
That's noble, and from slumber rouses it,
Saying, 'Get up, pay homage to the spring!'
And therefore Emily was remembering
To rise and celebrate the month of May.
Picture her clad in colours fresh and gay:
Her yellow hair was plaited in a tress
Behind her back, a yard in length I'd guess.
And in the garden, while the sun uprises,
She wanders here and there, and as she pleases
Goes gathering flowers, mixing white and red,
To weave a graceful garland for her head;
And like an angel out of heaven sang.

The great tower, that was so thick and strong,
Which was the castle's principal dungeon
Wherein the two knights languished in prison
Who were and are the subject of my tale,
Adjoined exactly to the garden wall
Where Emily was used to take her pleasure.
Bright was the sun that morning, bright and clear,
And Palamon, that wretched prisoner,
As was his way, by leave of his gaoler,
Was up, and roaming in an upper room
From which the noble city could be seen,
Also the garden, filled with greenery,
In which the fair and radiant Emily
Was wandering, and walking up and down.
This wretched prisoner, this Palamon
Walks in his chamber, pacing to and fro,
And to himself complaining of his woe
And wishing that he never had been born.
It chanced, as fate or luck would have it then,
That through a window, fenced with iron bars
Solid and big as any wooden beam,
He cast his eye upon Emilia:
At which he started back with a loud cry,
As though he had been bitten to the heart.
And at that cry Arcita leapt up
And said, 'Why do you look so deathly pale?
What is the matter, cousin? Are you ill?
Who has upset you? Why did you cry out?
I beg you, for the love of God, submit
With patience to our gaol, since it must be.
Fortune has dealt us this adversity:
Some malign aspect or disposition
Of Saturn in some adverse position
Has brought it on us; nothing's to be done:
It stood thus in our stars when we were born;
The long and short of it is this: Endure.'

    And to that, Palamon said in reply,
'Truly, cousin, you have the wrong idea.
Prison was not the reason for my cry,
For I was hurt just now, pierced through the eye

Right to the heart; the wound is killing me.
The beauty of that lady whom I see
There in that garden wandering to and fro,
Made me cry out; she's cause of all my woe.
I don't know if she's woman or goddess,
But it is really Venus, I would guess.'
With that Palamon fell upon his knees,
Exclaiming: 'Venus, if it be your wish
Thus to transform yourself in this garden
For me, a sorrowful and wretched man,
Will you not help us to escape from prison?
And if it be my destiny to die
As foreordained by eternal decree
In prison, then at least bestow compassion
Upon our house, brought low by tyranny!'
But while he talked, Arcita cast his eye
To where the lady wandered to and fro;
And at the sight, her beauty hurt him so
That if Palamon has been wounded sore,
Arcita is as badly hurt, or more.
And with a sigh, dejectedly he spoke:
'Beauty so fresh destroys me, as I look
On her who wanders yonder in that place.
Unless I win her mercy and her grace
That I at least may see her every day,
I'm better dead; what more is there to say?'
    Hearing those words, his cousin Palamon
Looked black, and angrily replied to him:
'Do you say that in earnest or in jest?'
'No, on my oath,' said Arcita, 'in earnest.
So help me God, I'm in no mood to clown.'
Knitting his brows together, Palamon
Retorted, 'It would do you no great honour
Did you prove either faithless or a traitor
To me who am your cousin, and sworn brother,
Each bound by solemn oaths, one to the other,
That even if it means we die by torture,
Neither of us would ever cross the other
In love or any other thing, dear brother,
Till death shall part the two of us for ever!

No, you must always come to my support
As loyally as I must come to yours:
This was your solemn oath, and mine also,
Which you dare not deny, as I well know.
Thus you're in my confidence, there's no doubt,
And like a traitor you are now about
To begin to make love to my own lady
Whom I must love and serve until I die!
No, you shall not, be sure of that, you liar!
I loved her first, and told you my desire
As to my confidant, to one who swore
To lend support, as I have said before;
Therefore you are committed, as a knight,
To help me on, if it lies in your might,
Or else I dare aver you are forsworn.'

    And Arcita disdainfully answered him:
'You'll be forsworn', said he, 'sooner than I;
Forsworn I tell you, forsworn utterly!
For I loved her first, and as a woman too.
What can you say? You can't tell even now
Whether she is a goddess or a woman.
Yours is no more than a religious feeling:
Mine is real love, love of a human being;
I told you what happened to me for that reason,
As to my cousin, as to my sworn brother.

    'But, granted that you loved her earlier,
Have you forgot the old philosophic saw
That goes like this, "All's fair in love and war"?
Love is a mightier law, upon my soul,
Than any made by any mortal rule;
For love, all man-made laws are broken by
Folk of all kinds, all day and every day.
A man is bound to love, against all reason.
Though it should cost his life, there's no escaping,
Whether she's a maid, a widow, or a wife.
What's more, you are not likely, all your life,
To win her favour, any more than I;
For as you yourself know too certainly,
Both you and I have been condemned to prison
For ever; and for us there's no escaping.

We bicker like the two dogs for a bone;
They fought all day for it, and yet got none;
For while they quarrelled, a kite came along,
And from between them both bore off the bone.
And therefore, brother, as in politics,
Each for himself—there isn't any choice.
Love if you wish; I love, and ever shall.
And truly, my dear brother, one thing's sure:
Here in this prison we must both endure,
And each of us must take his chance, that's all.'

　　Bitter and long the strife between the two,
Which, had I leisure, I'd depict for you;
But to the point: it happened—if I may
Make a long story shorter—that one day
A noble duke, whose name was Perotheus,
Who'd been a friend of the Duke Theseus
Since they were boys together, came to pay
A visit to his friend, and holiday
In Athens, as he often used to do;
There was no man on earth whom he loved so—
And Theseus loved him just as tenderly.
So great was their love, ancient writers say,
That when one of them came at last to die,
His friend went down and looked for him in hell.
But that's a tale I have no wish to tell.

　　Duke Perotheus loved Arcita well,
And had known him in Thebes for many a year.
And finally, at the request and prayer
Of Perotheus, and without ransom,
Duke Theseus let Arcita out of prison,
Free to go as it pleased him anywhere
On certain terms: I'll tell you what they were.

　　This, set down in plain language, was the pact
Between Theseus and Arcita: that
If so be Arcita were ever found
Alive by night or day on Theseus' land
And Arcita were caught, it was agreed
His head was to be cut off with the sword.
There was no other choice or help for it
But to take leave, and go home with all speed.

He'd better watch out, now his neck's forfeit!
    How sharp the agony Arcita suffers now!
He feels death itself pierce his heart right through.
He weeps, he wails, he laments pitifully,
Watches a chance to kill himself secretly.
He cried, 'Alas, the day that I was born!
For I'm in a worse prison than before.
Now it's my fate eternally to dwell
Not in a purgatory, but in hell!
Alas that ever I knew Perotheus!
Otherwise I'd have stayed with Theseus
Fettered for ever in his prison. Then
Happiness and not misery had been mine.
Though I may never win nor yet deserve
Her favour, yet the sight of her I serve
Would have sufficed to have contented me.
O my dear cousin Palamon!' cried he,
'It seems that in this case you've come out best,
How happily in prison you may rest!
In prison—no indeed, but paradise!
Yours is the luck in this throw of the dice,
For you have sight of her, I the absence.
It's possible, being in her presence,
And since you are a doughty knight, and able,
That by some chance—since Fortune is changeable—
You'll sooner or later attain your desire
While I, who am exiled and in despair,
So barren of hope that there's no living creature
That's formed of earth or water, flame or air,
That can yield comfort or a cure for this—
Well may I die in despair and distress!
Farewell my life, my joy, my happiness!
    'Alas, why is it that most folk complain
So much of God's providence, or Fortune,
That often grants them, in so many ways,
Far better favours than they could devise?
Here's someone wishes for enormous wealth,
And this leads to his murder, or ill-health;
Here's someone longing to get out of prison,
Whose servants murder him when he gets home.

Infinite harms from this would seem to flow;
We don't know what we pray for here below,
But, like a man drunk as a wheelbarrow,
Who knows he's got a home where he can go,
But doesn't know which is the right road thither—
For when you're drunk, then every road's a slither.
Yes, in this world, that's how it goes with us;
All frantically seeking happiness,
But oftener than not in the wrong place.
There's no doubt we can all of us say so.
Especially I, who conceived a great notion
That if I only could escape from prison
Then joy and perfect happiness must be mine,
Whereas I'm exiled from my well-being.
For since I cannot see you, Emily,
I might as well be dead; no cure for me.'

　　Upon the other hand, when Palamon
Came to realize that Arcita had gone,
He created such an outcry, the great tower
Resounded with his bellowings and clamour.
The very fetters round his shins were wet
With the salt bitter tears Palamon shed.
'Alas,' he cried, 'God knows you've gained the day
In this our quarrel, cousin Arcita!
Now you're at large in Thebes, walking free
And caring little for my misery.
You may, since you are resolute and shrewd,
Assemble all our kinsfolk and kindred,
And make so fierce an assault on this city
That by some chance, or through some kind of treaty,
You may gain her for your lady and your wife,
She for whose sake I needs must lose my life.
For, when one weighs the chances, one can see,
As you're at large, no prisoner but free,
And a prince too, how great is your advantage:
Greater than mine, here dying in a cage.
For I must weep and wail while I'm alive,
With all that prison brings with it of grief;
And with the added pangs of love also,
Which doubles all my torment and my woe.'

With that the fire of jealousy awoke
Within his breast, and took hold of his heart
So furiously, that Palamon turned white,
The white of boxwood or of cold dead ash.

Then he cried, 'O you cruel gods, who rule
This world, and bind it with your eternal
Decree, and on the adamantine tablet
Inscribe your will and your eternal fiat,
What's mankind to you? Of no more esteem
Than is the sheep that cowers in the pen?
For man dies, just like any animal,
Suffers imprisonment and gaol as well,
Endures great adversity and sickness;
Often as not he's innocent, alas!
What governing mind is in such prescience
That so torments the guiltless innocent?
And, what makes all my tribulation worse,
Man is bound to observe the divine laws,
And for the love of God must curb his will,
Whereas no restraint curbs the animal.
And when a beast is dead, it feels no hurt,
But after death man has to weep and wail,
Despite his cares and sorrows while on earth.
There isn't any doubt it may be so.
I leave it to theologians to reply,
But well I know this world's a misery.
Alas! I see some viper, or thief, who's done
Mischief enough to many an honest man,
At large, free to go where it pleases him:
But I must stay in prison, for Saturn
And Juno too, have in their jealous rage
Almost destroyed the whole lineage
Of Thebes, whose broad walls desolate lie.
And Venus undoes me in another way,
With fear and jealousy of that Arcita.'

Now I will pause and let Palamon rest,
Leave him to wait in silence in his gaol,
Turn to Arcita, and resume his tale.

The summer passes, and the nights are long,
Increasing and redoubling love's keen sting

For both the lover and the prisoner.
I don't know which of them has more to bear—
To put it in a nutshell, Palamon
Is condemned to perpetual prison,
In chains and fetters till the day he dies;
Arcita is on pain of death exiled
For evermore from Theseus' territory,
Never to look again upon his lady.

Now all you lovers, let me pose the question:
Who's worse off, Arcita or Palamon?
The one may see his lady every day,
But is shut up in prison for always;
Whereas the other, free to go or come,
May never see his Emily again.
Now make your choice between them, if you can;
I'll go on with the tale as I began.

PART TWO

Now when Arcita at last reached Thebes,
He fainted half the day, and cried, 'Alas!'
For he would never see his lady again.
And, to sum up in a few words his pain,
Such grief was never felt by any creature
That was or will be while the world endures.
Bereft of food, of drink, and of his sleep,
Arcita grew thin, dry as a stick;
His eyes were hollow, horrible to look at,
Sallow and pale his colour, like cold ash;
And he was always solitary and alone,
And bewailing his woes the whole night long;
If he heard the sound of music, or a song,
The tears came, and he could not leave off weeping.
So enfeebled were his spirits, and so low,
So changed was he, that nobody would know
His voice and speech for Arcita's, though he heard it.
So changed was he, Arcita went about
For all the world as if not merely lovesick,
But actually manic, suffering from

Some melancholic humour in his forehead,
Which is the seat of imagination.
All things, in short, had been turned upside-down
Both in the character and disposition
Of the lover Arcita, that sorrowful man.

    But why go on all day about his pain?
When he had endured for a year or two
This cruel torment and this pain and woe
In Thebes (his native land, as I explained)
One night, as there he lay asleep, it seemed
To him as if Mercury, the winged god,
Appeared before him, bidding him take heart.
He bore erect his drowsy caduceus
And wore a helmet on his glorious
Hair—for he noted that he was arrayed
As when he lulled Argus the hundred-eyed.
And the god said: 'To Athens you must go,
There waits the destined ending of your woe.'
At this Arcita gave a start, and woke.
'For sure, however heavy be the cost,
I'll go to Athens, and right now,' said he,
'No fear of death is likely to deter me
From seeing her whom I love and obey.
If I'm with her, what matter if I die?'

    And as he spoke, he picked up a large mirror,
And saw how his complexion had changed colour,
And that his countenance was now wholly changed.
Right then it came into Arcita's mind
That, since his visage was so much disfigured
By the affliction that he had endured,
Were he to keep a low profile, he might
Live quite unknown in Athens all his life,
And see his lady almost every day.
Whereupon Arcita changed, without delay,
His clothes for those of a poor labourer,
Then, all alone—save only for a squire
To whom he had confided his whole story,
And was disguised as shabbily as he—
Set off for Athens by the shortest route.
And so one day he turned up at the court

And offered his services at the gate,
To fetch and carry, any kind of work;
And, to cut short a tale already long,
He got a job under a chamberlain
Whose office was to work for Emily;
A cunning fellow who kept a sharp eye
On every servant serving his mistress.
As Arcita was young, strong as an ox,
And tall as well, and big-boned, he was good
At drawing water and at hewing wood,
And doing any job that he was asked.
He spent a year or two in this service
As chamber-page to the fair Emily;
Philostrate was the name they called him by.
But never was a person of his class
Half so beloved as he, in the whole court.
So gentlemanly was his disposition
All Theseus' palace rang with his renown.
They said that it would be a gracious act
If Theseus were to raise him up a step,
And find for him a worthier employment,
Where he might better exercise his talent.
So great his reputation grew in time,
Both for his helpfulness and courteous tongue,
That the Duke Theseus, to have him near,
Appointed Arcita a chamber-squire,
With money to maintain his new position.
And people also brought to him his income
From his own country yearly, on the quiet;
But his spending was so prudent and discreet
That no one wondered how he came by it.
So for three years he led his life like this,
And did his job so well, in peace and war,
There was no man whom Theseus valued more.
Let's leave him in this happiness; and I'll
Speak of Palamon for a little while.

    Buried in his impregnable prison,
In darkness and in horror, Palamon
These seven years has worn himself away
In anguish and distress. And who but he

Feels twofold grief and pain? Love stings him so
That he's gone clean out of his wits for sorrow.
And, more than that, he is a prisoner
Not just for one year, but for evermore.

Who could rhyme rightly in the English tongue
His torment? To be sure I'm not the man;
So I will skip the matter, if I may.

It happened in the seventh year, in May,
On the third night, as ancient writers tell
Who give the fullest version of this tale,
Whether by accident or destiny
—For when a thing is fated, it must be—
That not long after midnight, Palamon,
Helped by a friend, broke out of his prison,
And, fast as he could go, fled from the city.
He'd given his gaoler such a dose of clarry
(A narcotic made of a certain wine
Spiked with the finest Theban opium),
The gaoler slept, no matter how they shook him,
The whole night long, and could not be awoken;
And off Palamon goes, fast as he can.

The night was short and day was near at hand,
So at all costs Palamon had to hide;
And to a nearby wood, with fearful tread,
And stealthy foot, there tiptoed Palamon;
To cut it short, he thought it his best plan
To hide himself within the wood all day,
And then when night had come to make his way
Homeward to Thebes, and there beg assistance
From friends to go to war with Theseus;
And, in a word, he'd either lose his life
Or else win Emily to be his wife.
Such was his purpose, and such was his plan.

And now I'll turn to Arcita again,
Who little guessed how close he was to mishap,
Till Fortune chose her time to spring the trap.

The busy lark, the messenger of day,
With song is saluting the morning grey,
While burning Phoebus, rising up so bright
That all the east is laughing in the light,

Is with his long beams drying in the groves
The silver drops still hanging on the leaves.
And Arcita, who in the royal palace
Is now chief squire to the Duke Theseus,
Rises and looks out on the cheerful day:
And to pay homage to the month of May,
Yet thinking all the while of his desire,
On a horse prancing like a flame of fire
Rides to amuse himself, out to the fields
A mile or two beyond the palace walls;
And by some chance begins to shape his course
Towards the very wood of which I spoke,
To make himself a garland from the groves
Either of woodbine or of hawthorn leaves;
And in the sunlight he sings lustily,
'May, with all your flowers and greenery,
Welcome to you, fresh and lovely May!
I hope to garner some green leaf or spray.'

   And, leaping from his horse lightheartedly,
He swiftly thrusts his way into the wood.
Along a path he wanders up and down,
As chance would have it, near where Palamon
Lay hidden in a thicket out of sight,
Lurking in mortal terror of his life.
Who it could be, Palamon had no notion;
He would have thought Arcita the last person—
But it's been truly said, these many years,
That 'Fields have eyes, and even woods have ears'.
It's best a man should keep his wits about him,
For people turn up when you least expect them.
How little did Arcita imagine
His friend was near, to hear what he was saying,
For he crouched in the thicket very still.

   When Arcita had tired of wandering,
And ended was the joyful song he sang,
He suddenly began to muse, and fell
In a brown study, as these lovers will,
Now high in heaven, and now deep in hell,
Now up, now down, a bucket in a well;
Just like a Friday, if the truth be spoken,

One moment, sunshine; the next, pouring down;
Just so does Venus overcloud and darken
Her followers' hearts; just as her day is fickle
(Friday's her day), so is her mood changeable;
There's no day of the week that's quite like Friday.

    His song done, Arcita began to sigh,
And without more ado sat himself down.
'Alas!' he cried, 'that ever I was born!
For how long, Juno, pitiless goddess,
Will you continue to wage war on Thebes?
Alas! it's been brought to destruction,
The royal blood of Cadmus and Amphion,
Of royal Cadmus, first to build and plan
Thebes, and the first founder of the town—
Cadmus, who was the city's first crowned king.
Of his lineage am I, and his offspring
By the true line, and of the blood royal;
And now I am a serf, so miserable
A slave, that as a menial squire I
Serve him who is my mortal enemy.
Yet Juno heaps upon me still more shame,
For I dare not be known by my own name;
Am no more Arcita, but Philostrate,
Am Arcita no more, but Fiddlestick!
Alas, Juno! Alas, relentless Mars!
All of our line have perished through your wrath
Except for me and wretched Palamon,
Whom Theseus martyrs in a dungeon.
On top of all, to break me utterly,
Love with his burning arrow has pierced me
And so scorched through my true and troubled heart,
My death was sewn for me before my shirt.
From one look of your eyes, O Emily!
I perish; and because of you I die.
All the rest of my misery and care
I'd count as nothing, as not worth a straw,
If I could only please you, Emily.'
With that he swooned, and for a long time lay
Senseless upon the ground; and then leapt up.

    Palamon felt as if a cold sword slid

Suddenly through his heart; and shuddering
With anger, could remain no longer hidden,
But, when he'd heard all that Arcita said,
Sprang like a madman with face pale and dead
Out of the thick bushes, crying, 'Liar!
You foul, black, lying traitor, Arcita!
I've got you, you who love my lady so,
For whom I suffer so much grief and pain;
You, my blood brother, sworn confidant too,
As I've told you before, time and again;
You who have made a dupe of Theseus
And changed your name dishonestly like this—
All I can say is, one of us must die!
You shall not love my lady Emily,
None shall love her but I, and only I;
For I am Palamon, your enemy!
Though here, as luck will have it, I've no weapon,
For I am only just escaped from prison,
Never you fear, it's either you must die,
Or else give up your love for Emily.
Now take your choice, for you shan't escape.'

      Then Arcita, with hatred in his heart
When he'd recognized Palamon, and heard
His tale, fierce as a lion drew his sword,
And thus replied: 'By God in heaven above,
If it weren't that you're sick and crazed with love,
And if you were not here without a sword,
You'd never walk a step out of this wood
Alive, but die instead, here by my hand!
For I disown the covenant and bond
Which you have made, or so you say, with me.
Get this into your head, fool: Love is free,
And I will love her still, in your despite!
But seeing that you are a noble knight,
And ready to decide your claim in battle,
My word on it, tomorrow I'll not fail,
None knowing, to be here, as I'm a knight;
And I'll bring arms enough for you and me:
Choose you the best, and leave the worst for me.
Tonight I'll bring you enough food and drink,

And bedding too; and if so be you win
And kill me in this wood that we are in,
She shall be yours, as far as I'm concerned.'
    'My hand on that,' was Palamon's response.
And so they separated till the morrow,
Each having pledged himself to meet the other.
    O Cupid, lacking in all charity,
Allowing none to share thy rule with thee!
It's a true saying, neither Love nor Power
Willingly brooks a rival or compeer,
As Arcita and Palamon have found.
Now Arcita rides straight back to the town,
And in the morning, before daylight, he
Prepares two sets of armour secretly,
Fit and sufficient for them to settle
Their difference upon the field of battle;
And on his horse, alone as he was born,
He carries all his gear in front of him.
Within this wood, at the set time and place,
Both Arcita and Palamon are met.
And then the colour of their faces changed
Like those of Thracian huntsmen when they stand
Guarding a gap in covert with the spear
When hunting for the lion, or the bear,
And hear the beast come rushing through the groves,
And breaking through the branches and the leaves,
And think, 'Here comes a deadly enemy!
No question, one of us has got to die;
For I must either kill it breaking cover,
Or it must do me in, if I should blunder.'
It happened so with them; they altered hue,
So well each knight the other's prowess knew.
    And there was no 'Good-day' or other greeting;
With no preliminaries, or word spoken,
Each of them helped the arming of the other,
As friendly as a brother helping brother;
And then with sharp strong spears each thrust at each,
So long it was a wonder it could last.
To see them fight, you'd have thought Palamon
Had been a raging ravenous lion;

And Arcita a cruel ruthless tiger.
They ran against each other, mad with ire,
Like wild boars frothing white foam, till they stood
Fighting up to the ankles in their blood.
And, fighting thus, I'll leave them for a while,
For it's of Theseus that I have to tell.

   Destiny, paramount minister
That in this world executes everywhere
God's predetermined providence, is so strong
Things thought impossible by everyone,
Things which you'd swear could never ever be,
Shall yet be brought to pass, though on a day
That happens once a thousand years or so.
For certainly our passions here below,
Whether of war or peace, or hate or love,
Are governed by the providence above.

   All this bears on the great Duke Theseus,
Who is so keen and eager for the chase,
And most of all in May to hunt the stag,
That no day dawns that finds him in his bed,
But up and dressed, in readiness to ride
With horn and hounds and huntsman at his side.
For Theseus takes such delight in hunting,
The killing of the stag is his great passion;
Forsaking Mars, the mighty god of war,
He follows now the huntress Diana.

   As I have said, the day was fine and clear
When Theseus set out, joyous and gay,
With fair Hippolyta, his lovely queen,
And Emily, all of them clad in green,
Riding to hunt in royallest array.
Making his way straight on towards a wood
Hard by, where he'd been told there was a stag,
Duke Theseus rode directly to a glade
Where, as he knew, a stag would often break
From cover, leap the brook, and so away.
It was his hope to try a course or two
With hounds he had selected for the work.

   Now, having come into the glade, the duke,
Shading his eyes from the still rising sun,

Caught sight of Arcita and Palamon.
They might have been two boars, furiously clashing;
Back and forth the bright swords flickered, flashing
So fearsomely, it seemed their lightest stroke
Would be enough to fell the stoutest oak.
But who they were, he had no clue whatever.
The duke clapped spurs that instant to his courser,
And at a bound he was between the pair
With sword pulled out, and crying, 'Stop! No more!
Who strikes another blow must lose his head!
By Mars, the next man I see move is dead!
But tell me now what manner of men you are
Who've the audacity to duel here
With no umpire or other officer,
As if it were a royal tournament?'
　　To which Palamon answered the next moment,
Saying, 'My lord, what needs it to waste breath?
We both of us deserve no less than death.
We are two unhappy creatures, two captives,
Already overburdened with our lives;
And as you are a lawful prince, and judge,
Grant to us neither mercy nor refuge.
But kill me first, for holy charity,
And kill this fellow here as well as me.
Or first kill him, for little do you know
That this is Arcita, your deadly foe,
Banished on pain of death from your country,
For which alone he well deserves to die.
For this is he who turned up at your gate
And, saying that his name was Philostrate,
Has made a fool of you year after year;
And you have gone and made him your chief squire,
And he's the man in love with Emily!
And, as the day has come when I must die,
I may as well make a full confession:
I am that miserable Palamon
Unlawfully escaped from your prison.
I am your deadly enemy; it is I
Who burn with love for lovely Emily,
And in her sight, this instant, I would die!

I ask for sentence, and for death, therefore.
But at the same time kill this fellow here,
Since both of us deserve death at your hand.'
    'That's about it,' the noble duke returned,
'By this confession, out of your own mouth
You stand condemned; which sentence I confirm;
No need for torture to make you confess!
By red almighty Mars, for you it's death!'
    But then the queen, in womanly sympathy,
Began to weep, and so did Emily,
And all the ladies in the company.
Greatest of pities it would be, they thought,
That such a fate should ever be their lot;
For noble birth was theirs, and high estate,
And love alone the matter at debate.
They saw their bleeding wounds, so deep and wide,
And all together as one woman cried,
'Have pity, sir, upon us women all!'
And then upon their bare knees down they fell,
And would have kissed his feet, there where he stood;
Till his wrath slackened, altering his mood,
For pity soon repairs to noble hearts.
Though anger made him shake with rage at first,
He briefly reconsidered what they'd done,
Summed up the causes of their transgression,
And, although in his wrath they stood accused,
Yet by his reason they were both excused.
For, so he argued, in love there's not a man
Who will not give himself what help he can;
No less will he endeavour to break prison.
And in his heart too he took pity on
The women, for they never ceased from weeping.
And in his noble heart he thought again,
And to himself, under his breath, he said,
'Shame on the ruler who has no compunction
But acts the lion, both in word and deed,
With those who are repentant and afraid,
As well as with the proud and scornful, those
Who persist in the error of their ways.
He's not got much discernment if he is

Unable to discriminate in such cases,
But treats alike humility and pride.'
And when his anger had thus passed away
He looked up, and a gleam was in his eye
As he spoke aloud; and this is what he said:
   'The god of love indeed! Now God bless me,
How great, how powerful a prince is he!
His might prevails against all obstacles,
He's a real god: look at his miracles:
For in his own way he can always make
Just what he likes of every human heart.
   'Look at Arcita here, and Palamon,
Escaping scot-free out of my prison
To Thebes, where they could have lived like kings,
And, knowing that I am their mortal foe,
And that their lives are in my hands also—
In spite of all this, Love none the less brings
Both of them here with open eyes, to die!
Now isn't that the very height of folly?
What bigger fool than he who is in love?
Just look at them, by God in heaven above!
Look at the state they're in! See how they bleed!
That's how the god of love, their master, paid
Their fees and wages for their services!
Yet they suppose themselves, these devotees
Of Love, to be completely rational!
But just you wait, here's the best joke of all:
The cause of all their horseplay, this young lady,
Has no more reason to thank them than I;
And of these fiery goings-on knows no more,
God save us, than a cuckoo or March hare.
But we'll try anything once, hot or cold;
A man must be a young fool, or an old—
That's what I found myself, in days long gone:
I was one of Love's servants in my time.
And therefore, since I too have felt the sting
Of Love, and know how it can hurt a man,
As one who's been caught often in that noose,
I here forgive you wholly your trespass,
At request of the queen, who's kneeling here,

And also Emily, my sister dear.
Now both of you must swear an oath to me,
That you will never do my country harm,
And never war upon me, night or day,
But be my friends in every way you can.
And I forgive you wholly this trespass.'
    And, as he asked, they swore in proper form;
As overlord they asked for his protection,
Which Theseus granted. Then he said to them:
'Even though she were a queen or a princess,
Both of you are eligible, of course,
As far as royal blood and riches go,
To marry her some day; but none the less
—It's of my sister Emily I speak,
The cause of all your jealousy and strife—
Though you fought for ever, it remains the truth,
As yourselves know, she cannot marry both.
Like it or leave it, one of you, therefore,
Of necessity must go whistle for her.
In other words she can't have both at once;
It's no use being angry or jealous.
And therefore I will order matters so
That each of you shall win what destiny
May have decreed for him. Let me explain—
Here is your part in what I shall arrange.
    'To put an end to it once and for all,
Without more argument, this is my will,
Like it or lump it, each of you is free,
And without ransom or impediment,
To go wherever he may wish to go,
And this day twelvemonth, and no later, he
Shall bring along with him a hundred knights
Armed at all points, and equipped for the lists,
And ready to make good his claim to her
In battle; and I promise on my honour,
And as I am a knight, that without fail
That whichever is able to prevail,
In other words, whichever of the two
Can, with his hundred I spoke of just now,
Kill or drive from the lists his adversary,

I shall then give in marriage Emily
To whomsoever Fortune favours so.
I'll build the lists here; and so help me God
I'll prove a fair and even-handed judge.
This is the only outcome I'll permit:
One of you must be killed or made captive.
And if what I have said seems good to you,
Say so, and count yourselves fortunate too.
For both of you the matter's at an end.'
     Who looks happier now than Palamon?
Who but Arcita leaps up in delight?
What tongue is there to tell, what pen to write
Of the joy thus created by the generous
Gesture made there by the Duke Theseus?
Down on their knees they fell, all sorts of folk,
To render thanks with all their hearts and might,
And the two Thebans thanked him oftenest;
Then, with light hearts, and filled with cheerfulness
And hope, rode homeward after their farewells,
To Thebes with its broad and ancient walls.

                    PART THREE

No doubt I'd be accounted most remiss
Did I neglect to tell how Theseus
Spared no expense, as he went busily
To work to build the lists right royally;
And nowhere in the world, I dare aver,
Was to be seen a finer amphitheatre.
A mile in radius was the circuit,
Entirely walled with stone, and ditched without,
As round as any circle was its shape,
Filled with tiered seats rising to sixty feet,
And so designed, that in whichever row
You sat, you'd not obstruct your neighbour's view.
     At the eastern end stood a white marble gate,
And at the west its fellow opposite.
In the whole world there was no place like it,

Considering how quickly it was built;
For there was not a craftsman in the land
Skilled in mathematics, no artisan,
No portrait-painter, carver of images,
Whom Theseus did not pay with board and wages
To build and decorate his amphitheatre.
Above the eastern gate he'd raised an altar
And temple for his rites and sacrifices
In Venus' honour, who is Love's goddess;
And for Mars another like it, on the west,
Which cost a wagonload of gold at least.
Then, in a turret on the northern wall,
He'd set up a resplendent sanctuary
Of white alabaster and red coral,
A rich, magnificent oratory
For Diana, goddess of chastity.

    But I'd almost forgotten to rehearse
The splendid carvings, sculptures, and pictures,
The forms, the shapes, the faces and figures,
That were contained in these three oratories.

    First, in the temple of Venus you saw unfold,
Set on the walls, and moving to behold,
The broken sleeps, the shuddering and cold
Sighs, the sacred tears, and doleful wailings,
The fiery stings, the longings and desirings,
That all Love's servants in this life endure;
The oaths that bind and make their vows secure;
Pleasure, Hope, Desire, and Foolhardiness,
Beauty and Youth, and Laughter and Largesse;
Potions and Force, Falsehood and Flattery,
Extravagance, Intrigue, and Jealousy
With yellow marigolds for a garland
And with a cuckoo perched upon her hand;
Feasts, Music, Songs, and Joy and Display,
And Dances; all of Love's phenomena
That I have told you of and mean to tell,
Were painted in their order on the wall,
And many more than I can mention here.
For indeed, the whole hill of Cytherea
Where Venus has her principal residence,

Was figured on the walls in fresco-paint,
With all its garden and its gaiety.
Nor was the porter, Idleness, passed by,
Nor beautiful Narcissus, of times gone;
Nor yet the folly of King Solomon,
Nor the enormous strength of Hercules,
Medea and Circe with their witcheries,
Nor the proud-hearted Turnus' stern courage,
Nor wealthy Croesus as a wretched slave.
As you can see, not Wisdom nor Riches,
Strength nor Beauty, Cunning nor Boldness,
Can ever hold a candle to Venus,
Who steers the entire world just as she pleases.
You see, these folk were so caught in her noose,
Time and again they'd cry out in distress,
As one or two examples here will show,
Although I could provide a thousand more.

   The image of Venus was marvellous. She
Was naked, floating on a boundless sea,
And all was hidden, from the navel down,
With green waves bright as glass; and a cithern
Was held in her right hand, while fluttering
Above a lovely garland of fresh scented
Roses that she was wearing, her doves circled.
In front of her stood her son Cupid, who
Was winged, as he is often shown; blind too.
He bore sharp shining arrows and a bow.

   Why should I not tell you as well of all
The frescoes that were painted on the wall
Inside the temple of red Mars the great,—
Frescoed throughout its entire length and breadth,
Like the interior of that dismal place
That's known as the Great Temple of Mars, in Thrace,
In that most frigid, cold, and icy region
Wherein Mars has his principal mansion?

   First on the wall was painted a forest
Inhabited by neither man nor beast,
And filled with knotted, gnarled, old barren trees,
Jagged broken stumps, rotten and hideous,
Through which there ran a rumble and a sough,

As if a gale were breaking every bough.
And half-way down a hill, under a slope,
There stood the temple of Mars Armipotent,
All built of burnished steel; its entrance was
Exiguous, long, and dismal to look at.
From it there came a rush, a furious blast
Of air, so strong it made the whole gate shake.
And through the doors a wintry glimmer shone,
For the wall had no window—no, not one
Through which a glimpse of light might enter in.
The door was of eternal adamant;
Lengthwise and crosswise it was double-clenched
With toughest iron; and, to make all strong,
Each pillar that the temple stood upon
Was barrel-thick, and made of gleaming iron.

    There you could see the dark imaginings
Of Treachery, and all its contrivings;
And cruel Anger, red as burning coal;
The pickpocket; and Fear with visage pale;
The smiler with the knife beneath his cloak;
The farmstead burning under the black smoke;
The perfidy of the murder in the bed;
Stark War, with open wounds, all bebloodied;
Discord, with dripping knife and direful face.
And full of screeching was that gruesome place.
The killer of himself you could see there,
With his own heart's blood drenching all his hair;
The driven nail that split the sleeping head;
Stark Death upon his back, with mouth agape.
In the middle of the temple sat Mischance,
With comfortless and dismal countenance.
And you saw Madness, laughing in his rage,
Armed Revolt, Hue and Cry, and fierce Outrage;
The carcass with slit throat flung in a bush;
A thousand dead, and they not killed by plague;
The tyrant with the plunder he had reft;
The town obliterated and laid waste.
You saw the reeling ships burn on the sea;
The wild bears crush the hunter; and the sow
Devour the child right in the very cradle;

The cook scalded, for all his length of ladle;
All the misfortune that to Mars belongs—
Run over by his cart, the carter pinned
And lying on the ground beneath its wheel.
Also there were, among those Mars protects,
The barber, and the butcher, and the smith
Who forges on his anvil the sharp sword.
And high above, depicted on a tower,
You saw Conquest, seated in great splendour,
With the sharp sword-blade hung above his head
Suspended by a thin and slender thread.
Caesar's and Nero's murders were portrayed,
And Mark Anthony's, albeit none of these
Had yet been born; but none the less their deaths
And the foreseen malignancy of Mars
Were there, told by these paintings, as the stars
Tell who is to be killed, or die, for love.
One example taken from legend should serve;
Even if I wished, I could not tell them all.

   Mars' effigy, with dire and maniacal
Regard, stood armed upon a chariot;
And over his head two starry figures shone,
Which ancient books of geomancy name,
The one Puella, the other Rubeus;
The god of war was represented thus.
A wolf stood at his feet in front of him,
Eyes glowering, about to eat a man;
Subtle the pencil that portrayed this story
In reverence of Mars, and of his glory.

   Now I shall speed as quickly as I may
To the holy temple of chaste Diana
To give you a description of it all.
A painted fresco covered every wall:
Scenes of the hunt, or shamefaced chastity.
There you could see sorrowful Callisto
Who, when she had offended Diana,
Was transformed from a woman to a bear,
And after that became the northern star;
So it was pictured; I can tell no more.
Her son's a star as well, as you can see.

And there was Dana, turned into a tree;
No, I don't mean the goddess Diana,
But Penneus' daughter, who was called Dana.
And there was Actaeon, turned into a stag
For punishment; he'd seen Diana naked;
And there you saw how his own deerhounds caught
And ate him up, because they knew him not.
Again, a little further on, you saw
How Atalanta hunted the wild boar
With Meleager and others; Diana
Plagued him for this, and he was made to pay;
And many another scene as wonderful,
Which I'll not trouble memory to recall.

   High on a stag the goddess had her seat,
With small hounds playing round about her feet;
Beneath her feet was set a waxing moon,
Waxing at present, but about to wane.
Her effigy was clothed in green, with bow
In hand, and arrows in a quiver. Low
The eyes were cast, bent in the direction
Of Pluto and his dark dominion.
Before her was a woman, labouring
In travail, with a child too long unborn,
Who plaintively was calling on her name,
Crying for help: 'For only you alone
May help me'—and whoever painted it
Grudged not a penny on the colours, but
Knew how to paint the life, and knew his job.

   At last the lists were ready. Theseus,
Who had provided, at no little cost,
The temples and the arena with all
Their furnishings down to the last detail,
Was wonderfully pleased when it was done.
But that's enough of Theseus; it's time
To speak of Arcita and Palamon.

   The day of their returning is at hand,
When each of them must bring a hundred knights
To settle all by battle in the lists.
And so to Athens each of them has brought,
In order that their covenant might be kept,

A hundred knights, all well armed and equipped.
Indeed it was maintained, by many a man,
That never, since the world itself began,
Had so few ever made, on sea or land,
So far as knightly prowess is concerned,
So noble and renowned a company;
For all who took delight in chivalry,
And meant to make themselves a famous name,
Had begged and prayed to take part in that game;
And any who was chosen was in luck.
You know, if such an event were set up
—Either in England or no matter where—
Tomorrow, every able-bodied knight
And lover would be eager to be there,—
To battle for a lady, Lord bless me!
A sight worth seeing, that's what it would be!

    And such were those who came with Palamon.
For many were the knights who rode with him,
Some armed with breastplate and habergeon
With a light tunic under; others wore
Steel plates, or else full suits of body-armour;
One carried a buckler, one a Prussian shield;
One cased his legs in armour, and would wield
A battleaxe; another, a steel mace;
New weapons; but on older models based.
Thus everyone was armed as he thought best,
As I have told.

             And there you might have seen
Riding in company with Palamon,
Lycurgus himself, the great King of Thrace.
Black was his beard, and powerful his face;
And the round rolling eyeballs in his head
Gleamed with a light half yellow and half red;
With beetling shaggy brows he looked about him
As if he were an eagle-headed gryphon;
Huge were his limbs, and his thews hard and strong,
His shoulders broad, arms muscular and long.
As was the custom of his native country
High on a chariot of gold stood he,
Four white bulls in the traces; and he wore

Instead of surcoat over his armour,
A bearskin turned by age as black as coal,
Its yellow claws gilded as bright as gold.
And combed behind his back, his flowing hair
Was black and shining like a raven's feather
Under a wreath of gold upon his head,
Of immense weight, thick as your arm; all set
With gleaming jewels—rubies, diamonds.
Round and about his chariot, white wolfhounds,
Twenty and more, each one big as a steer,
And trained to hunt the lion and the deer,
Were following him with tightly fastened muzzles,
Filed leash-rings fitted to their golden collars.
A hundred lords came with him in his train;
All excellently armed, stout-hearted men.

   According to legend, with Arcita
The great Emetrius, King of India,
Upon a bay horse accoutred in steel,
And covered with a diapered cloth of gold,
Came riding, like the god of weapons, Mars.
His surcoat was of purple silk from Tars*
And overlaid with white pearls, huge and round;
His saddle was of fine new-beaten gold;
A sleeveless cloak was hanging from his shoulder,
Swarming with rubies, red as sparkling fire;
His hair was curling, and arranged in rings—
Yellow they were, and glittered in the sun.
A high nose; eyes the colour of citron;
Full rounded lips; a florid complexion;
He'd a few freckles sprinkled on his face,
Some yellow, and some shading into black,
And gazed about him glaring like a lion.
His age was twenty-five, or so I reckon.
His beard had sprouted, and was well begun;
His voice was like a trumpet thundering.
Upon his head he wore a gay green garland
Of laurel, fresh and pleasing to the eye.
For sport, he carried perched upon his hand
A falcon, tamed and whiter than a lily.
He had a hundred nobles with him there,

Bareheaded, but all armed with richest gear,
Fully equipped in every kind of way.
For, take it from me, dukes and earls and kings
Had gathered in this splendid company
For love and the advance of chivalry.
You saw, on every side about the king,
Tame lions and tame leopards gambolling.
And in this style these nobles, one and all,
Came on the Sunday to the citadel
About nine, and there alighted in the town.

    And when that valiant knight, Duke Theseus,
Had brought them all to Thebes, his city,
And had, according to rank and degree,
Found lodging for the whole great company,
He laboured for the comfort of his guests,
Regaling them with banquets and with feasts,
Till no one could have shown, so people said,
A better judgement, or improved on it.

    The music, service at the feast, and how
Great gifts were presented to high and low,
The splendid spectacle of Theseus' palace,
Who sat first, and who last, upon the dais,
Which ladies were the loveliest, or danced best,
Or which of them could best dance and sing,
Or which could speak of love with most feeling,
What hawks were sitting on the perch above,
What dogs were lying on the floor below,
Of all these things I shall say nothing now,
But give the gist of it; I think that's best.
But to the point—so listen, if you please.

    That Sunday night, before the break of day,
Palamon heard the lark begin its lay—
Although it was two hours before the dawn,
Yet the lark sang—and up rose Palamon,
In highest spirits and with devout heart
Ready to go upon his pilgrimage
To Cytherea, the blessed and benign—
I mean, to Venus and her honoured shrine.
In the hour ruled by her, he slowly trod
Towards the lists, where Venus' temple stood,

And kneeling down, with humble demeanour
And a full heart, he prayed as you shall hear:
   'Fairest of the fair, daughter to Jupiter,
And bride of Vulcan, O my lady Venus,
You who bring joy to mount Cytherea,
By that love which you bore for Adonis,
Take pity on my bitter smarting tears,
And take into your heart my humble prayer.
Alas, I have no words with which to tell
The nature or the torment of my hell;
My heart's not able to reveal its woe;
I am so confused I can only say,
"Take pity, radiant Lady, for you know
My thought, and see the wounds that hurt me so.
Think of all this, take pity on my sorrow,
And evermore, so far as lies in me,
Your true and faithful servant I shall be,
And wage eternal war on chastity."
If you will help me, this shall be my vow.
I have no wish to brag of feats of arms,
Nor that tomorrow should bring victory,
Nor for renown, nor for the hollow glory
Of honour won, trumpeted up and down;
But what I want is the sole possession
Of Emily, and to die serving you.
Do you devise the means, and show me how.
Whether the victory is theirs or mine
Means nothing, makes no difference to me,
So that I have my lady in my arms.
Though it be true that Mars is god of arms,
Your power is so great in heaven above,
That, if you wish, I'll surely gain my love.
I'll worship in your temple ever after:
Wherever I may go, upon your altar
I shall make sacrifice, and light the flame;
If this be not your will, sweet Lady, then
I beg you let Arcita drive a spear
Straight through my heart tomorrow. I won't care,
It will mean nothing when I've lost my life,
If Arcita should win her for his wife.

This is the sum and total of my prayer:
Give me my love, O blissful Lady dear.'

His prayer being ended, Palamon
Made sacrifice with all due rites, although
I shall not tell of his devotions now.
But in the end the statue of Venus shook,
And made a sign; and this Palamon took
To mean his prayer had been heard that day.
For though the sign betokened a delay,
He was quite sure his boon was granted him;
And so with cheerful heart he hastened home.

Three hours after Palamon set forth
To visit the temple of divine Venus,
Up rose the sun, and up rose Emily,
And to Diana's temple made her way.
The maidens whom she took with her had brought
With them the fire, all ready and prepared;
The vestments and incense, and all the rest
That appertains to making sacrifice;
The horns filled full of mead, as custom was;
Nothing was lacking for her sacrifice.
The temple, smoking with incense, was full
Of splendid hangings; with light heart, Emily
Washes herself in water from a well;
How she performed that rite, I dare not tell,
Unless it be in a most general way;
And yet it would be fun to hear it all.
For men of goodwill, such things are no harm;
But they're best left to the imagination.
Her shining hair was combed, untressed and loose;
A coronal of evergreen oakleaves
Was on her head, neatly and meetly set.
Two fires upon the altar being lit,
She then performed those rites which you may read
In old books such as Statius' *Thebiad*.
Then she began, when she had lit the fire,
To pray to Diana, as you shall hear:

'O you chaste goddess of the greenwood, you
Who look upon earth, heaven, and the sea,
Queen of Pluto's dark kingdom there below,

Goddess of virgins, who for many a year
Have understood my heart, known my desire,
O keep me from your vengeance and anger,
From which Actaeon suffered long ago.
O you chaste goddess, you know well that I
Desire to be a virgin all my life,
Never to be a mistress or a wife.
You know I'm still one of your company,
A virgin, and a lover of the chase,
Who would far rather roam the forests wild
Than ever be a wife, or be with child.
I'll never be companioned with a man.
Now help me, Lady, since you may and can
By virtue of your threefold deity.*
For Palamon, who has such love for me,
And Arcita, whose passion hurts him so,
This favour, and no more, I beg from you:
Set peace and amity between the two,
And from me let their hearts be turned away,
Till all their burning love and hot desire,
And all their feverish torment and fire
Be quite put out, or else turned otherwhere.
But if it happens you won't grant this favour,
Or if my destiny be ordained so
That needs must I must have one of the two,
Send me the one that most desires me.
Behold, O goddess of chaste purity,
These bitter tears upon my cheeks falling.
And since you are a virgin, and our guardian,
Do you defend and guard my maidenhood,
And while I live I'll serve you as a maid.'

The fires were burning clear upon the altar
While Emily was thus engaged in prayer.
But suddenly she saw a curious sight:
For all at once one of the fires went out,
And caught again; immediately after that,
The other fire dimmed and extinguished;
And as it went out, it began a whistling,
Making a noise like wet branches burning,
And there, out of the end of every faggot,

Ran blood, or what seemed blood, drop after drop;
At which Emily, all but terrified
Out of her wits and senses, gave a cry:
But it was only out of shock she cried,
Having no notion what it signified;
And she wept pitiably. But Diana
Chose at this very moment to appear
Clothed like a huntress, with her bow in hand,
And spoke: 'Dry your tears, daughter; understand
Among the gods on high it is affirmed,
The eternal word is set down and confirmed,
That you shall marry one of these two men
Who suffer so for you; but which of them,
I may not say. And now farewell, for I
May stay no longer. But the fires that burn
Upon my altar shall in time make plain
Before you leave here, what your destiny
In this affair may be.' And thereupon
Her arrows clattered in their case and rang;
The goddess vanished. Emily, amazed,
Exclaimed aloud, 'What can this mean, alas?
I place myself in your protecting care,
To dispose as you wish, O Diana!'
And home she went, taking the shortest way;
And that was all—there is no more to say.

An hour after this—the hour of Mars—
Arcita strode to the fierce god of war's
Grim temple, to perform his sacrifice
With all due pagan rites and ceremonies.
With deep devotion, and with suppliant heart,
He made his prayer thus, direct to Mars:

'O you strong god, honoured in the cold
Regions of Thrace, and there accounted lord,
Who hold in every kingdom, every land,
The bridle-reins of war firm in your hand,
You who can sway their fortunes as you please,
Accept of me my humble sacrifice.
And if you think my youth may so deserve,
And that my strength is sufficient to serve
Your godhead; if you count me as your man,

I pray you to take pity on my pain.
By those same pangs, and by that scorching fire,
Those flames in which you once burned with desire
When Venus' beauty was all yours to use,
Young, lovely Venus, fresh and generous;
And when at will you had her in your arms—
Although things fell out badly for you once,
That time when Vulcan caught you in his net,
And found you lying with his wife, alack!
For all the pain that then was in your heart,
Take pity too, I pray, on my sore hurt.
For I am young and ignorant, as you know,
More racked and torn with love, as I suppose,
Than any living creature ever was;
For she for whom I suffer all this pain
Cares not a button if I sink or swim.
Before she'll promise me her heart, it's plain
I must by main strength win her in the lists;
And well I know that without help or grace
From you, my lord, my strength will not avail.
Then give me aid tomorrow in the battle,
For that fire that once burned you long ago,
As well as for that fire that burns me now,
So that tomorrow brings me victory—
Let mine be all the doing, yours the glory!
Above all other places I shall honour
Your sovereign temple; I shall ever labour
For your delight in your hard trade of war;
And I shall hang my banner in your fane,
With all the weapons of my company,
And ever after, till the day I die,
Feed an eternal fire there for you.
I bind myself, moreover, with this vow:
My beard, and these long hanging locks of hair,
As yet untouched by razor or by shears,
To you I dedicate; and I shall be
Your true and faithful servant till I die.
Take pity on my burning sorrows, Lord;
Give me the victory; I ask no more.'
  When strong Arcita had ceased his prayer,

The rings that hung upon the temple door
Clattered together; the doors clanged as well;
At which Arcita flinched. The altar fires
Blazed up until they lighted the whole temple,
And from the ground emanated a sweet smell.
Arcita lifted up his hand, to cast
More incense on the fire; until at last
After more and other rites, the carven
Statue of Mars made its steel hauberk ring;
And with that sound he heard a murmuring,
Very low and soft; and it said, 'Victory!'
To Mars he gave the honour and the glory,
Then, full of hope that all will turn out well,
Arcita heads for home; he is as joyful
And glad as the birds are of the bright sun.

But in a trice a furious row began
Over this granted boon, in heaven above,
As between Venus, the goddess of love,
And Mars, the cruel god armipotent.
Jupiter was kept busy making peace
Till bleak old Saturn, versed in stratagems,
Was able, from his long experience,
To find an answer satisfying both.
The old, in fact, have a great advantage:
Wisdom, experience, belong to age.
You can outdo the old, but not outwit.
Though it's not Saturn's nature to discourage
Terror and contention, he was quick
To find a remedy for the whole dispute.

'My dear daughter Venus,' said Saturn,
'Mine is the widest orbit round the sun,
And so my power is greater than men suppose;
Mine are all drownings in the gloomy seas,
Mine is the prison in the dark dungeon;
Mine are all stranglings, hangings by the throat,
The mutter and rebellion of the mob,
All discontents and clandestine poisonings;
When I am in the sign of Leo, mine
Is vengeance, mine is fell retribution.
Mine is the ruin of high palaces,

The falling of the walls and of the towers
Upon the miner and the carpenter.
For I killed Samson, shaking the pillar;
To me belong all deadly sicknesses,
Black treacheries, deceits, conspiracies;
The pestilence is fathered by my glance.
Now weep no more; I'll use all diligence
To see that your own knight, your Palamon,
Shall win his lady as you promised him.
Though Mars must help his man, yet none the less
Between you two there must some time be peace,
Albeit your temperaments are opposed,
From which these endless squabbles take their rise.
I am your grandfather, ready to command;
So dry your tears, I'll do what you demand.'
    Now that's enough about the gods above,
Of Mars, and Venus the goddess of love;
And I'll tell you, as plainly as I can,
The outcome of the tale that I began.

PART FOUR

Great junketings were going on that day
In Athens, while the joyous month of May
So lifted up the spirits, thus enhancing
The general gaiety, that people passed
All of the Monday jousting, or in dancing,
Or else spent it in Venus' high service.
But, needing to rise early for the fight,
Early they took themselves to bed that night.
And in the morning, when the dawn was breaking,
In all the inns about there was a clattering
Of horses and armour. Bands and companies
Of noblemen on stallions and palfreys
Rode to Theseus' palace. You'd have seen there
Much preparing of marvellous armour,
Well-wrought and rich; steelwork, embroidery,
And goldsmithry; the glittering shields, and steel
Headpieces, trappings, golden helmets, mail,

And coats-of-arms; princes on war-horses,
Robed splendidly; attendant knights, and squires
Nailing the spearheads fast, and buckling on
The helmets; strapping shields with leather thongs;
With so much to be done there, none was idle.
You'd see the horses foam, champ the gold bridle;
You'd see the armourers spurring to and fro
With file and hammer, fast as they could go;
Yeomen on foot, commoners by the thousand,
All of them armed with short staves, thickly crowding;
Pipes, trumpets, kettledrums, and clarions
That howl for blood in battle and in war;
The palace filled with people everywhere,
In knots of two or three, or nine or ten,
Debating back and forth, and speculating
About the Theban knights; some of them saying
One thing, and some another; others laying
Wagers on different knights—some backing Blackbeard,
Some Baldhead, while yet others were for Thatch-haired,
'That one looks tough, he'll put up a good fight!'
'That axe of his is twenty pounds in weight!'
—Thus the whole hall was full of speculation
A long time after that day's sun had risen.

  The great Duke Theseus, from sleep aroused
By the music and the hubbub of the crowd
Outside his palace gates, kept to his chamber,
Till—for they treated them with equal honour—
They brought the Theban knights to the palace.
Duke Theseus was at a window seat,
Just like a god in splendour on his throne.
Thither the press of people hurried in
To see him, and to pay due homage, and
Listen to his directives and commands.
'Ho there!' a herald on a scaffold shouted
Until the noise of the crowd abated,
And, silence having fallen on them all,
He then announced the great Duke Theseus' will:
  'The prince has, in his prudence and wisdom,
Concluded that it would be mere destruction
Of noble blood, if this affair were fought

In terms of mortal combat, to the death.
And therefore he desires to modify
His first proposal, so that none shall die.
No man, therefore, upon pain of death,
May bring with him, or have sent to the lists,
Any kind of arrow, poleaxe, or short knife;
No short, sharp-pointed sword for stabbing with
May any draw, nor carry at his side.
And at the tournament no man may ride
More than one charge against his opponent
With spear unblunted; but for self-defence,
Thrusting on foot's permitted; any man
Who's down, must not be killed, but must be taken,
Brought to the stake that's fixed on either side,
Forcibly carried there, and there abide.
And should it chance that either of the captains
Is captured, or else kills his opponent,
That is the finish of the tournament.
And now, Godspeed! Forward, and lay on hard!
Fight your fill, gentlemen, with mace and sword!
Go ahead and begin: the prince has spoken.'

The people's voice rose to the roof of heaven,
So loud they cried, with so joyous a note:
And their cry was, 'God save so good a duke!
He'll have no wholesale spilling of good blood!'
Up go the trumpets, and the fanfares shrilled,
And in due order the whole company
Goes riding to the lists, through the great city
Hung with no plainer stuff than cloth-of-gold.

In princely state the noble Theseus rides
With the two Thebans upon either side;
Behind them rode the queen, and Emily,
And after them, another company
Of various folk, in order of degree.
And in this way they passed through the city
Untiil they reached the lists with time in hand.
It was still early in the morning, when
Theseus took his seat in state on high,
With Queen Hippolyta, and Emily,
And other ladies, each in their degree.

Meanwhile, a great crowd presses to the seats.
At the west end, there enters through the gates
Of Mars, Arcita with red banner and
The hundred knights belonging to his band;
And at the selfsame moment Palamon
Enters by the gates of Venus at the east,
With a white banner and defiant face.
No matter where you looked, you'd never find
Anywhere in the world two companies
So equally matched at every point as these;
None might, no matter how expert, contend
That any, in either, held an advantage
In years, in birth or rank, or in courage,
So evenly had each of them been chosen.
In two trim rows they ranged themselves. And when
The roll was called, and every name was read,
Their numbers checked to ensure no deceit,
Then were the gates shut, and up goes the cry:
'Now do your duty, show your mettle, knights!'
    The heralds leave off spurring up and down;
Now the loud trumpets, and the clarion
Ring out; and on the east side and the west
In go the spears, couched firm for the attack,
In go the spurs, sharp in the horse's side.
We'll soon see who can joust, and who can ride!
There on thick shields the shafts shiver and split.
One of them through the breast-bone feels the thrust.
Twenty feet in the air the spears leap up;
Out come the swords, like silver is their flash;
They hew at helms, and hack them all to bits;
And out in harsh red floods the blood now spurts;
Under their heavy maces the bones smash.
This one thrusts through the thickest of the press
Where strongest horses stumble; down go all;
One's rolling underfoot, just like a ball;
And one, on foot, thrusts with his broken shaft,
Another with his horse comes crashing down;
And one is wounded through the body, taken,
Manhandled to the stake, furiously fighting;
There he, according to the rules, must bide.

Another's captured on the other side.
From time to time Theseus makes them rest
To take refreshment, drink if they so wish.
Often have these two Thebans met in combat,
And each has done his opponent a mischief,
And both have been unhorsed by one another.
No tiger in the vale of Gargophia
Reft of its cub and turning on the hunter,
Could have been crueller than Arcita
Is in his jealous rage to Palamon.
And there's no lion hunted in Benmarin
More fell, more hunger-frenzied for its prey
And thirsty for its blood, than Palamon
Out to kill Arcita, his enemy.
The eager blows rain down and bite
Their helmets; and the red blood gushes out.
But soon or late, all things must have an end.
Before the sun went down, the mighty King
Emetrius had at length contrived to catch
Palamon fighting Arcita; his sword bit
Deep into Palamon's flesh; whom it took
Twenty to drag, unyielding, to the stake.
In coming to the aid of Palamon
The mighty King Lycurgus was knocked down,
While King Emetrius, for all his strength,
Was thrown out of his saddle a sword's length
By Palamon's last blow, so hard he hit;
But all for nothing—he's dragged to the stake.
Of no avail is his courageous heart:
There he must stay now that he has been caught,
Held there by force, and by the rules agreed on.

    Now who is in worse case than Palamon,
Since he may not go out again to fight?
And when Duke Theseus had seen it happen,
To everyone there fighting he called out:
'Ho there! No more! All's over now and done!
I'll be an honest judge, no partisan:
Arcita of Thebes shall have Emily,
The luck's with him, she has been fairly won.'
At once there rose a shout from one and all

For joy at this, so loud and thunderous
It seemed the very lists themselves would fall.
    Now what can Venus do, in heaven above?
What can she do or say, the Queen of Love,
But weep because she cannot have her wish,
Until her tears rain down upon the lists?
Cried she, 'Now I am thoroughly disgraced!'
    But Saturn answered, 'Daughter, hold your tongue!
Mars has his way, his knight has got his boon,
And, as I live, you'll be contented soon.'
    The trumpeters and the loud music blare;
Loudly the heralds yell and shout and cry
Happy as larks for the Prince Arcita.
But bear with me, and don't anticipate,
You'll hear what kind of miracle happened next.
    Noble Arcita, having taken off
His helmet, so that he can show his face,
Spurs the whole length of the great arena
All the while looking up at Emily,
Who casts on him, in turn, a friendly eye,
(For, generally speaking, all women
Follow whoever's favoured by Fortune)
And she was all his heart's delight and joy.
    Out of the ground there bursts a hellborn Fury,
From Pluto sent at request of Saturn,
At which his frightened horse begins to shy,
And leap aside, and stumble in leaping;
And before Arcita can react, he
Has been thrown off and pitched upon his head,
And lies in the arena as if dead,
With his chest smashed in by his saddle-bow.
Turning as black as coal, black as a crow,
He lay there, the blood rushing to his face.
Quickly they carried him out of the place
With heavy hearts, to Theseus' palace.
They cut the laces of his armour, then
Put him to bed without the least delay,
For he was conscious still, and still alive,
And calling all the while for Emily.
    And now Duke Theseus and his guests arrive

Back home at Athens, with great pomp and joy.
Despite what happened, he'd not cast a gloom
If he could help it, over everyone;
Besides, they said Arcita would not die,
But must recover from his injury.
They were as pleased about another thing:
Not one of all their number had been slain,
Though some were badly wounded, like the man
Who'd been thrust with a spear through the breast-bone.
As for their other wounds and broken arms,
Some of them had ointments, some had charms;
They also drank infusions and herb-medicines
To help regain the full use of their limbs;
For which the noble duke, as best he can,
Comforts and honours every one of them,
Holding high revel all the livelong night
For the foreign lords and princes, as was right.
No thought was there of victory or defeat
Any more than at a tournament or joust,
For, really, there was no disgrace. A fall
Need not be counted, it's incidental;
And to be hauled by main force to the stake
Unyielding, captured by a score of knights,
One man all on his own, and harried so,
Pulled and propelled with arm and foot and toe,
And his horse driven off with stave and cudgel
By yeomen, men on foot, and boys as well:
There's nobody would count that as disgrace,
Or who would dare to call it cowardice!
It was proclaimed, by order of the duke,
To put a stop to rancour and malice,
That neither side did better than the other,
But each matched each, as brother matches brother.
He gave appropriate gifts to one and all,
And for three days he held high festival,
And honourably escorted the two kings
As far as a day's travel from Athens.
Then every man went home the shortest way:
It was all over, bar 'Good luck!' 'Goodbye!'
About the tournament I'll say no more,

c.t.—5

But tell of Palamon and Arcita.
    Swollen and swelling is Arcita's breast,
The pain about his heart grows worse and worse.
The clotted blood, for all the doctors' skill
Corrupts and festers in his belly, till
Bleeding and cupping are no help for him,
Nor herbal draughts, nor any medicine.
For the expelling, or 'animal' power
Can neither eliminate nor expel
The venom from the other, 'natural', power.
The vessels of his lungs begin to swell
And every muscle, deep down in his chest,
With poison and with gangrene is corrupt.
Nothing is any use to save his life,
For he can neither vomit nor excrete.*
Broken and shattered is that part of him,
And Nature now has no domination.
All you can say, where Nature will not work,
Is, 'Goodbye, doctor! Take the man to church!'
The long and short of it is, he must die;
And so Arcita sends for Emily,
And for his dearest cousin, Palamon.
And this is what Arcita said to them:
'The heavy heart that is within my breast
May not declare a tithe of my sharp grief
To you, my lady, whom I love the best;
But I bequeath the service of my ghost
To you above all created beings, for
I know my life no longer may endure.
Alas the woe! Alas the bitter pain
That I have suffered for you for so long!
And alas death! Alas, my Emily!
Alas, the parting of our company!
Alas, queen of my heart! Alas, my bride!*
Lady of my heart, and causer of my death!
What is this world? What does man ask to have?
Now with his love, now in the chilling grave,
Alone, and with no kind of company!
Sweet enemy, farewell, my Emily!
Hold and fold me in your two arms gently

For love of God, and hear what I shall say.
   'For love of you there's been contention
Between me and my cousin Palamon,
Rancour and jealousy for many a day.
Now may wise Jupiter direct my heart
Fittingly and faithfully to portray
A lover's attributes and qualities,
Such as faith, wisdom, honour, chivalry,
Rank, birth, humility, magnanimity,
And all that's needed for the lover's art.
As I look to Jupiter for salvation,
In the whole world there isn't anyone
So worthy to be loved as Palamon,
Who serves you, and will serve you all his life.
And if you ever think to be a wife,
Do not forget the noble Palamon.'
And with these words, his speech began to fail,
For from his feet up to his breast there came
The chill of death, so that it vanquished him,
While in his arms the vital power dispersed.
The intellect that lived in his sick breast
Failed only when the heart was touched by death.
And then, with darkening eyes and flagging breath,
Upon his lady he still cast his eye.
His last word was, 'Have pity, Emily!'
His spirit changed its house and went on—where
I cannot say, for I was never there.
So I'll shut up; I'm no theologian;
There's nothing about souls in the volume
I found my story in; it's not my line
To talk about such theories, although
Much has been written about where they go.
Arcita's cold; may Mars direct his soul:
It is of Emily I have to tell.
   Emily shrieks; Palamon groans; and soon,
His sister having fallen in a swoon
Beside the corpse, the duke leads her away.
But what's the use of wasting precious time
In telling how she wept both night and day?
In cases like this women feel such sorrow

When they have lost their husbands, most of them
Will mourn and grieve and lament in this way,
Or very likely fall in a decline
So deep that in the end they're bound to die.

Unending were the laments, and the tears
Shed by the old, and those of tender years,
For the dead Theban, throughout the city.
The whole town wept for him, both man and boy;
Be sure there was not half the lamentation
When Hector, newly killed, was brought back home
To Troy. What a mourning there was here!
Scratching of cheeks, and tearing of the hair!
And women crying, 'O why did you die,
Had you not gold enough, and Emily?'

There was no man could comfort Theseus,
Excepting his old father, Aegeus,
Who understood the world's transmutations,
Having seen so many of its ups and downs,
Joy after woe, grief after happiness;
He gave examples of such happenings.

'Just as no man has ever died,' said he,
'Who has not lived in this world in some way,
Just so there never lived a man,' he said,
'Anywhere on earth, but at some time was dead.
This world is but a thoroughfare of woe,
And we are pilgrims, travelling to and fro.
All earthly troubles have an end in death.'
And he said much more to the same effect,
Exhorting people to be comforted.

Duke Theseus then gave the most careful thought
To finding the best place to build the tomb
Of good Arcita: one to honour him,
Appropriate to his rank and position.
At length he came to the conclusion
That where Arcita and Palamon
Had first fought one another for their love,
There in that very grove so fresh and green,
Where Arcita had felt the burning flame
Of love, and amorous desires, and sung
His complaint, there he would erect a pyre

Where all the funeral rites could be performed.
Then he commanded them to hack and hew
The ancient oaks, and lay them in a row
Of faggots, properly disposed to burn.
So on swift feet the duke's officers run
At his command. Next, Theseus bids them bring
A funeral bier, and over it he spread
A cloth-of-gold, the richest that he had.
And he had Arcita swathed in the same
Material, with white gloves on his hands,
His head wreathed with a fresh green laurel crown,
A keen and gleaming sword set in his hand.
He laid him, face uncovered, on the bier,
Then wept, till it would break your heart to hear.
When day broke, that it might be seen by all
He had the body brought into the hall,
Which echoed with the din of lamentation.
   Then the heart-broken Theban, Palamon,
Came with bedraggled beard, ash-matted hair,
In clothes of black, bespotted with his tears,
And, weeping more than any, Emily,
The saddest there of the whole company.
As Arcita was of the blood royal,
To dignify and enrich the funeral
Duke Theseus commanded them to bring
Three horses, all harnessed in glittering
Steel, covered with the arms of Arcita.
Each of these huge white horses had a rider,
One of them carrying the dead man's shield,
While high aloft another man upheld
His spear, and the third bore his Turkish bow
(Its quiver burnished gold, the trappings too),
And they rode sadly at a walking pace
Towards the greenwood grove, as you shall hear.
And following them the noblest of the Greeks
Bore on their shoulders Prince Arcita's bier
With even steps, with their eyes red and wet,
Across the city, along its main street
Spread with black draperies, hung from on high,
And draped with the same colour all the way.

On the right hand there walked old Aegeus,
And on the other side, Duke Theseus,
With vessels in their hands of finest gold,
All full of wine and honey, milk and blood;
Palamon next, with a great company,
And these were followed by poor Emily,
Bearing the fire—the custom in those days—
For her part in the funeral service.

   Splendid the work and preparation for
The funeral, and building of the pyre;
The green top of the pyre reached the sky,
Its base spread twenty fathoms—that's to say
The branches and the logs reached out that far.
First, they laid down load after load of straw—
But how they built the pyre as high as heaven,
How the trees were felled, or what their names were even,
—Oak, fir, beech, aspen, elder, ilex, hazel,
Willow, elm, plane, ash, box, poplar, lime, laurel,
Maple, thorn, beech, yew, dogwood, and chestnut—
Are things I'm not proposing to relate;
Nor how the demigods ran up and down,
Disinherited of their habitation,
In which they'd lived in quietness and peace,
Nymphs, dryads, fauns, and hamadryades;
Nor how the animals and birds all fled
In panic terror, when they felled the wood;
Nor how the ground blenched, aghast at the bright
Sun, being unaccustomed to the light;
Nor how the pyre was first laid with straw,
Then with dry sticks, and faggots split in three,
Then with green wood, and then with spicery,
Then cloth-of-gold, and gems and jewellery,
And then with garlands hung with many flowers,
With myrrh and incense, and all sweet odours;
Nor how Arcita lay amidst all this,
Nor what the treasure piled around him was;
Nor how Emily, according to usage,
Thrust in the funeral torch, and lit the blaze;
Nor how she fainted when the fire built up,
Nor even what she said, nor what she thought,

Nor what the jewels were that people cast
Into the fire when the flames blazed up;
I'll not tell how some threw in shield and spear,
Others the very clothing that they wore,
And goblets full of wine, and milk, and blood,
Into the roaring flames that blazed white-hot;
Nor how the Greeks, in a great band together,
Faced to the left, then with a loud shouting
Galloped their horses thrice around the pyre,
And round it thrice again, with spears clattering;
Nor how three times the women made their keen;
Nor how Emily was at last led home;
Nor how Arcita burned to ashes cold;
Nor shall I tell you how his wake was held,
The livelong night; nor how the Greeks contested
The funeral games, for I'm not interested
In who wrestled best, his body oiled and naked,
Or who made the best showing, though bested.
I will not even tell how they went home
To Athens, once the funeral games were done;
But make an end of my long story, and
Come to the point as quickly as I can.

    In time, after the passage of some years,
Ended at length the mourning and the tears
Of all the Greeks, by tacit agreement.
Then it appears they held a parliament
At Athens, to talk over various
Affairs and issues; among which there was
Some talk of making foreign alliances,
And of compelling Theban allegiance.
And therefore the good Theseus lost no time
In sending for the noble Palamon.
Not knowing for what cause he came, or why,
Dressed in his clothes of black, sorrowfully
Prince Palamon has hastened to obey.
Thereupon Theseus sent for Emily.
When all were seated, and the place was hushed,
For a short space of time Theseus paused.
Before speaking from the wisdom of his heart
He let his eyes rove over them. His face

Was serious. Then with a quiet sigh
He spoke his mind to the whole assembly:
   'When the First Mover, the First Cause above,
First created the great chain of love,
Great was His purpose, great the consequence.
He knew all whys and wherefores when He bent
With that great chain of love, water and land,
And air and fire, within fixed certain bounds
They may not go beyond. And that same Prince
And Mover', he continued, 'established
Here in this miserable world below
For all things that are engendered on earth,
Fixed seasons, days, durations, beyond which
They may last no longer, not a day; although
That period they may easily abridge.
There is no need to cite authorities;
Experience proves it; all I want to do
Is to make clear just what my meaning is.
Then from this divine order it is plain
The Mover is eternal, does not change.
It's clear to anyone, except a fool,
That every part derives from a great Whole,
For Nature did not take its beginning
From any part or portion of a thing,
But from a being perfect and immutable,
Descending thence to become corruptible.
And therefore in His provident foresight
He has so ordered His creation that
Things of all kinds, all processes, survive
By continual succession, do not live
For ever and ever. And this is no lie,
As anyone can see with half an eye.
Look at the oak, that has so long a growth
From the time it first begins to germinate,
And has so long a life, as is well known,
But in the end decays; the tree falls down.
   'Likewise consider how the hardest stone
Under our feet, the stone we tread upon
As it lies on the road, is worn away.
In time the broadest river will run dry;

Great cities we have seen decline and fall;
Thus we may see that an end comes to all.

'In the case of men and women, it's clear also
That at one time or another, they must go;
That is to say, in either youth or age
Die you must, whether you be king or page;
One dies in bed, another in the sea,
Another on dry land, it's plain to see;
It can't be helped, for all go the same way.
And so I can affirm all things must die.

'Who contrives this but Jupiter the King,
Who is the Prince and Cause of everything,
Who converts all back to its proper source
From which, in very truth, it first arose?
And against this it's useless, in the end,
For any living creature to contend.

'It's common sense, or so it seems to me,
To make a virtue of necessity,
Take what we can't avoid with a good grace,
Especially what's due to all of us.
Whoever mutters at this is a fool,
And rebellious to Him Who governs all.
The man who dies in his life's prime and flower
While sure of his good name, wins most honour,
For in that case he brings no shame to either
Himself or friends. And his friend ought to be
Gladder of his death when it's with honour he
Yields up his latest breath, than when his name
Has faded in the course of age and time,
When all his former prowess is forgotten.
And so it's best, as regards his good name,
To die when he is at the height of fame.

'Now to deny this is perversity.
Then why should we repine or be downcast
That good Arcita, flower of chivalry,
Has departed with honour and repute
Out of the foul prison of this life?
And why should these, his cousin and his wife,*
Lament his happiness, who loved them well?
Would he thank them? Not on your life: his soul

And themselves they offend, yet are no happier.
    'What conclusion is there for me to draw
From this long argument, save to advise
We should let gladness follow upon sadness,
And then thank Jupiter for all his goodness?
And now, before departing from this place,
I think that of two sorrows we should make
One perfect joy that will always last.
And look: there where we find the deepest sorrow,
There shall we first of all begin the cure.

    'Sister,' said he, 'it has my full consent,
And is confirmed here by my parliament,
That noble Palamon, your own true knight,
Who's served you with his whole soul, heart, and might,
As he has always done since first you knew him,
Deserves your favour, so take pity on him,
And take him for your lord and your husband.
We have agreed on this; give me your hand.
And now let's see your womanly compassion!
For after all, he's a king's brother's son;
Even if he were no knight, but a poor squire,
As he has loved and served you year by year,
And suffered for you such adversity,
That ought to be considered, for, believe me,
Noble compassion should outweigh justice.'
Then he addressed the knight, Palamon, thus:
'I take it there needs little arguing
To obtain your agreement to this thing.
Come here and take your lady by the hand.'
And so between them both was sealed the bond
Of matrimony, which some folk term marriage,
By the whole council and the baronage.
And thus with joy and with minstrelsy
Palamon has wedded Emily.
May God, Who created this world so wide,
Grant him His love, for he has dearly paid;
For Palamon from now on all is bliss,
He lives in wealth and health and happiness,
And Emily loves him so tenderly,
And he loves and serves her so devotedly,

That between those two was never spoken
A jealous word, nor so much as a cross one.
No more of Palamon and Emily,
And God save all this noble company!

[handwritten: competing points of view of { knight ⇒ idealism / miller ⇒ carnal]

THE MILLER'S PROLOGUE

Here follows the argument between the Host and the Miller

And when at last the knight's tale had been told,
There was not one among us, young or old,
Who did not say it was a noble story,
Well worth remembering; especially
All of the better sort. Laughing, our host
Swore, 'As I live, we're now on the right track!
A good beginning; we've unstrapped the pack.
And now let's see who'll tell another tale,
For there's no doubt the game is well begun.
Now tell me, Mister Monk, that's if you can,
Something to cap the knight's, and pay him out.'
The miller, half-seas over, was so pale
With drink that he could barely keep his seat
Upon his horse; his manners were quite lost,
He'd not doff hood nor hat, and wouldn't wait,
But, ranting like a Pilate on the stage,*
Began to swear: 'Christ's arms and blood and bones,
I've got a splendid tale for the occasion
To pay the knight out with, and cap his tale.'
Our host could see that he was drunk with ale,
And said, 'Hold hard, Robin! Watch it, brother!
Some better man must first tell us another,
So pipe down now; let's make a go of it.'
    'By all that's holy, that I won't,' said he,
'I mean to speak, or I'll be on my way.'
Answered our host, 'In Satan's name, say on!
You're nothing but a fool, your wits are drowned.'
    'Now listen,' said the miller, 'one and all!

[handwritten: Miller is a drunk, rouge]

But first I make a public avowal
That I am drunk; I can tell by the sound.
So, if I trip up on a word or two,
Blame it on Southwark ale, I beg of you.
For I'll tell a story of a carpenter,
And of his wife also; and how a scholar
Set his cap at her, made a fool of him.'

But the reeve interrupted, 'Hold your tongue!
Leave off your sottish rude obscenity.
It is a sin, and also a great folly,
To slander or aggravate any man,
And also to bring wives in disrepute.
You've many other things to talk about.'

The drunken miller made a quick retort.
Said he, 'We all know, don't we, dear old Oswald,
It's he who has no wife who is no cuckold.
But mind you, I'm not saying you are one;
There's plenty of good wives—for every one
That's bad, there are a thousand who are good,
As you should know, unless you're off your head.
Now why are you so worked up at my tale?
For, pardon me, I have a wife as well.
Yet not for all the oxen in my team
Would I push my luck so far as to presume
That I was one myself. I will believe
I'm not. We mustn't be inquisitive
About God's secret doings, or our wives'.
So long as you can find God's plenty there,
About the rest, you've no call to enquire.'

In short, the miller would not curb his tongue
Or language for the sake of anyone,
But told his vulgar tale in his own way.
I'm sorry that I must repeat it here.
And therefore, I entreat all decent folk
For God's sake don't imagine that I speak
With any evil motive, but because
I'm bound to tell, for better or for worse,
All of their stories, or else falsify
My subject-matter as you have it here;
And so, should anyone not wish to hear,

Turn the page over, choose another tale.
There's plenty of all kinds, to please you all:
True tales that touch on manners and on morals,
As well as piety and saintliness;
I'm not responsible if you choose amiss.
The miller is a lout, as you're aware;
So was the reeve; and so were many more.
They both told bawdy stories. Then beware,
And do not lay upon me all the blame,
Or take in earnest what is meant in fun.

THE MILLER'S TALE

At one time there was living at Oxford
A rich old gaffer, carpenter by trade,
Who took in paying guests; and he'd a lodger
Living with him, a needy hard-up scholar
Learned in the liberal arts; but all his fancy
Turned to the study of astrology:
He could work out a few propositions,
And thus calculate answers to questions,
When people came to ask him if the stars
Were auguring dry weather or downpours;
Or he'd forecast what events would befall,
One kind or another—I can't list them all.
  Fly Nicholas was what they called this scholar.
For love *sub rosa*, pleasing, or for pleasure
In bed or out of it, he'd a great knack;
And he was wily too, and close as wax,
Although he looked as demure as a maid.
In the house he lodged in, he'd a room and bed
All to himself, and prettily furnished
With sweet delicious herbs; he was as sweet
As ginger, or the root of licorice.
His *Almagest*,* and astrological
Treatises, with his textbooks great and small,
The instruments required for his science,
His astrolabe, and abacus-counters,
Were neatly stacked on shelves beside his bed;

His wardrobe-chest was draped with scarlet frieze.
A splendid psaltery hung overhead,
On which, at night, he'd play sweet melodies,
And fill the room with music till it rang;
'The Angel to the Virgin' he would sing,
And after, 'The King's Tune' would be his choice.
Folk often praised him for his cheerful voice.
And so this genial student spent his time,
Living on his friends' money and his own.

The carpenter had a new-wedded wife.
And he loved her; he loved her more than life;
She was no more than eighteen years of age.
Jealous he was, and kept her closely caged,
For she was wild and young, and he was old,
And thought she'd likely make him a cuckold.
And, since he was ignorant and unschooled,
He'd never come across Cato's advice,
Which lays it down that like should mate with like:
Men ought to wed according to their state,
For youth and age are often at debate.
But, seeing that he'd fallen in the trap,
He must put up with things, like other folk.

Young, comely was this wife; a lovely girl;
Her body slim and supple as a weasel.
She wore a cross-striped sash, all made of silk;
An apron also, white as morning milk,
She wore about her loins, gored to flare.
White was her smock; its collar, front and back,
Embroidered with black silk inside and out.
The ribbons of the white cap that she wore
Were also coal-black silk, to match the collar;
She'd a broad silken headband set back high.
And certainly she'd a come-hither eye.
Plucked to a slender line were her eyebrows,
And they were arched, and black as any sloes.
Sweeter was she by far to look upon
Than is a pear-tree in its early bloom;
And softer than the wool upon a wether.
And from her girdle hung a purse of leather
Tasselled with silk, spangled with beads of brass.

Roam the world up and down, you'd never raise
A man whose wit and fancy could dream up
A prettier poppet, or a girl like that.
Brighter the brilliance of her colouring
Than a new-minted Tower sovereign.
But when she sang, it was as brisk and clear
As any swallow perching on a barn.
And she would skip and frolic, and make play
Like any kid or calf behind its dam.
Her mouth was sweet as mead, or ale and honey,
Or store of apples laid in heather or hay.
She was as skittish as a frisky colt,
Tall as a mast, straight as a crossbow-bolt.
She wore a brooch upon her lower collar
Broad as the boss upon a shield or buckler.
The shoes upon her legs were laced up high.
She was a peach, a dolly, and a daisy!
Fit for a prince to lay upon his bed
Or some good retainer of his to wed.

    Now sir, and again sir! It so fell out
That this Fly Nicholas began one day
To flirt and play about with this young wife,
Her husband having gone off to Osney
(These scholars are so artful, and so sly!)
And on the quiet caught her by the cunt,
And said to her, 'Unless I have my way,
Sweetheart, for love of you I'll surely die.'
He held her by the haunches hard and tight,
'Now let's make love at once,' cried he, 'sweetheart!
Or it's the end of me, so help me God!'
She bucked and shied like a colt being shod,
And quickly wrenched away from him her head,
Saying, 'I'll not kiss you, on my word!
Let go,' she cried, 'now stop it, Nicholas!
I'll scream for help, I'll rouse the neighbourhood!
Take your hands off! It's no way to behave!'

    But Nicholas began to plead; he made
So good a case, offered himself so often,
That in the end her heart began to soften.
She gave her word, and swore by St Thomas,

[handwritten margin note, left:] common<

[handwritten margin note, left:] woman who is vigorous, happy, healthy → like a common woman.

That when she saw a chance, she would be his.
'My husband's eaten up with jealousy,
You must be circumspect in this affair.
So watch your step, and mind you're cautious,'
She said, 'or it will be the end of me.
So, just in case, you've got to keep it dark.'
'Don't worry about that,' said Nicholas,
'His time's been badly wasted, if a scholar
Can't get the better of a carpenter.'
And so the two of them agreed, and swore
To watch their chance, as I explained before.

When Nicholas had settled matters thus
He stroked her loins and gave her a sweet kiss,
And off he went and picked up his psaltery,
And strummed a loud and lively melody.

Now it so happened that, one fine saint's day,
This good wife visited the parish church
To make her devotions and worship Christ.
Her forehead gleamed as brightly as the day,
So hard she'd scrubbed it when she left off work.
Now in that church there was a parish clerk
Who answered to the name of Absolon.
His hair was curly, and like gold it shone,
And stuck out wide and broad, just like a winnowing
Fan from each side of a straight, even parting.
His face was red, his eyes grey as a goose.
In fantastically fenestrated shoes
And scarlet stockings, he dressed stylishly.
He wore a light blue jacket, fitting tightly,
A mass of fine tagged laces laced it neatly,
With over it a surplice white and gay
As blossom blooming on a branch of may.
Lord save and bless us, but he was a lad!
For he could shave and barber, and let blood,
Draw up a quittance or a conveyance.
In twenty different styles he'd jig and dance,
But in the Oxford mode, as was the fashion,
Flinging his legs in every direction;
He'd play upon a tiny two-stringed fiddle,
And sometimes he would sing, a loud falsetto;

And he could play as well on a guitar.
In the whole town there was no inn or bar
He'd not enlivened with his company,
The ones with lively barmaids, naturally.
But the fact is, he was a bit squeamish
Of farting; fastidious and prim in speech.
    This Absolon, high-spirited and gay,
Was taking the censer round on that saint's day,
Censing the women of the parish, when
He'd take his chance to cast sheep's eyes at them—
Especially at the carpenter's wife.
To look on her seemed happiness enough,
She was so neat and sweet and flirtatious.
Take it from me, if she had been a mouse,
And he a cat, he would have pounced at once.
He was so smitten with a love-longing,
This parish clerk, this gallant Absolon,
That when he went round with the collection,
He wouldn't take a penny from the women;
Good manners, so he told them, quite forbade.
    That night the moon shone bright, and Absolon
Took his guitar, meaning to stay awake
All through the livelong night for his love's sake.
And off he went, jaunty and amorous,
Until he came to the carpenter's house
Just before dawn, a little after cock-crow,
And took his stand beneath a casement-window
That jutted from the wall. Then soft and low
He sang, his voice well-tuned to his guitar,
'Now dearest lady, if it pleases thee,
I beg and pray, take pity upon me.'
The carpenter awoke, and heard him sing,
And then turned over to his wife, saying,
'What! Alison! Don't you hear Absolon
Yodelling away under our bedroom wall?'
And Alison gave him this answer back:
'Yes, John; as goodness knows, I hear it all.'
    And so things went on as you might expect.
He woos her daily, this lad Absolon,
Becoming, in the end, quite woebegone.

class tension between fly nicholas (scholar) and carpenter

All day, and all the night, he stays awake;
He combs his spreading hair, and spruces up;
He woos with messengers and go-betweens;
He swears that he will be her slave; he sings,
Quavering and trilling like a nightingale;
He sends her honey-wine, mead and spiced ale,
And waffles from the griddle, piping hot;
And, as she lives in town, he proffers cash.*
For there are some who will be won with riches,
And some with blows; and some again with kindness.
    And once, to show off his versatility,
He played King Herod in a Mystery,
High on an open stage; but what's the use?
Her heart is so set on Fly Nicholas
That Absolon can go whistle for her;
He only wins a snub for all his labour.
She made a monkey of him; all his earnest
Is turned by Alison into a jest.
No doubt of it, that proverb is no lie
Which goes, 'You'll always see the nigh and sly
Cut out the lover who is far away.'
Useless for Absolon to fume and fret:
Because he wasn't there, and out of sight,
On-the-spot Nicholas stood in his light.
    Show us your mettle now, Fly Nicholas!
Leave Absolon to wail, and sing 'Alas!'
For it so happened that one Saturday
The carpenter had gone off to Osney,
And this Fly Nicholas and Alison
Having conferred, came to the conclusion
That Nicholas must hatch some stratagem
To fool the silly jealous husband; when,
If everything went well and turned out right,
She'd sleep in the arms of Nicholas all night,
For that was his desire, and hers also.
And thereupon, without another word,
Nicholas, who would brook no more delay,
Carried up to his bedroom stealthily
Enough of food and drink to last a day
Or two, and told her that she was to say,

Should the carpenter ask for Nicholas,
She hadn't got a notion where he was,
And hadn't set eyes on him all that day;
And she believed he must have fallen ill,
As the maid could not rouse him with her call,
Loud as she cried, he'd answered not at all.

  So Fly Nicholas, all that Saturday,
Kept to his room, and stayed there quietly
Eating and sleeping, and what else he pleased,
Till Sunday, when the sun had gone to rest.
Then this poor carpenter was much astonished
At Nicholas, and wondered why he'd vanished.
Said he, 'I'm much afraid, by St Thomas,
Something must be amiss with Nicholas.
Perhaps he's been struck dead, which God forbid!
For to be sure, it's an uncertain world.
Today I saw a corpse borne to the church—
One who, on Monday last, I saw at work!'
Then to his servant-lad: 'Get a move on!
Shout at his door, or bang it with a stone!
See what's up, tell me straight out what it is.'

  At this the boy ran boldly up the stairs,
And there outside the bedroom door he stood,
Bawling away and hammering like mad:
'Hey, Mister Nicholas, what are you doing?
Hey! Hey! How can you sleep there all day long?'

  But all for nothing: he heard not a word.
A hole he found, low in a bottom board,
In and out of which the cat used to creep,
And through the cat's hole he took a good peep,
And in the end he caught a glimpse of him.
Fly Nicholas was sitting bolt upright
As if moonstruck; motionless, mouth agape.
So down the stairs he ran, and lost no time
Telling his master how he'd found the man.

  On hearing this, the carpenter began
To cross himself; and, 'Help us, St Frideswide!'
He said, 'No man can tell what may betide,
He's fallen in a fit, or some insanity,
And all because of all this astroboly,

As all along I thought that it would be!
One shouldn't pry into God's mystery.
Yes, the unlettered man is blessed indeed
Who doesn't know a thing except his Creed!
Much the same fate befell, it seems to me,
That other student of astroboly:
He walked the fields stargazing, to foresee
What might befall; and suddenly fell in
A claypit—something that he'd not foreseen.
But all the same, I swear by St Thomas
I'm most upset about Fly Nicholas.
He shall be scolded for his studying
If I've got anything to do with it—
Yes, that he shall, by Jesus, heaven's King!
Get me a staff, to pry against the floor,
While you, Robin, are heaving up the door.
He'll come out of his studying, I'll bet.'
And at the bedroom door he set to work.
His boy was a strong fellow for his size,
And heaved it off its hinges in a trice.
The door fell to the floor; the job was done.
And there sat Nicholas, still as a stone,
And kept on gaping up into the air.
The carpenter, thinking he was in a fit,
Took Nicholas by the shoulders, gripped them tight,
And shook him hard, and yelled with all his might:
'What, Nicholas! What! Look down for God's sake!
Think on Christ's suffering! Awake, awake!
The sign of the cross defend you from all harm,
From sprites and elves!' He gabbled a night-charm
On each of the four corners of the house,
And on the threshold of the door without:

> Jesus Christ, Saint Benedict,
> Evil spirits interdict:
> Night-hags fly this Paternoster!
> What happened to St Peter's sister?

And in the end this wily Nicholas
Gave a deep sigh, and spoke. He said, 'Alas,
Must the world now come to its end so soon?'
Answered the carpenter, 'What do you mean?

Have trust in God, like all us working-men.'

'Fetch me a drink,' was Nicholas' reply,
'And then I'll tell you—but confidentially—
Of a certain thing that touches you and me.
You can be sure I'll tell no other man.'

The carpenter went down and came again,
Bringing with him a huge quart of strong ale,
And then when each of them had drunk his fill,
Fly Nicholas got up, shut fast his door,
And sat himself down by the carpenter.

Said he, 'John, my dear host, you've got to swear
To me upon your word of honour here
Never to betray this secret to a soul,
For it is Christ's own secret that I tell;
For should you tell it to a soul, you're lost.
If you betray me, this must be the cost:
You'll go stark mad.' 'Which Jesus Christ forbid!
No, Christ forbid it, by His holy blood!'
Replied this simple soul. 'I'm not a blab,
And though I say it, I don't like to gab.
Say what you will, for I shall never tell
Man, woman, or child, by Him that harrowed hell!'

'Now, John,' said Nicholas, 'and I'll not lie,
I have found out, through my astrology,
By gazing in the moon, that's shining bright,
That on Monday next at about nine at night,
There'll be a fall of rain—so fierce a spate
Even Noah's flood was never half so great.
This world', said he, 'in less time than an hour
Must all be drowned, so frightful the downpour.
Thus all mankind must drown and wholly perish.'

The carpenter exclaimed, 'Ah, my poor wife!
Must she be drowned? Alas, poor Alison!'
He almost fell, he was so overcome,
And asked, 'Then is there no way out of this?'

'Why, yes of course,' replied Fly Nicholas,
'If you'll be guided by expert advice.
You mustn't act on ideas of your own.
For as Solomon very truly says,
"Don't act without advice, or you'll repine."

Now, if you'll act in accordance with mine,
I'll undertake—without a mast and sail—
To save her, you, and me; yes, without fail.
Haven't you heard how Noah was preserved,
When he had early warning from the Lord,
That all the world must sink beneath the waves?'
    'Yes,' said the carpenter, 'a long time ago.'
    'Haven't you heard', said Nicholas, 'also
Of the trouble Noah and the others had
Before they could even get his wife aboard?
I daresay he'd have swapped his prize black sheep
Yes, all of them, for her to have a ship
All to herself, an ark for her alone.
Have you a notion what's best to be done?
This calls for speed; when it's an urgent thing,
You can't delay, or waste time speechifying.
    'Now fetch into the house—and hurry up—
A kneading-trough, or else a brewing vat,
For each of us, but see that they are large
So we can float in them, as in a barge,
And have in them enough provision for
A day, that's all; we shan't need any more!
The waters will abate and go away
About nine in the morning of next day.
But neither your boy Robin, nor your maid
Gillian must know of this; they can't be saved.
Don't ask me why; for even if you did,
I wouldn't tell the secrets God keeps hid.
You should be satisfied, unless you're mad,
To have the same good fortune Noah had.
I'll see your wife is saved, so never fear;
Now off with you, make haste in this affair.
    'But when you've got these kneading-tubs—all three:
One for her, one for you, and one for me—
High in the rafters you must hang them then,
So that our preparations can't be seen.
And when you've done all that I've told you to,
And stowed our food in them—and an axe too,
So we can cut the rope, cast off and go
When the water comes—and when you've broken through

A hole high up there, up in the house gable,
On the garden side, and just above the stable,
So we can pass through freely on our way
When the deluge has stopped and gone away—
You'll paddle about as merrily, I bet,
As any white duck following its drake,
And then I'll shout: "Hi, Alison! Hi, John!
Cheer up there, for the floods will soon be down!"
And "Hi there, Master Nicholas!" you'll reply,
"Good morning! I see you plain, for it is day."
And then we'll be, for all the rest of life,
Lords of the world like Noah and his wife.

    'But there's one thing I must warn you about:
You'd better bear in mind that on the night
The three of us are embarked on shipboard,
Not one of us must speak a single word,
Call or cry out, but pray to God instead,
For that is the commandment of the Lord.
You and your wife must hang as far apart
As may be, because between you and her
There must be no sin, not a look or glance,
Much less the act: such is the ordinance.
Go, and good luck! Tomorrow night we'll creep
Into our tubs, when everyone's asleep,
And sit there, putting all our trust in heaven.
Now off with you, I haven't got the time
For further argument—as people say,
"A word to the wise"—which you are anyway:
You haven't any need of me to teach.
Be off and save our lives, I do beseech!'

    The simple carpenter went on his way.
Over and again he sighed, 'Alack the day!'
And told the secret to his wife; but she
Already knew, better by far than he,
What this ingenious plot was all about.
But none the less she put on a good act,
You'd think that she was frightened half to death.
'Alas!' she cried, 'Be on your way, make haste!
Help us escape, or all of us must perish!
As I'm your true and lawful wedded wife,

Go, dearest husband, help to save our lives!'
    How potent is a strong emotion!
Sometimes an impression can cut so deep
That people die of mere imagination.
This simple carpenter began to shake,
He really thought he was about to see
Noah's flood-waters rolling like the sea
To drown his Alison, his honey-pet.
He weeps and wails, the picture of misery;
Gives many a heavy sigh, many a sob.
Then, having got hold of a kneading-trough,
A brewing vat, and also one more tub,
He had them sent in secret to his home,
And hung them in the rafters on the quiet.
And then with his own hands he carpentered
Three ladders, shafts and rungs by which to climb
Up to the kneading-tubs hung in the beams.
Next he provisioned them, both tubs and trough,
With bread and cheese, and good ale in a jug,
Quite sufficient to last them for a day.
And having made all these arrangements, he
Packed his boy off, with Gillian the maid,
To London on some business that he had.
And on the Monday, as it drew to night,
He shut the door, and with no candle lit,
He arranged everything as it should be.
A moment later up they climbed, all three,
And for some little time sat quietly.

    'Say the Lord's prayer,' said Nicholas, 'Mum!'
And John said 'Mum!' and 'Mum!' said Alison.
The carpenter says a paternoster, then
Sits motionless, and says his prayer again,
Watches and waits, and listens for the rain.

    The carpenter, after his busy day,
Fell dead asleep, round curfew-time I'd say,
Or perhaps later. Nightmares made him groan;
And, as his head was lying the wrong way,
He snored and snored, again and yet again.
Then down his ladder tiptoed Nicholas,
And down hers, Alison as softly sped;

With no word uttered, they have gone to bed,
And there, where the carpenter used to lie,
There is the music, there the revelry!
And thus did Alison and Nicholas,
With fun and frolic for their business,
Lie till the bell for lauds began to ring,
And they could hear the friars in chancel sing.

　　The parish clerk, as usual woebegone
For love, this lovelorn amorous Absolon,
Happened to be at Osney on the Monday
With a party of his friends on holiday;
And on the offchance, quietly asked a canon
If he'd seen anything of carpenter John.
The man drew him aside, out of the church,
And said, 'I don't know; he's not been at work
Since Saturday; I think he's gone to get
Some timber that was sent for by the abbot.
He often goes for timber to the farm,
And there he stays, perhaps a day or two;
And if not, then for certain he's at home.
But where he is, I couldn't really say.'

　　The happy Absolon, filled with delight,
Thought, 'Now's the time to stay awake all night.
For certainly I haven't seen him stir
Since daybreak, in or out of his house-door.
And, sure as I stand here, at first cock-crow
I'll give a quiet tap on the window
That's set so low upon his bedroom wall.
Now I'll be able to tell Alison
About my lovelonging for her and all;
And what is more, I don't intend to miss
The chance of giving her at least a kiss.
You bet I'll get some kind of satisfaction.
My mouth has itched and itched the whole day long,
And that means kissing, at the very least.
And all night I was dreaming of a feast.
So I'll go and sleep an hour or two, and then
I'll stay awake all night and have my fun.'

　　When the first cock had crowed, just before dawn,
Up rose that joyful lover, Absolon,

c.t.—6

And dressed himself to kill, in his best clothes.
First he chewed cardamon and licorice
To make his breath sweet, then he combed his hair.
Under his tongue he carried herb-paris,
For in this way he hoped that he would please.
He sauntered off to the carpenter's house,
And placed himself beneath the casement window
Which barely reached his chest, it was so low,
And softly coughed; then, in a gentle tone:
'Where are you, honeycomb, sweet Alison?
My sweetest cinnamon, my pretty chick!
Awake and speak to me, sweetheart, awake!
It's little thought that you give to my sorrow,
Or what a sweat I'm in for love of you;
For it's no wonder that I swoon and sweat,
I'm yearning like a lambkin for the teat.
Truly, sweetheart, I am so much in love,
I yearn for you like any turtle-dove
After its mate; I eat less than a girl.'

   'Go from the window, jackanapes,' said she,
No kiss-me-quick for you—God save us all!
I love another—and small blame to me—
Better than you, by Jesus, Absolon!
Be off with you now, or I'll throw a stone,
Go in the devil's name, and let me sleep!'

   'Alas!' cried Absolon, 'Alas! alack!
Was true love ever so abused before?
Then kiss me, since I cannot hope for more,
For Jesus' love, and for the love of me.'

   'Will you be off when you've had it?' said she.

   'Yes, of course, sweetheart,' answered Absolon.

   'Get ready then,' she said, 'I'll be back soon.'
To Nicholas she whispered, 'Hush your mouth.
Hush now, and I'll give you a real good laugh.'

   Then Absolon went down upon his knees,
And said, 'Now I'm in clover, no mistake!
I hope there'll be more coming, after this!
Sweetheart, be kind, be kind to me, sweet chick!'

   The window was unfastened hastily.
'Come on,' she said, 'and get it over quick!

Get a move on, in case the neighbours see.'
  Absolon began wiping his mouth dry.
The night was dark as pitch, as black as coal;
Out of the window she put her arse-hole,
And Absolon, as luck would have it, kissed
Her with his mouth smack on her naked arse
Relishingly, not knowing what it was.
He leapt back, thinking something was amiss.
Girls don't have beards, as he knew well enough,
And what he'd felt had been hairy and rough.
'Foo!' he cried. 'What have I done? Foo, foo!'
  'Ha-ha!' she laughed, and clapped the window to,
And Absolon went off in sorry case.
  'A beard! A beard!' exclaimed Fly Nicholas,
'That's a good one, the best one yet, by God!'
  The hapless Absolon heard every word,
And in his rage and fury bit his lip,
And to himself he said, 'I'll pay you out.'
  Now who but Absolon rubs and scrubs his lips
With dust, with sand, with straw, with cloth, with chips?
Again and yet again he cries, 'Alas!
May the devil take my soul, I'd rather have
Revenge for this insult, than own the town!
Alas!' he cried, 'if only I'd steered clear!'
His burning love was cold and quite put down,
For from the moment that he kissed her arse
He was quite cured, and didn't give a curse
For lady-loves, but went denouncing them,
While crying like a child that's just been beaten.
Slowly he crossed the street to pay a visit
To a certain blacksmith they call Mister Gervase,
A man who specialized in forging ploughshares,
And who was sharpening coulters busily.
Absolon came and knocked, but quietly,
And said, 'Open up, Gervase, lose no time.'
    'What? Who are you?' 'It's me, it's Absolon.'
'What, Absolon! The Lord save and bless me!
For Christ's sweet sake, why are you up so early?
What's up with you? Some trollop, that I'll bet,
Has been leading you a dance, by St Neot!

That's it! You know well enough what I mean.'
  But Absolon, who didn't give a bean
For all this chaff, and had more fish to fry
Than Gervase guessed, made no kind of reply
Except to say, 'Do you see, old fellow,
There in the fireplace, that hot plough-coulter?
Please lend it for a job I have to do,
And soon enough I'll bring it back to you.'
  Gervase replied, 'As I'm an honest smith,
You could have it if it were made of gold,
Or as many sovereigns as a sack will hold.
But in Satan's name, what do you want with it?'
  Said Absolon, 'Let that be as it may;
I'll tell you all, but on some other day'—
And he picked up the coulter by the cool
End of the shank; out of the door he stole,
And made his way to the carpenter's wall.
To begin with he coughs, then taps once more
Upon the window, as he did before.
  At this Alison answered, 'Who's out there,
Knocking like that? I'm certain it's a thief.'
  'Why, no,' said he, 'the Lord knows, my sweet chick,
It's your own Absolon, my sweetest darling.
Look what I've brought for you,' said he, 'a ring
Of gold—my mother gave it me, by heaven!
It's a real beauty, skilfully engraven,
And I will give it to you for a kiss.'
  Now Nicholas had got up to piss,
And thought that he'd improve upon the fun,
Get Absolon to kiss him on the bum,
And so he quickly put the window up,
And stealthily stuck his whole arse right out,
Buttocks and all, as far as the hip-bone.
Meanwhile the parish clerk, our Absolon,
Said, 'Speak! I don't know where you are, sweetheart.'
  Upon this Nicholas let fly a fart,
So great it sounded like a thunderclap.
But Absolon, half-blinded by the blast,
Had got his iron ready, smoking hot;
Smack in the middle of the arse he smote

Nicholas. From his rump the skin flew off
A handsbreath round, the coulter was so hot;
And the smart stung him till he thought he'd die.
He yelled like frenzy in his agony:
'Help! Water! Water! Help! Help! For God's sake!'
   The carpenter, startled from out his sleep,
Heard someone yelling 'Water!' as if mad,
And thought, 'Alas! For here comes Nowell's flood!'
And he sat up without another word,
And with his hatchet hacked in two the cord,
And down went all, and stopped for nothing, till
He hit the cellar floorboards, and lay still.
   Up leapt Nicholas and Alison,
Crying, 'Help!' and 'Murder!' as they ran
Into the street; the neighbours, one and all,
Came running in to stare upon the man
Who was still lying stunned, white-faced and wan,
Because his arm was broken with the fall.
But he must put up with his misfortune:
For when he spoke, he was at once borne down
By both Fly Nicholas and Alison.
For they told everybody he was mad,
So frightened of a fancied 'Nowell's Flood'
That in his folly he had gone and bought
Three kneading-tubs, and hung them from the roof,
And that he had then begged them, for God's love,
To sit with him to keep him company.
   Folk began laughing at his lunacy;
Up at the roof they peered and stared and gaped,
And treated his misfortune as a joke.
No matter what the carpenter might say,
It was no use, none took him seriously.
Their sworn testimony so beat him down,
He was reputed mad by the whole town,
For all the scholars sided with the other,
Saying 'The man's a crackpot, my dear fellow',
So that the whole affair became a joke.
And that's how the carpenter's wife got poked,
Despite his vigilance and jealousy;
That's how Absolon kissed her bottom eye,

And how Nicholas got a blistered bum.
Now God save all of us, my tale is done!

THE REEVE'S PROLOGUE

When folk had had their laugh at this grotesque
Affair of Absolon and Nicholas,
Then different folk had different things to say,
But for the most part were amused, and laughed;
And none took umbrage at the tale, save only
Oswald the reeve, so far as I could see.
Because he followed the carpenter's craft,
A crumb of anger lingered in his heart,
And he began to carp at it a bit.

   He grumbled: 'Happen I could pay you back,
Tell how a swaggering miller got his eye
Well wiped—that's if I wanted to talk bawdy.
But I am old, and past the age for play;
Grass-time is done; for me it's winter hay;
And this white poll is witness to my years.
My heart has mouldered too, as have my hairs;
I feel just like a medlar, or split-arse,
And that's a kind of fruit gets worse and worse
Till rotten-ripe and laid in muck or straw.
All of us old men are like that, I fear;
It's not till we are rotten, that we're ripe;
We'll jig away, so long's the world will pipe.
For our lust's always caught against a snag:
A leek's green tail, to go with a white head,
Is what we want; for though our vigour's gone,
The flesh still longs for folly just the same.
We talk of what we can no longer do;
In cold raked ashes, there's a spark or two.

   'Four burning coals we have, as I can show:
Boasting, lying, avarice, and rage;
Four embers that belong to our old age.
Weak, feeble as our ancient limbs may be,
Desire never fails. And as for me,
There's life in the old dog yet; it's long ago

Since first my tap of life began to flow;
For surely it was Death, when I was born,
That drew the tap of life and let it run,
And it's been flowing ever since, so fast
There's little left in a near-empty cask,
A few drops only, on the barrel-rim.
My poor old tongue may rattle on and on
Of wickedness, and follies past and gone,
What else is left, save dotage, for old men?'

   But, having listened to this homily,
Our host addressed us magisterially:
'Now what does it add up to, all this wisdom?
Why go on Bible-thumping all day long?
It was the devil made a reeve a preacher,
A sailor or a sawbones of a cobbler!
Out with your tale, and let's waste no more time.
Look, it's half after seven, and Deptford's here!
That's Greenwich, full of scoundrels, over there!
High time you told your story, so begin.'

   Oswald the reeve replied, 'Well, gentlemen,
I hope that none of you will be upset
If I cap his tale and pull his leg a bit.
Tit for tat's only fair, so I'll hit back.

   'This drunken miller has just told us here
About the diddling of a carpenter;
As I'm one, it's to scoff at me, perhaps.
If you don't mind, I mean to pay him out;
It's his own loutish language that I'll speak.
I hope to God he goes and breaks his neck.
Though he can easily see a mote in mine,
In his own eye he cannot see the beam.'

THE REEVE'S TALE

At Trumpington, which isn't far from Cambridge,
There runs a brook, and over it a bridge;
And there's a mill that stands upon this brook;
And what I tell you is the honest truth.
For many years a miller lived in it:

He was as proud and gay as any peacock,
Could play the bagpipes, fish, and mend a net,
Turn cups upon a lathe, wrestle and shoot;
And ever at his belt hung a large knife
With a long blade, and sword of keenest edge.
And in his pocket he'd a nifty dirk:
Whoever touched him put his life at stake.
He packed a Sheffield carver in his hose.
Round was his face, and flattened was his nose;
He had a skull as hairless as an ape's.
He was a market braggart, out and out.
And nobody dared lay a finger on him
Without his swearing that he'd do for them.
Fact is, he was a thief of corn and meal,
And sly: he never missed a chance to steal.
He'd got a nickname: it was Show-off Simkin.
And he'd a wife; she came of noble kin
—It seems her father was the village parson:*
He'd had to settle on her a good dowry,
Brass pots and pans, before Simkin would marry.
She'd had her schooling in a nunnery
For Simkin wouldn't take a wife, he said,
Unless she were well-brought-up, and a maid,
Lest it mar his freeman status and degree.*
And she was proud and pert as a magpie.
They were a sight to see, that precious pair,
On Sundays, when he'd strut in front of her,
With his hoodscarf-tippet wrapped about his head,
While she came after, in a gown of red,
A gown that matched the stockings that he wore.
None dared to call her anything but 'Madam'
Or flirt with her, or even make a pass,
Unless he wanted to be killed by Simkin,
With his poinard or dagger or cutlass.
For jealous folk are always dangerous,
Or so they'd like their women to suppose.
And, as her pedigree was a bit smirched,
She stank with pride, like water in a ditch;
Was full of supercilious disdain
Because—or so it seemed to her—what with

Her family and her convent education,
A lady ought to keep herself aloof.

    Between these two a daughter had been born,
A girl of twenty; they'd no other children
Except a baby of six months, which lay
In cradle still; it was a bouncing boy.
The girl was plump, well-grown, and well set-up;
Pug was her nose, and grey as glass her eyes;
Her buttocks broad, her bosom round and high;
But she had lovely hair, and that's a fact.

    This village priest, as she was such a beauty,
Had planned to make her heir to his property,
To all of it, house, furniture, and goods,
So made it difficult for her to wed:
That she should marry well was his intent,
Into some noble house of ancient blood;
The wealth of Holy Church ought to be spent
On blood that's Holy Church's by descent.
For he would have his holy blood honoured
Though Holy Church itself should be devoured.

    Of course this miller had the monopoly
Of grinding corn for the surrounding country,
And in particular for a great college
That people call the Solar Hall at Cambridge,*
Whose wheat and malt were always ground by him.
It happened that its manciple suddenly
Fell sick; most people thought that he would die.
At this the miller soon began to steal
A hundredfold more of their corn and meal;
He'd only filched politely, earlier;
But now he was a barefaced plunderer.
And so the Warden makes a great to-do,
For which the miller doesn't give a straw,
Loudly defies and swears it is not so.

    Now at the college of which I've been speaking
Were two young hard-up students, headstrong chaps,
And game for anything. And just for kicks
They plagued the Warden for short leave, until
They'd leave to see their corn ground at the mill.
And each of them was game to stake his neck

The miller couldn't pinch a half a peck
Of corn off them, whether by force or cheating;
And in the end the Warden gave permission.
One of them was called John; Alan the other;
Both born in the same town, a place called Strother,
Far in the north—but I can't say just where.

  When Alan had collected all his gear,
Upon a horse he slung a sack of corn:
And so the pair set off, Alan and John,
Each with stout sword and buckler by his side.
John knew the way—they'd no need for a guide—
And when they reached the mill, threw down the sack.
Alan spoke first: 'Watcheer, Simon! How's yor wife,
And how's yor canny lass?'* 'Upon my life,'
Said Simkin, 'welcome, Alan! And John too!
How's things? What brings you here, the pair of you?'

  'Simon,' said John, 'by God, need knaws nae law;
Who hes no help, he needs must help hisself,
As learned folk say—or else he's but a fyeul.
Wor manciple—Aah doot that he's nigh dead,
His grinders keep on aching in his head;
And so Aah's cum, and also brought Alan,
To grind wor corn, and bring it hyem again;
Aah begs ye de the job fast as ye can.'

  'Trust me, I'll do just that,' replied Simkin:
'What will you do while I've the job in hand?'

  'By God, right by thon hopper Aah'sl stand,'
Said John, 'and Aah'sl watch how corn gans in.
Because in my born days Aah's nivver seen
Just how thon hopper wags, to-fro, to-fro.'

  To which Alan replied, 'Will ye de sae?
Then, John, Aah means te stand beneath, by gum!
And Aah'll be watching how the meal fa's doon
Into thon trough; and that'll be my game.
Be sure that you and me's the same sort, John:
For Aah's as bad a miller as ye be.'

  The miller grinned at their fatuity,
And thought, 'All this is nothing but a ruse.
They think that they can't possibly be fooled,—
As I'm a miller, I'll hoodwink them yet,

For all their learning and philosophy!
The more smart tricks that they try out on me,
The more I'll steal when it comes to the crunch.
Instead of flour I shall give them bran.
As the mare told the wolf, once on a time,*
"The greatest scholar's not the wisest man."
And for their learning I don't give a damn.'

   Seeing his chance, he tiptoed quietly
Out of the doorway, and looked stealthily
Around, and up and down, till he discovered
The students' horse where it was standing tethered
Behind the mill, beneath a leafy arbour;
And to the horse he gently sidled up,
And stripped it of its bridle on the spot.
Once it was loosed, the horse turned to the fen
Where the wild mares were running free; and then
Whinnying 'wee-hee!' raced off through thick and thin.

   The miller came back and said not a word,
Joked with the students, got on with his job
Until the corn was well and truly ground.
And when the flour had been sacked and bound,
John goes out, finds his horse is run away:
'Help!' and 'Way, marra!' he begins to cry,
'Wor horse is lost! Alan, by God's bones,
Stir thy stumps, man, and cum oot here at once!
Warden has tint his nag!' At this, Alan
Forgot meal, corn, and all; forgot his plan
To keep an eye on things—'What! Where's he gyen?'
He cried.

        The millers' wife came bounding in:
'Alas! your horse has run off to the fen
To the wild mares, as fast as he can go.
And no thanks to the hand that tethered him,
That should have better tied the bridle rein!'
'Alas!' cried John, 'for Jesus' sake, Alan,
Take off thy sword; Aah'll do the same also.
For Aah's as wick, God knows, as any roe;
Christ almighty, he'll not escape us both!
Why dinna ye put nag into thon barn?
Bad luck on it, but you're a gowk, Alan!'

And those poor lads ran off towards the fen
Hard as they could, Alan as well as John.

And when the miller saw that they had gone,
A whole half-bushel of their flour he took,
And bade his wife knead it into a cake.
Said he, 'I bet those students got a fright.
It seems a miller can still put one over
(No matter what his learning) any scholar.
Let them go to the devil their own way!
See where he goes! Well, let the children play.
They'll not catch him that easy, I'll be bound!'

Those silly students, running up and down,
Cried, 'Steady! Woa, woa! Hey up there!
Look ahint! Whistle, Aah'sl head him here!'
In short, although they tried with all their might,
They couldn't catch him till it was black night,
That horse of theirs kept galloping so fast;
But in a ditch they cornered him at last.

Weary and wet as cattle in the rain
Comes silly John, and after him Alan.
Says John, 'Black wes the day that Aah wes born!
We've been made look reet Charlies, fit to scorn.
Corn's pinched—it's gowks they'll call us, one and all,
Warden, our mates, and miller worst of all!'

Thus grumbles John on his way to the mill,
As, rein in hand, he leads his Bayard there.
He found the miller sitting by the fire,
For night was come; as they could go no further,
They begged him for God's sake to give them shelter,
A room to sleep in; and they offered money.

To this the miller answered, 'If there's any,
Such as it is, then you shall have your share.
Mine's a small house; but you've learned to dispute;
You'll find it easy to ratiocinate,
And with your syllogisms make a place
A mile wide out of twenty feet of space.
And now let's see if it is big enough—
Or make it bigger with your rhetoric.'

'Now, Simon,' returned John, 'by St Cuthbert!
Ye have us there—and ye will have yor joke.

"A man", they say, "sal tyek ane of twa things,
Sic as he finds, or else sic as he brings."
But, seriously, dear host, all Aah's asking's
Get us some food and drink, and do us well:
We'll pay for all, cash down, reet on the nail,
A man can't lure a hawk with empty hand:
And see here, there's our brass, ready to spend.'

   The miller sent his daughter to the town
For bread and ale, and roasted them a goose,
Tethered the horse that it might not run loose,
And in his own room made for them a bed,
With blankets and with sheets decently spread,
Not ten feet from his own, or maybe twelve.
His daughter had a bed all to herself,
Right in that very room, not far away.
This was the best they could do, and for why?
There wasn't any more room in the place.
They supped and talked, and made of it a party,
Drinking strong ale until they'd all had plenty,
And about midnight they retired to rest.

   The miller got himself properly pissed,
White as a sheet with drink, and not just flushed:
He was hiccupping and talking through his nose,
Croaking as if he'd a cold in the head;
To bed he goes, and with him his wife goes,
And she's as spry and merry as a grig,
Because she's got her whistle truly wet.
At her bed's foot the cradle has been set
That she might rock it, or give the child suck.
And when they'd drained the last drop from the jug,
The daughter went to bed, right there and then;
And Alan went to bed, and also John;
And that was it—no need for sleeping-draughts!
The miller had a skinful, that's for sure;
For in his sleep he snorted like a horse,
Honking at both ends; his wife bore the bass,
And joined him in the chorus with a will;
Two furlongs off you might have heard her snore,
And with them snored, *par compagnie*, the girl.

   The student Alan, hearing this music,

Gave John a poke and said, 'Be ye asleep?
Did ivver ye hear sic a sang before?
Just hark at that lot at their evening prayer!
The itch fa' on their bodies like wildfire!
Did ivver ye hear sic an eldrich thing?
Ay, and the worst of all bad ends to them!
For me, all this lang neet, there'll be nae rest.
Nivver ye mind, all sal be for the best.
For, John, as Aah may hope for heaven's bliss,
If that Aah can, Aah means to stuff thon lass.
The law allows us easement and redress;
For, John, there is a statute that says this:
"If in one way a man be made to suffer,
Then he maun be recompensed in another."
Wor corn is stolen, that you can't deny,
And us have had reet bad luck all today;
And, seeing that Aah'sl have nae amends
Against my loss, Aah'sl have recompense.
That's hoo it sal be, no way else, by gum!'

    To which John answered, 'Watch thy step, Alan.
Thon miller', said he, 'is a dangerous chep,
And gin he should be startled from his sleep,
Might do the pair of us an injury.'

    But, answering 'He cudna hurt a fly',
Towards the wench Alan began to creep;
The girl lay on her back, so fast asleep,
Before she knew, Alan had got so close
That it was far too late to raise a fuss;
To cut the story short, they soon were one.
It's John's turn now; let Alan have his fun.

    Now for ten minutes or so John lay still,
Then to himself began to grouse and grumble.
Said he, 'This is a poor sort of a joke;
Aah can say Aah's been made a monkey of.
But my marra's had some sort of recompense:
He's got thon miller's daughter in his arms.
He took a chance and now he's got his oats,
While here Aah's lying like a sack of dirt;
And when this jape is told aneuther day,
They'll think that Aah was daft, a proper sawney!

Aah'sl chance it and get up, gi' it a show.
Nowt venture, nowt to win, as people say.'
And up he got, and stealthily tiptoed
Up to the cradle, which he took away,
Then placed it quietly at his bed's foot.

Soon after this, the wife began to stop
Her snoring, woke up, and went out to piss,
Came back again, and then began to miss
The cradle, groping for it everywhere
And finding nothing. 'Oh dear,' said she, 'oh dear,
I almost went wrong, and I almost got
Into the students' bed. Eh, bless us! Then
In what a pretty pickle I'd be in!'
And on she went, until she found the cradle.
Her hand groped further, till it touched the bed,
Then, with no other thought than all was well,
Because she knew just where the cradle stood,
Not knowing where it was, as it was dark,
She fairly crawled into the students' bed,
And lay quite still, and would have gone to sleep.
Soon enough, John the student comes to life,
And lays on hard with this good miller's wife;
It's years since she had had so good a bout,
For he thrusts like a madman, hard and deep.
And what a ball they had, Alan and John,
Till the third cock, that crows before the dawn!

But with the dawn, Alan began to tire,
For he'd been toiling away all night long.
Said he, 'Goodbye, sweet Molly, day is here,
Aah can ne longer stay; but evermair
Wherever Aah may be, Aah'll be thy lad.'

'Then, dearest sweetheart, go,' said she; 'farewell.
But I'll tell you one thing before you go.
When you are on your way home past the mill,
There at the back, and just outside the door,
You'll find a half-bushel cake made of your flour,
The flour that I helped my father steal.
And now, my sweetheart, God save you and keep.'
At this the girl almost began to weep.

Alan got up and thought, 'Before daybreak

Ah'd best go back, and slip in next my mate,'
And touched the cradle with his hand. 'By Christ,'
Thought he, 'Aah's gyen aa' wrang; Aah's up shit creek.
Head's in a totter from my work to-neet,
Nae wonder then, gin Aah canna go reet.
And Aah can tell by cradle Aah's off course,
Miller and wife are kipping in thon bed.'
Then, as the devil would have it, he passed on
To the very bed the miller was lying in.
Supposing he was crawling in with John,
It was beside the miller that he crept;
And so he threw his arm about his neck
And whispered, 'John, ye hogshead, for Christ's sake
Wake up! Ye nivver heard a better joke!
By St James, it's the best yet! Thrice tonight
Aah hes stuffed miller's lass, flat on her back,
While you've been chicken—aye, and flade to death.'
    'You have, have you?' the miller cried. 'Blackguard!
You treacherous jackanapes! By holy God
I'll have your tripes for daring to dishonour
My daughter, nobly born of noble blood!'
And he seized Alan by his Adam's apple,
And he as heatedly returned the grapple,
And gave his nose a right belt with his fist;
A stream of blood ran down the miller's chest,
And on the floor, with broken nose and mouth.
Like two pigs in a poke they plunged about,
And up and down they had it, up and down,
Till the miller stumbled, tripping on a stone,
And down he fell, backward upon his wife;
She, quite oblivious of this battle royal,
Had fallen fast asleep with student John
Who had been keeping vigil the whole night,
And with the fall was startled out of sleep.
'Help, holy cross of Bromeholme!' she cried,
'*In manus tuas*! Lord, to Thee I call!*
The fiend's upon us! Wake up, Simon, wake!
My heart's fair bursting, I'm as good as dead,
There's someone on my belly! And on my head!
Simon! Those wretched boys are in a brawl!'

So John leaps out of bed fast as he can,
And feels along the walls, gropes to and fro
To find a stick; and she jumps up also,
But, more familiar with the room than John,
Finds a stick leaning by the wall at once.
She saw a little glimmering of light,
For through a hole the moon was shining bright,
And by that light could just make out the two,
Yet could not tell for certain who was who,
But only caught a glimpse of something white.
And when she saw this something white, she thought
The student had been wearing a nightcap,
So crept up near and nearer with her stick,
And thought to have hit Alan a good thwack,
And hit the miller plumb on his bald pate,
And down the miller goes, crying blue murder.
The students thrashed him soundly; left him there,
Threw on their clothes, collected horse and meal,
And so away; but stopped off at the mill,
And there they picked up the half-bushel cake,
All their own flour, beautifully baked.

That's how this cocky miller got well thrashed,
And lost out on the grinding of the wheat,
And paid for all that John and Alan ate,
Who also gave him a good going-over.
His wife's been tumbled, and so has his daughter,
What it is to be a miller and a cheat!
And so this proverb's true enough, say I,
The one that goes 'Do as you would be done by';
A cheater shall be cheated, soon or late.
And may God, high upon His heavenly seat,
Save all this company, both great and small!
And so I've done the miller with my tale.'

THE PROLOGUE OF THE COOK'S TALE

The cook from London, while the reeve spoke, looked
As pleased as if his back were being scratched.
'Ha ha!' laughed he, 'by Christ Jesus' passion,

I'd say that was a pretty sharp retort
The miller got, over the lodgings question!
And, in his own way, Solomon was right:
For, "Bring not every man into thine house"
He said; and it's a pretty risky business,
This giving a night's lodging; you can't be
Too careful about sharing privacy.
And may the Lord rain on me grief and care
If ever—sure as my name's Hodge of Ware—
I heard of a miller more completely duped!
That's a mean trick they played him in the dark!
And God forbid that we should leave off here;
And so, if you'll be good enough to hear
A story told by a poor chap like me,
Then I'll tell you, as well as ever I can,
A funny thing that happened in our city.'
    Our host answered: 'You're welcome, as for me.
Tell away, Roger, but mind it's a good one;
For many's the stale pasty, drained of gravy,
And warmed-up Jack-of-Dover pie you've sold,
That's been twice hotted up and twice left cold.
Many's the pilgrim who has been the worse
For the parsley stuffing in your fatted goose,
And has called down upon you heaven's curse,
Because your cookshop's always full of flies.
Now tell on, Roger, if that's your right name.
But if I tease a bit, pray don't be vexed,
For many's the true word that's said in jest.'
    Said Roger, 'On my oath, that's true enough.
But "A true joke's no joke"—so say the Dutch.
And so, before we go on, Harry Bailly,
Swear on your honour that you won't be angry
Even if my tale is of an innkeeper.
But all the same I will not tell it yet;
Before we part you'll be paid out, I bet.'
With that he laughed and cheered up. Then and there
He told his tale, which you're about to hear.

THE COOK'S TALE

A prentice lad once lived in our city,
Who earned his living at the victualling trade.
Gay was he as a goldfinch in the greenwood,
Goodlooking, stocky, as brown as a berry,
With long black hair, and rigged out stylishly.
So well he danced, so well and merrily,
That people came to call him Peter Playboy.
He was as full of love and lechery
As a beehive is full of sweetest honey;
So any girl who met with him was lucky.
At every wedding-feast he'd sing and caper;
He was fonder of the tavern than the counter.
When any procession rode by in Cheap,
Out of the shop and after it he'd shoot.
Then till he'd seen all there was to be seen
And danced his fill, he'd not come back again.
He gathered up a gang of his own sort
For dancing, singing, and that kind of sport;
And they would fix a rendezvous to meet
To play at dice in such-and-such a street;
For in all the town you'd find no other prentice,
No better hand to throw a pair of dice
Than Peter could; into the bargain, he
Was a free spender, albeit on the sly.
His master came to know this all too well,
For many a time he found an empty till.
You may be sure, where there's a playboy prentice
Who lives it up with women, dice, and parties,
It's his employer's shop that pays for him,
But has no part in any of the fun.
Such fun and games are theft, near as no matter:
One calls the tune, the other pays the piper.
When a man's poor, high living and honesty
Are all the time at odds, as you can see.

    This frisky prentice managed to stay on
Till his apprenticeship was nearly done,
Although reproved and rated day and night,
And sometimes hauled with fanfares to Newgate.*

But in the end, one day while casting up
Accounts, his master chanced to recollect
A proverb going like this, word for word:
'Best throw the rotten apple from the hoard
Before it has a chance to rot the remnant.'
It's just the same with an unruly servant,
It's much less harm to put him out to grass
Than let him spoil the others in the place.
And so his master gave him his release,
Told him to go, with curses on his head;
And thus the frisky prentice took his leave.
Now he can live it up all night; or not.
And since there's never thief without a mate
Ready to help him swindle, fleece, or cheat
Anyone he can rob or sponge upon,
He quickly sent his bed and baggage on
To a boon companion, one of his own sort,
As fond as he of dice and other sport,
Whose wife kept, as a respectable front,
A shop; but earned a living with her cunt.

Fragment II (Group B¹)

INTRODUCTION TO THE
SERGEANT-AT-LAW'S TALE

What the Host said to the pilgrims

Our host saw that the bright sun had traversed
A quarter part—plus half an hour or so—
Of the arc it runs from sunrise to sunset,
And though not well versed in the art, was sure
That it must therefore be the eighteenth day
Of April, herald to the month of May;
Having noted that the shadow of each tree
Was equal to its height—that is to say,
Long as the upright body casting it—
From the shadow, therefore, he could calculate
That Phoebus, which was shining clear and bright,
Was forty-five degrees in altitude;
That, reckoning the date and latitude,
The time was ten o'clock. And suddenly
He pulled his horse around:
                              'Now, gentlemen,
I have to warn all in this company
A fourth part of the day's already gone.
Now, for the love of God and of St John,
Lose no more time than you can help, I say;
I tell you, sirs, that Time wastes night and day
And steals from us in secret while we're sleeping,
And through our carelessness when we are waking,
Just like a stream that never turns again,
Descending from the mountain to the plain.
Seneca and many a philosopher
Laments for time lost more than golden treasure;
For, as he says, lost wealth's reparable,
But time, once lost, is irrecoverable.
It won't come back, any more than Molly

Gets back the maidenhead lost by her folly;
And so let's not grow mouldy doing nothing.
    'Now, Mister Lawyer, as you hope for heaven,
Tell us a tale, according to your bargain.
Since you have given us your free assent
That in this case you'll stand by my judgement.
Acquit yourself, make good your commitment,
And then you'll have at least a clear conscience.'
    'Good host,' said he, '*depardieux*, I assent;
For I've no thought of breaking my engagement.
A promise is a debt; I'll gladly pay it;
I can't say any fairer. And, by rights,
He who lays down the law ought not to break
The law himself, but rather to obey it:
So goes the code. But none the less I'm sure
I don't know any first-rate tale that Chaucer,
For all his little skill in rhyme and metre,
Has not—in language such as he can master—
Told long ago, as many are aware;
If he's not told them in one book, dear sir,
It is because he's told them in another.
For he has told of lovers of all kinds,
And more than Ovid mentions, or you'll find
In his *Epistles*, which are very old.
Why should I tell what's been already told?
    'In youth he wrote of Ceix and Halcyon;
Since when he's celebrated every one
Of those noble ladies, and their loves as well.
And anyone can look out, if he will,
His huge tome called *The Legend of Good Women*
And read about the wounds, so wide and gaping,
Of Babylonian Thisbe, and Lucrece;
The sword of Dido, dying for Aeneas;
Of Phyllis, hanging herself from a tree
For love of Demophon; the elegy
Of Dejaneira and Hermione,
Of Hypsipyle, and Ariadne;
The barren island standing in the sea;
And of Leander drowning for Hero;
The tears of lovely Helen, and the woe

Of Cressida; and yours too, Laodamia;
And of your cruelty too, Queen Medea,
Your little children hanging by the neck
Because your Jason proved himself a jilt.
Alcestis, Hypermnestra, Penelope,
How highly Chaucer praised your womanhood!

    'You can be certain he writes not a word
About that dreadful tale of Canace
Who once loved her own brother sinfully;
(And shame on such damnable tales, say I)
Nor tells the story of Apollonius
Of Tyre, and how King Antiochus
Despoiled his daughter of her maidenhead—
That story is so horrible to read
Where he flings her down upon the paving-stones!
And therefore he, with due deliberation,
Would never speak in any of his poems
Of such unnatural abominations,
And if it can be helped, neither will I.*

    'But what shall I do for a tale today?
I'd surely hate to be compared with those
Muses that people call Pierides
—If you have read the *Metamorphoses*
Of Ovid, then you'll know just what I mean—*
But nevertheless I don't give a bean
If what I offer, coming in his wake,
Seems like baked haws, the plainest of plain fare;
I'll speak in prose; it's up to him to make
The poetry.' Then he, with solemn face,
Began his tale, which you're about to hear.

THE PROLOGUE OF THE
SERGEANT-AT-LAW'S TALE

    Hateful poverty, of all evils worst!
With thirst, with cold, with hunger so confounded!
To ask assistance shames you to the heart;
Yet if you ask for none, you are so wounded

That absolute need uncovers all the wound hid!
Indigence forces you, in spite of all,
To borrow for your keep; or beg, or steal.

You may blame Christ, observing bitterly
He misapportions wealth that's temporal,
Or you reproach your neighbour sinfully,
Saying you've not enough, while he has all.
'When his tail's burning in the fire of hell
He'll pay for it one day,' says you, 'by God!
He's never helped the needy in their need!'

Hear what is said about it by the wise:
It's better to be dead than to be poor,
And one whom all your neighbours will despise,
For goodbye all respect, when you are poor!
And here is yet another sage old saw:
'Horrible are the lives of the penurious!'
Beware of being driven to that pass!

If you are poor, you're hated by your brother,
And shunned by all your friends! O full of riches,
You merchants, O you prudent folk and worthy,
You've all the luck, no losing double aces,
But have your bags well stuffed with fives and sixes,
And runs of luck at throwing the best chance;*
At Christmas time, how gaily you can dance!

For gain and profit you scour lands and seas;
And like wise men, are kept informed about
The state of kingdoms; you're a fount of news
And stories, tales of peace, war, and debate.
Were it not for a merchant, I'd be out
Of tales right now. He's been dead many a year,
But he taught me a tale, which you shall hear.

THE SERGEANT-AT-LAW'S TALE

PART ONE

In Syria there was once a company
Of prosperous traders, sober honest men,
Exporting far and wide their spicery,
Their cloth-of-gold and richly hued satin.
So novel were their goods, and such a bargain,
That every man was desirous to deal
With them, and bring them merchandise to sell.

It chanced the leading merchants of this group
Made up their minds that they would go to Rome,
Either on business, or for pleasure—but
In any case they determined to come
Themselves and send no delegate; whereupon
They put up in the quarter they supposed
Would be best suited for their purposes.

These traders had been living in the town
Some time, as suited their convenience,
When rumours of the excellent renown
Of the daughter to the emperor, Constance,
Fully detailed with every circumstance,
Came to these Syrian traders in a way
I shall describe. They heard from day to day

What was the common talk of every man:
'Our Emperor of Rome has got a daughter
(May God preserve him!). Since the world began,
If you reckon up her beauty with her virtue,
There never was another such as her,
Whom God uphold in honour, and sustain!
And of all Europe she should be the queen.

'Hers is most perfect beauty, without pride;
Youth, but without its greenness or folly;
In all her actions, virtue is her guide;
All arrogance quelled in humility.
She is a mirror of all graciousness,
Her heart a very shrine of holiness,
Her hand, a liberal instrument of largesse.'

All this report was true, as God is true.
But to the story let us turn again.
These traders had their ships loaded anew,
And when they'd looked upon this happy maiden,
Back to Syria they sailed contented home,
And there pursued their business as before,
And thrived thereafter—I can say no more.

These merchants had good standing, as it chanced,
With him who then was Sultan of Syria;
For when they came from any foreign place,
He would, with the most gracious courtesy,
Regale them, while enquiring curiously
The news of various countries, and thus learn
The wonders that they might have heard or seen.

Now among other things, particularly
These traders told him of the Lady Constance,
Detailing her great worth so earnestly,
Her image captured the imagination
And so obsessed the heart of this sultan,
That his sole concern and his one desire
While he had life and breath, was to love her.

Perhaps it was inscribed in that great book
Which people call the sky, set out in stars
When he was born, that it should be his luck,
His destiny to die for love, alas!
For in the stars, clearer than in a glass,
Is written, for whoever cares to read,
The death of every man; no doubt of it.

In stars, many a winter before their birth,
Was written the fate of Hector, Achilles,
Of Pompey, Julius Caesar, and their death;
The Theban war, the death of Hercules,
Of Samson, Turnus, and of Socrates,
Were written there; but men's wits are so dull
There's none who can interpret them in full.

Sending for his privy council, the sultan
—Here I am cutting a long story short—
Made what he had in mind quite plain to them,
Telling them that unless he had the luck
To win Constance, and to win her forthwith,
He'd surely die, unless they speedily
Discovered or devised some remedy.

Various counsellors made various
Suggestions; they debated up and down;
Many a subtle argument was brought forth;
Some spoke of magic and conjuration;
But finally, and in conclusion,
In all of these they saw no advantage,
And no way out for him save marriage.

But here they foresaw great difficulty
In putting it in practice—to be plain,
Seeing there was such great diversity
Between the two, in law and religion,
'No Christian prince', they said, 'would be willing
To let his child be wed under the cherished
Laws taught to us by Mahomet, our prophet.'

And he replied, 'Rather than I should lose
Constance, I will be christened and baptized;
I must be hers; I have no other choice.
Leave off your arguing, and hold your peace.
Go save my life, and neglect no device
To obtain her, in whose hands my life lies;
For I may live no longer in this grief.'

No need for further expatiation:
I'll say, by treaty and by embassy,
Helped on by the Pope's aid in mediation,
Backed by the clergy and nobility,
All were agreed, as you shall shortly hear,
To the destruction of idolatry
And to the spreading of Christ's blessed law.

For the sultan, with his whole baronage,
And all his subjects also, were to be
Christened, and Constance given in marriage,
Dowered with gold, but in what quantity
I cannot tell. With sufficient surety
This bargain was sworn to by either side,
And now, fair Constance, may God be your guide!

Now some will wish and expect, I imagine,
That I should speak of all the large provision
That the emperor in his magnificence
Made for the wedding of his daughter Constance.
But you should know so great a preparation
For an occasion of such high importance
Is not to be recounted in a sentence.

Bishops had been assigned to go with her,
With lords and ladies, knights of great renown,
And plenty of other folk to follow after.
And he had it proclaimed throughout the town
That all must pray, with due devotion,
To Christ, that He would bless their marriage,
And grant a swift and prosperous voyage.

At last the day comes of her departing,
That melancholy, fatal day has come
When there can be no further tarrying,
And all prepare to set forth and be gone.
And now Constance, with sorrow overcome,
Rises with pale face, ready to depart,
Knowing too well there is no help for it.

Alas, what wonder is it if she wept,
Who must be sent away to a strange nation
Far from the friends who so tenderly kept
And cared for her; to be bound in subjection
To one of whose character she knows nothing?
All husbands are good men, and always were,
As all wives know; but I dare say no more.

'Father,' she said, 'your wretched child, Constance,
Your young daughter, brought up so tenderly,
And you, my mother, my most precious
Joy above all, excepting Christ on high,
Since I must go to Syria, once more I
Commend myself, your Constance, to your grace,
Never again to see you with these eyes.

'It is to Barbary, the heathen nation,
That I must go, because it is your will,
May Christ, Who perished for our salvation,
Give me strength His commandments to fulfil,
Though I die, wretched and miserable!
Women are born to bondage, suffering;
To live beneath the dominance of men.'

No, not at Troy, when Pyrrhus breached the wall,
Before Ilium burned; when Thebes was down;
No, not at Rome, harried by Hannibal,
When he'd vanquished its legions a third time,
Was heard weeping so tender or heart-broken
As in that room, where she bade them adieu;
But, weep or sing, she has no choice but go.

O Primum Mobile, you unpitying sphere,
Whose diurnal eternal motion sways
All things from east to west, and every star,
That naturally would go the other way!
Your thrusting set the heaven in such array
That at the outset of this grim voyage,
Unfavourable Mars blasts the marriage.

Aries presages, with his oblique ascent,
Misfortune; cadent Mars, helplessly thrust
Out of his angle into the darkest house,
Is in this case a baleful influence.
O powerless Moon, how feebly you are placed
In conjunction with no favourable sign,
Thrust from the auspicious to the malign!*

That reckless Emperor of Rome! Alas,
Was no astrologer in all the town?
Is timing of no matter in such a case?
No choosing of a favourable time
For persons of high rank, when they embark?
Not when one knows the hour of their birth?
Alas, it's either ignorance, or sloth.

   The lovely and unhappy girl is led
To the ship with pomp, and with all circumstance.
'Now Jesus Christ be with you all,' she said.
All they could say was, 'Farewell, fair Constance!'
She tries to keep a cheerful countenance;
And so I leave her there to sail away,
And tell of happenings in Syria.

   The sultan's mother—that well-spring of vices!
Seeing the course on which her son was bent,
How he'd forsake their ancient sacrifices,
Summoned her counsellors to come at once;
They soon appeared, to learn of her intent.
She, when these folk had assembled together,
Sat herself down, and spoke as you shall hear.

   'My lords,' she said, 'you all know that my son
Is now upon the point of giving up
The holy hallowed laws of our Koran,
Given by God's apostle, Mahomet.
But I make one vow to almighty God—
Sooner the life shall be torn from my breast
Than from my heart the faith of Mahomet!

'What can this new faith bring us, if not ill?
Bodily suffering, bondage, and remorse,
And afterwards to be dragged down to hell
For renouncing Mahomet and our faith!
But, my good lords, if you will swear to this,
To follow my advice, do as I say,
I shall make us safe for ever and a day.'

They swore, and they all promised, every one,
To stand by her, with her to live and die;
And that, as best he could, each one of them
Should recruit all his friends to fortify
Her cause. And so the sultaness has taken
The enterprise in hand, as you shall hear;
And she addressed them all in this manner:

'First pretend to accept the Christian faith,
Cold water will not do us any harm!
And I'll prepare a banquet, such a feast
As will settle all accounts with the sultan;
For let his wife be christened never so white,
She shall have need to wash away the red,
Though she'd water by the fontful at her side!'

O sultaness! Termagant! Root of evil!
Virago! Semiramis the second!
You serpent hidden in the form of woman,
Like to the serpent fettered deep in hell!
Two-faced, treacherous woman, through your malice
All that confounds virtue and innocence
Is bred in you, you breeding-place of vice!

O Satan, envious ever since the day
That you were chased out of our heritage!
You know of old just how to get your way
With women; you made Eve bring us to bondage;
You mean to wreck this Christian marriage!
Thus, more's the pity, when you would beguile,
You choose, alas, a woman as your tool.

This sultaness, whom I accuse and curse,
Having dismissed her council secretly
—But why spin out the tale? I'll not digress—
Rode out to see the sultan one fine day,
And told him that she would renounce her faith,
And at the hands of priests receive baptism,
Repenting having stayed so long a heathen,

Beseeching him to let her have the honour
Of inviting all the Christians to a feast—
'How best to please them shall be my endeavour.'
The sultan said, 'It shall be as you ask,'
And, kneeling, he thanked her for her request.
He was so glad he knew not what to say.
She kissed her son and took her homeward way.

PART TWO

These Christian folk landed in Syria,
A grand, imposing host; when they arrived
The sultan sent a message straightaway
To his mother first, then all the countryside,
With sure news of the coming of his bride;
He begged her to ride out to meet his queen
With welcome, for the honour of his realm.

Thick was the press, and splendid the array,
When the Syrians and the Romans met together;
The sultan's mother, richly dressed and gay,
Received her in so pleased and fond a manner,
She might have been a mother with her daughter;
And then in solemn pomp the two rode slowly
In state toward the neighbouring city.

I don't suppose the triumph of Julius
The poet Lucan brags so much about,
Could have been more splendid or more sumptuous
Than was the turn-out of this happy crowd;
But she, for all her flattering friendliness,
That evil ghoul, that sultaness, that scorpion!
Planned covertly to plant a deadly sting.

The sultan comes himself soon after this,
And in such splendour that you'd not believe;
Greets Constance with all joy and happiness,
And in that happiness I shall take leave
Of them, to keep my story plain and brief.
And in due course of time, folk thought it best
To end the revels and go take their rest.

Now the time came when this old sultaness
Prepared the banquet of which I have told;
And the Christians made them ready for the feast,
Yes, all without exception, young and old;
It was a royal banquet to behold,
More dainties there than I can tell you of.
Before they rose, they bought them dear enough!

O sudden sorrow, ever the successor
To bliss on earth, salted with bitterness!
End of the joy of our earthly labour!
For sorrow subsumes all our happiness.
So if you would play safe, heed this advice:
When things are going well, just bear in mind
That unforeseen misfortune comes behind.

For to give the facts as briefly as I'm able,
The sultan and the Christians, every one,
Were stabbed and hacked to pieces at the table,
All but the Lady Constance, she alone.
The sultaness, that damnable old crone,
Helped by her friends, has done this evil thing;
She means to rule the country as its queen.

And all the Syrians who had been converted
And who were in the sultan's confidence,
Before they could escape, were hacked to pieces.
No time was lost in capturing Constance:
Aboard a ship—one that was rudderless—
They bundled her: 'Sail off and find your way
From Syria back again to Italy!'

Some of the treasure that she brought with her,
And, to be fair, provisions in great plenty,
They've given her; also what clothes she wore.
And forth she sails upon the bitter sea,
O my kind Constance, fount of charity!
O loved young daughter of the emperor!
He who is lord of Fortune be thy star!

Crossing herself, she prayed with piteous voice
Before the cross of Christ; and thus prayed she:
'O bright and blessed altar, holy Cross,
Red with the compassionate blood that washed away
The world's inveterate iniquity,
Defend me from the devil and his claws
When I am drowning in the deep sea waves.

'Victorious Cross, shield of the faithful, you
Who were the only one worthy to bear
The King of Heaven, His wounds all fresh and new,
The white Lamb, pierced through with the deadly spear!
Banisher of the fiend from him or her
Marked with your sign, over whom your arms extend,
Save me, and grant me power to amend!'

And so she floated many a year and day,
Across the Aegean sea, into the Strait
Of Gibraltar, as fortune would direct.
Many a scant and meagre meal she ate,
Many a time she thought that she must die,
Before the weltering waves would cast her up
To land her at the place ordained by fate.

You may well ask me why she was not slain
With others at the feast? Who was there to save?
To that demand this answer I return:
Who rescued Daniel from the fearsome den
Where everyone but he, master and man,
Was eaten by the lion, nor might escape?
No one but God, whom he bore in his heart.

God chose to show His miraculous power
Through her, that we might see His mighty works;
And Christ, the remedy for every sorrow,
As learned men know, chooses His instruments
For purposes that are obscure and dark
To human wit, because our ignorance
Can never wholly grasp His providence.

Since at the feast she was not murdered, who
Was it kept her from drowning in the sea?
Who succoured Jonah in the fish's maw
Till he was spouted up at Nineveh?
All of you know that it was none but He
Who saved the Hebrew people from their drowning,
Dry-footed through the parted waters passing.

Who commanded the four spirits of tempest
That have the power to vex land and sea,
Both north and south, and also east and west,
'Vex not a leaf, vex neither land nor sea'?
None can have given that command but He
Who thus preserved from wind and storm this woman
Continually, whether awake or sleeping.

Where found she food and drink to keep alive?
How did her food last for three years and more?
Who fed Egyptian Mary* in the cave
Or in the desert? None but Christ, be sure.
As great a miracle as when with five
Loaves and two fishes, He contrived to feed
Five thousand. God sent His plenty in her need.

She was driven out into our own ocean,
And over our fierce seas, until at last
Under a castle—I don't know its name—
Far in Northumberland, the wild caves cast
Her ship upon the sand, which held it fast,
So that it would not budge for a whole tide;
It was Christ's will that there she should abide.

The governor of the castle soon came down
To see the wreck. He searched throughout the ship,
And found the woman, weary and careworn;
He also found the treasure that she brought.
In her own tongue for mercy she besought.
'Cut the life from my body,' she prayed him,
'And free me of the misery I am in.'

A kind of corrupt Latin was her speech,
But none the less she made them understand.
The governor, when he had seen enough,
Brought the poor woman safe ashore to land.
She kneels and thanks God for deliverance;
But who or what she was she would not tell,
Nothing could make her speak, for good or ill.

Her wits were so bedevilled by the sea
That she had lost her memory, she said.
The governor felt for her such sympathy,
And his wife too, that both for pity wept.
She was so diligent, so tireless
To serve and please everyone in that place,
That all loved her who looked upon her face.

The governor, and Hermengyld his wife,
Were infidels, like everybody there.
To Hermengyld she became dear as life,
And Constance made so long a sojourn there,
Giving herself to weeping and prayer,
That Lady Hermengyld, the governor's wife,
Became a convert through the grace of Christ.

In all the land no Christians dared assemble,
All Christian folk had fled from that country
Because the infidels had conquered all
The regions of the north by land and sea.
To Wales, last retreat of Christianity,
Fled the old Briton dwellers of this isle;
Here was their sanctuary for a while.

Yet the Christian Britons were not so exiled
That there were not some left, who secretly
Still worshipped Christ, and fooled the infidels.
And as it happened, three such lived near by
The castle; one was blind, and could not see,
Unless it were with those eyes of the mind,
The eyes through which men see when they are blind.

  Bright was the sun upon the summer's day
On which the governor, and his wife too,
With Constance took their way toward the sea,
For a brief outing, half a mile or so,
To take the air and wander to and fro.
And while they were upon this walk they met
The blind man, old and bent, with eyes fast shut.

'Lady Hermengyld!' the old Briton said,
'In Jesus' name, give me my sight again!'
The lady, at these words, grew terrified,
Fearing the governor would have her slain
If he knew of her love for Jesus Christ.
But Constance made her bold. 'Now do your work
As Christ wills, like a daughter of His church.'

  The governor, dismayed by what he saw,
Exclaimed, 'What is the meaning of all this?'
And Constance answered, 'Sir, it is the power
Of Christ, Who saves men from the devil's snare.'
And she began to tell him of our faith
With such effect, that before fall of night
He was converted to belief in Christ.

This governor was by no means the lord
Of the place I speak of, where Constance was found;
For many winters he'd held watch and ward
Over it for Alla of Northumberland,
The same who curbed the Scots with iron hand,
Who was, as all men know, an astute king;
But let me now take up my tale again.

Satan, who's always waiting in ambush
To trick us, noted Constance's perfection.
Casting about to make her pay for it,
He made a young knight living in that town
Burn for Constance with such a lustful passion
He quite believed, unless he had his way
Just once with Constance, he must surely die.

So the knight woos her, but it's all in vain,
She won't be got to sin in any way.
In his resentment he devised a scheme
By which she was to die a death of shame.
He waited till the governor was away,
And then one night in secrecy he crept
Into Hermengyld's bedroom while she slept.

Worn and tired out with prayer and vigil,
Constance is sleeping; Hermengyld also.
This knight, enticed and tempted by the devil,
Crept up to the bed softly, on tiptoe,
And cut the throat of Hermengyld in two.
Beside Constance he laid the bloody knife,
And then—God's curse upon him!—he made off.

Soon afterwards the governor came home,
And with him Alla of Northumberland,
To find his wife had been cruelly slain,
At which he broke down, wept, and wrung his hands;
And in the bed the bloody knife he found
Beside Constance. Alas, what could she say,
Out of her mind with sorrow and dismay?

This calamity was told to the king,
And where and when and how they found the lady
Wrecked in a ship; they told him everything
All the details that you have heard already.
Whereupon the king's heart was moved to pity,
Seeing so gentle and so good a woman
Brought to such misery and tribulation.

For as a lamb is brought to slaughter, so
She stands, this innocent, before the king.
And the false lying knight who did it, now
Accuses her of having done this thing.
But none the less there rose a murmuring
Among the people, saying they'd not believe
That Constance could have done so foul a deed.

For they had known her always virtuous,
One who loved Hermengyld as dear as life.
To this the entire household bore witness,
All but the man who killed her with his knife.
This public testimony strongly moved
The noble king, who thought he would enquire
Deeper in this, that the truth might appear.

Alas! Constance, you have no champion,
Neither can you defend yourself; but still,
He who once perished for our salvation
And bound Satan, who yet lies where he fell,
Must prove your mighty champion on this day:
For unless Christ vouchsafes a miracle
Innocent as you are, you'll surely die.

She sank down on her knees, and thus she prayed:
'O Thou immortal God, Who saved Susanna
From lying tongues, and thou, merciful Maid—
Mary I mean, the daughter of St Anna—
Before whose Child the angels sing hosanna,
If I am guiltless of this felony,
Come to my succour; or else I must die.'

Have you not seen at some time a pale face
Among a crowd, of one who is led out
Toward his death, when there is no reprieve?
Such is its colour you can single out
That face among all others, so beset
With peril, from the faces of the rest.
Gazing about her, Constance has that look.

O you who are living in prosperity,
Queens, duchesses, and ladies, every one,
Have pity on her in her adversity!
An emperor's daughter; yet she stands alone;
She has no one to whom she now can turn
For sympathy. O it is royal blood
Stands in jeopardy, far from friends at need.

And yet King Alla had such compassion,
—For noble hearts are open to pity—
That from his eyes the tears came running down.
'Now lose no time, but fetch a book,' said he,
'And if this knight will swear that it was she
Who killed this woman, then we will consider
Whom to appoint as her executioner.'

A Gospel, written in the British tongue,
Was brought, and on this book he swore the guilt
Was hers; that she had murdered Hermengyld.
At which a hand smote him on the neck-bone
So that he fell that instant, like a stone,
With his two eyes both bursting from his face,
In sight of everybody in that place.

A voice was heard by all who were present,
Saying, 'You have defamed an innocent
Daughter of Holy Church, before the king!
This you have done, and shall I hold my tongue?'
At this marvel the whole crowd was aghast.
They one and all stood there, in dread of vengeance,
Like people in a dream; save only Constance.

Great was the awe, also the penitence,
Of those who'd wrongly held in suspicion
This blessed saintly innocent, Constance;
And it was through this miracle, in conclusion,
(Constance assisting with her mediation)
The king, and many another in place,
Were all converted, thanks be to Christ's grace.

That lying knight was at once put to death,
Sentenced by Alla for his perjury;
Yet Constance felt great pity for his death.
And afterwards, Jesus of His mercy
Made Alla wed, with due ceremony,
This holy maiden, radiant and serene;
Thus Jesus Christ has made Constance a queen.

But who grieved at the wedding? Why, none other
Than Donegild, if what I hear is true.
She was the king's tyrannic old mother;
She felt her wicked heart must burst in two,
For what her son had done she hated so.
She thought it a dishonour he should take
So strange a foreign creature for his mate.

I've no desire to pad out my story
With chaff and straw; I'll only give the corn.
Why should I have to tell how royally
They married, or what courses were laid on,
Who blew the trumpet, or who wound the horn?
It all boils down to this: what can you say
But that they eat and drink, sing, dance, and play?

They go to bed, as is both meet and right;
For although women are most saintly beings,
They've got to take in patience at night
Such customary necessary things
As please the folk who wedded them with rings,
And lay aside their saintliness a bit
For the time being; there's no help for it.

In good time he begot on her a son,
And to a bishop, and the governor,
He entrusted his wife while he was gone
To Scotland to hunt down his foemen there.
The mild and gentle Constance, being far
Gone with the child, keeps always to her room,
And patiently awaits the will of heaven.

In due course a male child was born to her,
And at the font they baptized him Maurice.
The governor summoned a messenger,
And wrote to Alla to give him the news
Of how the happy event came to pass,
With other things he felt he ought to say.
He took the letter up and went his way.

    This courier, careful of his interests,
Rides swiftly to the mother of the king,
Whom courteously in his own tongue he greets,
And says to her, 'You may rejoice, madam,
And give a hundred thousand thanks to heaven!
The queen has borne a child, no doubt of it,
To the whole kingdom's joy and delight.

'Here's a sealed letter with news of this thing,
Which I must carry with all haste I may.
If you've a message for your son, the king,
Remember I'm your servant, night and day.'
'Never mind that,' was Donegild's reply,
'But for tonight I'd like you to stay here;
Tomorrow I will tell you my desire.'

    Of ale and wine the courier drank deep,
His letter, meanwhile, was filched secretly
Out of his box, while he slept like a pig;
And in its place a skilful counterfeit
Was fabricated, and maliciously
Addressed to Alla from the governor
About this business, as you are to hear.

The letter said the queen had given birth
To so horrible and fiendlike a creature,
That in the castle none was brave enough
To dare stay in it for one moment longer.
It said the mother was a witch; sent there
By fate, or else by spells or sorcery;
That no one could endure her company.

Grief-stricken was King Alla when he read
This letter; but he told his grief to none,
And with his own hand he wrote back and said,
'For ever welcome be Christ's dispensation
To me, that am instructed in His doctrine!
Lord, welcome be Thy pleasure and Thy will!
For I have placed my will at Thy disposal.

'So keep the child, whether it be foul or fair,
And my wife too, until my homecoming.
Christ, when it pleases Him, may send an heir
More acceptable than this, and more pleasing.'
He seals the letter, silently weeping,
And hands it over to the courier, who
Takes it and sets off without more ado.

O you messenger! Sodden and awash!
Breath stinking, staggering limbs, and wits astray,
And with distorted and contorted face,
All that's confided to you you betray,
Your mind all gone, and chattering like a jay!
Anywhere where drunkenness rules the roost,
You can be pretty sure no secret's safe.

O Donegild, what English I command
Cannot do justice to your cruelty
And malice—I consign you to the fiend:
And let him celebrate your treachery.
O you virago! No, by God I lie!
You fiend in human form! for I know well
That though you walk the earth, your soul's in hell.

Returning from the king, this messenger
Arrives at the court of Donegild again
And is made much of by the king's mother,
Who tries to please in every way she can.
He drinks, and stuffs his girdle well with wine,
He sleeps, and like the hog he is, he snores
All night until the sun begins to rise.

Again she stole his letters, every one,
And counterfeited others which ran thus:
'The governor is commanded by the king
On pain of hanging and condign justice.
He must on no account allow Constance
To remain in his kingdom, or reside
More than three days and quarter of a tide.

'But in the same ship in which she was found,
She, her young son, and all her goods and gear,
He is to place; and thrust her from the land,
And tell her she must never return here.'
O my Constance! Well may your spirit fear,
And, in your sleep, the nightmare ride your dreams,
When Donegild contrives such evil schemes!

   When morning had aroused the messenger,
He went to the castle by the shortest road,
And gave the letter to the governor,
Who, when its grievous message had been read,
Exclaimed again—'Alas! Lord Christ!' he said,
'How is it that the world so long endures,
With so much wickedness in its creatures?

'Almighty God, if it should be Thy will,
Since Thou are a just Judge, how can it be
Thou sufferest the innocent to be killed,
While wicked folk reign in prosperity?
Alas, kind Constance, it is woe to me
That I must be your executioner, or die
A shameful death; there is no other way.'

   Then young and old, everyone in the place,
Wept at the accursed letter the king sent.
And Constance, with a pale and deathlike face
On the fourth day towards her vessel went;
Yet nevertheless humbly obedient
To Christ, she knelt and prayed upon the strand,
'Lord, let me always welcome what you send.

'For He who has saved me from lying blame
While I was upon land, as you all know,
Can defend me from harm as well as shame
On the salt sea, though I cannot see how.
As strong as He has been, so is He now,
In Him I trust, and in His mother dear,
My sail and rudder, and my guiding star.'

Her little child lay weeping on her arm;
And, kneeling, tenderly to him she said,
'Hush, little son, I will do you no harm.'
With that she drew the kerchief from her head,
Over his little eyes that bandage laid,
And in her arms she lulled him gently, as
Up to the heaven above she cast her eyes.

    'Mary, bright Maid and Mother,' thus prayed she,
'True is it that it was through woman's act
Mankind was lost, for ever doomed to die,
For which your child upon a cross was racked.
Your blessed eyes saw all His agony;
So there is no comparison between
Your grief and any grief man may sustain.

'You saw your child being killed before your eyes;
And yet my little child is living still.
Bright Lady, to whom all in trouble cry,
Glory of womanhood, and beautiful
Maid, haven of refuge, bright star of day,
Take pity on my child; your gentleness
Takes pity on the pitiful in distress.

    'O little child! alas, what is your guilt?
Who never sinned as yet, I dare avow?
Why does your cruel father want you killed?
Dear governor, take pity on him now,
Only let my little child stay here with you;
And if you do not dare, for fear of blame,
Then kiss him once, and in his father's name.'

And having prayed, she looked back at the land:
'Farewell, pitiless husband!' she said aloud,
And up she rose and walked along the strand
Toward the ship, followed by the whole crowd,
And, hushing her little baby all the while,
She takes her leave; and with a devout heart
Crosses herself, and goes aboard the ship.

The ship was well provisioned, never fear,
More than enough to last her a long time;
And of what other things she might require
There was enough, praise be to God in heaven.
May God almighty temper wind and weather
And bring her home! Over the open sea
She's driven on; that's all that I can say.

PART THREE

Alla the king comes home soon after this,
Back to the castle of which I have told;
And he asks where his wife and his child is.
At which the governor feels his heart grow cold,
And tells him plainly all that I have told
About the matter—I cannot tell it better—
And shows the king his seal, also his letter:

'Sir,' said he, 'the things you commanded me
To do on pain of death, these I have done.'
The messenger was tortured until he
Had to confess and make all clear and plain,
And tell where he had lodged each night; and then
By inference, and skilful questioning,
They guessed the source from whence the mischief sprang.

   In the end they recognized the hand that wrote
The letter—though I don't know how they did—
And all the venom of that wicked plot.
Be sure the upshot was, that Alla had
His mother killed, as elsewhere you may read,
Because of her treachery and malevolence.
Thus ended old Donegild, and good riddance!

The grief that consumes Alla night and day
For his lost wife, and for his child also,
There is no tongue can tell, nor words to say.
But now I'll turn again to Constance, who
Five years and more was drifting on the sea,
Enduring hardship it pleased Christ to send,
Before her vessel drew near to the land.

I can't find its name in my authority,
But under yet another heathen castle
She and her child were cast up by the sea.
May God almighty, Who protects us all,
Remember them—for they're about to fall
Once more into the hands of heathen men,
And almost die—as you will shortly learn.

Down from the castle many came to gape
Upon the vessel, and Constance as well.
Until one night—to cut the story short—
The castle steward (may God damn his soul,
He was a rogue, a renegade as well!)
Came to the ship alone, and told her that
Whether she would or no, he'd be her mate.

The wretched woman was in great distress;
Her child cried out; and she cried piteously.
But the blessed Virgin helped her none the less:
She fought, and as she struggled desperately,
Overboard went that scoundrel suddenly,
And drowned; which retribution was his lot.
Thus Jesus Christ kept Constance without spot.

See the result of loathsome lechery!
O you foul vice, you debilate man's mind,
And more than that, you ruin a man's body.
The outcome of your work, and of your blind
Desires is grief. How many may one find
Killed or destroyed—not even for the act
Of sin, but merely for intending it!

How could this feeble woman find the strength
To shield herself against that renegade?
How was it Goliath measured his huge length
Upon the ground, crushed and subjugated
By one so young and unarmed as David?
How dared he look upon that direful face?
We know that it was only through God's grace.

Who gave Judith courage and hardihood
To murder Holofernes in his tent,
And deliver the chosen race of God
Out of their misery? My argument
Is that, just as the Lord in heaven sent
Courage and strength to save them from disaster,
So He sent unto Constance strength and power.

Her ship drove on between the narrow mouth
Of Gibraltar and Ceuta, making way
Sometimes west, and sometimes north and south,
And sometimes east, for many a weary day;
Until Christ's mother, blessed eternally,
Of her neverfailing goodness determined
That all her sorrows should come to an end.

Now that's enough of Constance for a while.
Let's speak about the Roman emperor.
From letters out of Syria, he's heard all:
The massacre of Christians; the dishonour
Done by that lying traitress to his daughter—
I mean the accursed wicked sultaness
Who had them slaughtered at the wedding feast.

The emperor despatched his senator
And, God knows, many another lord, at once,
And with them his imperative order
To exact full and summary vengeance.
They burned and killed and wasted the Syrians
For many a day, and when their task was done,
They turned and set their homeward course for Rome.

The senator returned with victory
To Rome; and, sailing home in princely style,
Came on the ship—according to the story—
In which sat Constance, forlorn all the while;
He knew not who she was, nor how nor why
She came to be like this; nor would she say
To save her life, one word about her history.

He brought her back to Rome, and to his wife
Entrusted her, and her young son also,
And at the senator's she lived her life.
Thus may Our Lady bring from out of woe
Forlorn Constance, and many more also.
And with the senator, as was her fortune,
Ever doing good, she lived for a long time.

The senator's wife turned out to be her aunt,
But for all that she was no better able
To recognize her niece, the Lady Constance.
Enough of that; let's now turn to King Alla,
Still sorrowing for his wife, still miserable,
And leave the Lady Constance in the care
And the safe keeping of the senator.

One day King Alla felt such keen remorse
For the killing of his mother, that he went
(If I may cut so long a story short)
To Rome, there to submit to what penance
The Pope might ask, and to his governance
In everything, and to beg Christ for pardon
For all the evil deeds that he had done.

News was soon spread throughout the town of Rome
That Alla had come on a pilgrimage,
By couriers who rode ahead of him;
The senator, according to usage,
Rode with his family to the meeting-place,
As much to impress with magnificence,
As to receive a king with reverence.

King Alla and this noble senator
Soon exchanged courtesies, each trying to
Outdo the other paying the most honour.
And it so happened, in a day or two,
The senator was invited to go
To dine with Alla; and, if I'm not wrong,
One of the party was Constance's son.

Some say it was at Constance's request
He went to the banquet with the senator;
But all such details are beyond my scope—
Be as it may, at any rate he was there.
It's true it was at Constance's desire
The child stood, while the banquet ran its course,
In front of Alla, gazing at his face.

Seeing the child, the king was struck with wonder,
And questioned the senator thereupon:
'Whose is that handsome child that's standing yonder?'
'I've no idea, by God and by St John!
He has a mother, but no father, none
That I know of,' said he. Then, turning round,
He told the king how the child had been found.

'But heaven knows,' the senator went on,
'None more virtuous than she, in all my life,
Of living women, whether maid or matron,
I ever heard of or set eyes upon!
I'm certain she would rather have a knife
Thrust through her breast than be adulterous:
There's no man who could bring her to that pass.'

Now this young child was as like to Constance
As is possible for anyone to be.
Her face was fixed in Alla's remembrance,
And he began to muse if there might be
Some chance the mother of the child was she
Who was his wife; and secretly he sighed,
And, rising, left the table with all speed.

'By heaven, my head is filled with fantasy!
It's clear to any rational judgement
My wife is dead, and drowned in the salt sea.'
Then he thought of another argument:
'How do I know that Christ may not have sent
My dear wife hither from across the sea,
Just as He sent her to my own country?'

And Alla went home with the senator
That afternoon, to look into this chance.
The senator received him with great honour,
And lost no time in sending for Constance.
Believe me, she was in no mood to dance
When she knew why, and whom she was to meet;
Scarcely could Constance stand upon her feet.

    When Alla saw his wife, he greeted her
And wept, till it was pitiful to see;
For from the moment that he looked on her,
He knew at first glance it was really she.
She, on her part, stood rooted like a tree,
For sorrow dumb, her heart shut in distress
When she remembered his unkindnesses.

Before his eyes she twice fell in a faint;
And Alla wept, explaining brokenly,
'As God,' said he, 'and all His holy saints
Shall ever have upon my soul mercy,
Of the harm done to you I swear that I
Am as innocent as is my son, whose face
Is so like yours—else let my soul perish!'

    Their tears and anguish did not soon subside,
It was long before their sad hearts found relief;
Most heart-breaking it was to hear them weep,
For weeping served but to increase their grief.
However, I beg you all to let me off
Telling of it—it would take till tomorrow;
I'm worn out with describing scenes of sorrow.

But finally, when the truth was manifest
That Alla was guiltless of her suffering,
A hundred times and more, I swear, they kissed;
And between them both such happiness begins,
That, save the joy of heaven which never ends,
The like has not been seen by any creature,
Or ever will be seen while earth endures.

Then she meekly begged her husband—to repay
The long and grievous sorrow she had borne—
To make an invitation specially
To the emperor her father, asking him
To condescend to come one day to dine.
On no account, she begged, was he to say
A word concerning her in any way.

Some people would claim that the child Maurice
Delivered this message to the emperor,
But it's my guess the king was not so foolish
As to send one of sovereign honour,
Of Christendom the glory and the flower,
A child like that; far better to suppose
He went himself; it seems that's how it was.

The emperor consented courteously
To come to dinner, as he had been asked;
And I have read that he looked curiously
Upon the child, and thought upon Constance;
Alla, returning to his residence,
Made every preparation for the feast
He could think of, to ensure its success.

When morning came, King Alla and his wife
Made themselves ready to go out to meet
The emperor. Joyfully they rode forth,
And when she saw her father in the street,
She alighted from her horse, fell at his feet,
'Father,' she cried, 'your young child, Constance,
Is now clean gone out of your remembrance.

'I am your daughter, your Constance,' said she,
'Whom long ago you sent to Syria.
It is I, father, who on the salt sea
Was thrust all by herself, and doomed to die.
Now, father dear, I beg of your mercy
Send me away to heathen lands no more,
But for his kindness thank my husband here.'

How touching was their joy! And who could tell
What happiness was theirs, when these three met?
But it is time for me to end my tale;
The day wears fast; so I'll not draw it out.
These happy folk sat down to their banquet
Where I'll leave them, delighting in their joy,
A thousand times happier than I can say.

   Their child Maurice was made emperor
By the Pope later; he lived Christianly,
Bringing to Holy Church the greatest honour,
But I'll pass over all his history,
Because my tale's concerned with Constance only.
In the old Roman chronicles you'll find
Maurice's life, for it's gone from my mind.

   King Alla, when he saw the time had come,
With his Constance, so angelic and sweet,
Journeyed straight back to England and his home,
And there they lived in happiness and peace,
But not for very long; I can promise
No earthly joy will last; time will not stay,
But changes like the tide; night follows day.

   Who ever lived in happiness for a day
Without being irked by guilt or by conscience,
Fear of some sort, by passion or envy,
Anger or pride, desire or resentment?
All this I point out for this reason only:
Short was the time of happiness and content
That Alla had to share with his Constance.

For death, who takes his toll of high and low,
After about a year—or that's my guess—
Snatched up King Alla from this world below,
For which Constance was filled with heaviness.
Now let us pray to God his soul to bless
While Lady Constance—to wind up my story—
Homeward to Rome, her city, makes her way.

To Rome this saintly being is come home,
And finds that all her friends are safe and sound,
All her adventures over now and done.
And when at length her father has been found,
Down on her knees she falls upon the ground;
Weeping womanly tears, with happy heart,
A hundred thousand times she praises God.

In virtue, and dispensing holy alms,
They lived for ever after; nor again
Were parted, until death divided them.
And now farewell! My tale is at an end.
May Jesus Christ, Who has the power to send
Joy after grief, so guide us in His grace,
And guard all of us who are in this place!

Amen.

THE EPILOGUE OF THE
SERGEANT-AT-LAW'S TALE

Our host stood in his stirrups there and then,
And said, 'Good people, listen all of you!
That was a first-rate tale we heard just now!
Mister Parish Priest, by God's bones,' he went on,
'Tell us a story, as you undertook.
I can see that you educated folk
Know heaps of good things, yes by God you do!'
    The parson answered him: 'Bless us!' said he,
'What ails the man to swear so wickedly?'
Our host returned, 'O Holy Joe, that's you!
I think I smell a Lollard in the wind.*

'Good people all, hear me,' our host exclaimed,
'Now just you wait! For by Christ's holy Passion
The next thing we'll be getting is a sermon.
This Lollard here is going to preach a bit.'
   'No, by my father's soul, that he shall not,'
Said the sea-captain, 'he's not going to preach,
Instruct us or expound some gospel text.
We all believe in God above,' said he,
'But he would only sow some heresy,
Or scatter weeds and tares in our clean wheat.
And so I warn you in advance, good host,
My handsome self has got a tale to tell,
A merry tale, and one to ring the bell,
One that will wake up the whole company:
Only it won't have any philosophy,
Or phisoboly,* jargon or law-argot.
I haven't got much Latin in my gob.'

Fragment VII (Group B²)

THE SEA-CAPTAIN'S TALE

There was a merchant living at St Denis
—As he was rich, most people thought him wise—
Who had a wife, a woman of great beauty,
A sociable girl, and fond of parties,
Which is a thing that causes more expense
Than all the regard and the compliments
Which men pay them at dinners and at dances
Is worth. Such pretences and salutations
Pass like a passing shadow on a wall;
But hard on him who has to pay for all!
The wretched husband always has to pay;
It's for the sake of his own standing he
Keeps us in dresses and in finery,
In which array we revel merrily!*
And if it turns out that he can't endure,
Or won't put up with such expenditure,
But thinks it all a waste and a dead loss,
Then someone else has got to pay for us,
Or lend us cash—and there the danger is.

    Now this good merchant kept an open house
In splendid style: you'd marvel at the crowds
Drawn daily there, for he was hospitable
And had a lovely wife—but hear my tale.
Among other of his guests, both high and low,
There was a monk—a handsome, pushing fellow,
—I'd guess he'd seen some thirty years or so—
Who was forever visiting the place.
This young monk—he'd a prepossessing face—
Had grown so intimate with the good man
From the time that their acquaintanceship began,
That he was as familiar in the house
As it is possible for a friend to be.
    As for this kindly merchant, seeing that he

And the monk too, were born in the same town,
The monk claimed kinship with him; which in turn
The merchant took no trouble to deny,
But was as happy as a bird at dawn,
For to his heart it was a source of joy.
So they were linked in everlasting friendship,
And each of them swore to the other he
Would be a brother to him while life lasted.

A free spender, Brother John: especially
While staying in the house; most generous,
Eager to please, and never mind the cost.
He'd not forget to tip the meanest page
In the whole house; for when he came, he gave
His host, and all the servants in the place,
Some gift that was appropriate to their standing;
And so they were as happy at his coming
As the birds are when the sun uprises.
No more of that for now; it suffices.

Now it happened that this merchant one fine day
Made plans to visit Bruges, there to buy
A quantity of goods and merchandise;
So he despatched a messenger to Paris
Immediately, entreating Brother John
To spend a day or two at St Denis
With him and his wife, for a holiday,
Before he left for Bruges as arranged.

Now this good monk that I am speaking of,
Being dependable, and a bailiff,
Had from his abbot warranty to range
Just as he liked, whenever he might wish,
To inspect the granges and outlying barns;
So lost no time in coming to St Denis.
Who was so welcome as milord the monk?
Our dearest cousin, gracious and urbane?
He brought a gift of wine, as was his wont,
A cask of malmsey, and another, full
Of sweet Italian red; and some wildfowl.
And so I'll leave the merchant and the monk
To entertain themselves, and eat and drink.

Three days went by; and then the merchant rose,

And soberly took stock of his affairs;
So up into his counting-house he goes,
To reckon up how matters stood that year,
What his expenses and outgoings were,
Whether he'd made a profit or a loss.
He spread his books and money-bags across
The counting-board in front of him, then shut
And locked the door (his treasure-hoard was great),
And, having made quite sure that for the mean time
He wouldn't be disturbed at his accounting,
Remained there until past nine in the morning.

The monk, who'd risen with the dawn also,
Was walking in the garden to and fro,
Having recited, most punctiliously,
His office.
                 Quietly the good lady
Stole to the garden where he paced sedately,
Greeted him as she'd often done before.
She had a little girl for company,
A pupil under her authority,
Quite young, and as yet subject to the rod.
'My dearest cousin, Brother John,' she said,
'What ails you, that you are so early up?'

'Niece,' answered he, 'it ought to be enough
To take no more than five hours' sleep at night
Unless you are some decrepit old man
Like any of these married chaps, who crouch
Cowering like a tired hare in its form
Half-dead after the hounds have hunted him.
But why are you so pale, my dearest niece?
I'm pretty sure of it that our good man
Has been at work on you since night began.
Hadn't you better go and have a rest?'
And saying this, he gave a merry laugh,
And at his secret thought blushed a bright red.

At this the pretty lady shook her head
And answered him, 'The Lord knows all,' said she,
'No, cousin dear, it's not like that with me;
For by that God Who gave me soul and life,
In all the land of France there is no wife

Who gets less pleasure from that sorry game.
Though I can sing, "Alas and woe is me
That I was born, yet to no one', said she,
'Dare I say how things really stand with me.
I am so full of misery and dread,
I'm thinking that I ought to go away
Or end it all.'
              Then the monk stared at her,
And said, 'Alas my niece! May God forbid
That you should ever do yourself away
For any fear or grief. Tell me what's wrong,
The chances are I can, in your misfortune,
Give some help or advice; tell me therefore
What worries you, and it will go no further.
See, I take oath here on my prayer-book
That never while I live, by hook or crook,
Shall I betray what you confide to me.'

  'I swear the same again to you,' said she.
'By God and by this prayer-book I swear,
Though I were to be torn to pieces here,
I'll never, even if I go to hell,
Breathe any word of anything you tell,
And not because of any cousinship,
But truly out of love and trust and friendship.'
And so they swore; and thereupon they kissed,
And then told one another what they pleased.

  'Cousin,' said she, 'if only I'd the time,
Which I haven't—least of all in this garden—
I'd tell the story of a martyred life,
And what I've been through since I was a wife
With that husband of mine, though he's your cousin.'

  'No!' cried the monk, 'by God and by St Martin!
He is no cousin of mine, no not he,
No more than that leaf hanging on this tree!
I call him that, by St Denis of France,
As an excuse for better acquaintance
With you, whom I have always loved above
All other women, and I speak the truth.
I swear it on my monkhood! Now make haste,
Tell me your troubles, then off with you, lest

He should come down out of his counting-house.'
   She answered, 'O my dear love, Brother John,
I'd keep this secret if I could, be sure,
But it must out, I can't stand any more;
Because to me my husband's the worst man
That ever lived since the world first began.
But it won't do, seeing that I'm a wife,
To tell another of our private life
Whether in bed, or any other place;
And God forbid I should, for goodness' sake!
A wife should never speak of her husband
But to his credit; that I understand;
And yet this much to you alone I'll say,
So help me God, he isn't worth a fly.
What most upsets me is his stinginess.
And you know well enough, by nature women
Desire six things—and I'm at one with them:
They want a husband to be courageous,
Intelligent, rich, and what's more, generous;
Complaisant to his wife, lusty in bed.
But by our blessed Lord above, Who shed
His blood for us, it seems I've got to pay
For clothes I bought—and all to do him credit!
A hundred francs, and that by next Sunday.
And if I don't, I shall be quite undone!
Indeed I'd rather never have been born
Than live discredited and put to scorn;
And if my husband ever finds it out,
I am as good as done for: so I pray,
Lend me this sum—or it's all up with me!
Dear Brother John, lend me these hundred francs,
And I'll not disappoint you with my thanks;
If you will only do the thing I say,
I'll pay you back upon the day you fix,
And do you any favour or service
I can—whatever you like to suggest.
And if I don't, then may my punishment
Be worse than that of Ganelon of France!'*
   To which the worthy monk made this reply,
'Indeed, indeed, my very own dear lady,'

Said he, 'I feel so very sympathetic
I swear to you—and here's my hand upon it—
I'll help you out—soon as your husband's gone
To Flanders—from the trouble that you're in;
For then I'll bring to you a hundred francs.'
And saying this, he caught her by the flanks,
Kissed her time and again, and squeezed her tight.
'And now be off, as quiet as quiet,
And as soon as you can manage, let us dine,'
Said he, 'my pocket sundial says it's nine.
Now go, and be as true as I shall be.'

    'God forbid that I shouldn't!' answered she,
And off she goes, as happy as a lark,
To tell the cooks that they must hurry up,
So that they all could dine without delay.
Then up to find her husband goes the lady,
And knocks upon his office door so boldly.

    'Qui là?' says he.—'It's me, for heaven's sake!
And tell me, sir, when do you mean to eat?
And how long are you going to be at
Your sums and ledgers and accounts and stuff!
The devil take part in all such reckonings!
As if God hadn't given you enough!
Come down, and leave your money-bags alone.
Aren't you ashamed to think that Brother John
Has been miserably fasting all day long?
Come, let us hear a mass, and then we'll dine.'

    'Dear wife,' said he, 'how little you realize
The cares of business, its complexities!
Lord save us! Of us merchants, by St Ive,
Out of a dozen, two will barely thrive,
Or make a steady profit while they live.
All we can do is keep up appearances,
Put on a good face, live as best we can,
Quietly go on with our businesses,
And keep our affairs secret till we die,
Or go on pilgrimage, to get away
From creditors. Therefore it's necessary
For me to keep an eye upon this strange
World; business being ever at the mercy

Of fortune, chance and circumstance and change.
    'I'm off to Flanders at the break of day,
But I'll be back again, soon as I can.
So, dearest wife, I beg that you will be
Obliging, compliant to everyone.
Mind you look after all our goods and gear,
And see to it the house is properly run
For you've enough of everything, and more,
A thrifty household needs to keep in store;
And you've no lack of clothes or provision,
Or money for your purse, should you want some.'
And saying this, he shut the office door,
And came downstairs without delaying more.
And thereupon a mass was quickly said,
And after that the tables were soon laid;
They lost no time in sitting down to eat,
And the merchant fed the monk with splendid fare.

    Soon after dinner, with a serious air,
Taking him aside to speak to privately,
The monk said to the merchant: 'Cousin dear,
I see you're off to Bruges—so Godspeed!
May St Augustine be your guard and guide!
Take care, I beg you, cousin, when you ride;
Take care also to moderate your diet—
Be temperate, especially in this heat.
Between us two, no need for ceremony:
So God keep you, dear cousin, and goodbye!
And if there should be anything whatever
You'd like to ask of me, that's in my power,
No matter what, count on me day or night;
It shall be done exactly as you'd like.

    'But may I ask one thing before I go?
If you can manage it—and that's to lend
A hundred francs, just for a week or so?
It's for some cattle that I've got to buy,
To stock one of the farms upon our land.
Lord save us, but I wish that it was yours!
Be sure I'll pay you back upon the day.
If it were a thousand, there'd be no delay!
But let me beg you, keep this business quiet,

For I have yet to buy the beasts tonight.
Now, my dear cousin, let me say goodbye;
And thanks for all your hospitality.'

'Dear cousin,' the good man returned politely,
'Now surely that's a very small request!
My money's yours whenever you may want it,
Not just my money, but my merchandise.
For heaven's sake don't stint! Take what you please!
But there's one thing about us, as you know:
With businessmen, their money is their plough.
We can get credit while we've a good name,
But when we're out of cash, why, that's no fun.
When it's convenient, you can pay it back:
I'm glad to do my best to help you out.'

He brought the hundred francs out there and then,
Handed them on the quiet to Brother John:
And no one in the world knew of this loan,
Only the merchant and the monk alone.
They stroll about, and drink and talk and loiter,
Till Brother John rides back home to his cloister.

And so when morning came, the merchant rides
To Flanders, with his apprentice as guide,
And after a good journey, reaches Bruges.
There he goes busily about his business,
Buying and borrowing, but never dicing,
And never dancing, but in short behaving
Just like a businessman—so there I'll leave him.

Upon the Sunday following his departure,
Who should arrive, with fresh-shaved face and tonsure,
At St Denis but the monk, this Brother John?
Down to the very smallest serving-boy
All of the household staff were filled with joy
Since 'milord Brother John' was back again.
But to the point: in brief, this Brother John
And the pretty little wife have struck a bargain;
That for these hundred francs, he'd have the right
To have her flat upon her back all night;
Which agreement was duly acted on.
A happy busy time they had till dawn,
When Brother John arose, and said goodbye

To all the household staff, and went his way.
Not one of them, and no one in the town,
Has the least suspicion of Brother John;
Off he goes to his abbey, and rides home
Or where he likes; I'll say no more of him.

In good time, at the closing of the fair,
The merchant sets off to St Denis, where
He wines and dines his wife, to whom he says
That goods are now so dear, he has to raise
A loan, because he'd given a surety,
And now had twenty thousand crowns to pay.
And so this merchant is to Paris come,
To borrow of his friends a certain sum
In francs; the rest of it he'd brought with him.
As soon as he had arrived in the city
The first man that this merchant went to see
For his own pleasure, was this Brother John;
All out of fondness and deep affection,
And not to seek or borrow any money,
But to see him, ask after his welfare,
And gossip over business and affairs,
As old friends do when they are met together.
The merchant was made much of by the other,
And had a hearty welcome; for his part
The merchant gave details of his good buys,
And (thank the Lord!) bargains in merchandise.
There was one snag: he'd somehow got to raise
As best he might, a loan to meet his debt,
Before he could relax in peace and comfort.

'I'm truly glad to see that you've come home
From Bruges safe and sound,' said Brother John.
'And, heaven be my witness, were I rich,
For twenty thousand crowns you would not lack.
It's after all only the other day
That you so kindly lent those hundred francs—
By God above, and by St James, I say
I'm hardly able to express my thanks!
But I've returned that money, none the less;
I took it to your home, to your good lady
Your wife, and laid it on your counter; she'll

Be sure to know of it, as I can tell,
I gave her certain vouchers—Now farewell,
If you'll excuse me; for I can't stay long.
Our abbot's on the point of leaving town,
I'm in his party, and must go with him.
Give my love to our lady, my sweet niece,
And so goodbye, dear cousin, till we meet.'

   This merchant, having borrowed on credit
—No flies on him, I tell you!—paid the money
To the hands of Lombard bankers in Paris
Who gave him back his surety; home he goes
As merry as a grig, for well he knows
That over and above his gross outlay
He stood to make a thousand francs that trip.

   He wife stood ready waiting at the gate
To meet her husband, as she always did,
And they rejoiced together all that night,
For he was in the money, clear of debt.
Next day the merchant started to embrace
His wife again; he kissed her on the face,
And up he goes, and makes it strong and stiff.

   'Now stop!' she cried, 'Lord knows you've had enough!'
And she again began her amorous play,
Till in the end the merchant turned to say:
'By heaven, but I am a little vexed
With you, dear wife, though much against my wish.
And do you know why? If I'm right, my guess
Is that you've created some sort of coolness
Between me and my cousin Brother John.
You should have let me know before I'd gone
That he had paid to you a hundred francs
In ready money; he thought it poor thanks
When I spoke to him of borrowing; at least
It seemed so to me when I saw his face.
But none the less, as God is heaven's king,
I never thought to ask him anything.
So please don't do it ever again, my dear,
And always tell me, when I leave you here,
If any debtor's paid in my absence,
Lest I should ask him, through your negligence,

To pay me something he's already paid.'
    His wife was neither frightened nor dismayed,
And thereupon she boldly answered him:
'Pooh to that lying monk, that Brother John!
And for his vouchers I don't give a bean.
It's true enough he brought a certain sum
Of ready cash—bad luck on his monk's snout!
For God knows that I thought there was no doubt
He'd given it to me all for your sake,
To spend myself and make myself look smart,
And because we are cousins; also for
The many times we've entertained him here.
But as I see I'm in an awkward spot,
I'll give you a short answer: this is it:
Few of your debtors pay as soon as I!
For I'll pay you in full, and readily,
And every day; and should I fall behind,
Why, I'm your wife; so chalk it up, and I'll
See to it that you are soon satisfied.
I swear I've wasted none, but laid out all,
Every penny of it, upon clothes to wear,
And as I've laid the money out so well
To look a credit to you, then my dear
Don't be so vexed; for goodness' sake, I say
Let's laugh and have a good time, you and I;
Here is my pretty body for a pledge!
And I'll not pay you back except in bed!
And so forgive me, my own dearest husband,
I'll cheer you up if only you'll turn round.'
    The merchant saw there was no remedy,
That scolding would be nothing more than folly,
For the thing was past mending. 'Wife,' said he,
'I'll let you off, but don't you dare to be
So free again. Mind you take better care
Of what belongs to me; and that's an order.'
So my tale ends, and while we live may He
Who lives in heaven, send us tail in plenty!
                        Amen.

What the Host said to the Sea-Captain and the lady Prioress

'Well told, by corpus dominus!'* cried our host,
'Long may you, master mariner, sail the coast!
God send that monk a cartload of bad luck!
Oho boys, keep a lookout for such tricks!
How that monk made a monkey of the fellow,
And, by St Augustine, his wife also!
Never ever bring a monk into the house!
   'But let's get on now, and see who'll be first
Of all this crowd to tell another tale.'
This said, he spoke politely as a girl:
'Excuse me please, my lady Prioress,
If you don't mind—if only I were sure
It wouldn't put you out—I'd say it was
Your turn to tell a story, if you'd care.
Now will you condescend, my dearest lady?'
'Gladly,' said she. And now you'll hear her story.

THE PROLOGUE OF THE PRIORESS'S TALE

Domine dominus noster

'O Lord, Our Lord, how marvellous is Thy name
Which is spread abroad throughout the world,' said she;
'Not only is Thy most excellent fame
Proclaimed by those who hold authority,
But in the mouths of children Thy glory
Finds utterance, for sometimes even those
Who suck the breast may manifest Thy praise.

'Wherefore in praise of Thee, as best I can,
In praise of Thee, and that white lily flower
That gave birth to Thee and remained virgin,
My tale shall be, and all my endeavour;
Although I cannot augment her honour,
For she herself is honour; next her Son,
The source of goodness, and of souls the balm.

'O mother Maiden, maiden Mother free!
O unburned bush that burned in Moses' sight!
Thou who didst draw down from the Deity
Through thine humility, the Holy Spirit
By whose power, when He had lit your heart,
The Word was conceived and made flesh! Help me
To tell my tale, and tell it to your glory.

'Lady, thy magnificence and goodness,
Thy divine power and humility,
There is no tongue nor skill that can express:
For sometimes, Lady, when we pray to thee,
Thou givest first, of thy benignity,
Bringing to us the light, through thy prayer,
That leads and guides us to thy Son so dear.

'So feeble is my skill, O blessed Queen,
Even to declare thy consummate goodness
Is a weight that I'm not able to sustain;
I'm like a child twelve months of age, or less,
Scarce able yet to utter or express
Any word at all; therefore I pray thee
To guide the song that I shall sing of thee.'

THE PRIORESS'S TALE

There was in Asia a great Christian city
In which a Jewish quarter was maintained
By the great lord who governed that country,
For their foul lucre, by usury gained,
—Hateful to Christ, by Christian folk disdained—
And through its street the people came and went,
For it was free and open at either end.

Down at the further end of it there stood
A little Christian school, in which there were
A flock of children, all of Christian blood,
Who in that school were given year by year
Such teaching as was customary there,
That's to say, they were taught to sing and read,
Such things as infants learn in their childhood.

Among these children was a widow's son,
A little schoolboy, seven years of age;
Daily to go to school was his custom,
Also, whenever he saw the image
Of Christ's dear mother, it was his practice,
As he'd been taught, to kneel down and to say
An 'Ave Maria' and go on his way.

And so the widow's little son was taught
Always to honour thus our blessed Lady,
Dear mother of Christ, and he never forgot;
For a good child will always learn quickly.
But every time I think about him, I
Find myself thinking of St Nicholas;
At the same tender age, he honoured Christ.

This little child was in the school learning
His little book; and, sitting at his primer,
Heard 'Alma redemptoris'* being sung
By other children who were practising
Out of their anthem-books. And he drew nearer,
Near as he dared, to hear the words and music,
Until he had the opening verse by heart.

He had no notion what the Latin said,
Being so young, and of such tender years;
Till one day he took it into his head
To ask a friend to make a paraphrase,
Or tell him why the anthem was in use;
He begged him to translate it and explain—
On his bare knees he begged him many a time.

At length his friend, an older boy than he,
Answered him thus: 'The song, as I've heard say,
Was made about our blessed gracious Lady,
To greet and to beseech her, so that she
May be our help and succour when we die.
That's all that I can tell you of the matter,
I'm learning singing, and don't know much grammar.'

'And is the anthem sung in reverence
Of Christ's dear mother?' said this innocent.
'See if I don't, but I shall try my hardest
To learn it all before Christmas be past.
Even if, because my primer isn't learnt,
They scold or beat me three times in an hour,
I mean to learn it for Our Lady's honour.'

Daily, in secret, on his homeward way,
His friend taught him till he knew it by heart,
And in the end he sang it perfectly,
Confidently word for word, tuned to the note.
Twice every day the song passed through his throat.
Once on the way to school, once coming back;
On Christ's dear mother his whole heart was set.

This little child, as I have said, would sing
In the Jews' quarter, going to and fro;
Sing merrily, and always the same song:
'O Alma redemptoris', loud and clear.
The sweetness of Christ's mother had pierced through
His heart until he could not, come what may,
Cease singing of her praise upon his way.

The serpent Satan, our first enemy,
Who has his wasps' nest in the hearts of Jews,
Swelled up: 'O Hebrew people!' was his cry,
'Is it an honourable thing, think you,
That such a boy should walk where he may choose,
In scorn of you, and make of you his scoff,
Singing songs that are an insult to your faith?'

So from then on all of the Jews conspired
To hunt to death this innocent young boy.
And to this end an assassin was hired
Who lay in ambush for him in an alley.
This cursed Jew, as the little child passed by,
Grabbed him and held him in a cruel grip,
And cut his throat and threw him in a pit.

It was a cesspit that they threw him in,
Where these Jews used to go to purge their bowels.
O Herods of our day! O fiendish nation!
What may your malice and your hate avail?
Murder will out; be sure it will not fail,
Especially where God's glory shall be spread;
The blood cries out upon your fiendish deed.

    O martyr, constant in virginity!
Now mayest thou ever follow with thy song
In heaven the white celestial Lamb—said she—
Of which the great evangelist, St John,
In Patmos wrote; who says that those who sing,
Going before the Lamb with a new song,
Have never known the bodies of women.

    The wretched widow waited all that night
Watching for her little child; he never came.
And so, as soon as it was morning light,
With anxious fearful face, all pale and wan,
At school and everywhere she looks for him,
And in the end she finds that he had been
In the Jews' quarter, where he last was seen.

With a mother's pity bursting in her breast,
She goes, as she were half out of her mind,
Everywhere she could think of, where she guessed
There was some likelihood that she might find
Her little child; till, calling all the while
Upon the meek and gentle mother of Christ,
She looked for him among the Jews at last.

She besought and entreated piteously
Of every Jew inhabiting the place
To tell if he had seen her child go by,
But they said no. Yet Jesus in His grace
Put it into her head, before too late,
That while there she should call out for her son,
Near to the pit in which he had been thrown.

Almighty God, bringing to pass Thy laud
In mouths of innocents, behold Thy power!
This gem of chastity, this emerald,
Ruby of martyrdom, as bright as fire,
Though on his back with slit throat lying there,
'O *Alma redemptoris*' loud he sang,
So loud he sang it that the whole place rang.

Then from the street the Christians passing by
Came crowding in to marvel at this thing.
Posthaste they sent for the magistrate; he
Came on the instant, without tarrying.
He renders praise to Jesus, heaven's king,
Also His mother, glory of mankind;
And then commands the Jews to be fast bound.

This child, with pitiful lamentation,
Was lifted up, singing continually;
And with great pomp, in solemn procession,
Carried into the neighbouring abbey.
Fainting beside his bier his mother lay;
And scarcely could the people who were there
Part her, this second Rachel,* from his bier.

Every Jew, by order of the magistrate,
That knew about the murder had to die
A shameful death by torture on the spot.
Such wickedness he would not tolerate.
'For evil must have evil's just desert.'
Therefore he had them by wild horses torn,
To be hanged later, as the laws ordain.

Upon his bier he lies, this innocent,
Before the high altar, while mass is sung,
And then the abbot with the whole convent
Hastened to give him burial; but when
They sprinkled holy water over him,
Again, at the first touch of holy water,
He sang, 'O *Alma redemptoris mater*'.

This abbot, who was a most saintly man
As all monks are—at least they ought to be—
Questioned the little boy, and thus began:
'I beseech you, my dearest child,' said he,
'And in the name of Holy Trinity,
To tell me how it is that you can sing,
Although it seems your throat is cut in twain.'

'My throat is cut right to the bone, I know,'
Answered the child, 'and by all natural law
I should have died, died a long time ago,
But Jesus Christ, as holy books declare,
Wills His abiding glory to endure;
So, for the honour of His mother dear,
I still can sing 'O *Alma*' loud and clear.

'Wellspring of mercy, sweet mother of Christ,
Her I have loved, so far as in me lay;
And when I was about to lose my life,
She came to me and bade me sing this lay,
Even in death, as you have heard today;
And, soon as ever I began my song,
It seemed she laid a pearl upon my tongue.

'Therefore I sing, as I must always sing,
In honour of that blessed gracious Lady,
Until the pearl is taken from my tongue;
For after that, Christ's mother said to me,
"My little child, I shall fetch you away
When from your tongue the pearl I gave is taken.
Be not afraid, you shall not be forsaken." '

This saintly monk—by which I mean the abbot—
Pulled out his tongue, and took away the pearl;
And very gently he gave up the ghost.
And when the abbot saw this miracle,
With salt tears trickling down like rain, he fell
Flat on his face upon the ground. Prostrate
He lay, as still as if chained to the spot.

And the whole convent on the pavement lay
Weeping also, and giving praise to her,
Christ's mother. Then they rose and went their way,
And lifted up this martyr from his bier;
And in a shining marble sepulchre
His tender little body was enclosed.
May God grant that we meet where he now is!

Young Hugh of Lincoln,* who was killed also
By cruel Jews—who hasn't heard of that?
For it was but a little while ago—
Pray for us, who are weak and sinful folk,
That in His mercy mercifullest God
May also multiply His boundless mercy
On us, in reverence of His mother Mary.

                                                    Amen.

THE PROLOGUE TO SIR TOPAZ

What the Host said to Chaucer

When she had told this legend, every man
Fell silent: it was wonderful to see.
Till in the end our host again began
To crack his jokes; and his eye fell on me
At length—'What sort of chap are you?' said he,
'You look as if you'd lost sixpence and found
A penny—you keep staring on the ground.

'Come over here, and look up cheerfully!
Watch out sirs—room and plenty for this chap!
He's as well-made around the waist as me,
And what a cuddle—think of it!—he'd make
For any woman with a pretty face!
And from the look of him, he's a bit fey:
Besides, he never speaks to anybody.

'Now tell us something, since the others have;
A tale to make us laugh—and lose no time.'
'Host,' I replied, 'please don't take it amiss:
I don't know any other tale but one
That I learned long ago, and it's in rhyme.'
'That's good enough,' said he, 'we're bound to hear
Something worth hearing, to judge by his air.'

SIR TOPAZ

Here Chaucer's Tale of Topaz begins

THE FIRST FIT

Listen, sirs, with right goodwill,
And believe me I shall tell
    Of the merry capers
Of that knight with so much mettle
Whether for tournament or battle
    Whose name was Sir Topaz.

He was born in a far country,
In Flanders far beyond the sea,
    And Poperinghe was the place.
His father was of high degree,
For he was lord of that country,
    Thanks be to Heaven's grace.

A stalwart swain Sir Topaz grew;
White was his face as whitest dough,
    His lips as red as rose;
And like a scarlet dye his hue,
And it's the truth I'm telling you,
    He had a handsome nose.

And saffron was his beard and hair
That to his girdle fell so fair,
    Of Spanish hide his shoes;
His brown hose came from Bruges Fair,
His silken gown beyond compare
    Had cost him many sous.

A huntsman he of savage deer,
And he'd ride hawking by the river
  A goshawk on his wrist;
At that he was a good archer,
At wrestling you'd not find his peer,
  He always won his bets.

  Many a maiden in her bower
Had sighed for him with wild desire
  ('Twere better she had slept);
But he was chaste and no lecher
And sweeter than the bramble flower
  That bears a scarlet fruit.

  Of a verity I say
It so befell upon a day
  Sir Topaz out would ride;
He clambered on his steed so grey,
And lance in hand he rode away,
  A long sword at his side.

  He galloped through a fair forest
Filled with many a savage beast,
  Aye, both buck and hare;
And as he galloped east and west
I shall relate how he almost
  Fell to a grievous snare.

  There flourished herbs of every sort,
Like licorice and ginger-root,
  And cloves and many more;
And nutmegs which you put in ale
Whether it be dark or pale,
  Or put away in store.

  And birds were singing, I must say!
The sparrowhawk and popinjay,
  Till it was joy to hear;
The throstlecock piped up his lay,
And the wood-dove upon the spray
  Piped up both loud and clear.

And when he heard the throstle sing,
The knight was filled with love-longing,
    And spurred away like mad;
His good steed kept on galloping
Wet as a rag, so much 'twas sweating,
    With sides all drenched in blood.

    Then Sir Topaz so weary was
From galloping over the tender grass,
    So fiery was his courage,
That he alighted there and then
To give his horse a breather, when
    He also gave it forage.

    'O Saint Mary, Heaven bless me!
Why must this love so distress me
    And bind me with its rope?
All last night I dreamed, dear me,
An Elf-Queen should my sweetheart be,
    And sleep beneath my cloak.

    'I'll only love a Fairy Queen;
No woman I have ever seen
Is fit to be my mate
                In town;
    All other women I forsake,
I'll follow in the Elf-Queen's track
    Over dale and down!'

    Then he climbed into his saddle,
Galloped over stile and puddle,
    A Fairy Queen to find;
He rode so long at gallop and trot
Till at last he found, in a secret spot,
    The country of Fairyland
                So wild;
For in that country there was none
That dare to show his face to him,
    Neither wife nor child;

Until there came a burly giant,
His name it was Sir Elephant,
   A dangerous man indeed.
He said, 'Sir Knight, by Fee Fo Fum!
I live round here, so gallop home
   Or I will slay your steed.
                       With mace!
For it is here the Fairy Queen
With harp and flute and tambourine
   Has made her dwelling place.'

The knight said, 'Sir, believe you me,
Tomorrow I shall meet with thee,
   When I've my armour on;
And on my word, if I've the chance,
You'll pay for it with this stout lance,
   And sing another song.
                  Your gob
Shall be run through from cheek to chine
Before it's fully half-past nine,
   And here I'll do the job.'

Sir Topaz beat a quick retreat;
This giant pelted him thereat
   With stones from a terrible sling;
But he escaped, did Childe Topaz,
And it was all through Heaven's grace
   And his own noble bearing.

Yet listen, masters, to my tale
Merrier than the nightingale,
   And I shall make it known
How Sir Topaz of the slender shanks
Galloping over braes and banks
   Is come again to town.

His merry men commanded he
To make mirth and revelry
   For he had got to fight
A monstrous giant whose heads were three,
All for the love and levity
   Of one that shone so bright.

'Call hither, call hither my minstrels all,'
He said, 'and bid them tell some tale,
   The while I gird my armour on;
Some romance that is really royal
Of Bishop, Pope and Cardinal
   And also of a lover lorn.'

   First they brought him delicate wine,
Mead in bowls of maple and pine,
   All sorts of royal spices,
And gingerbread as fine as fine,
And licorice and sweet cummin,
   And sugar that so nice is.

   He put on next his ivory skin
Breeches of the purest linen,
   He also donned a shirt.
And next his shirt he did not fail
To have wadding and a coat of mail
   For to protect his heart.

   And over that a fine hauberk
—It was a most expensive work,
   Made of the stoutest steel;
And over that his coat-armour
Whiter than the lily flower,
   In which to take the field.

   His shield was of the gold so red
Emblazoned with a great boar's head,
   And a carbuncle beside;
And then he swore by beer and bread,
That giant shortly would be dead,
   Betide what may betide!

   His greaves were of tough leather; he
Sheathed his sword in ivory,
   And wore a helm of brass;
A whalebone saddle he sat on,
And like the sun his bridle shone,
   Or like the moon and stars.

His spear was of the best cypress,
'Twas meant for war, and not for peace,
   So sharp its tip was ground;
His charger was a dapple-grey
It went an amble all the way
   And gently paced around
                              The land,
Well, gentlemen, that's the first fit!
If you want any more of it,
   I'll see what comes to hand.

THE SECOND FIT

   Now hush your mouth, for charity,
Each gentle knight and fair lady,
   And listen to my tale
Of battle and of chivalry,
Of courtship and of courtesy
   That I'm about to tell.

   They talk about those grand old stories
Of Horn and of Sir Ypotis,
   Of Bevis and Sir Guy;
Of Libeaus and Sir Pleyndamour,
But Sir Topaz bears away the flower
   Of royal chivalry!

   He bestrode his noble grey
And forth he glided on his way
   Like a spark from flame;
Upon his crest he bore a tower
Wherein was stuck a lily flower,
   God shield him from all shame!

   This knight was so adventurous
He never slept in any house,
   But wrapped him in his hood;
His pillow was his shining helm,
While his charger grazes by him
   On herbs so fresh and good.

And he drank water from the well
As did the knight Sir Percival
Whose armour was so fine;
Till on a day—

THE PROLOGUE TO THE TALE OF MELIBEUS

Here the Host interrupts Chaucer's Tale of Sir Topaz

'No more of this, by God!' our host declared,
'This arrant drivel of yours makes me tired!
God be my witness, it makes my ears ache
To listen to you spout the filthy stuff!
The devil take such jingles! I suppose
It's what's called doggerel.'
                                                    Said I, 'Why so?
Why cut my story short and not another's,
Seeing it's the best ballad that I know?'

   'By God,' said he, 'to put it in a word,
Your shithouse rhyming isn't worth a turd!
You're wasting time, that's what, and nothing else.
I tell you flat, sir, no more of your verse!
Now see if you can tell, in poetry,
Some tale worth hearing, some old history,
Or anything in prose, that will at least
Be either edifying, or amuse.'

   'Gladly,' said I,' by everything that's holy!
I shall tell you a little thing in prose
You ought to like, unless you're hard to please.
It is an edifying moral story,
Though different folk have told it differently,
As I'm about to indicate and explain.

   'For instance, you know how each Evangelist
When writing of the Passion of Jesus,
Never puts matters quite in the same dress
As any of the others; none the less
Each tells the truth, and all agree in essence,
Though in the telling there's a difference.
For some of them say more, and some say less,
When they are dealing with His piteous Passion—

I'm talking of Mark, Matthew, Luke, and John—
But without doubt, the substance is the same.
And therefore I beseech you, gentlemen,
If it should seem to you I've changed the wording—
For instance, if I put in a few more
Proverbs than you remember having heard
Included in this little treatise here,
To strengthen the effect; and furthermore,
If I don't use exactly the same words
As you have heard used in the tale before,
Don't fault me, I entreat; because nowhere
Will you find any vital difference
Either in meaning, content or substance,
With that other little tract from which I drew
This entertaining tale I wrote for you,
So listen to what I'm about to tell,
And, please, this time you'll let me end my tale.'

THE TALE OF MELIBEUS

The 'little thing in prose' which Chaucer related to the Pilgrims
after the Host had put a stop to 'Sir Topaz', his burlesque parody
of the metrical romances of the day, turned out to be an im-
mensely long example of the didactic allegories that were so
popular in the Middle Ages. The *Tale of Melibeus* is a close trans-
lation of the French *Livre de Melibé et de Dame Prudence*, which
was in turn a paraphrase of the *Liber Consolationis et Consilli* by
Albertanus of Brescia. It is not so much a story as a debate on the
subject of the horrors of war and a plea for conciliation and agree-
ment among enemies, and it bristles with maxims and quotations
from recognized authorities. As the general reader would un-
doubtedly find the *Tale of Melibeus* wearisome I have omitted it.
But W. W. Lawrence has pointed out that it has an important
place in the scheme of *The Canterbury Tales*, for from it derives
the discussion on marriage—whether the wife or the husband
should have the authority—which is the theme round which
the tales of the Nun's Priest, the Wife of Bath, the Scholar, and
the Merchant are centred, and which is resolved in the *Franklin's
Tale*.

Here is a brief summary of the story. A rich young man called Melibeus and his wife Prudence had a daughter called Sophie. While Melibeus was away from home three of his enemies broke into his house and beat up his wife and daughter, leaving the latter for dead. On his return his wife advised him to have patience and consult what he should do with his friends and relatives. Melibeus did so; and some advised vengeance, but others recommended caution. Prudence herself enjoined him not to be overhasty, but Melibeus said he would not be guided by her because of the danger of following female advice, and because if he followed her counsel it would seem he had yielded his authority to her; whereupon Prudence defended the excellence of women's advice, quoting numberless authorities in support, till Melibeus gave in and agreed to do as she counselled. After this she gave him a good deal more advice and finally sent for his enemies and persuaded them to give Melibeus satisfaction if he wished; but in the end Melibeus forgave them completely.

THE PROLOGUE OF THE MONK'S TALE

What the Host said to the Monk

When I'd wound up my tale of Melibeus
And of Prudence his wife, and her goodness,
Our host exclaimed, 'As I'm a true believer,
And by St Madrian's holy bones,* I'd rather
That Goodelief, my wife, had heard this tale
Than lay hands on a barrel of good ale!
For she is nothing like as patient
As was this Melibeus' wife, Prudence.
By God's bones! when I beat my serving-lads
She bounds out, bringing me the big club-staves,
Yells, "Murder every man-jack of the swine!
Break every bone, and break their backs for them!"

And if one of my neighbours fails to nod
To her in church, or has the hardihood
To slight her in some way, when she comes back
She's on the rampage, screaming in my face,
"You miserable rat, avenge your wife!

By corpus bones, I'd better have your knife,
And you can take my distaff and go spin!"
From dawn to dusk, that's how she carries on.
"Alas!" she says, "that it should be my fate
To wed a milksop, yes, a gutless ape
Who's been shoved round by everyone all his life,
And doesn't dare to stand up for his wife!"
    'So it goes on, unless I pick a fight;
I've got no option but to sally forth—
She sees to it my life's not worth the living
Unless I act like a mad raging lion.
I'm pretty sure she'll make me kill someone
One of these days—I'll end up on the run.
For I'm a dangerous fellow with a knife,
Even if I daren't stand up to the wife,
For she's got big strong arms, as you'll find out
—Cross her, that's all, or try to contradict!
But now let's change the subject.
                                        My lord Monk,
Cheer up, for it's your turn,' our host went on,
'Indeed, you've got to tell us all a story.
Look where we are! Rochester stands hard by.
Ride forward, my good sir, don't spoil our game.
But on my honour, I don't know your name,
Whether to call you milord Brother John,
Or Brother Thomas, or else Brother Alban?
Which monastery's yours, in heaven's name?
I swear to God you've a delicate skin,
There's plenty of good grazing where you're from,
You're no repentant sinner, no thin shade!
Some kind of supervisor, on my faith!
A sacristan perhaps, or cellarer.*
For, by my father's soul, I'd say you were
Someone in authority when at home:
No wretched cloisterer, no poor novice,
But an administrator, shrewd and wise,
And moreover a big and brawny chap,
And a most personable one, at that!
God confound him, I pray, whoever first
Led you to take up the monastic life,

For you'd have been a rare cock with the hens.
If you had freedom, as you have the power,
To copulate as much as you desire,
A fellow like you would have fathered dozens!
For pity's sake, why do you wear the cope?
God damn my soul, but if I were the Pope,
Not only you, but every lusty man,
Tonsure and all, should be allowed a woman;
For otherwise the world is like to perish.
Religion has got hold of all the best;
As for us laymen, we're no more than sprats.
Your feeble tree engenders feeble shoots.
All this ensures our offspring are so weak
And scrawny, they can scarcely copulate.
No wonder that our wives want to try out
Clerics like you, for you pay Venus' debt
Far better than we can—as God's my witness,
The coin you pay with isn't counterfeit!
Take no offence, sir, if I joke like this;
There's many a true word that's said in jest.'

    All this the good monk bore with patience,
And answered: 'I will do my very best
To tell you, so far as seems consistent
With decency, a tale or two; or three.
I'll narrate, if your taste lies in that quarter,
The life of Edward, saint and confessor;
Or the kind of tale that's classed as Tragedy,
Of which I've hundreds in my monastery.
Tragedy means a certain kind of story
As ancient books remind us, of some man
Who was once living in prosperity,
And fell from high estate to misery,
And who came to a calamitous end.
And they are versified; most usually
In six-foot verses known as hexameters.
Many have also been composed in prose,
As well as in all sorts of different metres.
That's all—this explanation should suffice.

    'Now pay attention, if you want to hear.
But first, before proceeding any further,

If I don't tell these stories in due order,
Whether of popes, or emperors, or kings,
According to the chronologic sequence
As written in the books; and if you find
That I put some before, and some behind,
Just as they chance to come into my mind,
I beg you to excuse my ignorance.'

THE MONK'S TALE

Here the Monk's Tale begins: De Casibus Virorum Illustrium

I shall lament, and in the Tragic Mode,
The sufferings of those who once stood high,
Who fell from eminence, so that none could
Deliver them out of adversity.
For when Fortune makes up her mind to fly,
Her course no man is able to withhold;
Let no one trust in blind prosperity;
Be warned by these examples true and old.

LUCIFER

Although Lucifer was an archangel
And not a man, with him I shall begin.
For although Fortune cannot hurt an angel,
From his high station, owing to his sin,
Down into hell he fell, there to remain.
Lucifer, brightest angel of them all,
Never to escape—for now you are Satan—
Out of that misery into which you fell!

ADAM

There's Adam, who upon Damascus' plain
Was made by the finger of the Lord on high,
And not begotten of man's filthy sperm,
Who ruled all Paradise, save for one tree.
No man on earth has ever ranked so high

As Adam, until he, for disobeying,
Was driven from his blessed felicity
To labour, and to hell and misfortune.

SAMSON

There's Samson, whom the angel heralded
Well in advance of his nativity;
Who was to God almighty consecrated,
Honoured by all, so long as he could see.
There was never such another man as he
For strength, allied with daring hardihood;
But to his wife his secret he betrayed,
So had to kill himself for misery.

Samson, that noble and almighty champion,
With his bare hands, having no weapon by,
Once killed and tore to pieces a huge lion
Met on the road upon his wedding-day.
His treacherous wife cozened him cunningly
Till she had gained his confidence; and then
Betrayed his secret to the enemy,
And forsook him and took another man.

Three hundred foxes he took in his ire,
Their tails he tied together in a band,
And then he set the foxes' tails on fire,
For to each tail he tied a burning brand;
And they burned all the crops throughout the land,
And all the vines, and all the olive trees.
A thousand men he slew with his right hand,
His only tool the jawbone of an ass.

When they were killed, so great a thirst had he
That he was like to perish; so he prayed
God to take pity on his agony,
And send him drink; or he must soon be dead.
And from that ass's jawbone, sere and dry,
Out of a molar tooth, there sprang a well
(Look in the Book of Judges for the story)
From which, God helping him, he drank his fill.

And once, at Gaza, in a single night,
Although the place was filled with Philistines,
By main force he uprooted the town gates;
Alone upon his back he carried them
High on a mountain where they could be seen.
O noble, mighty, and beloved Samson,
Had you not told your secret to the women,
You'd not have had an equal under heaven!

By command of the messenger divine,
Scissors and razors never touched his hair,
And Samson never touched strong drink or wine,
For all his strength resided in his hair.
For fully twenty winters, year by year
He had all Israel in his governing.
But he must soon weep many a bitter tear,
For women are to bring him down to ruin.

It was his beloved Delilah whom he told
That it was in his hair that his strength lay;
On which the woman sold him to his foes.
When he was sleeping in her lap one day,
She had his hair cut off or clipped away,
And thus Delilah let his enemies
Discover where his strength and vigour lay;
They bound him fast, and put out both his eyes.

But before Samson's hair was clipped and shorn,
No bonds of theirs were strong enough to bind;
But he's imprisoned now in a cavern
Where at a handmill he is forced to grind.
O noble Samson, strongest of mankind!
O sometime Judge, in wealth and splendour living;
Well may you weep, because your eyes are blind,
And your prosperity become affliction.

This was the end of that poor prisoner:
His enemies prepared a feast one day,
Making him play the fool before them there,
And this was in a temple of great splendour,

But in the end he attacked savagely,
Shaking its two stone pillars till they fell.
Temple and all crashed down, and there it lay—
He killed himself, his enemies and all.

That is to say, the princes every one;
Three thousand bodies altogether, slain
By the falling of that temple built of stone.
Of Samson I have nothing more to say:
This old and simple tale is meant to warn
All husbands from confiding to their wives
Anything that they'd rather not have known,
If it means danger to their limbs or lives.

HERCULES

His labours sing the laud and great renown
Of Hercules, that sovereign conqueror,
For in his day he was the paragon
Of strength: he killed the Nemean lion,
And took its skin; humbled the proud Centaurs;
He killed the Harpies, cruel birds and fell;
He stole the golden apples from the Dragon,
He dragged out Cerberus, the hound of hell;

He killed the cruel tyrant, Busirus,
And made his horse devour him, flesh and bone;
Killed Hydra, fiery and poisonous;
Of Achelous' two horns, he broke off one;
And he killed Caecus in his cave of stone;
He killed the mighty giant, Antaeus,
And the Erymanthean boar, hideous and grim;
And on his neck bore the whole weight of heaven.

There's no one since the beginning of time
Who killed as many monsters as did he;
And throughout all the wide world ran his fame
For boundless strength and magnanimity;
He visited all kingdoms and countries.
He was too strong for any to oppose.

At each end of the world, Tropheus says,*
He set a pillar up as boundary.

This noble hero had a lover who
Was called Dejaneira, as fresh as May;
And if what these learned writers say is true,
She sent a fine new shirt to him one day
—A fatal shirt! Alas, alackaday!
It had been steeped so cunningly in venom,
He hadn't worn the shirt for half a day
Before it stripped his flesh from off the bone.

None the less there are scholars who excuse her
And blame one Nessus, for he made the shirt,
But be that as it may, I won't accuse her;
Still, he wore it upon his naked back
Until the poison made his flesh turn black.
And when he saw there was no remedy,
Hot burning coals about himself he raked,
And so, disdaining poison, chose to die.

Thus died the famed and mighty Hercules,
Now who can trust in Fortune for a moment?
He who has the whole world pressing on his heels
Will often be laid low before he knows it.
Whoever knows himself, is truly wise!
Watch out: when Fortune wants to play a trick,
She bides her time before she overthrows
Her victims in a way they least expect.

NEBUCHADNEZZAR

The royal majesty, the precious treasure,
The glorious sceptre, and the mighty throne
Belonging to King Nebuchadnezzar,
Can scarcely be described by human tongue.
Not once, but twice, he took Jerusalem;
He carried off the vessels of the Temple.
His glory and delight was Babylon,
Which city he made his chief capital.

The fairest children of the blood royal
Of Israel he castrated; each of them
He forced into his service as a thrall,
And among others, Daniel was one,
And Daniel was the wisest of them all,
For he could interpret what the king dreamt
When in the whole of Chaldea there was none
Able to understand what his dreams meant.

That proud king had a statue made of gold,
Seven cubits broad and sixty cubits high;
To which image he ordered young and old
To bow themselves in reverence and awe,
Or in a furnace, in red roaring fire,
All who would not obey him must be burnt.
But to that action neither Daniel nor
The two youths who were with him would assent.

This king of kings was arrogant and proud,
And thought that God, Who reigns in majesty,
Could not divest him of his royal crown.
But it was taken from him suddenly,
And in his imagination he became
An animal; and like an ox ate hay,
And roamed with wild beasts for a certain time,
Lodging in rain, under the open sky;

And like an eagle's feathers grew his hair,
Like a bird's claw his nails; until the Lord
At length released him after certain years,
And gave him back his reason; when with tears
He thanked God, and thereafter was afraid
While he had breath, to sin or to trespass;
And till the day they laid him on his bier,
He knew that God was full of power and grace.

BELSHAZZAR

He had a son who was called Belshazzar,
Who ruled the kingdom when his father died.
Unable to take warning by his father,

He lived in great magnificence and pride,
And was an inveterate idolater.
His great position fortified his pride,
But Fortune without warning cast him down,
Dividing both his kingdom and his crown.

One day Belshazzar held a feast for all
His lords and nobles, bidding them make merry;
Then he directed all his officials:
'Go bring the plate and vessels here,' said he,
'Those that my father reft triumphantly
From Jerusalem, from the Temple treasure-house;
And let us give thanks to our gods on high
For the honour that our fathers left to us.'

His wife, his nobles, and his concubines
Drank, for as long as any felt the want,
Out of those holy vessels, various wines.
But it so happened that he cast his glance
Upon a wall, and saw an armless hand
Write rapidly; he sighed, and shook with terror.
The hand that had so frightened Belshazzar
Wrote, *Mene, tekel, peres*, and no more.

There was no magician in the whole land
Who could interpret what this writing meant
But Daniel, who in due course explained:
'O King,' said he, 'God to your father sent
Glory and honour, revenue, rule, and wealth;
But he was proud, and had no fear of God;
God therefore dealt him a harsh punishment,
And took away the kingdom that he had.

'He was cast out of human company,
And made with asses his habitation,
And ate hay like a beast in wet and dry,
Until he understood, through grace and reason,
That God Who reigns in heaven has dominion
Over every realm and every creature;
And in the end the Lord God had compassion
On him, restored his realm and human figure.

'Now you, who are his son, are proud also,
And know these things to be the verity,
Yet rebel against God, and are His foe.
You drank out of His vessels brazenly;
Your wife and concubines all sinfully
From these same holy vessels drank their wine;
And as you worship false gods wickedly,
There is laid up for you great suffering.

'That hand was sent from God, take it from me,
That wrote *Mene*, *tekel*, *peres* on the wall.
Your reign is done, you're nobody at all,
Your kingdom is divided, and shall be
Given to the Persians and the Medes,' said he.
And on that very night the king was slain,
And Darius was there to occupy
Though with no legal right, Belshazzar's throne.

The moral here, ladies and gentlemen,
Is that there's no security in power;
Because when Fortune means to ditch a man,
She takes away his kingdom and his treasure,
And takes all of his friends too, for good measure.
The friends that a man makes in good fortune
Become his enemies in bad, I'll wager;
A proverb that's both true and widely known.

ZENOBIA*

Zenobia, the Queen of Palmyra,
Whose fame's recorded by the Persians,
Was so expert and courageous in war
She was surpassed in valour by no man,
Not in upbringing nor in lineage either.
Descended from the blood of Persian kings,
I won't say that there was no woman fairer,
But she'd a figure that you couldn't better.

I find that from her childhood she avoided
All women's work; she'd go off to the wood
Where with broad-bladed arrows she would shed
The blood of many a wild deer she shot.
She'd even catch them, for she was so fleet;
Later, when she grew older, she would kill
Leopards and lions, and tear bears apart,
And with her bare hands deal with them at will.

She dared to seek out wild beasts in their dens,
To roam about the mountains in the dark,
And sleep beneath a bush; and she'd the strength
To wrestle; she could subdue by main force
Any young man, no matter how stalwart;
No one who wrestled with her could withstand
Her arm; she kept herself inviolate,
Disdaining to be bound to any man.

Yet her friends got her married in the end
To Odenathus, prince of that country,
Although she kept them waiting a long time.
All the same you must realize that he
Had the same fanciful ideas as she.
But none the less, when they were joined together
They lived in joy and felicity,
For each was loved so dearly by the other.

Save for one thing: she never would consent
By any means, that he should ever lie
More than once with her; it was her intent,
So that the human race might multiply,
To bear a child; and so, as soon as she
Found she was not with child after the act,
Then she would suffer him to have his way
Once more, but only once; and that was that.

And if she were with child on that occasion,
It was the last time he might play that game
Till a clear forty weeks had come and gone,
When she would let him do it once again.

He might be mad for it, but all the same
He'd get no more from her; and she would tell him
It was a lecherous and shameful thing
To play in bed for any other reason.

Two sons had she by this Odenathus,
Whom she brought up in learning and virtue.
But to resume our tale: I'll tell you this,
You'd never find so praiseworthy a creature,
So wise, so generous (but not overmuch),
So courteous, and so resolute in war,
And indefatigably able to endure
Its toil, though you should search the world throughout.

How splendidly she lived! It can't be told,
Her magnificent plate and gorgeous dresses.
She was entirely clad in gems and gold,
Nor, though she loved to hunt, would she neglect
To gain command of different languages
When she had leisure; for her great delight
Was studying in books, from whose learned pages
She taught herself to lead a virtuous life.

But to cut short the story, I will say
Her husband was as valiant as she;
And thus they conquered many a mighty state
In eastern lands, and many a fine city
Belonging to the imperial majesty
Of Rome; and in a firm grip held them fast;
Their foes could never gain the victory
Until the day Odenathus breathed his last.

If any of you wish to learn about
Her wars with King Sapor, and others too,
And want to know how these events turned out,
Why she made conquests, and her claims thereto,
And of her later misfortunes and woe,
How she was besieged and made prisoner,
Let him turn to my master Petrarch,* who
Wrote quite enough, believe me, on this matter.

When Odenathus died she held on firmly
To all these conquests, and with her own hand
Battled against her foes so savagely
There was no prince or king in all the land
But counted himself lucky if he found
She had no wish to wage war on his country.
They sued for peace, made treaties of alliance
With her and let her go her own sweet way.

Not Claudius, the Roman emperor,
Nor Gallienus, emperor before him,
Nor any Arabian or Egyptian,
Or any Syrian or Armenian
Managed to summon up the nerve to dare
To take the field against her in a fight,
For fear of being slaughtered at her hands,
For fear her army should put theirs to flight.

And her two sons were always clad like kings,
They were heirs to the kingdom, after all;
Hermano and Thymalao were their names,
Or so they called them in the Persian tongue.
But with her honey Fortune mingles gall:
No longer may she rule, this mighty queen;
She lost her throne, for Fortune made her fall
Into the pit of misery and ruin.

For when into Aurelian's hands there came
The government of Rome, without delay
He planned to exact vengeance from the queen,
Marched with his legions on Zenobia,
And in the end—to cut short a long tale—
Put her to flight, and took her prisoner,
And chained her up, and her two sons as well,
And then returned to Rome a conqueror.

Among the many trophies that he won,
There was Zenobia's golden chariot;
This mighty Roman, great Aurelian,
Had it brought back with him that all might see it.

Zenobia walked before him at his triumph,
And hanging from her neck were golden chains,
Upon her head a crown, as well befitted
Her rank; her dress encrusted with rich gems.

Alas, Fortune! She who at one time was
The bane of kings, and feared by emperors,
Is for the mob to gape upon, alas!
She who went helmed to fight in furious wars,
And stormed the stoutest citadels and towers,
Must now wear on her head a woman's cap;
And she who bore a sceptre bound in flowers
Must carry a distaff, and earn her keep.

OF PEDRO, KING OF SPAIN*

Noble and honoured Pedro, glory of Spain,
Whom Fortune held so high in majesty,
It is your pitiful death we must bemoan;
Your brother drove you out of your country,
And later, at a siege, by treachery
You were betrayed, and brought to his pavilion
There to be killed by his own hand; when he
Succeeded to your revenues and kingdom.

Who contrived all this wickedness and sin?
It was a black eagle on a field of snow,
Caught in a limed twig coloured red as flame;
A nest of evil helped the assassin,
Not Charlemagne's Oliver, who was so
Mindful of loyalty and honour, but
A Breton Ganelon-Oliver, who
Took bribes, and lured the king into a trap.*

OF PETER, KING OF CYPRUS*

O noble Peter, King of Cyprus, who
Won Alexandria by great generalship,
And many of the heathen brought to grief,
For which your own liege subjects envied you;

For nothing but your chivalrous exploits
They killed you in your bed, early one morning;
Thus Fortune guides her wheel, and turns it so,
And brings us all from happiness to mourning.

OF BERNADO OF LOMBARDY*

Your ill fortune, great Bernardo, Viscount
Of Milan, O you scourge of Lombardy,
God of enjoyment, why should I not recount,
Since in the world's eyes you once climbed so high?
Your brother's son—and doubly your ally,
Being your nephew and your son-in-law,
Shut you within his prison, there to die;
And you were killed, I don't know how or why.

OF UGOLINO, COUNT OF PISA

The plight of Ugolino, Count of Pisa,
There is no tongue can tell of it, for pity!
A short way out of Pisa stands a tower
Wherein he was kept in captivity,
His little children with him—there were three,
The eldest being just five years of age.
O Fortune! Who could have the cruelty
To put such pretty birds in such a cage?

He was condemned to perish in that prison,
For Roger, who was bishop then of Pisa,
Had brought against him a false accusation,
So that the people rose up in their anger
And shut him up, as you have heard me say,
In prison, where what food and drink they had
Could barely suffice them, it was so meagre,
And moreover it was both poor and bad.

One day it happened—round about the hour
At which their food and drink used to be brought—
The gaoler shut the doorways of the tower.
He heard it plainly, but he did not speak.

And then into his heart there came the thought
It was from hunger they meant him to die.
'Alas!' cried he, 'that ever I drew breath!'
And thereupon the tears fell from his eyes.

His youngest son, who was three years of age,
Said to him, 'Father, tell me why you weep.
When will the gaoler bring us broth to eat?
Is there no bit of bread you have kept back?
I am so hungry that I cannot sleep.
I would to God that I might sleep for good!
Then hunger would not creep into my gut.
There's nothing I would rather have than bread.'

Thus, day by day, the little child would cry,
Till in his father's bosom down he lay,
And saying 'Farewell, father, I must die'
He kissed his father, dying the same day.
And when his grieving father saw him die,
Such was his sorrow that he bit his arm,
And cried, 'Alas, Fortune! What can I say?
I blame your fickle wheel for all my harm.'

His children thought that it was out of hunger
He bit upon his arm, and not from grief.
'Alas!' they cried, 'don't do that, dearest father,
But eat our flesh instead: it is the flesh
That you gave us; so take our flesh and eat.'
These were the very words the children said.
And in a day or two, soon after that,
Both of them lay down in his lap and died.

And he, despairing, also starved to death;
The mighty Count of Pisa ended thus,
Cut down by Fortune from his high estate.
This telling is enough, and should suffice;
Whoever would hear more, I would advise
To go and read that great Italian
Poet whose name is Dante: he describes
All in detail, and he won't let you down.*

NERO

Now although Nero was as vicious
As any fiend that lives in deepest hell,
He held—or so we're told by Suetonius—
The wide world in subjection to his rule,
Both east and west, and north and south as well.
His clothes were embroidered from head to foot
With jewels—ruby, sapphire, and white pearl,
For gems and jewels were his great delight.

No emperor was more sumptuous in display,
Or more fastidious and superb than he;
He'd only wear the same clothes once; when they
Were banished from his sight and thrown away.
Nets made of golden mesh he had in plenty
To fish the Tiber with, when he inclined.
His every wish he made law by decree:
Fortune herself obeyed him as her friend.

Just for the fun of it, he burned down Rome;
Killed all the senators another day,
Only to hear how they would weep and scream;
He killed his brother; with his sister lay;
Dealt with his mother most unspeakably,
And had her womb slit open, to see where
He'd been conceived—alas, alas that he
Should show so little feeling for his mother!

No tear dropped when he saw that dreadful sight—
All he said was, 'A handsome woman, she!'
You may well wonder how he ever might
Stand and pass judgement on her dead beauty.
He ordered them to bring him wine; when he
Drank it at once, but showed no other grief.
When power is conjoined with cruelty,
Alas, the poison will go in too deep!

In youth the emperor had a tutor who
Taught him booklearning, manners, courtesy;
He in his time was held to be the flower
Of moral wisdom, if the books don't lie;
And while this tutor held authority,
Nero was made so docile and so clever,
Long was it before vice and tyranny
Dared show themselves in him. This Seneca,

The man I'm talking of—for the good reason
That Nero stood in awe of him—for he'd
Always chastise him, but with tact, for sin,
Never with a blow, but only with a word:
'Sir,' he would say, 'an emperor should indeed
Be virtuous and an enemy of despotism'
—Just for this saying, Nero made him bleed
To death in a bath, with both his arms cut open.

And it was Nero's custom, when a boy,
Always to stand up in his tutor's presence,
Which later seemed to him great cause for grievance,
And so he made him perish in this way.
But none the less that wise man, Seneca,
Chose rather to die in a bath like this
Than undergo some other and worse torture;
Nero made his loved tutor perish thus.

Now the time came when Fortune would no longer
Cosset this Nero's overbearing pride;
For although he was strong, yet she was stronger.
She reasoned thus: 'By God! I must be mad
To set a man so crammed with every vice
High in the world, and call him emperor!
By God! I'll topple him out of his seat,
And he will fall when he expects it least.'

The people rose against him one dark night
Rebelling at his crimes; upon which he
Hastened alone out of his palace gate
And went where he expected help to be,

And hammered at the door; the more he cried,
The faster all the doors were shut and barred.
Then he realized how he'd been self-deceived;
Not daring to call out, he went away.

The people muttered, crying everywhere,
And he with his own ears heard what they cried.
'Where's that damned tyrant, Nero? Is he here?'
Almost he went out of his wits for fear,
Most pitifully to his gods he prayed
For succour, but it wasn't any good.
For fear of this he thought he would have died,
And ran into a garden, there to hide.

And Nero found two workmen in this garden
Seated by a huge fire, blazing red,
Whereupon he entreated these two workmen
To take his life by cutting off his head,
So that no outrage might be committed
Upon his body after he was gone.
He killed himself; there was no help for it,
And Fortune laughed; for she had had her fun.

OF HOLOFERNES*

Now there was no king's captain in his day
Who overthrew and conquered more countries,
None mightier in the field in every way,
Or in his time more honoured and famous,
More magnificent in his arrogance
Than Holofernes, whom Fortune embraced
Lovingly, then led up the garden path
Until, before he knew, his head was off.

Not only did all men hold him in awe
For fear of losing wealth or liberty,
He forced them to renounce their faith also.
'Nebuchadnezzar is a god,' said he,
'Thou shalt worship no other god than he.'

And no one dared to dispute his behest
Save in Bethulia, a strong city,
Where one Eliachim was a priest.

But mark Holofernes' death, and be warned!
In the middle of his army, drunk one night,
He lay inside his tent, big as a barn,
And yet, despite his splendour and his might,
Judith, a woman, as he lay asleep
Struck off his head; quietly from his tent
She stole, so quietly that no one saw it;
Back to her city with his head she went.

OF THE ILLUSTRIOUS KING ANTIOCHUS*

As for that mighty king, Antiochus,
Need I rehearse his royal majesty,
His evil actions and huge arrogance?
There never was another such as he:
Read in the Book of Maccabees and see.
There you may read the proud boasts that he made,
And why he fell from great prosperity
To perish wretchedly on a hillside.

Fortune had so exalted him in pride
He actually believed he could attain
High as the highest star that's in the skies,
And in the balance weigh the highest mountain,
And even hold in check the tides of ocean.
Towards God's people he turned all his hatred,
And had them tortured cruelly, and slain;
He thought his pride would never be abated.

And because Timothy and Nichanor
Had been vanquished by Jews so crushingly,
Such was his hatred for the Jews therefore,
He bade his soldiers make his chariot ready
With utmost speed; disdainfully he swore
To march at once upon Jerusalem
And on it wreak his rage pitilessly;
But he was quickly thwarted of his plan.

For God smote him grievously for this threat
With an invisible and cureless wound
That cut and bit its way into his guts
Until the pain of it could not be borne.
But certainly the punishment was just,
For he had racked the guts of many men.
And yet, spite of the pain, he'd not give up
His damnable and hell-begotten plan,

But bade his army to prepare forthwith;
When suddenly, before he even knew it,
God put down all his pride and boastfulness:
He fell so heavily out of his chariot
That all his limbs and skin were lacerated,
So that he could no longer walk nor ride;
And in a chair they carried him about,
So sorely was he bruised in back and side.

God's retribution smote him cruelly;
Throughout his flesh the vile worms crawled and crept,
And moreover he stank so horribly
That nobody in his household could bear it,
No matter if he were awake or slept;
The stink was something no one could endure.
In this torment he lamented and wept,
And knew God to be lord of every creature.

To his whole army, to himself also,
So nauseous was the stench of his carcass,
He found no man to carry him; and so,
In this stink, in this horrible distress,
Most wretchedly upon a hill he perished.
And so this spoiler and this homicide,
The cause of so much lamenting and tears,
Has won such reward as pertains to pride.

OF ALEXANDER

The story of Alexander is well known,
And anybody who knows anything
Has heard something or all of his fortune.

In short, the whole wide world, by force of arms
He won, or vanquished through his great renown:
Men were so keen to sue for peace to him,
Wherever he went, from here to the world's end,
The pride of man and beast came tumbling down.

Even now no comparison can be made
With him and any other conqueror;
Before him the whole world once quaked with dread.
Chivalry's and magnanimity's flower,
Fortune made him the sole heir of her honour,
And only wine or women could abate
His great designs and ambitious endeavour,
So like a lion's was his fighting spirit.

How could it boost his fame, even if I told
Of Darius, and a hundred thousand more,
Of kings and princes, dukes and barons bold,
All brought to ruin by this conqueror?
Journey to the world's end, as far as far,
The earth was his—what more can I report?
Were I to write or talk for evermore
Of his prowess, I'd even then fall short.

He reigned twelve years, it says in Maccabees,
The son of Philip, King of Macedon,
Who was the first king of the land of Greece.
O noble, great Alexander, alas
That such a fate as yours should have befallen!
For it was your own subjects gave you poison,
And Fortune turned your six-spot to an ace, *
And yet she shed no tear for you—not one.

Now who will give me tears for lamenting
The death of one so noble and courteous,
Who ruled the whole wide world as his domain,
Yet in his heart thought it did not suffice,
His spirit was so filled with high courage?
Alas! who will assist me to indict
The treachery of Fortune, and rebuke
Poisoners?—I blame both for all this grief.

OF JULIUS CAESAR

Through wisdom, valour, and immense labour,
From humble birth to royal majesty,
Rose Julius Caesar, the great conqueror,
Who won the occident, by land and sea,
By either force of arms, or by treaty;
Making each realm tributary to Rome:
And, later, Emperor of Rome was he,
Till the time came when Fortune turned on him.

O mighty Caesar, who in Thessaly
Fought with your father-in-law, great Pompey,*
He who led all the orient's chivalry
As far as where begins the dawn of day:
All killed or taken in captivity
By you, bar Pompey and the few that fled;
And thus you held the entire east in awe,
Thanks be to Fortune and her signal aid.

But now let me lament here for a little
That noble Pompey, once the governor
Of Rome, who fled when he had lost the battle.
One of his men it was, a base traitor,
Who cut his head off, hoping to win favour
From Julius, and brought his head to him.
Alas Pompey! The east's great conqueror!
That Fortune should bring you to such an end!

To Rome again returning, Julius
Held there his triumph, crowned with laurels high,
But the time came when Brutus Cassius,*
Who looked on his success with envious eye,
Plotted an underhand conspiracy
Against this Julius, with cunning guile;
He chose the very spot where he would die
Stabbed with their daggers, as you'll hear me tell.

Now Julius went up to the Capitol
Of Rome one day, just as he always used;
And there met with a sudden surprisal:
False Brutus and his other enemies
Fell upon him and stabbed him with their knives;
Bleeding from many wounds they let him lie;
But he groaned only at one of these blows,
Two at most, unless history is a lie.

So noble was Julius Caesar's heart,
So dear were honour and propriety
To him, he did not mind the deadly smart
Of wounds, but threw his cloak across his thigh
That nobody might see his private parts;
For, as he lay there dying in a swoon
And thinking he was dead in reality,
Yet he was not neglectful of decorum.

I refer you for this history to Lucan
And Suetonius, and to Valerius too,
Because from first to last they have set down
How Fortune was first friend, and then a foe
To both of these great conquerors. And so
Let no one ever trust in Fortune's favours;
Be on your guard, whatever else you do:
Be warned by all these mighty conquerors.

CROESUS

The wealthy Croesus, King of Lydia once,
Of whom the Persian Cyrus stood in awe,
Was taken in his pride and arrogance
And led away to be burned in the fire.
But such a deluge poured down from the sky,
It killed the fire, and let him escape;
Yet he had not the good sense to beware,
Till Fortune hung him gaping from a gibbet.

For when he'd escaped he could not resist
Beginning to wage new war yet again.
Fortune, he was convinced, had so worked it
That he escaped through a chance fall of rain,
Therefore it followed he could not be slain
By any foe. He dreamed a dream one night
Which made him so self-confident and vain,
He set his heart on getting his own back:

Up in a tree he was, or so he thought,
And there Jupiter washed him, back and side;
And a fine towel was by Phoebus brought
To dry him with. This dream puffed up his pride;
He asked his daughter, standing by his side,
In whom he knew that deep insight abounded,
To tell him what this strange dream signified,
And this is how his vision was expounded:

She said to him, 'That tree stands for a gallows,
And Jupiter represents snow and rain;
And as for Phoebus with his fair clean towel,
These signify, I'd say, rays of the sun.
You are to be hanged, father, that's certain;
The rain will wash you, and the sun will dry.'
Thus Croesus' daughter warned him, blunt and plain.
Phania was the name he called her by.

And hanged indeed was Croesus the proud king,
Even his royal throne was no avail.
The burden of all tragedies is the same:
A song of lamentation to bewail
How Fortune is ever ready to assail
With sudden stroke the kingdoms of the proud;
For when you trust in her, then she will fail,
Cover her shining face as with a cloud.

THE PROLOGUE OF THE NUN'S PRIEST'S TALE

'Halt!' said the knight, 'no more of this, good sir!
What you have said is true enough, I'm sure;
And more than true; but still, a little sadness
Goes a long way with most folk, by my guess.
And as for me, it is a real discomfort
To hear of folk who live in wealth and comfort,
And then, alas, learn of their sudden ruin.
But on the other hand it's gratifying
To hear about a man of low estate,
How he climbs up and becomes fortunate,
Thenceforth abiding in prosperity.
Such things are pleasanter, it seems to me,
And make a proper subject for a tale.'
'That's right!' agreed our host, 'by St Paul's bell!
What you say's true; this monk goes booming loud
About how Fortune covered with a cloud
I don't know what; and about Tragedy
As you've just heard; how it's no remedy,
God save us all, to bewail or lament
When what's done's done; what's more, it's a penance,
As you've remarked, to hear these tales of woe.

   'Mister Monk, no more of this, the Lord bless you!
Your tales are boring all of us to death,
And all this kind of talk is waste of breath,
No fun in it, it doesn't entertain.
So, Brother Peter—if that's your right name—
I beg you on my knees, tell something else:
Were it not for the jangling of those bells
Hanging and dangling from your bridle-rein,
By Him who died for us, by heaven's King,
I'd have dropped off to sleep long before this,
And fallen in the mud, deep as it is,
And then your tale would have been told in vain.
You know, the scholars have an axiom:
If a man's got no audience—why then,
It's of no use to go on lecturing.

   'For I have it in me, and I can tell,
To pay attention to a well-told tale.

Tell something about hunting, if you please.'
    'No, I'm in no mood for frivolities.
It's time for someone else to tell his story
As I have,' said the monk. Our host addressed
The nun's priest in his rough and ready way:
'You priest, come over here, you Brother John!
Give us a tale to make our hearts feel gay.
Cheer up, forget that nag you're riding on:
Scruffy your horse may be, all skin and bone,
But if he does his job, who cares a bean?
See that you always keep a merry heart.'
    'Yes indeed,' he replied, 'I swear you're right.
Yet, Mister Host, yes, I'll be much to blame
If I'm not merry.' Right then he began
His tale; and this is what we heard from him,
That pleasant priest, that genial Brother John.

THE NUN'S PRIEST'S TALE

*Here begins the Nun's Priest's Tale of the Cock
and Hen, Chantecleer and Pertelote*

A hard-up widow, getting on in age,
Once on a time lived in a small cottage,
Beside a coppice, standing in a dale,
This widow, about whom I tell my tale,
Had, since the day when she was last a wife,
In patience led a very simple life,
For she'd few goods, and what she earned was small.
By making do with what God let her have,
She kept both her two daughters and herself.
She had three pigs—three good-sized sows in all—
Three cows, besides a sheep that she called Moll.
Her bed- and living-room was thick with soot,
And in it many's the scanty meal she ate.
She had no need of any piquant sauce,
No dainty morsel ever passed her lips;
Her diet matched the cottage where she lived,

So too much eating never made her sick;
Her only medicine was a temperate diet,
And exercise, and a contented heart.
She was not stopped from dancing by the gout,
No apoplexy ever hurt her head.
She never touched wine, neither white nor red;
Most of the food she ate was white and black—
Milk and brown bread, in which she found no lack,
Grilled bacon and an egg or two sometimes:
She was a dairy-woman of a kind.

    She had a closed yard that was fenced about
With wooden palings, a dry ditch without,
In which she kept a cock called Chantecleer.
In all the land, at crowing he'd no peer.
His voice was mellower than the mellow organ
You hear in church on feast-days, sweetly playing;
And where he lived, his crowing told the hour
Better than any clock in abbey-tower.
He knew by instinct each revolution
Of the equinoctial circle in that town,
For every fifteen degrees, on the hour,
He crowed to perfection with all his power.*
His comb was redder than the choicest coral,
And crenellated like a castle wall;
His beak was black, and like jet its gloss;
Like lapus-lazuli his legs and toes,
Each with nails whiter than the lily flower;
And like the burnished gold was his colour.
This peerless cock had at his disposition
Seven hens for his delight and delectation,
Who were his sisters and his mistresses,
Their colouring amazingly like his;
And the one with the brightest-feathered throat
Was called the lovely lady Pertelote.
She was so gentle, kind and courteous,
And sociable, with such pretty ways,
That since the day that she was a week old
She'd Chanticleer's heart firm in her hold,
Locked up with her, captive in every limb,
He loved her so, that all was well with him.

And what delight it was to hear them sing
At sunrise, when the day began to spring,
'My love has gone away!' in sweet accord.
For in those far-off days, as I have heard,
The animals and birds could speak and sing.

    And it so came about, one early morning,
As Chanticleer was sitting among all
His wives upon the perch inside the hall,
And next to him the pretty Pertelote,
He groaned, and went on groaning in his throat,
Like a man badly troubled with a dream.
And so, much frightened, she exclaimed, 'Dear heart,
What's wrong with you? What makes you groan like that?
You're a fine sleeper, you are—fie for shame!'

    And this is how he answered her: 'Madam,
Pray do not take offence—but goodness me!
I dreamt I was in desperate jeopardy
Just now—my heart's still fluttering with fright.
May God', said he, 'make my dream turn out right,
And keep me out of any filthy dungeon!
I dreamt that I was walking up and down
Inside our yard, and there I saw a beast
Much like a dog, which was about to seize
Hold of my body and then kill me dead!
Its colour was a kind of yellow-red,
Its tail and both its ears were tipped with black,
Not like the other hairs upon its back;
Its snout was narrow, with two glowing eyes—
The way they looked at me, I nearly died!
So if I groaned, that was the cause of it.'

    'Get along with you! Shame on you, faintheart!
Alas!' cried she. 'For, by the Lord above,
Now you have lost my heart, lost all my love.
I cannot love a coward, that I swear!
For if we can, we women all desire
Whatever any of us say, to have
Husbands who're generous and wise and brave
And discreet; not a skinflint nor a fool,
Nor one who is afraid of naked steel,
No, nor a braggart, by the Lord above!

How can you have the face to tell your love
That anything can make you feel afraid?
Have you no man's heart, and yet wear a beard?
Alas! and can you be afraid of dreams?
Nothing, God knows, but nonsense is in dreams.
Dreams come from overeating, flatulence,
From temperamental change, which happens if
One of the body humours is excessive.*
That dream which you met with tonight, be sure
Comes from a surplus of red bile, or choler,
Which, pardon me, makes people have bad dreams
Of fiery arrows, and red roaring flames,
Red ravening beasts that are about to bite,
Of fighting, dogs of every size and shape;
Just as the melancholy, or black humour,
Makes many cry out in their sleep for fear,
Dreaming of a black bull, or a black bear,
Or of black devils come to haul them off.
Of other humours I could tell enough,
Which trouble many people in their sleep,
But I'll pass on as quickly as I can.
　'Look at Cato, who was so wise a man,
Didn't he say, "Take no account of dreams?"'
　'Now sir,' said she, 'when we fly from these beams,
You'll take, for goodness' sake, some laxative:
Upon my life and soul, the best advice
That I can give you is, go purge yourself
Of the red choler and black melancholy.
To save time, as there's no apothecary
Here to be had, I'll be your guide myself,
And show you herbs to benefit your health;
And in our own yard I shall find those herbs
Which have a natural property to purge
From top to bottom, above and beneath,
So don't go and forget, for heaven's sake!
Yours is a most choleric temperament:
Be careful that the sun in his ascent
Doesn't catch you brimful of hot body humours.
And if it does, I'm quite prepared to wager
You're likely to go down with tertian fever,

Or catch an ague which might be your death.
First you must take some worms as digestives
A day or two before your laxatives,
Which might be spurge-laurel, centuary,
And hellebore, or else fumitory,
For all of them grow in our garden here;
Or catapuce, buckthorn, or herb ivy,
All growing in our yard so prettily;
Peck 'em up where they grow, and eat 'em up!
For your good name's sake, husband, do cheer up!
And fear no dream! I can't say any more.'

'Madam, a thousand thanks', said Chanticleer,
'For your advice; but none the less, as touching
This Mister Cato, whose renown for wisdom
Is so immense: although he may have said
That dreams are nothing to be worried at,
If you read ancient books you'll find, by God,
That many a man of more authority
Than ever Cato was, believe you me,
Subscribes to just the opposite opinion;
They have discovered from experience
That dreams are certainly foretokenings
Of joys as well as the tribulations
That in this present life we undergo.
There is no need to argue about it:
One's own experience shows it for a fact.

'One of our greatest authors, Cicero,
Writes thus: Once on a time two friends set out
Upon a pilgrimage, with hearts devout,
And it so happened they came to a town
Where such a press of folk was crowding in,
And such a shortage of accommodation
They couldn't find so much as a cottage
To put them both up. So they were obliged
Just for that one night, to part company.
And each of them went to a hostelry
To take his chance of any bed at all.
Now one of them found shelter in a stall
Down in a distant yard with plough-oxen;
The other man lodged reasonably well,

As was his luck, or maybe his good fortune;
For luck has power over one and all.
   'And it so happened that, long before dawn,
As this man lay in bed, he had a dream;
He dreamed he heard his friend cry out and call,
Saying, "Alas! for in an ox's stall
Tonight I shall be murdered where I lie!
Come to my aid, dear brother, or I die!
Come in all haste!" And so the man, in panic,
Started from out his sleep; but once awake,
Turned over, and took no more heed of it.
His dream was an absurdity, he thought.
But in his sleep he twice had the same dream.
And yet a third time. His companion came,
Or so he thought—"I am now killed," he said,
"Look at my bloody wounds, all gaping wide!
Rise early, rise up early in the morning,
And you'll see at the west gate of the town,"
Said he, "a cart that's loaded full of dung,
In which my body's hidden. Have it held,
Have that cart stopped and seized immediately.
The truth is, I've been murdered for my gold."
He told him in detail how he'd been killed,
His face most pitiful, all pale its hue.
And, never doubt, he found the dream was true.
For the next day, as soon as it was dawn,
He made his way to his companion's inn,
And when he found this ox-stall, he began
To shout and call for his companion.
   'It was the innkeeper who answered him:
"Mister," he said, "your friend's already gone,
For he left town as soon as it was dawn."
   'The man, remembering what he had dreamt,
Became suspicious, and set off at once
To the town's western gate: and there he found
A dung-cart on its way to dung the ground
Or so it seemed—loaded in just the way
You heard the dead man saying it would be.
And so with full confidence he began
Calling for law and vengeance on the crime:

"My friend's been murdered, murdered in the night!
He's lying stiff and stark upon his back
Here in this cart! I want the magistrate
Who should be keeping order in this town!
Help! Help! Alas, here's my friend lying dead!"
Such is the tale—and what more need I add?
Folk rushed out, tipped the wagon to the ground,
And in the middle of the dung they found
The dead man, newly murdered.

                                        'Blessed art Thou,
O Lord our God, as Thou art just and true,
Who never sufferest murder to be hid!
"Murder will out"—we see it every day.
Murder is so hateful and abominable
To God, Who is so just and reasonable,
That He will not allow it to be hidden,
Though it may wait a year or two, or three.
Murder will out—and that's my firm opinion!
And in a trice the officers of the town
Had seized the carter and the innkeeper,
Tortured one, put the other on the rack,
Till they had confessed their criminal act,
Whereupon they were both hanged by the neck.
    Thus we can see that dreams are to be feared.
And indeed in the same book I have read,
Right in the very chapter after that—
Lord bless me, I'm not making all this up—
About two men who would have crossed the sea
For a certain purpose, to some far country,
Had it not been the wind was contrary,
So that they were kept waiting in a city
Set pleasantly enough beside a harbour;
Until one day, as light began to fade,
The wind began to alter in their favour.
Cheerful and glad, the two men went to bed,
Resolved that early next day they would sail,
Had it not been for a great miracle.
For one of them, as he lay there sleeping,
Dreamed a strange dream just as the day was breaking:
It seemed to him a man stood by his bed,

And told him that he must remain, and said,
"All I have got to say to you is this:
If you should sail tomorrow, you'll be drowned."
He woke, and told his friend what he had dreamed,
And he implored him to put off his journey
And stay there where he was, just for one day.
His friend, who had a bed in the same room,
Began to laugh, and made great fun of him.
"No dream", said he, "can frighten me enough
To make me even think of putting off
Going about my business. I don't care
A damn about your dreamings—not a straw.
They're only a delusion and a snare.
People dream all the time of apes and owls,
And such enigmas as will puzzle fools;
Of things that never have been nor will be.
But you mean to stay dawdling here, I see,
And miss your tide, from sheer perversity.
Lord knows I'm sorry for it; so goodbye."
And so he took his leave, and went his way,
But before his voyage was half over
Don't ask me why, or what caused the disaster,
But the ship's bottom split, through some misfortune,
And as it chanced both ship and man went down
In sight of other vessels by their side,
Which had sailed out with them on the same tide.
And so, my lovely Pertelote, you may gather
From such time-honoured instances, disregard
Of dreams is something no one can afford,
For as I say, there is no doubt whatever
In general most dreams are to be feared.

'What about Kenelm's dream, of which I read
In the life of St Kenelm, Kenulphus' son,
The noble King of Mercia?* How Kenelm
Dreamed something one day, only a short time
Before they murdered him, and how he saw
His murder in a dream. His nurse explained
The dream in full, and warned him to beware
Of treachery; but he was only seven,
And therefore he would pay but scant attention

To any dream, so holy was his heart.
And by the Lord in heaven, I'd give my shirt
For you to read his story, as I have!
Madame Pertelote, this is the plain truth:
Macrobius, who wrote of Scipio's dream
In Africa, lends his support to them,
And he confirms that dreams are forewarnings,
And that they tell of future happenings.
Please, madam, take a careful look as well
At the Old Testament—see if Daniel
Supposed that dreams were an absurdity!
Read about Joseph too, and there you'll see
Whether or no dreams are— I don't say all—
Warnings of things that afterwards befall.
Think of the King of Egypt, Lord Pharaoh,
And of his baker and his butler too:
Did they find dreams of no effect?* Those who
Study the history of various realms
May read of many marvels about dreams.
What about Croesus, King of Lydia,
Did he not dream that he sat on a tree,
Which meant he would be hanged? And what of her,
Andromache, she who was Hector's wife?
That very night before he was to die
She dreamed that Hector was to lose his life
If on that day he ventured forth to fight.
She warned him, but it was of no avail;
He sallied out to battle none the less,
But was killed soon enough by Achilles.
But that's too long a tale for me to tell,
Besides, it's nearly dawn, and I must fly.
To wind up, let me say just this to you:
To me this dream portends adversity.
And furthermore, I have to tell you this:
I don't set any store by laxatives,
For I know all too well that they are poison,
I hate them, and I say to hell with them!
  'Let's talk of something pleasant, and drop this.
Madame Pertelote, as I hope for heaven,
One thing I have, one great grace God has given:

When I look on the beauty of your face,
And see those scarlet circles round your eyes,
Then all the terror that affrights me dies.
For it's God's truth that "*In principio*
Mulier est hominis confusio"*
—Madam, the meaning of this Latin is,
"Woman is man's whole joy and happiness."
For when I feel at night your gentle side,
Although our perch is so narrowly made
I may not mount upon your back, alas!
I am so filled with joy and happiness
That I defy all visions and all dreams.'
And, saying this, he flew down from the beams,
For it was day, with his wives one and all,
And at his cluck they answered to his call,
For he had found corn fallen in the yard.
Royal was he, he was no longer scared,
And twenty times he feathered Pertelote,
Trod her as often too, by nine that morning.
He looks as if he were a rampant lion,
And on his toes goes strutting up and down,
And does not deign to set foot on the ground.
He cluck-clucks when a grain of corn is found;
His wives come running to him, one and all.
Thus royal, as a prince is in his hall,
I'll leave our Chanticleer to go on feeding;
I'll tell you later of what happened to him.

    Now when the month in which the world began,
The month called March, when God first created man,
Had ended, and since its beginning, two
And thirty days and nights had passed also,*
It chanced that Chanticleer, in all his pride,
His seven wives all walking by his side,
Having cast his eyes up to the brilliant sun,
Which in the sign Taurus the Bull had run
Twenty and one degrees, and somewhat more,
Knew by no teaching other than nature
That it was nine a.m. With merry note
He crowed and said, 'The sun has now climbed up
Forty-one degrees, and a bit more, I'd guess.

Now Madame Pertelote, my earthly bliss,
Hark at those happy birds, hark how they sing,
And see the pretty flowers, how they spring!
My heart is filled with joy and content!'
But trouble came upon him in a moment.
For ever the latter end of joy is grief,
God knows all earthly happiness is brief.
(And if a proper poet were to write,
That's good enough to be put in a book
As a most notable and striking fact.)
Now pay attention, if you know what's best:
This tale is just as true, I do attest,
As is the story of Sir Lancelot,
That tale which women hold in great esteem.
But let me take my subject up again.

   A black fox, iniquitous and sly,
Who'd lived for three years in the wood near by.
As was predestined by divine foresight,
Burst through the hedges on that selfsame night
Into the yard where stately Chanticleer
And all his wives used often to repair;
And in a bed of cabbages he lay
Quite still till near the middle of the day,
Biding his time to fall on Chanticleer,
As is the way of every murderer
Who lies in wait to kill his fellow-men.
Treacherous assassin, lurking in your den!
O second Iscariot, new Ganelon!
You lying dissembler, you new Sinon,
That Greek who carried utter grief to Troy!*
O Chanticleer, accursed be the day
You flew into that yard, down from those beams!
For you had ample warning from your dreams
That day, for you, would prove most perilous;
But that which God foresees, must come to pass
—Or such is the opinion of most scholars.
Any accomplished scholar will bear witness
That there has been a great altercation
Upon this in the schools; much disputation
About the question of predestination;

It's been debated by a hundred thousand!
But here I cannot sift chaff from the grain
As can that sainted theologian
St Augustine, or Bishop Bradwardine,
Or Boethius, and say whether God's divine
Foreknowledge constrains me to do a thing
Of necessity—'simple' necessity—
Or whether, if free choice be granted me
To do that very thing, or not to do it,
Though before the doing of it, God foreknew it,
Whether His foreknowledge does not bind me,
Except by 'conditional' necessity.*
But all these questions are not my affair;
My tale is of a cock, as you can hear,
Who took his wife's advice, worse luck I say,
To go into the yard the very day
After he'd had the dream you heard me tell.
Women's advice is fatal as a rule:
A woman's advice brought us first to woe,
And out of Paradise Adam had to go,
Where he had been so happy and at ease.
But as I don't know whom it may displease
If I depreciate the advice of women,
Forget it, it was only said in fun.
Read the authorities that treat this problem,
And you'll hear what they have to say of woman!
For these are the cock's words, and not my own:
I can't conceive of harm in any women!

    The lovely Pertelote was happily
Taking a dustbath, with her sisters by,
In sunshine; while Chanticleer joyously
Sang merrier than a mermaid in the sea
(Physiologus in his *Bestiary*
Confirms they sing both well and merrily).
And it so happened, when a butterfly
Among the rows of cabbage caught his eye,
He was aware of a fox there, crouching low.
At this he never felt less wish to crow,
But, chattering a 'cok-cok', he leapt up
Like someone in a panic, terror-struck;

For any animal will instinctively
Try to escape his natural enemy
Once he has seen it, although it may be
He's never set his eyes on one till then.
    And so when Chanticleer caught sight of him
He would have fled, had not the fox exclaimed,
'Good sir, where are you off to? I'm your friend!
Alas, that you should be afraid of me!
Surely you won't think I am such a fiend
As to wish you any injury or harm?
It's not to spy your secrets that I've come;
Indeed, indeed, the reason for my coming
Was only this: to listen to your singing.
Indeed, indeed, you have a voice as pleasing
As any angel has up there in heaven!
And, moreover, you've more musical feeling
Than Boethius, or anyone now singing.
Your noble father (may his soul be blessed),
Your mother, in the goodness of her heart,
Have both been in my house, to my great pleasure;
Be sure I'd love to make you welcome, sir!
But since we mentioned singing, I'll say this,
As I hope to have the use of my two eyes,
Except for you, I've not heard anyone
Sing in the morning as your father sang.
Sure it came from the heart, all that he sung!
And he, to make his voice more loud and strong,
Would strain until he'd have to screw both eyes
Tight shut; he'd have to stand on his tiptoes
Stretch his long slender neck—then how he'd crow!
He was a man of much discernment, too;
No man the country round was half so wise,
Or half so good a singer as he was.
Now I've read in that book called *Brunel's Ass*
Among other verses, of that famous cock
Who, when a parson's son gave him a knock
And broke his leg (the lad was young and foolish),
Saw to it that he lost his benefice.*
But certainly there's no comparison
Between your father's wisdom and discretion

And judgement, and that cock's ingenuity.
Now sing, sir, sing for sweet saint charity!
Show me if you can emulate your father!'

Without suspecting treason, Chanticleer
Began to flap his wings, enchanted by
The fox's blandishments and flattery.

Alas, my lords! Many's the treacherous fawner
Dwells in your courts, many's the flatterer
Who's far more pleasing to you, on my oath,
Than he who tells you nothing but plain truth.
Read Ecclesiasticus on flattery;
Beware, my lords, beware of treachery.

High stood our Chanticleer on his tiptoes
Stretching his neck; and with both eyes tight closed,
Began to crow as loud as ever he could.
And Mister Russell Fox at once leapt up,
And took hold of Chanticleer by the throat,
And bore him on his back towards the wood,
For there was none as yet to give pursuit.

O Destiny none of us can avoid,
Alas that Chanticleer flew from those beams,
Alas, his wife had no belief in dreams!
It was a Friday brought this misadventure.

O divine Venus, goddess of pleasure,
Seeing that Chanticleer was your worshipper,
And served you to the utmost of his power,
Much more for delight than to multiply
The world, how can you suffer him to die
On Friday of all days—for it's your day?

O Geoffrey de Vinsauf, you sovereign
Poet who, when Richard Lionheart was slain,
Elegized so movingly his death,*
If only I'd your learning and your art
To rail at Friday half as well as you
—For he was killed upon a Friday too—
Then I'd show you how well I could lament
For Chanticleer, his terror and torment!

Sure such an outcry and lamentation
Was never made by ladies when Ilium
Was lost, and Pyrrhus with his naked sword

Had seized hold of King Priam by the beard
And killed him, as we're told in the *Aeneid*,
Than all those hens made in the widow's yard,
At seeing their Chanticleer carried off.
Loudest of all shrieked Madame Pertelote,
And louder even than Hasdrubal's wife
When she saw how her husband took his life
After the Romans had burned down Carthage—
She was so full of agony and rage
That in cold blood she leapt into the fire,
And with a steadfast heart burned herself there.
    O all you woeful hens, you screamed as high
As they, when Nero burned down the city
Of Rome, and all of the senators' wives
Shrieked out to see their husbands lose their lives;
Though they were guiltless, Nero had them slain.
Now I'll turn to my story once again.
    This poor old widow, both her daughters too,
Hearing the screeching and hullabaloo
Made by these hens, ran straight out of the house
In time to see the fox head for the coppice
And carry off the cock upon his back.
They raised an outcry: 'Help! A fox! A fox!
Halloo! A fox!' and after him they ran,
With sticks and cudgels and a crowd of men,
With Coll the dog, and Talbot, and Garland,
And Malkin with the distaff in her hand,
The cow and calf, even the very hogs
Ran fit to burst, scared by the barking dogs
As well as by the shouting men and women.
They yelled and yodelled like the fiends in hell,
The ducks squawked as if going to be killed;
The geese, in fright, went flying over trees;
Out of the hive there came a swarm of bees.
God bless us all, so hideous was the din,
Not even Jack Straw and his mob of men
Ever let out a clamour half as shrill
When hunting Flemings down to lynch and kill,*
As they let out the day they chased the fox.
Trumpets they brought, of brass and bone and box

And horn, on which they hooted and they blew;
What with their whooping and their screeching too,
— It seemed as if the very heaven would fall.
Now, good sirs, please to listen, one and all!

See how Fortune overturns instantly
The hope and conceit of her enemy!
For the cock, slung upon the fox's back,
Managed, for all his dreadful fright, to speak,
And said, 'Good sir, if I were in your place,
So help me God, I'd turn round and say this:
"Go home, you stupid yokels! Plague on you!
Now I'm at the wood's edge, what can you do?
Trust me, I'll keep the cock, and eat him up!"'

'Good idea,' said the fox, 'I'll do just that.'
He'd barely said the words, when in a flash
The cock broke deftly from the fox's mouth,
And flew high up a tree to perch thereon.
And when the fox saw that the cock was gone,

'Alas!' he cried, 'Dear Chanticleer, alas!
I've behaved badly to you, I confess,
Inasmuch as I made you so afraid
When I snatched up and took you from the yard.
But, sir, I did it with no bad intent;
Come down and I shall tell you what I meant.
And I'll speak honest truth, so help me God.'

'No, I'll see us both damned first,' said the cock,
'But myself first and worst, both blood and bones,
Before you trick me oftener than once!
You'll not, with your soft soap and flatteries
Get me to sing again, and close my eyes!
To him who shuts his eyes when he should look,
And that on purpose, the Lord send bad luck!'

'No,' said the fox, 'may God rather send
Bad luck to him who knows no better than
To talk too much when he should hold his tongue.'

Now see what comes of taking it too easy,
And placing heedless trust in flattery!

But if you think this tale a trumpery
About a fox, and of a cock and hen,
Don't overlook the moral, gentlemen!

For everything that's written, says St Paul,
Is written, surely, to instruct us all.
So take the corn, and let the chaff lie still.
Now, gracious Father, if it be Thy will,
As Our Lord promised, make us all good men,
And bring us to His heavenly bliss.

                                    Amen!

EPILOGUE TO THE NUN'S PRIEST'S TALE

At this our host remarked, 'Mister Nun's Priest,
Your breeches and your very balls be blessed!
That was a splendid tale of Chanticleer.
But on my word, were you a secular,
Then you'd be a rare cock among the hens!
If you would as you could, one imagines
There'd be a need for hens—yes, seventeen
Times seven hens and more! Just look at him!
Look at the muscles on this splendid priest!
What a great neck he has, what a broad chest!
And brighter than a sparrowhawk's, those eyes!
What a complexion too! He needs no dyes,
Scarlets from India or from Portugal
To touch it up! Bless you, sir, for your tale!'
    Thereupon he, with cheerful demeanour,
Spoke to another of us, as you'll hear.

experience vs. authority

Fragment III (Group D)

THE PROLOGUE OF
THE WIFE OF BATH'S TALE

'Experience—and no matter what they say
In books—is good enough authority
For me to speak of trouble in marriage.
For ever since I was twelve years of age,
Thanks be to God, I've had no less than five
Husbands at church door—if one may believe
I could be wed so often legally!
And each a man of standing, in his way.
Certainly it was told me, not long since,
That, seeing Christ had never more than once
Gone to a wedding (Cana, in Galilee)
He taught me by that very precedent
That I ought not be married more than once.
What's more, I was to bear in mind also
Those bitter words that Jesus, God and Man,
Spoke in reproof to the Samaritan
Beside a well—"Thou hast had", said He,
"Five husbands, and he whom now thou hast
Is not thy husband." He said that, of course,
But what He meant by it I cannot say.
All I ask is, why wasn't the fifth man
The lawful spouse of the Samaritan?
How many lawful husbands could she have?
All my born days, I've never heard as yet
Of any given number or limit,
However folk surmise or interpret.
All I know for sure is, God has plainly
Bidden us to increase and multiply—
A noble text, and one I understand!
And, as I'm well aware, He said my husband
Must leave father and mother, cleave to me.
But, as to number, did He specify?

He named no figure, neither two nor eight— *times to marry*
Why should folk talk of it as a disgrace?
    'And what about that wise King Solomon:
I take it that he had more wives than one!
Now would to God that I might lawfully
Be solaced half as many times as he!
What a God-given gift that Solomon
Had for his wives! For there's no living man
Who has the like; Lord knows how many a bout
That noble king enjoyed on the first night
With each of them! His was a happy life!
Blessed be God that I have married five!
Here's to the sixth, whenever he turns up.
I won't stay chaste for ever, that's a fact.
For when my husband leaves this mortal life
Some Christian man shall wed me soon enough.
For then, says the Apostle Paul, I'm free
To wed, in God's name, where it pleases me.
He says that to be married is no sin,
Better it is to marry than to burn.
What do I care if people execrate
The bigamy of villainous Lamech?
I know that Abraham was a holy man,
And Jacob too, so far as I can tell;
And they had more than two wives, both of them,
And many another holy man as well.
Now can you tell me where, in any age,
Almighty God explicitly forbade
All marrying and giving in marriage?
Answer me that! And will you please tell me
Where was it He ordained virginity?
No fear, you know as well as I do, that
The Apostle, where he speaks of maidenhood,
Says he has got no firm precept for it.
You may advise a woman not to wed,
But by no means is advice a command.
To our own private judgement he left it;
Had virginity been the Lord's command,
Marriage would at the same time be condemned.
And surely, if no seed were ever sown,

each point is right in it's own sense.

From what, then, could virginity be grown?
Paul did not dare command, at any rate,
A thing for which the Lord gave no edict.
There's a prize set up for virginity:
Let's see who'll make the running, win who may!
    'This teaching's not for all men to receive,
Just those to whom it pleases God to give
The strength to follow it. All I know is,
That the Apostle was himself a virgin;
But none the less, though he wished everyone
—Or so he wrote and said—were such as he,
That's only to *advise* virginity.
I have his leave, by way of concession,
To be a wife; and so it is no shame,
My husband dying, if I wed again;
A second marriage can incur no blame.
Though it were good for a man not to touch
A woman—meaning in his bed or couch,
For who'd bring fire and tow too close together?
I think you'll understand the metaphor!
Well, by and large, he thought virginity
Better than marrying out of frailty.
I call it frailty, unless he and she
Mean to live all their lives in chastity.
    'I grant all this; I've no hard feelings if
Maidenhood be set above remarriage.
Purity in body and in heart
May please some—as for me, I make no boast.
For, as you know, no master of a household
Has all of his utensils made of gold;
Some are of wood, and yet they are of use.
The Lord calls folk to Him in many ways,
And each has his peculiar gift from God,
Some this, some that, even as He thinks good.
    'Virginity is a great excellence,
And so is dedicated continence,
But Christ, of perfection the spring and well,
Did not bid everyone to go and sell
All that he had, and give it to the poor,
And thus to follow in His tracks; be sure

need to procreate to make virgins

He spoke to those who would live perfectly;
And, sirs, if you don't mind, that's not for me.
I mean to give the best years of my life
To the acts and satisfactions of a wife.
    'And tell me also, what was the intention
In creating organs of generation,
When man was made in so perfect a fashion?
They were not made for nothing, you can bet!
Twist it how you like and argue up and down
That they were only made for the emission
Of urine; that our little differences
Are there to distinguish between the sexes,
And for no other reason—who said no?
Experience teaches that it is not so.
But not to vex the scholars, I'll say this:
That they were fashioned for both purposes,
That's to say, for a necessary function
As much as for enjoyment in procreation
Wherein we do not displease God in heaven.
Why else is it set down in books, that men
Are bound to pay their wives what's due to them?
And with whatever else would he make payment
If he didn't use his little instrument?
It follows, therefore, they must have been given
Both to pass urine, and for procreation.
    'But I'm not saying everyone who's got
The kind of tackle I am talking of
Is bound to go and use it sexually.
For then who'd bother about chastity?
Christ was a virgin, though formed like a man,
Like many another saint since time began,
And yet they lived in perfect chastity.
I've no objection to virginity.
Let them be loaves of purest sifted wheat,
And us wives called mere barley-bread, and yet
As St Mark tells us, when our Saviour fed
The multitude, it was with barley-bread.
I'm not particular: I'll continue
In the condition God has called us to.
In married life I mean to use my gadget

As generously as my Maker gave it.
If I be grudging, the Lord punish me!
My husband's going to have it night and day,
At any time he likes to pay his dues.
I shan't be difficult! I shan't refuse!
I say again, a husband I must have,
Who shall be both my debtor and my slave,
And he shall have, so long as I'm his wife,
His "trouble in the flesh". For during life
I've "power of his body" and not he.*
That's just what the Apostle Paul told me;
He told our husbands they must love us too.
Now I approve entirely of this view—'
    Up leapt the pardoner—'Now then, madam,
I swear to you by God and by St John,
You make a splendid preacher on this theme.
I was about to wed a wife—but then
Why should my body pay a price so dear?
I'll not wed this nor any other year!'
    'You wait!' said she. 'My tale has not begun.
It is a different cask that you'll drink from
Before I've done; a bitterer brew than ale.
And when I've finished telling you my tale
Of tribulation in matrimony
—And I'm a lifelong expert; that's to say
That I myself have been both scourge and whip—
You can decide then if you want to sip
Out of the barrel that I mean to broach.
But you had best take care if you approach
Too near—for I've a dozen object-lessons
And more, that I intend to tell. "The man
Who won't be warned by others, he shall be
Himself a warning to all other men."
These are the very words that Ptolemy
Writes in his Almagest: you'll find it there.'*
    'Let me beg you, madam,' said the pardoner,
'If you don't mind, go on as you began,
And tell your tale to us and spare no man,
And teach all us young fellows your technique.'
    'Gladly,' said she, 'if that's what you would like;

[margin annotation] physical temptation

But let no one in this company, I beg,
If I should speak what comes into my head,
Take anything that I may say amiss;
All that I'm trying to do is amuse.
    'And now, sir, now, I will begin my tale.
May I never touch a drop of wine or ale
If this be not the truth! Of those I had,
Three were good husbands, two of them were bad.
The three good ones were very rich and old;
But barely able, all the same, to hold
To the terms of our covenant and contract—
Bless me! you'll all know what I mean by that!
It makes me laugh to think, so help me Christ,
How cruelly I made them sweat at night!
And I can tell you it meant nothing to me.
They'd given me their land and property;
I'd no more need to be assiduous
To win their love, or treat them with respect.
They all loved me so much that, heavens above!
I set no store whatever by their love.
A wily woman's always out to win
A lover—that is, if she hasn't one.

Since I'd got them in the hollow of my hand,
And they'd made over to me all their land,
What point was there in taking pains to please,
Except for my advantage, or my ease?
Believe you me, I set them so to work
That many a night I made them sing, "Alack!"
No flitch of bacon for them, anyhow,
Like some have won in Essex at Dunmow.*
I governed them so well in my own way,
And kept them happy, so they'd always buy
Fairings to bring home to me from the fair.
When I was nice to them, how glad they were!
For God knows how I'd nag and give them hell!
    'Now listen how I managed things so well,
You wives that have the wit to understand!
Here's how to talk and keep the upper hand:
For no man's half as barefaced as a woman
When it comes to chicanery and gammon.

It's not for knowing wives that I say this,
But for those times when things have gone amiss.
For any astute wife, who knows what's what,
Can make her husband think that black is white,   *manipulatior*
With her own maid as witness in support.
But listen to the kind of thing I'd say:
   "So this is how things are, old Mister Dotard?
Why does the woman next door look so gay?
She can go where she likes, and all respect her,
—I sit at home, I've nothing fit to wear!
Why are you always over at her house?
She's pretty, is she? So you're amorous!
What did I catch you whispering to the maid?
Mister Old Lecher, drop it, for God's sake!
And if I've an acquaintance or a friend,
You rage and carry on just like a fiend
If I pay him some harmless little visit!
And then you come back home pissed as a newt,
And preach at me, confound you, from your bench!
What a great shame—just think of the expense—
To marry a poor woman, so you tell me.
And if she's rich, and comes of a good family,
It's hell, you say, to put up with her pride,
And her black moods and fancies. Then, you swine,
Should she be beautiful, you change your line,
And say that every rakehell wants to have her,
That in no time she's bound to lose her honour,
Because it is assailed on every side.
   "You say that some folk want us for our riches,
Some for our looks, and others for our figures,
Or for our sex appeal, or our good breeding;
Some want a girl who dances, or can sing,
Else it's our slender hands and arms they want.
So the devil takes the lot, by your account!
None can defend a castle wall, you say,
For long if it's attacked day after day.
   "And if she's plain, why then you say that she's
Setting her cap at every man she sees:
She'll jump upon him, fawning like a spaniel,
Till someone buys what she has got to sell.

Never a goose upon the lake so grey
But it will find its gander, so you say.
Says you, it's hard to manage or control
A thing no man would keep of his own will.
That's how you talk, pig, when you go to bed,
Saying that no sane man need ever wed,
Nor any man who hopes to go to heaven.
Wretch, may your withered wrinkled neck be broken
In two by thunderblast and fiery lightning!

"And then, you say, a leaky roof, and smoke,
And nagging wives, are the three things that make
A man flee from his home. Oh, for God's sake!
What ails an old man to go on like that?

"Then you go on to claim we women hide
Our failings till the knot is safely tied,
And then we show them—A villainous saying,
A scoundrel's proverb, if I ever heard one!

"You say that oxen, asses, horses, hounds,
Can be tried out and proved at different times,
And so can basins, washbowls, stools, and spoons,
And household goods like that, before you buy;
Pots, clothes and dresses too; but who can try
A wife out till he's wed? Old dotard! Pig!
And then, says you, we show the faults we've hid.

"You also claim that it enrages me
If you forget to compliment my beauty,
If you're not always gazing on my face,
Paying me compliments in every place,
If on my birthday you don't throw a party,
Buy a new dress, and make a fuss of me;
Or if you are ungracious to my nurse,
Or to my chambermaid, or even worse,
Rude to my father's kinsfolk and his cronies,
That's what you say, old barrelful of lies!

"And about Jankin you've the wrong idea,
Our apprentice with curly golden hair
Who makes himself my escort everywhere—
I wouldn't have him if you died tomorrow!
But, damn you, tell me this—God send you sorrow!—
Why do you hide the strongbox keys from me?

It's mine as much as yours—our property!
What! I'm the mistress of the house, and you'll
Make her look like an idiot and a fool?
You'll never be, no matter how you scold,
Master of both my body and my gold,
No, by St James! For you'll have to forgo
One or the other, take or leave it! Now,
What use is all your snooping and your spying?
I sometimes think you want to lock me in
That strongbox of yours, when you should be saying
"Dear wife, go where you like, go and have fun,
I shan't believe the tales they tell in malice,
I know you for a faithful wife, Dame Alice."
We love no man who watches carefully
Our coming and going; we want liberty.

   "Blessed above all other men is he,
That astrologer, Mister Ptolemy,
Who set down in his book, the *Almagest**
This proverb: "Of all men he is the wisest
Who doesn't care who has the world in hand."
From which proverb you are to understand
That if you have enough, why should you care
A curse how well-off other people are?
Don't worry, you old dotard—it's all right,
You'll have cunt enough and plenty, every night.
What bigger miser than he who'll not let
Another light a candle at his lantern—
He won't have any the less light, I'm thinking!
If you've enough, what's there to grumble at?

   "And you say if we make ourselves look smart
With dresses and expensive jewellery,
It only puts at risk our chastity;
And then, confound you, you must quote this text,
And back yourself up with the words of Paul,
As thus: 'In chaste and modest apparel
You women must adorn yourselves,' said he,
'And not with braided hair and jewellery,
Such as pearls and gold; and not in costly dress.'
But of your text, and your red-letter rubric,
I'll be taking no more notice than a gnat!

"And you said this: that I was like a cat,
For you have only got to singe its skin,
And then the cat will never go from home;
But if its coat is looking sleek and gay,
She won't stop in the house, not half a day,
But off she goes the first thing in the morning,
To show her coat off and go caterwauling.
That's to say, if I'm all dressed up, Mister Brute,
I'll run out in my rags to show them off!

"Mister Old Fool, what good is it to spy?
If you begged Argus with his hundred eyes
To be my bodyguard—what better choice?—
There's little he would see unless I let him,
For if it killed me, yet I'd somehow fool him!

"And you have also said, there are three things,
Three things there are that trouble the whole earth,
And there's no man alive can stand the fourth—
Sweet Mister Brute, Jesus cut short your life!
You keep on preaching that an odious wife
Is to be counted one of these misfortunes.
Really, are there no other comparisons
That you can make, and without dragging in
A poor innocent wife as one of them?

"Then you compare a woman's love to Hell,
To barren lands where rain will never fall.
And you go on to say, it's like Greek fire,
The more it burns, the fiercer its desire
To burn up everything that can be burned.
And just as grubs and worms eat up a tree,
Just so a woman will destroy her husband;
All who are chained to wives know this, you say."

'Ladies and gentlemen, just as you've heard
I'd browbeat them; they really thought they'd said
All these things to me in their drunkenness.
All lies—but I'd get Jankin to stand witness
And bear me out, and my young niece also.
O Lord! the pain I gave them, and the woe,
And they, heaven knows, quite innocent of course.
For I could bite and whinny like a horse.
I'd scold them even when I was at fault,

For otherwise I'd often have been dished.
Who comes first to the mill, is first to grind;
I'd get in first, till they'd be glad to find
A quick excuse for things they'd never done
In their whole lives; and so our war was won.
I'd pick on them for wenching; never mind
They were so ill that they could barely stand!
　'And yet it tickled him to the heart, because
He thought it showed how fond of him I was.
I swore that all my walking out at night
Was to spy out the women that he tapped;
Under that cover, how much fun I had!
To us at birth such mother-wit is given;
As long as they live God has granted women
Three things by nature: lies, and tears, and spinning.
There's one thing I can boast of: in the end
I'd gain, in every way, the upper hand
By force or fraud, or by some stratagem
Like everlasting natter, endless grumbling.
Bed in particular was their misfortune;
That's when I'd scold, and see they got no fun.
I wouldn't stop a moment in the bed
If I felt my husband's arm over my side,
No, not until his ransom had been paid,
And then I'd let him do the thing he liked.
What I say is, everything has its price;
You cannot lure a hawk with empty hand.
If I wanted something, I'd endure his lust.
And even feign an appetite for it;
Though I can't say I ever liked old meat—
And that's what made me nag them all the time.
Even though the Pope were sitting next to them
I'd not spare them at table or at board,
But paid them back, I tell you, word for word.
I swear upon my oath, so help me God,
I owe them not a word, all's been paid back.
I set my wits to work till they gave up;
They had to, for they knew it would be best,
Or else we never would have been at rest.
For even if he looked fierce as a lion,

Yet he would fail to get his satisfaction.
    'Then I would turn and say, "Come, dearest, come!
How meek you look, like Wilkin, dear old lamb!
Come to me, sweetheart, let me kiss your cheek!
You ought to be all patient and meek,
And have ever such a scrupulous conscience—
Or so you preach of Job and his patience!
Always be patient; practise what you preach,
For if you don't, we've got a thing to teach,
Which is: it's good to have one's wife in peace!
One of us has got to knuckle under,
And since man is more rational a creature
Than woman is, it's you who must forbear.
But what's the matter now? Why moan and groan?
You want my quim just for yourself alone?
Why, it's all yours—there now, go take it all!
By Peter, but I swear you love it well!
For if I wished to sell my pretty puss,
I'd go about as sweet as any rose;
But no, I'll keep it just for you to taste.
Lord knows you're in the wrong; and that's the truth!"
    'All arguments we had were of that kind.
Now I will speak about my fourth husband.
    'My fourth husband was a libertine;
That is to say, he kept a concubine;
And I was young, and passionate, and gay,
Stubborn and strong, and merry as a magpie.
How I would dance to the harp's tunable
Music, and sing like any nightingale,
When I had downed a draught of mellow wine!
Metellius, the dirty dog, that swine
Who with a club beat his own wife to death
Because she drank—if I had been his wife,
Even he would not have daunted me from drink!
And after taking wine I'm bound to think
On Venus—sure as cold induces hail,
A greedy mouth points to a greedy tail.
A woman full of wine has no defence,
All lechers know this from experience.
    'But, Lord Christ! when it all comes back to me,

And I recall my youth and gaiety,
It warms the very cockles of my heart.
And to this day it does my spirit good
To think that in my time I've had my fling.
But age, alas, that cankers everything,
Has stripped me of my beauty and spirit.
Let it go then! Goodbye, and devil take it!
The flour's all gone; there is no more to say.
Now I must sell the bran as best I may;
But all the same I mean to have my fun.
And now I'll tell about my fourth husband.

　'I tell you that it rankled in my heart
That in another he should take delight.
But he was paid for it in full, by God!
From that same wood I made for him a rod—
Not with my body, and not like a slut,
But certainly I carried on with folk
Until I made him stew in his own juice,
With fury, and with purest jealousy.
By God! on earth I was his purgatory,
For which I hope his soul's in Paradise.
God knows he often had to sit and whine
When his shoe pinched him cruellest! And then
How bitterly, and in how many ways,
I wrung his withers, there is none can guess
Or know, save only he and God in heaven!
He died when I came from Jerusalem,
And now lies buried under the rood beam,*
Although his tomb is not as gorgeous
As is the sepulchre of Darius
That Apelles sculpted so skilfully;
For to have buried him expensively
Would have been waste. So goodbye, and God rest him!
He's in his grave now, shut up in his coffin.

　'Of my fifth husband I have this to tell
—I pray God keep and save his soul from hell!—
And yet he was to me the worst of all:
I feel it on my ribs, on each and all,
And always will until my dying day!
But in our bed he was so free and gay

And moreover knew so well how to coax
And cajole when he wanted my *belle chose*,
That, though he'd beaten me on every bone,
How quickly he could win my love again!
I think that I loved him the best, for he
Was ever chary of his love for me.
We women have, I'm telling you no lies,
In this respect the oddest of fancies;
If there's a thing we can't get easily,
That's what we're bound to clamour for all day:
Forbid a thing, and that's what we desire;
Press hard upon us, and we run away.
We are not forward to display our ware:
For a great crowd at market makes things dear;
Who values stuff bought at too cheap a price?
And every woman knows this, if she's wise.

'My fifth husband—may God bless his soul!
Whom I took on for love, and not for gold,
Was at one time a scholar at Oxford,
But had left college, and come home to board
With my best friend, then living in our town:
God keep her soul! her name was Alison.
She knew me and the secrets of my heart
As I live, better than the parish priest:
She was my confidant; I told her all—
For had my husband pissed against a wall,
Or done a thing that might have cost his life—
To her, and also to my dearest niece,
And to another lady friend as well,
I'd have betrayed his secrets, one and all.
And so I did time and again, dear God!
It often made his face go red and hot
For very shame; he'd kick himself, that he
Had placed so great a confidence in me.

'And it so happened that one day in Lent
(For I was ever calling on my friend,
As I was always fond of having fun,
Strolling about from house to house in spring,
In March, April, and May, to hear the gossip)
Jankin the scholar, and my friend Dame Alice,

And I myself, went out into the meadows.
My husband was in London all that Lent,
So I was free to follow my own bent,
To see and to be seen by the gay crowd.
How could I know to whom, and in what place,
My favours were destined to be bestowed?
At feast-eves and processions, there I was;
At pilgrimages; I attended sermons,
And these miracle-plays; I went to weddings,
Dressed in my best, my long bright scarlet gowns.
No grub, no moth or insect had a chance
To nibble at them, and I'll tell you why:
It was because I wore them constantly.

'Now I'll tell you what happened to me then.
We strolled about the fields, as I was saying,
And got on so well together, he and I,
That I began to think ahead, and tell him
That if I were a widow we could marry.
For certainly—I speak without conceit—
Till now I've never been without foresight
In marriage matters; other things as well.
I'd say a mouse's life's not worth a leek
Who has but one hole to run to for cover,
For if that fails the mouse, then it's all over!

'I let him think that he'd got me bewitched.
It was my mother taught me that device.
I also said I dreamed of him at night,
That he'd come to kill me, lying on my back,
And that the entire bed was drenched in blood.
And yet I hoped that he would bring me luck—
In dreams blood stands for gold, so I was taught.
All lies—for I dreamed nothing of the sort.
I was in this, as in most other things,
As usual following my mother's teachings.

'But now, sirs, let me see—what was I saying?
Aha! Bless me, I've found the thread again.

'When my fourth husband was laid on his bier
I wept for him—what a sad face I wore!—
As all wives must, because it's customary;
With my kerchief I covered up my face.

But, since I was provided with a mate,
I wept but little, that I guarantee!
  'To church they bore my husband in the morning
Followed by the neighbours, all in mourning,
And one among them was the scholar Jankin.
So help me God, when I saw him go past,
Oh what a fine clean pair of legs and feet
Thought I—and so to him I lost my heart.
He was, I think, some twenty winters old,
And I was forty, if the truth be told.
But then I always had an itch for it!
I was gap-toothed; but it became me well;
I wore St Venus' birthmark and her seal.*
So help me God, but I was a gay one,
Pretty and fortunate; joyous and young;
And truly, as my husbands always told me,
I had the best what-have-you that might be.
Certainly I am wholly Venerian
In feeling; and in courage, Martian.
Venus gave to me lust, lecherousness;
And Mars gave me my sturdy hardiness.
Taurus was my birth-sign, with Mars therein.
Alas, alas, that ever love was sin!
And so I always followed my own bent,
Shaped as it was by my stars' influence,
That made me so that I could not begrudge
My chamber of Venus to a likely lad.
I've still the mark of Mars upon my face,
And also in another secret place.
For, sure as God above is my salvation,
I never ever loved in moderation,
But always followed my own appetite,
Whether for short or tall, or black or white;
I didn't care, so long as he pleased me,
If he were poor, or what his rank might be.
  'There's little more to say: by the month's ending,
This handsome scholar Jankin, gay and dashing,
Had married me with all due ceremony.
To him I gave all land and property,
Everything that I had inherited.

But, later, I was very sorry for it—
He wouldn't let me do a thing I wanted!
My God, he once gave my ear such a box
Because I tore a page out of his book,
That from the blow my ear became quite deaf.
I was untameable as a lioness;
My tongue unstoppable and garrulous;
And walk I would, as I had done before,
From house to house, no matter how he swore
I shouldn't; and for this he'd lecture me,
And tell old tales from Roman history;
How one Simplicius Gallus left his wife,
Left her for the remainder of his life,
Only because one day he saw her looking
Out of the door with no head-covering.

  'He said another Roman, Whatsisname
Because his wife went to a summer-game*
Without his knowledge, went and left her too.
And then he'd get his Bible out to look
In Ecclesiasticus for that text
Which with absolute stringency forbids
A man to let his wife go gad about;
Then, never fear, here's the next thing he'd quote:
"Whoever builds his house out of willows,
And rides a blind horse over the furrows,
And lets his wife trot after saints' altars,
Truly deserves to be hung on the gallows."
But all for nothing; I cared not a bean
For all his proverbs, nor for his old rhyme;
And neither would I be reproved by him.
I hate a man who tells me of my vices,
And God knows so do more of us than I.
This made him absolutely furious;
I'd not give in to him, in any case.

  'Now, by St Thomas, I'll tell you the truth
About why I ripped a page out of his book,
For which he hit me so that I went deaf.

  'He had a book he loved to read, that he
Read night and morning for his own delight;
Valerius and Theophrastus,* he called it,

Over which book he'd chuckle heartily.
And there was a learned man who lived in Rome,
A cardinal who was called St Jerome,
Who wrote a book attacking Jovinian;
And there were also books by Tertullian,
Chrysippus, Trotula, and Heloise,*
Who was an abbess not far from Paris,
Also the parables of Solomon,
Ovid's *Art of Love*, and many another one,
All bound together in the same volume.
And night and morning it was his custom,
Whenever he had leisure and freedom
From any other worldly occupation,
To read in it concerning wicked women:
He knew more lives and legends about them
Than there are of good women in the Bible.
Make no mistake, it is impossible
That any scholar should speak good of women,
Unless they're saints in the hagiologies;
Not any other kind of woman, no!
Who drew the picture of the lion? Who?*
My God, had women written histories
Like cloistered scholars in oratories,
They'd have set down more of men's wickedness
Than all the sons of Adam could redress.
For women are the children of Venus,
And scholars those of Mercury; the two
Are at cross purposes in all they do;
Mercury loves wisdom, knowledge, science,
And Venus, revelry and extravagance.
Because of their contrary disposition
The one sinks when the other's in ascension;
And so, you see, Mercury's powerless
When Venus is ascendant in Pisces,
And Venus sinks where Mercury is raised.
That's why no woman ever has been praised
By any scholar. When they're old, about
As much use making love as an old boot,
Then in their dotage they sit down and write:
Women can't keep the marriage vows they make!

[margin handwritten note:] reference to Aesop's Fable — subjectivity, distortion, self-benefit

'But to the point—why I got beaten up,
As I was telling you, just for a book:
One night Jankin—that's my lord and master—
Read in his book as he sat by the fire,
Of Eva first, who through her wickedness
Brought the whole human race to wretchedness,
For which Jesus Himself was crucified,
He Who redeemed us all with His heart's blood.
Look, here's a text wherein we plainly find
That woman was the ruin of mankind.

'He read to me how Samson lost his hair:
He slept; his mistress cut it with her shears,
Through which betrayal he lost both his eyes.

'And then he read to me, if I'm no liar,
Of Hercules and his Dejaneira,
And how she made him set himself on fire.

'He left out nothing of the grief and woe
That the twice-married Socrates went through;
How Xantippe poured piss upon his head,
And the poor man sat stock-still as if dead;
He wiped his head, not daring to complain:
"Before the thunder stops, down comes the rain!"

'And out of bloody-mindedness he'd relish
The tale of Pasiphaë, Queen of Crete—
Fie! say no more—it's gruesome to relate
Her abominable likings and her lust!

'Of the lechery of Clytemnestra,
How she betrayed her husband to his death,
These things he used to read with great relish.

'He also told me how it came about
That at Thebes Amphiarus lost his life:
My husband had a tale about his wife
Eriphile, who for a golden brooch
Had covertly discovered to the Greeks
Where they might find her husband's hiding-place,
Who thus, at Thebes, met a wretched fate.

'He told of Livia and Lucilia,
Who caused their husbands, both of them, to die;
One out of love, the other out of loathing.
Hers, Livia poisoned late one evening,

Because she hated him; ruttish Lucilia
On the contrary, loved her husband so,
That she mixed for him, so that he should think
Only of her, an aphrodisiac drink
So strong that before morning he was dead.
Thus husbands always have the worst of it!
    'Then he told me how one Latumius
Once lamented to his friend Arrius
That there was a tree growing in his garden
On which, he said, his three wives, out of dudgeon,
Had hanged themselves. "Dear friend," said Arrius,
"Give me a cutting from this marvellous tree,
And I shall go and plant it in my garden."
    'Concerning wives of later days, he read
How some had killed their husbands in their bed,
And let their lovers have them while the corpse
Lay all night on its back upon the floor.
And others, while their husbands slept, have driven
Nails through their brainpans, and so murdered them.
Yet others have put poison in their drink.
He spoke more evil than the heart can think.
On top of that, he knew of more proverbs
Than there is grass and herbage upon earth.
"Better to live with a lion or dragon,"
Said he, "than take up with a scolding woman.
Better to live high in an attic roof
Than with a brawling woman in the house:
They are so wicked and contrarious
That what their husbands love, they always hate."
He also said, "A woman casts off shame
When she casts off her smock," and he'd go on:
"A pretty woman, if she isn't chaste,
Is like a gold ring stuck in a sow's nose."
Now who could imagine, or could suppose,
The grief and torment in my heart, the pain?
    'When I realized he'd never make an end
But read away in that damned book all night,
All of a sudden I got up and tore
Three pages out of it as he was reading,
And hit him with my fist upon the cheek

So that he tumbled back into our fire,
And up he jumped just like a raging lion,
And punched me with his fist upon the head
Till I fell to the floor and lay for dead.
And when he saw how motionless I lay,
He took alarm, and would have run away,
Had I not burst at last out of my swoon.
"You've murdered me, you dirty thief!" I said,
"You've gone and murdered me, just for my land!
But I'll kiss you once more, before I'm dead!"

     'He came close to me and kneeled gently down,
And said, "My dearest sweetheart Alison,
So help me God, I'll not hit you again.
You yourself are to blame for what I've done.
Forgive it me this once, for mercy's sake."
But once again I hit him on the cheek:
"You robber, take that on account!" I said.
"I can't speak any more; I'll soon be dead."
After no end of grief and pain, at last
We made it up between the two of us:
He gave the reins to me, and to my hand
Not only management of house and land,
But of his tongue, and also of his fist—
And then and there I made him burn his book!
And when I'd got myself the upper hand
And in this way obtained complete command,
And he had said, "My own true faithful wife,
Do as you please from now on, all your life:
Guard your honour and look after my estate."
—From that day on we had no more debate.
So help me God, to him I was as kind
As any wife from here to the world's end,
And true as well—and so was he to me.
I pray to God Who reigns in majesty,
For His dear mercy's sake, to bless his soul.
Now if you'll listen, I will tell my tale.'

The dispute between the Summoner and the Friar

The friar laughed, when he had heard all this.
'Now madam,' cried he, 'as I hope for bliss,

That was a long preamble to a tale!'
And when the summoner heard the friar bawl,
'See here!' he cried. 'By God's two arms! A friar
Will butt in all the time, and everywhere!
Good folk, they're all the same, these flies and friars,
Falling in people's foodbowls and affairs.
What are you talking of—"perambulation"?
Amble, trot, or shut up and sit down!
This kind of thing is ruining our fun.'

   'Oh indeed, Mister Summoner, is that so?'
Returned the friar. 'My word, before I go
I'll tell a tale or two about a summoner,
And raise a laugh from everybody here!'

   'Try it and see, Friar,' said the summoner,
'And damn your eyes! And damn my own as well
If I've not got two or three tales to tell
Concerning friars, that will make you mourn
Before I get as far as Sittingbourne.
For I can see you've lost your temper now.'

   'Now you shut up!' our host cried. 'Hold your row!'
He went on: 'Let the lady tell her tale.
You look as if you had had too much ale.
Madam, begin your tale: that would be best.'

   'I'm ready, sir,' said she, 'just as you wish,
That is, if I have leave of this good friar.'

   'Tell on, madam,' said he, 'and I will hear.'

THE WIFE OF BATH'S TALE

In the old days, the days of King Arthur,
He whom the Britons hold in great honour,
All of this land was full of magic then.
And with her joyous company the elf-queen
Danced many a time on many a green mead.
That was the old belief, as I have read:
I speak of many hundred years ago.
But now elves can be seen by men no more,
For now the Christian charity and prayers
Of limiters* and other saintly friars
Who haunt each nook and corner, field and stream,

Thick as the motes of dust in a sunbeam,
Blessing the bedrooms, kitchens, halls, and bowers,
Cities and towns, castles and high towers,
Villages, barns, cattle-sheds and dairies,
Have seen to it that there are now no fairies.
Those places where you once would see an elf
Are places where the limiter himself
Walks in the afternoons and early mornings,
Singing his holy offices and matins,
While going on the rounds of his district.
Women may now go safely where they like:
In every bush, and under every tree,
They'll find no other satyr there but he:
And he'll do nothing worse than take their honour.

    Now it so happened that this King Arthur
Had in his court a bold knight-bachelor
Who one day was hawking by the river,
And it so chanced, as he was riding home,
He met a maiden walking all alone,
And thereupon, though she fought long and hard,
The knight took by main force her maidenhood;
And this outrage occasioned a great stir,
So much petitioning of King Arthur,
That the knight was, in due course of law,
Condemned to death, and would have lost his head
According to the law as it then stood,
Had not the queen and many another lady
Importuned the king so long for mercy
That in the end he granted him his life
And gave him to the queen to dispose of:
Either to execute, or spare his life.

    The queen gave the king thanks with all her heart,
And some time afterwards spoke to the knight
One day when she saw opportunity:
'Your fate is in the balance still,' said she,
'You cannot yet be certain of your life,
But you shall live if you can answer me,
What is the thing that women most desire?
Your neck is forfeit to the axe—beware!
And if you cannot tell me here and now

I shall, however, give you leave to go
A twelvemonth and a day, to seek and find
An answer that will satisfy my mind.
And you must pledge, before you can depart,
Duly to yield yourself up in this court.'

Sad was the knight; sorrowfully he sighed;
But there! it's not as if he'd any choice.
And so at long last he made up his mind
To go, and to come back at the year's end,
With whatever answer heaven might provide;
And so he took his leave, and off he rode.

He visited every house, and every spot
Where he might have the luck to find out what
The thing is that we women most desire;
But could find in no country anywhere
Two people to agree with one another
Upon this subject.
                          Some said we love best
Riches and wealth; and others said, honour;
Some said, fine clothes; and others, happiness;
Some said it is the pleasures of the bed,
And to be often widowed, often wed.
And others said we're happiest at heart
When complimented and well cosseted.
Which is pretty near the truth, and that's no lie.
A man can win us best by flattery;
And with attentiveness, assiduity,
We're ensnared, one and all.
                          Some say that we
Love best to have our own way and be free,
To have no one reprove us for our follies,
But say how wise we are, how far from foolish.
If someone touches on a tender spot,
There isn't one of us—indeed there's not—
Who won't kick, just for being told the truth!
Just try it, and you'll find out soon enough.
However faulty we may be within,
We want to be thought wise, and free from sin.

And others say that we take great delight
In being thought dependable and discreet,

Able to hold steadfastly to one purpose,
Never revealing what a person tells us.
As for that notion, it's not worth a button,
Because we women can keep nothing hidden.
Witness King Midas—would you hear of him?

   Ovid, among some other trifles, said
That under his long hair King Midas had
Two asses' ears growing upon his head,
Which blemish he kept hid, as best he might,
Most artfully from everybody's sight,
So that, but for his wife, none knew of it.
Above all things he loved and trusted her;
And he implored her never to make mention
Of his deformity to anyone.

   No, not for anything in the world, she swore,
Would she do such a mean and sinful thing,
And bring discredit to her husband's name.
If only for her shame's sake, she'd not tell.
But none the less, she thought that she would die
If she had to keep a secret for so long;
So hard against her heart it seemed to swell,
That she must speak or burst; till finally
As she dared tell the secret to no man,
Down to a marsh close by her home she ran—
Till she got there, her heart was all afire—
And, like a bittern when it makes its boom,
Placing her mouth beneath the water's surface,
'Do not betray me, water, with your noise,'
Said she, 'to you I tell it, no one else:
My husband has got two long asses' ears!
I feel ever so much better now it's out.
I couldn't keep it in another minute!'
Which shows that though we may hold on a bit,
Yet out it must; we can keep nothing secret.
If you'd like to hear the ending of this tale,
Read Ovid's book: and there you'll find it all.

   Now when the knight, the subject of my story,
Found that he was no nearer the discovery
Of what it is that women love the best,
How heavy was the heart within his breast!

And home he went, for he could not remain;
The day was come when he had to return.
On his way home it happened that he rode,
Much troubled, by the borders of a wood
Where he, all of a sudden, caught a glimpse
Of four-and-twenty ladies in a dance;
And eagerly drew nearer, on the chance
That he would hear of something he could use.
Lo and behold! Before he quite got there,
The dancers vanished, he could not tell where.
No living creature was there to be seen
Save for a woman sitting on the green—
You couldn't imagine an uglier.
At the knight's coming, this old woman rose.
'There's no road on from here, Sir Knight,' she says,
'But tell me what you're looking for. Who knows,
You'll do yourself a good turn, it may be;
We old folks know so many things,' says she.

    'My dear good mother,' said the knight, 'for sure,
I am as good as dead, if I can't tell
What the thing is that women most desire.
If you could tell me that, I'd pay you well.'

    'Put your hand in mine and pledge your word,' said she,
'That you will do the first thing I require
Of you, so be that it lies in your power,
And I shall tell it to you before night.'

    'Agreed: you have my promise,' said the knight.

    'Then,' said she, 'I'll go so far as to say
Your life is safe: for I will stake my head
That what I say is what the queen will say.
Now let's see if the proudest of them all
That wears a headkerchief or jewelled snood
Will have the face to deny or refute
What I'll teach you. Say no more; let's go on.'
Then, whispering a few words in his ear,
She told him to cheer up and have no fear.

    The knight, on his arrival at the court,
Said he had kept, according to his word,
His day, and that he had his answer ready.
Many a maiden, many a noble lady,

And many a widow (widows are so wise),
The queen herself in the chair of justice,
Had all assembled in the court to hear;
And then the knight was ordered to appear.

All were commanded to observe silence,
And the knight to tell, in formal audience,
What it is mortal women love the most.
Instead of standing there dumb as an ox,
The knight resolved the riddle there and then
In ringing tones, so the whole court heard him:

'In general, my liege lady,' he began,
'Women desire to have dominion
Over their husbands, and their lovers too;
They want to have mastery over them.
That's what you most desire—even if my life
Is forfeit. I am here; do what you like.'
In the whole court there was no wife nor maid
Nor widow who'd contradict what he said,
But all declared that he deserved his life.
Upon this, the old woman whom the knight
Encountered sitting on the forest green,
Jumped up and cried: 'My sovereign lady queen,
Before the court disperses, do me right!
It was I who taught his answer to the knight.
For which he gave his promise on the spot
That he would do the first thing that I asked,
If so be that it lay within his might.
And so before the court I ask, Sir Knight,'
Said she, 'that you take me to be your wife.
For well you know that I have saved your life.
If this be false, deny it upon oath!'

'Alas!' replied the knight, 'alack, alas!
I know too well that such was my promise.
So for the love of God, choose something else!
Take all my goods and let my body go.'

'Never! A curse on us both if I do!
For though I may be ugly, old and poor,
I'd not, for all the gold and metal ore
That's buried under ground, or lies above,
Be other than your wife, and your true love!'

'My love?' cried he. 'You mean my damnation!
Alas! that ever any of my family
Should undergo such foul degradation!'
But it was all for nothing; finally
He was compelled to see he needs must wed;
And, taking his aged wife, goes off to bed.

Now some of you will say of me, perhaps,
That I don't trouble, out of laziness,
To tell of all the gaiety and joy
Seen at the feast upon that marriage-day:
To which I'll give a short and simple answer,
There was no feasting and no fun whatever,
Nothing at all but misery and mourning,
For he married her in secret in the morning,
And all that day hid himself like an owl,
Moping because his new wife looked so foul.

And now what bitter thoughts oppressed the knight
When he was brought to bed with his aged wife!
He tossed and twisted back and forth, the while
His wife lay there and never ceased to smile,
But said, 'My dearest husband! Bless me! Do
All knights who marry wives behave like you?
Is this the custom in King Arthur's house?
Is every knight of his so hard to please?
I am your own true love, also your wife,
And I am also she who saved your life.
And surely I have never wronged you yet?
So why behave like this on our first night?
You're acting like a man who's lost his wits.
What have I done? Now tell me, for God's sake,
And if I can, I shall soon set it right.'

'Set it right! Never, never!' cried the knight,
'Nothing can ever set it right again!
You are so hideous, so old and plain,
And what is more besides, so basely born,
It's little wonder if I toss and turn.
I only wish to God my heart would burst.'

'Is that', she asked, 'the cause of your distress?'
'Indeed yes, and no wonder,' said the knight.
'Now sir,' said she, 'all this I could put right

Before three days are up,—that's if I liked,
And you were to behave more courteously.

  'But since you talk of such gentility
As is derived from ancient wealth; and claim
On that account to be a gentleman—
Such affectation isn't worth a bean.
Look for the man who's always virtuous
In private and in public, does his best
Always to do what gentle acts he can,
And count him for the greatest gentleman.
For Christ wants us to claim nobility
From Him, and not from our rich ancestry,
For though they may have left us all their wealth,
For which we claim to be of gentle birth,
They are by no means able to bequeath
Their goodness, or their virtuous way of life
Which earned for them the name of gentlemen,
And points to us to follow in their steps.

  'Upon this Dante, that wise Florentine
Poet, has spoken with great eloquence;
Now listen: Dante's verses go like this:
"It's rarely man climbs to excellence by
His own thin branches; God in His goodness
Wills us to claim from Him nobility."*
For from our forebears we can only claim
Material things, which may injure and harm.

  'And everybody knows as well as I,
Were Nature to implant gentility
In any single family, so the line
Inherited it—why then, they'd never cease
In private and in public from behaving
Like gentlemen; moreover, they would be
Incapable of villainy or crime.

  'Take fire, convey it to the darkest house
That's between here and coldest Caucasus,
And shut the doors on it, and go away;
As brightly will that fire blaze and burn,
As if a thousand folk were looking on;
I'll stake my life, that fire will perform
Its natural function always, till it die.

Thus you can plainly see that nobleness
Has no connection with ancestral riches;
People aren't always on their best behaviour
As fire is—for fire is always fire.
And God knows one can often enough find
A lord's son who behaves just like a fiend.
And he who prizes his gentility
Because descended from a noble house,
From ancestors both noble and virtuous,
Yet who himself performs no noble deed
Like his own noble ancestor who's dead,
He is not noble, be he duke or earl;
For churlish actions are what make the churl.
For nobility's no more than the renown
Of your forebears, by their great virtue won,
Nothing to do with you, or your person;
Your nobility comes from God alone.
Thus our true nobility comes by grace,
Is not bequeathed along with our position.

   'And think how noble, as Valerius says,
Was Tullus Hostilius, who rose
From poverty to the highest rank of all.*
Read Seneca, and Boethius as well,
And there you will find that it's made quite plain
It's noble deeds that make the nobleman.
And therefore, my dear husband, I conclude,
That though my ancestors were rough and rude,
I might be granted yet, by God on high
(And so I hope) grace to live virtuously.
I'm truly noble then, if I begin
To live in virtue and to cast off sin.

   'As for my poverty, which you reprove,
The Lord on high, in Whom we both believe,
Willingly chose a life of poverty.
To every man, matron, and maid, surely
It's plain as day that Jesus, Heaven's King,
Would never choose a vicious way of life.
As Seneca and others say, in truth
Cheerful poverty is an honest thing.
Whoever is contented with his lot,

Poor as it is, I count him to be rich,
Though he may have no shirt upon his back;
Whoever covets anything is poor,
Because he wants what isn't in his power.
The man with nothing, who would nothing have,
Is rich, though you may count him as a slave.
The nature of true poverty is to sing;
On this Juvenal has a happy saying—
"The poor man, when he goes a-journeying,
Can laugh at thieves." Poverty's a hated boon,
And, as I'd guess, an efficient expeller
Of anxieties; also a great improver
Of wisdom, when it is patiently borne.
That is poverty, hard as it may seem:
It is an asset no one wants to claim.
Poverty will often, if you're humble,
Teach you to know God, and yourself as well.
Poverty's like an eyeglass, I declare,
Through which you can see who your real friends are.
In this I am not harming you; therefore
You can't go on complaining I am poor.

'And as for your reproach that I am old,
Were there no book whatever to uphold
Authority for it, yet all the same
It's said by honourable gentlemen
Just like yourself, that people should respect
An old man, call him "sir" for manners' sake:
I could find texts that say so, I expect.

'As for your point that I'm loathsome and old,
You've then no fear of being made cuckold;
For ugliness and age, it seems to me,
Are the best bodyguards for chastity.
But, since I know what gives you most delight,
I'll satisfy your sensual appetite.

'Choose now, choose one of these two things,' said she,
'To have me old and ugly till I die,
And be to you a true and faithful wife,
And never to displease you all my life;
Or else to have me beautiful and young,
And take your chances with a crowd of men

All flocking to the house because of me,
Or to some other place, as it may be.
Choose for yourself which of the two you please.'

   He turns it over in his mind, and sighs,
And in this way the knight at last replies:
'My lady and my love, my dear wife too,
I place myself in your wise governance;
Choose for yourself whichever's the most pleasant,
Most honourable to you, and me also.
All's one to me; choose either of the two;
What pleases you is good enough for me.'

   'Then I've the mastery of you,' said she,
'Since I may choose and decide as I wish?'

   'Yes, certainly,' said he, 'I think it best.'

   'Kiss me, and we won't quarrel any more,
For I'll be both to you, upon my honour!
That's to say, beautiful as well as good.
May death and madness be my lot,' she said,
'If I am not a wife as good and true
As ever wife was since the world was new.
And if I'm not as pretty as a queen,
As any empress that was ever seen
From east to west, before tomorrow's dawn,
Then you can deal just as you like with me.
And now, lift up the curtain: look and see.'

   And when the knight saw it was really so,
And that she was as lovely as she was young,
He caught her up in both his arms for joy,
With his whole heart bathed in a bath of bliss;
They kiss; a thousand thousand times they kiss.
And she obeyed him in all things that might
Afford him satisfaction or delight.

   To their lives' end they lived in perfect joy;
And may Christ Jesus send us husbands who
Are meek and young, and spirited in bed;
And send us grace to outlive those we wed;
And I pray Jesus to cut short the lives
Of those who won't be governed by their wives;
And as for all old and ill-tempered skinflints,
May heaven rain upon them pestilence!

THE PROLOGUE OF THE FRIAR'S TALE

That excellent limiter, the good friar,
Kept casting black looks at the summoner,
Yet had been able, so far, to hold back
From swearing at him, for good manners' sake.
At length, addressing the goodwife of Bath,
'Madam, God bless you with a happy life!'
Said he; 'believe me, you have touched upon
A difficult academic problem.
Some points you make are excellent, I'd say;
But, madam, as we ride upon our way,
All we need talk about is what amuses:
Let's leave citations of authorities
To schools of learning and to sermonizers,
For the Lord's sake! But, if the company please,
I'll tell you a good story, to make game
Of summoners; for as God's my witness,
You know you only have to hear the name
Of summoner to hear no good of them.
No offence meant! but a summoner is
A chap who runs about with summonses
For adultery and fornication,
Gets himself beaten up in every town.'
   Our host broke in with: 'Hey! Now watch it, sir.
One of your standing should be civiller:
We'll have no quarrelling in our company,
So tell your tale, and let the summoner be.'
   'No,' said the summoner, 'let him say to me
Whatever he likes: when my turn comes, by God!
He'll find himself hoist with his own petard.
You bet I'll teach him just how great an honour
It is to be a lying limiter;
I'll show him what kind of a job he has!'
   'Pipe down!' returned our host, 'enough of this!'
A moment later he addressed the friar:
'Begin your story, if you please, dear sir.'

THE FRIAR'S TALE

In my part of the world lived an archdeacon
Once on a time; a man of high position,
A stern executant of the retribution
The law imposes upon fornication,
Slander, and witchcraft, and church-robbery,
On procuration and adultery,
Forging of wills and breaches of contract,
Usury and simony and neglect
Of sacraments, and other kinds of crime
We need not enter into at this time.
He'd castigate whoremongers most of all;
If he caught them at it, how he'd make them squall!
And as for those who hadn't paid their tithes,
He came down on them like a sack of bricks
If any parish priest reported them;
He never missed a chance to take a fine.
For a skimped tithe, or scanty offering,
How piteously he'd make people sing!
Before the bishop caught them with his crook,
They'd be put down in the archdeacon's book,
Whereupon, being in his jurisdiction,
He had it in his power to penalize them.
And he'd a summoner ready to his hand,
There was no craftier rascal in England;
For he'd a secret set-up; private spies
Told him of things that he could put to use,
And he'd let off a whoremonger or two
If they could lead to half a dozen more.
For though it drives him mad as a March hare,
I don't propose to spare the summoner
The tally of his devilish misdeeds.
I need not worry about prosecution:
Over us friars they've no jurisdiction,
Nor will have till the ending of their days—

   'By Peter! So are the women of the stews
Out of our charge!' the summoner exclaimed.

   'Pipe down, be damned to you, I say pipe down!'
Cut in our host; 'and let him tell his tale.

Now go on, though it makes the summoner howl;
Hold nothing back, dear sir; spare no detail.'
   That thief, the summoner (the friar went on)
Had pimps ever ready at his beck and call,
Like lures to fetch a hawk; and they'd tell all
The secrets that they came across, or knew;
For their acquaintanceship was nothing new.
They served as his informers; secretly
He won himself a great profit thereby;
The archdeacon didn't always know how much.
For he could summons some illiterate
Without a written warrant, on the threat
Of excommunication and Christ's curse;
And they were glad enough to fill his purse,
And stand him dinners at the alehouses.
And just as Judas kept his Master's purse,
And was a thief, just such a thief was he;
The archdeacon got less than half his fee.
He was, if I'm to give him his just due,
A thief; a pimp; and a summoner too.
Moreover, he had harlots at command,
And so, if Reverend Robert, or Reverend
Hugh, Tom, Dick, or Harry, or whoever
Had one of them, it reached the summoner's ear;
Then, since the girl and he were in collusion,
He'd whip out a faked document to summon
The pair before the chapter court; and so
He'd fleece the man, and let the woman go.
And then he'd say to him, 'Friend, for your sake
I'll see her name is struck from our black list.
Trouble yourself no further about this;
Remember I'm your friend, and at your service.'
To tell of all the fiddles that he knew
Would take a year at least, or maybe two.
And there's no hunting dog on earth that's better
At picking from the herd a wounded deer,
Than he at finding an adulterer,
A concubine, or some sly whoremonger.
And since he got most of his income from it,
He gave his full attention to the matter.

And it so came about, that one fine day,
On the lookout as usual for his prey,
This summoner I'm talking of rode out
To summons an old widow, poor old bitch,
Having some trumped-up charge to extort cash;
When he saw, by the margin of a wood,
A jolly yeoman riding just ahead.
He bore a bow, with arrows bright and sharp,
And on his back he had a short green coat,
A hat upon his head, all fringed with black.

'Greetings, sir,' cried the summoner, 'well met!'
'The same to you and all good men,' said he.
'Where are you riding under the greenwood tree?
Going far today?'
                         Answered the summoner,
'No, I'm just riding to a place near by,
I've to collect a rent that's fallen due.'

'So you're a bailiff then?' 'I am,' said he,
But did not dare admit, for very shame,
He was a summoner—a filthy name!

'Lord bless you,' said the yeoman, 'you're a brother;
You are a bailiff, and I am another!
I'd like, as I'm a stranger in these parts,
To get to know you; perhaps afterwards
Become your friend and comrade if you like.
I've gold and silver laid up in my box,
If you ever happen to come to our shire
It's all yours; just as much as you desire.'

'Upon my soul, a thousand thanks!' replied
The summoner; and, shaking hands, the pair
Swore they would be as brothers all their lives.
Discoursing pleasantly, the two rode on.

Now this summoner was as full of chat
As butcher-birds, they say, are full of spite,
And always asking about everything.
Said he, 'Dear brother, tell me where you're living,
In case I come and look you up one day?'
The yeoman answered in his quiet way,

'My friend, I live far in the north country,*
Where I shall hope to see you one fine day.

I'll direct you, before we go our ways,
So carefully, you'll never miss the place.'

   'Well, brother,' the summoner said, 'seeing
You, like me, are a bailiff, while we're riding
Along the way, I'd like to ask you if
There's some dodge you could teach me? Now tell frankly
How I can make most profit in my job.
And don't, for fear of sin, or conscience' sake,
Hold anything that you can think of back.
Now tell, as between friends, how you make out?'

   'Upon my word, my dear chap,' he replied,
'My wages are, if I'm to tell the truth,
Too low; in point of fact, I'm poorly paid;
My master is a tight man, and a hard;
Also my job is pretty onerous.
If I didn't put the screws on I'd not live.
In fact, I take whatever folk will give
By hook or crook, through trickery or force.
From year to year I manage to subsist.
And frankly, that's the best that I can say.'

   'Well,' said the summoner, 'it's the same with me.
As God knows, I'll take anything like a shot
Unless it be too heavy or too hot!
What I get on the side, or privately,
I do not scruple over—no, not I,
For I'd starve if I didn't put the screws on.
And I'm not one to mention at confession
Such tricks as those. I have no conscience, none;
Not I; nor bowels of compassion.
Damn father-confessors, damn them I say!
By heaven, we two are well met, you and I.
But, my dear fellow, tell me, what's your name?'
The yeoman, as the summoner rattled on,
Began to smile at him a little.
                    Then,
'My friend,' said he, 'do you want me to tell?
I am a fiend; my dwelling is in Hell;
I'm riding here on business, and to see
If folk have anything to give to me.
What I pick up makes my whole revenue.

It seems that you're on the same errand too,
Lining your pocket, never minding how;
The same as me— for I'd set off right now
To the world's end and back, to find a prey.'
      'What!' cried he, 'Lord bless us, what's that you say?
I took you for a yeoman, certainly;
And you've a human form, the same as me.
But have you any definite fixed shape
In Hell, where you are in your natural state?'
      'No indeed,' said the other, 'we have none;
But when we like, we can assume a form
Or make it seem to you that we've a shape
Sometimes just like a man, or like an ape;
Or like an angel I can go about.
There's really nothing wonderful in it;
For any lousy conjurer can deceive,
And, pardon me, I've a more skilled technique.'
      'Why', asked the summoner, 'do you go around
In different shapes, instead of the same form?'
      'Because', said he, 'we prefer to assume
Whatever shape best suits to snare our game.'
      'What is it makes you go to all this labour?'
      'Very many reasons, Mister Summoner,'
He answered, 'but for everything there's a time.
The day is short; already it's past nine,
As yet I've taken nothing all today.
Now I'll attend to business, if I may,
And not to divulging everything we know,
Which, my good friend, your wits are far too slow
To understand, even if I told it you;
But, since you ask me why we labour so,
It's because, sometimes, we're God's instruments,
A means to carry out the Lord's commandments
Upon His creatures, as it pleases Him,
In diverse ways, in diverse shapes and forms.
It's true we have no power without Him
Should He please to oppose us. And sometimes
He grants, at our request, leave to maltreat
The body of a man, but not the spirit;
Job for example, whom we tormented.

And sometimes we have power over both,
That is to say, body and soul alike.
And sometimes we're permitted to harass
A man and vex his soul, but not his flesh;
And, as you see, it all works for the best.
For when a man resists our temptation,
It may contribute to his salvation,
Even if it was never our intention
He should be saved, but that Hell should catch him.
Sometimes we act as servants to some man,
For instance the archbishop, St Dunstan.
And I myself served the Apostles too.'

      'Now tell me', asked the summoner, 'if it's true
You make yourselves new bodies in this way
Out of the elements?' 'No,' the fiend replied,
'Sometimes we simulate them; sometimes rise
In bodies of the dead, in various ways,
And speak as fluently and well as ever
Dead Samuel did, raised by the witch of Endor.
(Although some people say it wasn't he;
But I've no time for your theology.)
But—I'm not joking—let me tell you this:
Hereafter, friend, you're going to a place
Where you will have no need for me to teach.
First-hand experience is what you'll get
My friend, which will enable you to lecture
As if from a professorial chair
Better than Virgil, when he was alive,
Or Dante either. Now let's ride on quickly,
For I would like to keep you company
Till it so happens that you break with me.'

      'Never!' the summoner cried, 'I never shall!
I am a yeoman, known to one and all;
I'll keep my promise to you in this matter.
For if you were the devil Lucifer,
Yet I would keep my promise to my brother,
The oath that we have sworn to one another,
To be a faithful partner in this matter,
And go about our business together.
You take your share, whatever people give,

And I'll take mine; in this way, we'll both live.
If one of us should get more than the other,
He's to play fair, and share it with his brother.'
   'Agreed,' the devil said. 'You have my word.'
And upon this they set off on their road.
Just at the entrance of the village where
The summoner had it in mind to go,
They saw a carter with a load of hay
Driving his cart along the public way.
The road was deep in mud; so the cart stuck.
The carter laid about him with his whip,
Yelling like mad: 'Hup Brock!' and 'Hup Scot!
Hup Brock! Hup Scot! Hup! Hup! Why stop for stones?
The devil take you,' cried he, 'body and bones
Sure as you're born! What I've been through today!
The devil take the lot—horse, cart, and hay.'
   Said the summoner: 'Now we'll have some fun.'
As if he'd noticed nothing, he drew near
The fiend, and slyly whispered in his ear,
'Hear that, brother? On my word, just listen!
Don't you understand what that carter's saying?
Take it at once, he's given it to you,
Hay, cart and all—and the three horses too!'
   'Lord no, not a bit of it,' said the fiend,
'Trust me, that isn't at all what he meant.
Just go and ask him, if you don't believe me;
Or hold on for a minute, and you'll see.'
   The carter thwacked his horses on the croup,
The team began to strain and heave and tug.
'Hup, now, hup! May Christ bless you and all
His handiwork, and creatures great and small!
Well tugged, old grey!' he shouted. 'That's my boy!
God keep and save you all, by St Eloi!
Thank God, that's got my cart out of the mud.'
   'See there, what did I tell you?' the fiend said,
'It only goes to show you, my dear brother,
The yokel said one thing, but meant another.
We'd best be getting on, for I can see
It's plain that there's no rake-off here for me.'
   When they had gone a short way out of town

The summoner whispered his companion,
'Brother, this place belongs to an old trout,
An old girl who would rather cut her throat
Almost, than yield a penny of her goods.
I'll get twelve off her, though it drive her mad!
If not, I'll have her summonsed to our court,
Though heaven knows the old bag's not at fault.
But as you don't seem able, in these parts,
To earn your keep, I'll show you how it's done.'

   The summoner banged at the widow's gate,
'Come out!' he shouted, 'you old harridan!
You've got some priest or friar there, I bet!'

   'God bless me, who's that knocking?' cried the woman.
'God save you, sir! What might your honour want?'

   'I have with me', he said, 'a bill of summons.
See to it that tomorrow you present
Yourself before his reverence the archdeacon,
On penalty of excommunication,
To answer to the court for certain things.'

   'O Lord! So help me Jesus, King of kings!
I swear to you I really cannot go.
I have been ill, and that for many a day.
I could not walk nor even ride so far.
It'd be the death of me, my side hurts so.
May I not have a copy of the paper,
Good Mister Summoner, and let my lawyer
Answer such charges as are laid to me?'

   'Right,' said the summoner, 'pay up—let's see,
Twelve pence will do*—and I'll not prosecute,
Though I don't stand to make much out of it:
My master takes the profit, and not me.
Come on—can't you see I'm in a hurry?
Give me twelve pence—I can't stand here all day.'

   'Twelve pence!' cried she. 'Our Lady St Mary
Deliver me from trouble, grief and sin!
I swear if the wide world were mine to win,
There's not twelve pence in the house anywhere!
And you know well enough I'm old and poor.
Show charity to a poor wretch like me!'

   'Never!' cried the summoner, 'the foul fiend fetch me

If I excuse you, though it be your ruin.'
　'Alas!' cried she. 'God knows I've done no wrong.'
　'Pay up!' said he, 'or else, by sweet St Anne,
I'll carry off your fine new frying-pan
To pay that debt that you owe me of old;
That time you made your husband a cuckold
I paid your fine for you to the archdeacon.'
　'You lie!' said she, 'as Christ's my salvation
Never have I, as widow or as wife,
Been summoned to your court in my whole life!
No, never ever has my body sinned!
I give you to the black and bristling fiend,
Body and soul and frying-pan also!'
　Said the devil, when he heard her cursing so
Upon her knees: 'Come now, good mother Mabel,
Are you in earnest? And mean what you say?'
　'The devil fetch him, frying-pan and all,
Unless he will repent him here and now.'
　'Not likely, not a hope there, you old cow,
I've no mind to repent', the summoner said,
'For anything of yours that I have had;
I only wish that I could have your smock
As well as every last stitch on your back!'
　'Now take it easy, brother,' said the fiend,
'Your body and this pan are mine by right,
And you must off with me to Hell tonight,
Where you'll learn more concerning our affairs
Than any theological professor.'
So saying, the foul devil fastened on him,
And he, body and soul, went with the fiend
To where all summoners have their heritage.
May God, Who created after His image
Mankind, guide and protect us, most and least,
And teach these summoners to mend their ways!
　Gentlemen, I could have told you (said the friar)
Had I permission from this summoner here,
On the authority of Paul, and John,
Of Christ, and many a theologian,
About such torments and such agonies
As would shake you, which no tongue can describe,

Though for a thousand winters I should tell,
The pangs of that accursèd house of Hell.
But, so to keep us from that dreadful place,
Watch, and pray Jesus, for His mercy's sake,
To guard us all from Satan's temptation.
And here's a proverb to reflect upon:
'The lion's always lurking in his den
To kill the poor and innocent if he can.'
Dispose your hearts constantly to withstand
The bondage and enslavement of the fiend;
But he may not tempt you beyond your might.
For Christ will be your champion and your knight.
And pray that all these summoners repent them
Of their misdeeds, ,before the devil gets them!

THE PROLOGUE OF THE SUMMONER'S TALE

High in his stirrups stood the summoner,
He was so wild with anger at the friar,
That like an aspen leaf he shook with ire.
   'Gentlemen,' said he, 'I've only one desire;
Let me entreat you, of your courtesy,
Now that you've heard this two-faced friar lie,
You will permit me to begin my tale.
How familiar this friar is with hell!
And, Lord knows, that's little cause for wonder;
Friars and fiends are not so far asunder.
For, bless us, you must often have heard tell
About the friar who was snatched to hell
In spirit once. It was a dream, a vision;
And when an angel led him up and down
To show him all the torments they had there,
It seems he didn't see a single friar
In the whole place; but lots of other folk
In trouble; so the friar turned and spoke:
   "Now, sir," said he, "are friars in so much favour
None of them ever seems to fetch up here?".
   "Far from it," said the angel, "there's a million!"
And led him down to have a look at Satan.

"Look," said the angel. "Satan's got a tail.
As big or bigger than a barge's sail.
You there, Satan! Lift up your tail," said he,
"Show us your arse, and let the friar see
The place where all the friars have their nest!"
And in a minute or two, more or less,
Just as bees come swarming from a hive,
A troop of twenty thousand friars drove
Out of the devil's arse, and swarmed through hell,
And then swarmed back, as fast as possible,
And crept into his arsehole, one and all.
He clapped his tail upon them, and lay still.
And, later, when the friar had looked his fill
At all the torments of that terrible place,
God in His mercy fetched his spirit back,
Restored it to his body, and he woke.
Yet even then his terror made him quake,
Because he couldn't get out of his mind
The true and natural home of all his kind,
The devil's arse. God save you all, bar one—
This damned friar here! And so my prologue's done.'

THE SUMMONER'S TALE

Gentlemen, in Yorkshire I believe there is
A marshy region known as Holderness,
In which a limiter* used to go about
Preaching to folk—and begging too, no doubt.
Now one day it so happened that this friar
Preached, in a certain church, his regular
Sermon exhorting folk to find the money
For masses for the dead; and above all
To give, for the glory of God, the wherewithal
For building yet more sacred edifices
Wherein to celebrate divine services;
Not where it's wasted, thrown away and squandered;
Or to bestow it where it isn't needed,
To clergy with good livings, for example,
Whose means (thanks be to God) are more than ample.

'Such masses', said he, 'fetch from Purgatory
The souls of all your friends, both old and young,
Yes, when rattled off and quickly sung;
And not by some pert priest who takes it easy,
Never singing more than one mass in the day!
O deliver those poor souls posthaste!' he cried,
'Twisting upon the spit, with flesh-hooks clawed!
How horrible it is to bake, to burn!
Now for Christ's sake make haste, and lose no time!'
And when he'd said all he'd in mind to say,
With 'qui cum patre'* he went on his way.
    When folk in church had given what they thought right,
Then off he went; no longer would he wait.
With bag for alms, tipped staff, gown tucked up high,
He'd go around the houses, poke and pry,
Begging for cheese or flour, wheat or corn.
His comrade carried a staff tipped with horn,
Waxed tablets backed with ivory to write on,
A beautifully polished stylus pen,
And always wrote the names down on the spot
Of those who gave—it didn't matter what—
As if to guarantee that he would pray
On their behalf. 'A bushel, now, of rye,
Or wheat, or malt; or else a cut of cheese,
Or what you like, it's not for us to choose;
A little cake for God, or a half penny;
Or will you give a penny for a mass,
Or just a bit of brawn, if you have any—
Or else a scrap of blanket, sweetest madam,
Our dearest sister—here's your name set down!—
Bacon, or beef, whatever you can find.'
A sturdy rascal always walked behind,
Their convent servant; and he bore a sack
To carry what folk gave them on his back.
No sooner than he'd got outside the door,
The friar would smooth out every single name
He'd written on the tablets earlier;
What he dished out was flummery and hokum—
    'No, there you lie, you summoner!' cried the friar.
    'Be quiet, for the love of Christ's sweet mother,'

Shouted our host, 'go on and tell your tale:
Mind you leave nothing out; let's hear it all.'
   'Trust me,' replied the summoner, 'I shall.'
   On went this friar from house to house, till he
Came to a dwelling where he used to be
Better looked after than in all the others.
But as for the good man whose house it was,
Ill and bedridden on a couch he lay.
'*Deus hic!** Thomas! Thomas, my friend, good day!'
The friar said in a mild, courteous tone:
'Thomas, my friend, God be with you, I say!
Many's the happy hour I've passed upon
This bench; and many's the good meal I've eaten!
And from the bench he shooed away the cat,
Then, laying down his alms-bag and his hat,
And staff as well, sat comfortably down.
(His mate had gone on ahead into town,
Taking their man with him, for he proposed
To spend the night there at a lodging-house.)
   'O my dear good sir,' said this poor sick man,
'How've you been managing since March began?
I've not seen you this fortnight, maybe more.'
'Lord knows I've been hard at it,' said the friar;
'For your salvation, in particular,
I've offered up many a costly prayer,
And for our other friends—God send them grace!
I have today been to your church for mass,
And preached, according to my modest wit,
Not quite conformably to Holy Writ,
Which I imagine you find hard to follow;
That's why I must interpret it for you:
To make the thing quite clear, you need a gloss.
For as we clerics say, "The letter killeth."
I was teaching them how to be charitable,
To make donations where it's reasonable;
And there I saw your wife—now, where is she?'
   'Out in the garden, I expect,' said he.
'Now don't you stir, she's bound to come in soon.'
   'Well, sir! you're very welcome, by St John!'
The woman cried. 'And keeping well, I hope?'

Gallantly rising to his feet, the friar
Gives her a hug, and sweetly kisses her,
Chirruping like a sparrow with his lips:
'Madam,' said he, 'never better in my life!
Your servant in all things! In the whole church
Today, I didn't see a prettier woman,
As sure as God above is my salvation!'
  'Well, may God mend my blemishes,' said she.
'Upon my word, you're welcome anyway!'
'Thanks, madam, it is what I've always found.
But pray excuse me—if you'd be so kind—
Don't be offended now—is that a promise?
I'd like to have a little word with Thomas.
These priests are much too slack and dilatory
To probe into a conscience tenderly
At confession; preaching's my special skill;
I'm deeply read in Peter and in Paul;
I roam about to fish for Christian souls,
To render unto Christ what's due to Him;
To speed His gospel is my one sole aim.'
  'Then if you don't mind, my dear sir,' said she,
'Give him a talking to! By the Trinity,
He gets as cross and angry as a bear,
Though he has everything he can desire;
I cover him at night and keep him warm,
Fling my leg over him, or else an arm,
But he just grunts like the pig in our sty.
That's all the fun he's got to offer me!
And there's no pleasing him in any way.'
  'O Thomas! Thomas! Thomas! *je vous dis!*
That's devil's work, and must be remedied.
Wrath is a thing almighty God forbade
Concerning which, I'll say a word or two.'
  'Now sir,' the wife put in, 'before I go,
What would you like for dinner? I'm about
To see to it.' 'Madam, *je vous dis sans doute*
Just let me have the liver of a chicken,
Some of your soft bread—just a slice—just one—
And after that, a roast pig's head maybe
—Though I'd not wish an animal to die

On my account—that's quite sufficient.
A simple, homely meal is all I want.
My spirit's nourishment is in the Bible;
This body's so inured to keeping vigil
That my poor appetite is quite destroyed.
Don't, I beseech you, madam, be annoyed
If I confide, as to a friend, in you.
Lord knows I tell these things to very few.'

    'O sir, just one short word before I go,'
Said she. 'My baby died two weeks ago,
Not very long after you last left town.'

    'I saw his death in a revelation
Back home in our dormitory,' said the friar.
'I daresay that in less than half an hour
After his death he was borne up to heaven.
As God's my judge, I saw it in a vision!
So did our infirmarian and our sacristan,
Both trusty friars for half a century:
They've reached (the Lord be thanked!) their jubilee,
And now may walk alone,* praise be to Him.
And up I rose, the whole convent as well,
Silently, with no clattering of bells;
The tears ran down my cheeks, how fast they fell!
Te Deum was what we sang, and nothing else,
Save that I offered up an orison
To Christ, to thank Him for His revelation;
For, sir and madam, it's undeniable
Our orisons are more effectual,
And we see more of Christ's most secret things
Than laymen may, even though they be kings.
We live in poverty and abstinence,
The laity in wealth and in abundance
Of food and drink, and in unclean delights.
All worldly satisfactions we despise.
Dives and Lazarus led different lives,
And so gained different guerdons when they died.
Those who would pray must fast, keep pure and clean,
Fatten the soul, but keep the body lean.
We live as the Apostle has advised:*
Clothes, food, however poor, are all we need.

The purity and fasting of us friars
Ensures that Jesus Christ accepts our prayers.
 'Think, Moses forty nights and forty days
Fasted, before almighty God on high
Spoke with him on the mountain of Sinai.
With empty belly, after his long fast,
He was permitted to receive at last
The Law, by God's own finger written down!
And Elijah on Horeb, it's well known,
Spent days in fasting and in contemplation
Before he spoke with God, our souls' physician.
Aaron, who was the Temple's governor,
As well as all the other priests, would never
Drink anything that might intoxicate
Before they went in by the Temple gate
To pray for the whole nation; but instead
Abstained from food and drink, and watched and prayed
Lest they should perish. Take heed what I say!
If you are not abstemious when you pray
For others—but enough! and mark my words!
Never forget how Jesus Christ, Our Lord,
Was our example, as the Bible says;
Think how He prayed and fasted forty days.
Therefore we mendicants, we simple friars,
Are wed to poverty and continence,
Charity, humility, abstinence,
Persecution for the sake of righteousness,
To tears, to pity, and chaste holiness.
And therefore it's quite plain that all our prayers
—I'm talking of us mendicants and friars—
Are to almighty God more acceptable
Than yours, with your feasts at the dinner-table.
If I'm not wrong, it was for greediness
That Adam was first chased from Paradise;
It's certain he was chaste in Paradise!
 'Now listen, and mark what I say, Thomas!
Though there's no text for it, as I suppose,
It's clear to me, from the commentaries,
That our dear Lord was speaking, when He said
"Blessed are the poor in spirit", of us friars.

Go through the rest of the New Testament,
And there you can see whether what it says
Is nearer to the vows of mendicants,
Or those who wallow in their endowments.
Shame on their pomp! And shame upon their greed!
And I despise them for their ignorance.

   'It seems to me they're like Jovinian,*
Fat as a whale, and wambling like a swan,
Like a bottle in a buttery full of wine.
How reverent, their prayers for the dead!
Just listen to them sing that psalm of David:
"Burp! Burp!" they go, *"cor meum eructavit!"**
Who follows best Christ's gospel and His path,
But us, the poor and holy, pure and chaste,
Doers not hearers of the word of God?
And as a hawk vaults high into the air
Upon its upward swoop, just so do prayers
Of charitable, chaste and busy friars
Swoop upward into the two ears of God!
O Thomas, Thomas! As I live and breathe,
If you were not our brother, you'd not thrive,
No, that you wouldn't, Thomas, by St Ive!
We all pray in our chapter day and night
To Christ, to send you health, that through His might
You'll soon regain the use of all your limbs.'

   'Lord knows, I don't feel the least difference!
So help me Christ!' said he, 'these last few years
I've spent a fortune on all kinds of friars,
And in the end been none the better for it!
I've used up nearly all I own, in fact.
I can kiss my gold goodbye—for it's all gone!'

   'O Thomas!' cried he. 'Is that what you've done?
Now what need have you, Thomas, to seek out
"All kinds of friars"? With the best physician,
Why look for other doctors in the town?
Your changeability will be your ruin.
So you think that I, or rather my convent
Is ineffectual, or insufficient,
To pray for you? Thomas, it's past a joke!
You don't give us enough, that's why you're sick.

"Hey! Give this convent half a load of oats!"
"Hey! Give that convent four and twenty groats!"
"Hey! Give this friar a penny—and be off!"
No, Thomas, it's not nearly good enough!
What's the use of a farthing split in twelve?
Anything whole and intact is itself
Stronger than when divided and dispersed.
Thomas, you'll get no flattery from me:
You want to have us work for you for free.
The Lord on high, Who made the world, has said
"The labourer is worthy of his hire."
For myself, Thomas, I have no desire
To touch a single penny of your money;
It's that our convent prays incessantly
For you, and for the building of Christ's church.
Thomas, if you would learn to do good works,
Your model is St Thomas: read his life
And what he did in India; then you'll see
If it be good to build a church for Christ.
You're lying here, full of the wrath and ire
With which the devil set your heart on fire,
Scolding and scolding this poor innocent,
Your wife, when she's so biddable and patient!
And therefore Thomas—take it how you like—
For your own good, don't wrangle with your wife;
And here's a maxim you can bear in mind
Concerning this; a saying of the wise:
"Do not be as a lion in thy house,
Nor be to household servants tyrannous,
Nor make thine acquaintance to flee from thee."*
I charge you, Thomas, once again I say,
Beware of her who in your bosom sleeps,
Beware also the snake that slyly creeps
Under the grass, to sting so cunningly.
Beware, my son, and hear me patiently,
For twenty thousand men have lost their lives
Through feuding with their sweethearts and their wives.
Since you've got such a sweet and saintly wife,
Thomas, what point is there in causing strife?
You'll nowhere find a serpent half so cruel

And deadly, even if you trod its tail,
As woman in her wrath, blinded with anger:
Vengeance is then the one thing they desire.
Anger's a sin, one of the deadly seven,
Abominable to the Lord in heaven,
And to the sinner himself spells destruction.
As any unlearned priest or half-taught parson
Can tell you, wrath engenders homicide.
Wrath is, in fact, the minister of pride.
My homily would last until tomorrow
Were I to tell of all the grief and sorrow
That anger brings. And therefore, day and night,
I pray to God above with all my might
He grants no power to the wrathful man!
Pity it is, and an abomination,
When such a one is set in high position.
    'For there was once a choleric magistrate:
During his term upon the judgement seat,
There were two knights went riding out together
One day. As luck would have it (says Seneca),*
One of them came back home, the other not.
This knight was brought before the judge forthwith,
Who said, "You murdered your companion.
And so I sentence you to die the death."
And to another knight he gave direction:
"Go, lead him to his death! Do as I say!"
But as it chanced, while they were on their way
To the appointed place of execution,
The knight whom they all thought was dead rode by.
So they decided it was the best plan
To bring both knights before the judge again.
But when they said, "Sir, the knight did not kill
His friend, for here he stands, alive and well"
—"So help me God!" the judge replied, "you die!
I mean not one, or two, but all the three!"
Then, turning to the first knight, the judge said,
"You were condemned: you must be executed.
And you also will have to lose your head,
Because you are the cause of your friend's death."
Then, turning to the third, the judge spoke thus:

"You had your orders, yet did not obey."
And so he had them put to death, all three.
    'The choleric Cambyses was a sot,
Playing the bully was his great delight.
And one day one of his attendant lords
A friend to virtue and morality,
Privately addressed him in these words:
"That lord is done for, who lives viciously;
And drunkenness, especially in a lord,
Stains his repute; there's many an eye and ear
Keeps watch upon him, and he can't tell where.
Be moderate when you drink, for heaven's sake!
Think how ignominiously wine can sap
All a man's control over mind and body."
    "It's just the other way about, you'll see,"
The king said. "You yourself shall testify
Drink does no harm to people in that way.
I'd like to see the wine that could suspend
My steadiness of eye or foot or hand."
Derisively he drank a great deal more,
A hundred times what he had had before;
Then the miserable, bloody-minded wretch
Gave orders for the knight's son to be fetched.
"Stand there in front of me," he told the boy,
And of a sudden he snatched up his bow,
And, drawing back the bowstring to his ear,
Let fly; the arrow killed the child right there.
"Now have I got a steady hand or no?
Or have I lost my strength and judgement too?"
Said he. " Has drink deprived me of eyesight?"
What use to give the answer of the knight?
His son was killed; there's no more to be said.
So watch out when you're dealing with a lord!
But sing "Placebo!"* "I shall if I can"
Unless it happens to be some poor man;
For in that case it's quite all right to tell
A man his faults—but not if he's a lord,
Not even if he's going straight to hell.
    'Or there's Cyrus, the choleric Persian
Who demolished the river of Gysen,

Because a horse of his had drowned therein
When he set out to conquer Babylon.
He made the river shrink by draining it
Until the women could wade over it.
Who can teach better than great Solomon?
"Make no friendship", said he, "with an angry man,
And with a furious man thou shalt not go
Lest it repent thee"*—I shall say no more!

   'Now, my dear brother Thomas, no more ire!
You'll find me just as true as a set-square.
Don't press the devil's knife against your heart;
It's your own anger does you so much hurt;
Instead, make me a full confession.'

   Cried the sick man, 'No, by St Simeon!
My parish priest has shriven me today:
I've told him all about my condition;
There's no need to confess again,' said he,
'Unless I choose, out of humility.'

   'Then give me gold, to build our monastery!
For to raise it—while others have lived well—
Mussels and oysters and the like', said he,
'Have been our food; and the Lord knows there's still
The foundations to complete, and not a tile
Of pavement yet laid down where we are living.
By God, there's forty pounds for stone still owing!
Help us, Thomas, by Him that harrowed hell,
For otherwise we've no choice but to sell
Our library. Did you lack our instruction,
Then the whole world would go down to destruction!
He who deprives the world of us—your pardon
Thomas—takes from the universe its sun,
For who can teach and labour as we can?
And this is not at all a recent thing.
For from the time of Elijah,' said he,
'Or Elisha, it's a matter of record
That there were friars, workers in charity,
For which let us devoutly thank the Lord.*
Now, Thomas, help, for holy charity!'
And down he went upon his bended knee.

   At this the sick man grew half mad with ire,

And would have loved to fling him in the fire,
Him and his lies and false hypocrisy.
'I can give you nothing, except what I have
Such as it is, in keeping here,' said he.
'You were saying just now that I was your brother?'
    'Indeed yes, there's no question,' said the other,
'I brought our letter of fraternity*
Sealed with our seal, to your good lady here.'
    'Well then,' said he, 'there's something that I'll give
Your holy convent while I'm still alive;
You'll have it in your hand, and have it soon,
On this condition, and on this alone:
That you shall so divide it, my dear brother,
That each friar gets as much as any other;
This without fraud or cavil you must swear
By the vows you vowed when you became a friar.'
    'I swear it by my faith,' the friar said.
His hand upon the other's hand he laid.
'I give my word! I'll never let you down!'
    'Now then, put your hand in, right down my back,'
Said the sick man, 'feel carefully behind,
And there, beneath my buttocks, you will find
A thing that I hid there for secrecy.'
    The friar thought, 'Ah! That will do for me,'
And thrust his hand right down into the cleft,
Hoping that there he'd find the promised gift.
And when the poor old sick man felt the friar
Groping about his arsehole here and there,
Full in the friar's hand he let a fart,
And no carthorse that ever drew a cart
Ever let out a fart as thunderous.
    He sprang up like a lion, furious.
'By God's bones!' shouted he, 'you two-faced clod!
That's an insult! You did it on purpose!
I'll see you're paid out for this fart, by God!'
    Hearing the row, the servants of the house
Came running in, and chased away the friar;
And off he went, rage working in his face,
To find that mate of his, who kept their gear.
And you'd have taken him for a wild boar;

c.t.—14

He ground his teeth, he was so furious.
He marched up smartly to the manor-house,
Because a man of rank was living there,
And he had always been his confessor.
This worthy was the lord of the village.
The friar came in, beside himself with rage,
Almost unable to get out a word,
Where, dining at his table, sat the lord;
But in the end brought out a 'God bless you!'

   The lord stared at the friar. '*Benedicite!*
What's the matter, Friar John? What's ado?
That something is amiss is plain to see.
You look as if the wood were full of thieves.
Sit down, and tell me what the trouble is:
I'll put it right if I am able to.'

   'I've been insulted,' said the friar. 'Today
Down in your village—not the meanest potboy
Would put up with my treatment in your town!
But nothing shocks me more than that old clown
With white hair, who blasphemed our convent too.'

   'Now, Master,' said the lord, 'I beg of you—'

   'Not Master, sir, but servant,' said the friar,
Although the Schools have done me that honour,*
It does not please the Lord that men should call
Us "Rabbi" in the market, or your hall.'

   'Never mind that,' said he, 'tell me what's wrong.'

   'Sir,' said the friar, 'a heinous calamity
Has fallen on my order, and on me,
And therefore also falls—*per consequens*—
On Holy Church, and its whole hierarchy,
But may the Lord in heaven amend it soon!'

   'Sir,' said he, 'you know best what should be done.
You are my confessor; don't be upset.
You are the salt and savour of the earth!
So pull yourself together, for God's sake!
Tell me your trouble.' And he did just that,
Told the whole story of—you all know what.

   The lady of the house sat there quite quiet,
And listened till she'd heard the friar out.
'Ah, Mother of God! Ah, holy blessed Maid!

Is that all? Tell me truly, now,' she said.
   'Madam,' he asked, 'what do you make of it?'
   'What do I make of it? May I be saved,
I'd say a lout has done a loutish act.
What can I say? The Lord send him bad luck!
His old sick head is filled with foolishness.
If you ask me I think he's a bit touched.'
   'By God, madam,' said he, 'to tell the truth,
Unless I get revenge some other way,
I'll pillory him everywhere I preach,
That blasphemer who told me to split up
What can't be split, and share it equally
With everyone—the foul fiend fetch the fellow!'
   The lord of the manor sat there quietly
Like someone in a trance, while he turned over
The matter in his mind—'How could the fellow
Have the imagination to set up
A poser like that, to perplex the friar?
I never heard of such a thing before.
I bet the devil put it in his mind!
In all the mathematic art till now
The like of that conundrum you'd not find.
How can one prove each gets an equal part
In the noisesomeness and noise of a fart?
Curse it all, gentlemen,' the lord exclaimed,
'Whoever heard of such a thing before?
To everyone alike, an equal share—
You tell me! It's impossible, can't be done!
The rumbling of a fart, like every sound,
Is a reverberation of the air,
No more, which little by little dies away.
There's none who could judge properly, I swear,
Whether it were divided equally.
What, one of my villagers at that! Yet he
Fairly took it out of you, my confessor!
In my opinion he's a lunatic.
And now, forget the fellow, and eat up!
Let him go hang himself—the devil take it!'

What the Lord's squire and carver said about the division
of a fart into twelfths

Now the lord's squire, who stood at the sideboard
To carve the meat for them, heard every word,
All that I've just related to you. Then,
'If I may be so bold, sir,' he began,
'Just for a bit of cloth to make a gown
—But only if it doesn't rouse your anger—
I think that I could tell you, Mister Friar,
How such a fart might equally be shared
Among your convent—that is, if I dared.'

'Tell, and you'll get a gown-cloth on the spot,
By God and by St John!' answered his lord.

'Sir,' said he, 'when the weather is set fair,
With no wind or disturbance of the air,
Have a cartwheel brought here into the hall.
See it has all its spokes—for as a rule
A wheel has twelve. Then you must bring to me
Twelve of the friars, and I'll tell you why:
Thirteen make up a convent, I suppose.
Your noble confessor, for his great merit,
Shall bring the number up to thirteen friars.
Then they must all of them kneel down together
So that each spoke's end has a friar's nose
Set firm against it. And your good confessor,
May the Lord save and bless him! shall stick his
Right in the middle, underneath the hub.
Then have this fellow, belly stiff and taut
As any drum, brought here into the hall,
And set plumb in the middle of the wheel,
Upon the hub, and make him let a fart.
And then—for I will stake my life on it—
You'll all be given demonstrable proof
That it will travel, both the stink and sound,
Fairly and equally to each spoke-end;
Except that this good man, your confessor,
Because he is a man of great honour,
Shall have first helping of the fart, which is
Fitting enough, for it is still the custom

Among these friars—and an excellent one—
To serve the worthiest among them first.
And in his case, it's certainly deserved.
Today he's taught all of us so much good
There in the pulpit, preaching where he stood,
I'm willing to assign him, for my part,
(So will the convent) first smell of three farts,
For he behaves in such fine saintly fashion.'

    The lord and lady, in fact everyone
Except the friar, all of them agreed
That Jankin spoke as wisely as Euclid
Or Ptolemy himself about the matter.
As for the rest: concerning the old fellow,
They said that only shrewdness and great wit
Enable him to speak out as he did,
That he was neither fool nor lunatic.
And as for Jankin, he's earned a new gown.
That's all; we've almost come to Sittingbourne.

Fragment IV (Group E)

Clerk's Tale (handwritten)

THE PROLOGUE OF
THE OXFORD SCHOLAR'S TALE

scared girl virgin (handwritten margin note)

'Now, Mister Oxford Scholar,' our host said,
'Today I haven't heard you speak a word.
You ride as shy and silent as a maid
Who's newly married, sitting at the table;
You're meditating some philosophical
Proposition or other, it would seem!
But Solomon has told us there's a time
For everything; and now, for mercy's sake,
This is no time for study: so cheer up!
Spin us some rattling yarn—because, by heaven,
Anyone, once he's entered on a game,
Must keep the rules to which he gave assent.
Mind you don't preach, and try to make us weep
For our past sins, as friars do in Lent;
Nor let your story send us all to sleep!

    'Let's have some jolly tale of adventure,
And keep your flowers of rhetoric in store,
Your figures of speech and so forth, to give wings
To the high-flown language that men keep for kings.
Just for once speak in simple terms, we pray,
So we can understand the things you say.'

    This the good scholar courteously answered:
'Host,' said he, 'I am subject to your rod.
For the time being you rule over us,
Therefore I will do as you say I must,
As far as is reasonable, certainly.
I shall tell you a tale, a tale that I
Learned at Padua from an excellent
Scholar—his every word and action went
To prove it. He's now dead, nailed in his coffin;
God grant, I pray, his soul may rest in heaven!

    'His name was Francis Petrarch,* laureate

"If you tell me what to do, I'll do it"— scholar (handwritten)

Poet, whose most eloquent rhetoric
Illumined Italy with poetry,
As did Lignano* with philosophy
And other fields of learning, such as law;
But Death won't suffer us to linger here
For longer than the twinkling of an eye.
He killed them both; and all of us must die.

    'But to go on about that famous man
Who taught this tale to me, let me explain
He made, in the rhetorical 'high style'
Before writing the main body of the tale,
A prologue; in the course of which he paints
Saluzzo and the country round Piedmont;
And speaks about the Apennines, those high
Mountains which form the bounds of Lombardy;
And in particular of Monte Viso
Where, in a little well, the river Po
Has taken its beginning and its source,
Becoming ever larger on its course
Eastward to Aemilia, Ferrara, till
Venice is reached—a thing too long to tell;
All of which—certainly in my judgement—
Seems to be on the whole irrelevant,
Except in so far as it serves to set
The scene. But here's his tale; now listen to it.'

THE OXFORD SCHOLAR'S TALE

    There is, on the west side of Italy,
Just at the foot of Viso, bleak and cold,
A rich and fertile plain, where you can see
Many a town and towering stronghold
That our forefathers built in days of old,
And many another pleasant sight also;
This superb region is called Saluzzo.

    A marquis was once ruler of that land,
As his great ancestors had been before;
Obedient, ever ready to his hand,

Were all his subjects, both the rich and poor;
So he lived happily, year after year,
Beloved and feared—through favour of Fortune—
Both by his nobles and the common men.

And moreover, as regards lineage,
He was the noblest born in Lombardy,
Handsome of person, strong, and young in age,
Honourable, the flower of courtesy,
Prudent enough in ruling his country,
Save in some things for which he was to blame;
And Walter was this young potentate's name.

I blame him, that he never would consider
What time might bring, or any future need,
But concentrated on the moment's pleasure,
On hawking and on hunting far and wide.
Almost all other business he let slide,
And he would not—and this was worst of all—
Come what come may, wed any wife at all.

But that one point his people took so hard,
One day they gathered in a flock and went
To him; and one, the wisest and most learned,
—Or one the prince would listen to, and consent
To be told what the deputation meant,
Or who could best explain a case like this—
Spoke for them, as you'll hear, to the marquis.

'O noble marquis, your humanity
Gives us the confidence to have the boldness
As often as may seem necessary,
To tell you of whatever weighs on us.
Permit us now, sir, in your graciousness
To complain, which we do with sorrowful hearts,
And do not let your ears disdain my voice.

'Although I am no more concerned in this
Than any other person in this place,
Yet inasmuch as you, my lord marquis,

Have ever shown me favour and kindness,
I am the more encouraged now to ask
An audience, to put forward our request
That you, my lord, may act as you think best.

   'Indeed, my lord, you and your actions please
Us all, and always have, so much that we
Could not ourselves imagine or conceive
How we might ever live more happily,
But for one thing, my lord; for, pardon me,
If only it pleased you to go and find
A wife, your people would have peace of mind.

   'O bow your neck beneath that happy yoke,
Which is dominion, but not servitude,
That men call matrimony or wedlock;
And in your wisdom please consider, lord,
Our days, in one way or another, speed;
Whether we sleep or wake, or ride or roam,
Time's always flying and will wait for none.

   'And though your green youth flourishes as yet,
Age creeps the nearer, silent as a stone;
Death threatens at all ages, and will strike
All ranks of men, for escape there is none;
And just as certainly as everyone
Knows that he has to die, so we are all
Uncertain of the day when death shall call.

   'Trust the sincerity of our intent,
Who never yet disobeyed your command,
And we will, lord, if only you'll consent,
Choose a wife for you now, right out of hand,
Born of the noblest house in all the land,
And greatest also—one that, in our view,
Must seem an honour both to God and you.

   'Deliver us from all this anxious dread
And take a wife, for God in heaven's sake!
For if it so fell out—which God forbid—

That at your death your line should terminate
And that a strange successor came to take
Your heritage—alas for those alive!
Therefore we beg you, marry with all speed.'

Their humble plea and suppliant address
Inclined the marquis' heart to swell with pity:
'My beloved people,' said he, 'you would press
What I never thought of doing, upon me.
I've been so happy in my liberty,
A thing that's seldom found in marriage;
Where I was free, I shall be in bondage.

'But as I can see it's honestly meant,
And I, as I have always done, rely
On your good sense, freely I shall consent
To take a wife as soon as ever I may.
As for the offer which you made today,
To choose one, I'll relieve you of that burden;
I beg you to forget about the notion.

'For children are, as God knows, like as not
To differ from their elders gone before;
All goodness comes from God, not from the stock
From which they were begotten, that's for sure.
I trust in heaven's goodness, and therefore
Commit to Him my marriage, happiness,
And peace of mind, submissive to His wish.

'Leave me alone in choosing of my wife,
That is a burden which I mean to shoulder.
But this I beg of you, as you love life,
To promise me that you will always honour
Whatever wife I take, while she has breath,
With word and deed, both here and everywhere,
As you would the daughter of an emperor.

'And furthermore, this you must swear to me:
Neither to oppose nor to disapprove
My choice; for if I forgo liberty

At your request, sure as my soul's to save,
There where my heart is set, I mean to wive;
And if you won't consent to such a promise,
I beg you say no more about the business.'

    With hearty goodwill they gave their consent
And swore to everything; none backed away;
They only asked of him, before he went,
That he would name to them a definite day
To hold the marriage on, soon as might be,
For even yet the people were afraid
That after all the marquis would not wed.

    With them he fixed a day that suited best,
On which he would be married without fail;
Saying he did all this at their request,
And they with humble hearts began to kneel
Upon the ground, reverent, dutiful;
All thanking him; and then they, having gained
All that they wanted, to their homes returned.

    And thereupon he bids his officers
To make arrangements for the wedding day,
And gives to his personal knights and squires
All such directives as are necessary;
And all that he commands them they obey,
And each without exception does his best
To make a success of the wedding feast.

PART TWO

Not far from the magnificent palace
In which the marquis made his plans for marriage,
Stood situate in a most pleasant place
A hamlet, where the poor folk of the village
Would keep their livestock, and where they would lodge,
And where they'd make a living from their toil,
Depending on the richness of the soil.

Now among these poor people lived a man
Supposed to be the poorest of them all:
And yet the Lord, Who dwells in heaven, can
Sometimes rain blessings on a cattle-stall;
He had a daughter, none more beautiful;
Folk in the village called him Janicula,
And the young girl was known as Griselda.

But when it comes to virtue and beauty,
Then there was none more fair beneath the sun
Than she, brought up in want and poverty;
Luxurious pleasures were to her unknown.
It was not from the winecask, but the spring,
She used to drink; since she loved virtue, work
Was better known to her than idle comfort.

But though the girl was still of tender age,
There was, enclosed within her virgin breast,
Maturity of spirit, steadfastness.
With deep devotion, love, and tenderness,
She kept her father in his poor old age.
For wool for spinning she kept a few sheep,
Was never idle till she fell asleep.

When she came homeward she would bring with her
Some roots or other herbs often as not,
Which she would shred and boil for provender,
And make her bed—which was by no means soft—
Her father being always her first care,
Treated with all devotion and deference
With which a child may honour its parent.

Upon this penniless girl, poor Griselda,
The marquis many a time had cast an eye
While hunting, as he rode upon his way;
Yet when he happened to catch sight of her
It was not with the wanton glance of folly
He looked upon her, but would contemplate
With sober eye her bearing; in his heart

Appraising not only her femineity
But goodness also; in both looks and acts
Surpassing anyone as young as she.
For though most people have no great insight
Into such things, the marquis judged aright
Her quality, and very soon decided
To wed her only, if he ever wedded.

The day of the wedding came: but none could say
Who or what woman was to be the bride.
And many wondered at this oddity,
And privately to one another said,
'Must our prince even now pursue his folly?
Will he not wed? Alas, the pity of it!
Why must he fool himself and us like this?'

But none the less the marquis had them make
With jewels set in gold and in azure,
Brooches and rings, all for Griselda's sake;
And he had dresses made to fit her measure,
Modelled upon a girl of a like stature;
And all the other ornaments as well,
That go with any wedding done in style.

And now the morning of the actual day
Fixed for the marquis' wedding is at hand;
And the whole palace was put on display,
Both the banqueting-hall and private rooms;
Kitchens and pantries stuffed with abundance,
And overflowing with the choicest viands
In the whole length and breadth of Italy.

The regal marquis, in his richest dress,
With lords and ladies in a company,
All who had been invited to the feast,
Being thus assembled, took the shortest way
With many a strain of mingled melody,
And all the young knights of his retinue,
Towards the village I spoke of to you.

Lord knows Griselda had no clue at all
It was for her this pomp had been prepared.
She'd gone off to fetch water from a well,
Was hastening, fast as she could, homeward,
For on this day the marquis, as she'd heard,
Was to be married; and she hoped she might
Be lucky and see something of the sight.

'I'll stand with all the other girls,' she thought,
'With my companions in our door, and see
The marchioness; and so I shall make shift
To finish off, as quickly as can be,
The work that's waiting there at home for me,
Then I'll have time to see her if she should
Go to the marquis' castle by this road.'

About to cross the threshold of her home,
She saw the marquis make his arrival;
He called her, and she set her pitcher down
Beside the threshold, in a cattle-stall,
And down upon her knees Griselda fell.
With downcast look she kneels there quietly,
Till she has heard what the lord's will might be.

The marquis pensively addressed the maid
In earnest tones; and thus he spoke to her:
'Where is your father, Griselda?' he said.
She made a reverent and humble answer,
Saying, 'He's here and at your service, sir.'
And she delayed no longer, but went in
And brought her father out to meet the prince.

The marquis took the old man by the hand,
And said, when he had taken him aside,
'Janicula, I neither should nor can
Conceal, nor any longer try to hide,
My heart's desire; but, if you are agreed,
No matter what, before I go I'll take
Your daughter here for wife until her death.

'You're loyal to me—that I know for certain,
And you're my faithful vassal born and bred;
Whatever pleases me, I dare be sworn
Will please you too; and therefore, on that head,
Say what you feel concerning what I've said—
The matter I spoke of to you just now—
Will you accept me for a son-in-law?'

This sudden offer so astonished him
That he blushed red, almost deprived of speech;
But managed, while he quaked in every limb,
To utter, 'Sir, my wish is as your wish—
I'd not stand in your way for anything—
You are my beloved lord and governor,
Arrange this matter just as you desire.'

'Yet I'd like', said the marquis quietly,
'To hold a conference—you, she, and I,
Here in this room; and I shall tell you why.
I mean to ask of her if it should be
Her wish to be my wife, and ruled by me.
And all this must be done while you are here,
I will not speak unless you're there to hear.'

While they were talking over, in that room,
Their marriage treaty (about which more later)
Folk gathered in a flock outside their home
Wondering at the diligence and care
With which the girl had cherished her aged father;
It might well be she wondered even more,
She'd never seen a sight like this before.

No wonder that she was amazed to see
So great a visitor come to that place;
Unused to having such a guest as he,
She paled, and all the colour left her face.
But to pursue the tale, and keep it brief,
Here are very words the marquis said
To that true-hearted, kind and loyal maid.

'Griselda,' said he, 'you must understand
It seems good to your father and to me
That you and I should wed; and so we can,
If, as I think, you wish to marry me.
But I must ask these questions first,' said he,
'Because it must be done at once or never.
Do you consent, or wish to think it over?

'I ask if you're prepared with all your heart
To submit to my will, so that I may,
As I think best, bring happiness or hurt
To you, and you'll not murmur, night or day?
That to my "Yes" you do not answer "Nay"
Either by word or frowning countenance?
Swear this, and here I swear to our alliance.'

Bewildered by these words, trembling with awe,
'Sir, I am all unfitted and unworthy',
She answered, 'to accept so great an honour;
Your wish is mine, whatever it may be.
And here I swear I'll never wilfully
Disobey you in thought or deed, even if
(And I am loth to die) it costs my life.'

'My own Griselda, that will do!' cried he,
And with grave countenance went to the door
And stepped outside; and after him came she.
Then he addressed the people who stood there:
'This is my wife,' he said, 'she who stands here.
I ask whoever loves me to love her
And honour her; I have no more to say.'

In order that none of her former gear
Should come inside his house, the marquis bade
The women to undress her then and there.
These ladies of the court were none too glad
To handle garments in which she'd been clad,
But none the less they clothed the lovely girl
From head to foot in fresh new apparel.

They combed her hair, that loose and tumbled lay,
And with their slender fingers set a garland
Upon her head; and next they loaded her
With brooches and with jewels of every kind.
But why make a long tale of her adorning?
They scarcely knew her in her loveliness,
She was transfigured by such magnificence.

Then with a ring brought for that very reason,
The marquis married her, and had her set
Upon a horse, snow-white and gently pacing,
And with no more delay had her escorted,
Helped by a happy crowd who came to meet
And lead her to the palace; thus they spent
The day in revel till the sun's descent.

To hasten on the story, let me say
That to the new-created marchioness
God showed His favour so abundantly
It was impossible that one could guess
That she'd been born and bred a country lass,
And not brought up in an emperor's hall,
But in a hovel or a cattle-stall.

She grew to be so loved and so revered
That people in the place where she was born,
Who from her birth had known her year by year,
Hardly believed it, for they would have sworn
She was no daughter of Janicula,
The old man whom I spoke of earlier;
She seemed to them to be another person.

For though she always had been virtuous,
She had increased so much in excellence,
Rooted in goodness were her qualities;
Herself so modest and so eloquent,
So kind, with so much claim to reverence,
And over people's hearts she had such power,
That all who looked upon her face loved her.

Nor was it only in Saluzzo town
There spread abroad the goodness of her name,
But many another neighbouring region;
If one said well, another said the same:
At length her goodness won so wide a fame
That men and women, old and young together,
Would travel to Saluzzo just to see her.

Thus Walter humbly—not so, royally!—
Wedded with honour and with good fortune,
Lived in God's peace comfortably at home,
And in the outside world his stock stood high;
Since he saw the good that's often hidden by
A humble station, he was held to be
A man of judgement—that's a rarity.

And not only was Griselda adept
In wifely and domestic arts; she could
If need be when the case required it,
Herself help to promote the public good.
There was no grievance, rancour, or discord
In all the land, that she could not compose,
And wisely draw to harmony and peace.

And even when her husband was away,
If any, whether commoner or noble,
Fell out, she'd reconcile their enmity;
Her sayings were so wise and seasonable,
Her judgements so acute and equitable,
That people thought she had been sent from heaven
To save them from all wrongs, and to amend them.

No long time after, she was brought to bed
And gave birth to a daughter; and although
She'd rather it had been a son, how glad
The marquis was, and all the people too;
For though a girl was first to come, they knew
She was not barren, and in time she would
Achieve a male child, in all likelihood.

PART THREE

It happened, as it sometimes does, that while
The child was being suckled, the marquis
Conceived so great a longing to make trial
Of Griselda, to try her steadfastness
And constancy, that he could not resist
This strange impulse to put her to the proof
And scare (needlessly, as God knows) his wife.

For he had put her to the proof before,
And always found her sterling; so what need
To try and test her ever more and more,
Though some applaud, and think that he was shrewd?
But as for me, I think it wrong and bad
For a man to test his wife when it is needless,
And subject her to fright, dismay, and anguish.

The marquis set about it in this way:
One night he came with stern and troubled face
Alone into the chamber where she lay.
'Griselda,' said he, 'you recall the day
I rescued you from poverty and distress,
And raised you to your present high estate—
I think you have not quite forgotten that?

'I'm only saying that I don't suppose
This high position I have placed you in
Makes you at all forgetful how it was
I took you up: when your wretched condition
Held for you little hope of happiness.
And now mark every word I say to you:
There's no one here to hear it but us two.

'For you yourself well know how you came here
Into this house: it's not so long ago;
And though to me you are beloved and dear,
Among my noblemen it is not so.
They're saying that for them it's shame and sorrow
To be in servitude and have to owe
Allegiance to a village girl like you.

'And there's no doubt whatever they have been
Talking like this, and saying things like these,
Particularly since your child was born.
But I desire to live with them in peace
As I have always done. I can't take risks,
I must do for your daughter what is best,
Not as I would, but as my people wish.

'And yet, God knows, all this is hateful to me;
But none the less, I promise to do nothing
Without your knowledge. But I wish', said he,
'To have your acquiescence in this thing.
Now let me see you practising your patience,
As you swore and promised me down in the village
The day on which we two were joined in marriage.'

When she had heard all this, she did not change,
Whether in look, or bearing, or in word;
Remaining undistressed, or so it seemed.
'All lies at your disposal, sir,' she said,
'What you wish shall wholeheartedly be obeyed.
My child and I are yours; and you may kill
Or spare what is your own; do as you will.

'As I pray God on high my soul to save,
Nothing that pleases you can displease me;
Nothing is there that I desire to have
Or fear to lose but you alone,' said she.
'This is my heart's wish, and shall always be,
Which neither time nor death is to erase,
Nor turn my heart to any other place.'

Happy as the marquis was at her reply,
Still he pretended that he was not so;
All grim and gloomy was his air as he
Stepped to the chamber door and turned to go.
Soon afterwards—within an hour or two—
He'd given secret orders to a henchman,
And told him to go to Griselda's room.

A kind of bodyguard, this trusty man,
Whom he had often found reliable
In weighty matters; and such fellows can
Do people's dirty work, and do it well.
The prince knew he was loved and feared by him;
And when he understood his master's will,
Into Griselda's room he softly stole.

'Madam,' said he, 'you must forgive me, though
I do what I must do, in duty bound;
You are too wise and sensible not to know
One cannot well evade a lord's command;
Though it may be lamented, or condemned,
Yet when he wants a thing, folk must obey,
And so must I; that's all that I can say.

'My orders are to take away this child.'
Here he broke off, and seized hold of the infant
With cruel hands, and made as if he would
Slaughter the little child before he went.
Griselda has to suffer and consent,
And like a lamb she sits there meek and still,
And lets the cruel fellow do his will.

Ominous was the repute of this man,
Ominous was his face, his words also,
Ominous the hour in which he came.
As for her little girl, whom she loved so,
She thought he'd murder her right there and then.
Yet none the less she neither sighed nor wept,
But, as her lord desired, acquiesced.

Yet in the end Griselda found her tongue,
And, turning to the fellow, humbly prayed
That, as he was a generous-hearted man,
He'd let her kiss her child before it died.
Upon her breast the little child she laid,
Her face most sad; and began lulling it,
And gave it first a blessing, then a kiss.

And she spoke to it in her gentle voice,
'Farewell, my child, whom I shall never see
Again—but I have signed you with the cross
Of that same Father—blessed may He be!—
Who died for all of us upon a tree.
Thy soul to Him, my baby, I commit,
For you must die because of me tonight.'

I'd say that for a nurse it would have been
Past bearing, such a sight as this to see.
Well might a mother have made outcry then!
And yet so firm and resolute was she,
That she endured all this adversity,
And gently to the bodyguard she said,
'Here is the child. Take back your little maid.

'Now go,' said she, 'do as your master says,
But one thing as a favour I would ask,
Unless my lord should have forbidden it.
Bury this little body in some place
Where neither bird nor beast can get at it.'
But to her request he made no reply;
Picked up the child, and went upon his way.

The henchman, on returning to his master,
Reported in detail, in brief plain words,
What Griselda had said, and her behaviour,
And then he handed over his dear daughter.
It seemed as if the prince felt some remorse,
But none the less held to his purpose still,
As lords do, when they mean to have their will.

He bade his henchman take it secretly.
And gently swathe it round and wrap it up
With all possible care, and tenderly
Carry it in a chest, or lapped in cloth,
And, if he did not want his head cut off,
To let no one know what he meant to do,
Whence he had come, or whither he would go;

He was to take the child to Bologna,
Where his dear sister was still living, who
Was at that time Countess of Panago,
And explain the whole thing, and beg her to
Bring up the child as one of noble blood;
And whose the child was, that she must keep hid
From everyone, no matter what she did.

He went off and performed his master's bidding;
But to the marquis let us now return,
Because he is now busy wondering
If he could ever tell from his wife's bearing,
Or else from any word of hers discern
That she had changed; but he could never find
Her other than still constant, and still kind.

As cheerful, meek, and ready to obey
And to love him, as she was used to be,
Was she to him in every kind of way;
And of her daughter not a word she'd say.
No outward mark of grief or misery
Was to be seen; never would she again
Utter, for any cause, her daughter's name.

PART FOUR

So matters stood, while four years passed away
Before Griselda was again with child;
And she, as God would have it, bore a boy
To Walter—none more comely than this child,
His son and heir; and, when the news was told,
Not only he, but the whole land was glad
At the child's birth, praising and thanking God.

When it was two, and taken from the breast,
The marquis once again felt a desire
To try his wife still further, if he might;
How needlessly was she made to endure
These tests and trials, against all nature!
But there's no holding back these married men
Once they have found a truly patient woman.

'My dear wife,' said he, 'as you know already
—And most especially since our son was born—
My people take our marriage very badly.
Now it is worse than it has ever been;
My soul is pierced through with their mutterings,
The voice of complaint is so keen and sharp
My spirit is half broken, like my heart.

'For now they're saying this: "When Walter's gone,
Then Janicula's family must succeed,
And lord it over us; choice we have none!"
People, be sure, are saying things like these,
And murmurs of this kind I'm bound to heed;
It's notions of that sort I'm always fearing,
Though not openly uttered in my hearing.

'I want, if possible, to live in peace;
Therefore I've made my mind up absolutely,
As I dealt with his sister in the night,
To deal with him, my son, as secretly.
I'm warning you, lest you should suddenly
Break out and go beside yourself with grief;
But over this be patient, I entreat.'

She answered, 'I have said, and always shall,
That I wish nothing, and refuse nothing,
But as you wish. I am not grieved at all,
Though my daughter and my son should both be slain
—That is, at your command, and by your will;
I've had no share nor part in my children
But sickness first; and after, grief and pain.

'You are our master; therefore, with your own
Do as you please; ask no advice of me.
For as I left at home all my clothing
When I first came to you, just so', said she,
'Did I leave my will behind, and liberty,
When I put on your dress; therefore I pray
Do what best pleases you; I shall obey.

'Indeed, had I the prescience to know
Your wish before you told me what it was,
I'd have done whatever you would have me do;
But now I know your will, and what you wish,
You can be sure I shall abide by it;
For if I knew my death would make you happy,
And it would please you, I would gladly die.

'Death itself is as nothing compared with
Your love,' said she. And when the marquis saw
The steadfast, staunch constancy of his wife,
He cast down both his eyes, and wondered how
All this she could so patiently endure;
And so he goes away with gloomy face,
His heart inwardly filled with happiness.

And that grim henchman has, in just the same
Manner—or worse, if a worse way there be—
As he had seized her daughter, seized her son,
Who was so young and beautiful to see;
But none the less so patient was she,
She gave no sign of sorrow or distress,
But blessed her son, first giving it a kiss;

Only she begged the fellow to at least
Bury her little son deep under ground
And so keep safe from every bird and beast
His tender and delicate-looking limbs.
No kind of answer would the man vouchsafe;
As if it mattered nothing he went off,
But brought it to Bologna safe and sound.

The more the marquis pondered it, the more
He wondered at her patience; and if he
Had not known of a certainty before
Griselda loved her children perfectly,
He'd have thought it was from craft or cruelty,
From rancour, or from sheer hard-heartedness,
She endured this with an untroubled face.

But he knew well enough that next to him
She loved her children best in every way.
And now I'd like to ask of all women,
Were these tests not enough? What more could any
Husband devise, however relentless,
To prove her loyalty and steadfastness
To one as inexorable as he?

None the less there are folk of such a kind,
That when they have once determined to take
A certain course, can never change their mind,
But, just as if they'd been bound to a stake,
Hold to their first resolve, and won't retreat.
In just this way the marquis determined
To test his wife, as he had first designed.

He watches for a word or look to show
That she had changed towards him in her heart;
There was no alteration he could see.
Unchanged as ever were her face and heart;
As she grew older, the more true was she,
The more in love, if that were possible,
More devoted and indefatigable.

In the end it seemed as if between those two
There was one will alone; what Walter wished,
That very wish became her wish also.
Thank heaven it all worked out for the best!
She showed, no matter what the tribulation,
A wife should have no wishes of her own,
But that her husband's wish should be her wish.

But Walter's ill repute spread far and wide.
Because he'd married a poor woman, in
The wickedness of his cruel heart, he had
Put secretly to death his two children—
This sort of rumour among folk was common.
No wonder either: for the people heard
No other report than they had been murdered.

And so, whereas his people had before
Loved him, opprobium of his ill fame
Made them begin to hate him more and more.
The name of murderer is a hateful name.
But for no consideration, all the same,
Would he give over his merciless plot;
Testing his wife occupied all his thought.

Now when his daughter was twelve years of age,
He sent messengers to the court of Rome,
Which had been secretly told his real purpose,
Requesting them such documents to contrive
As might be needful for his cruel plan;
And that the Pope, to set folks' minds at rest,
Should bid him to remarry if he wished.

Yes, he requested them to fabricate
A papal bull to say he had permission
To put aside Griselda, his first wife,
As if by special papal dispensation,
To put an end to rancour and dissension
Between his people and him—so ran the bull.
All this was published widely, and in full.

And the ignorant, as is not surprising,
Implicitly believed this rigmarole;
But when they brought to Griselda the tidings,
I can imagine what grief filled her soul!
But, steadfast now as always, she resolved
That she would undergo most patiently,
Poor creature, all Fortune's adversity,

Ever waiting on his pleasure and desires
To whom she had been given, heart and all,
Who was to be her one true earthly solace.
But, not to make of this too long a tale,
The marquis wrote a letter to detail
All that he had in mind, confidentially,
And sent it to Bologna secretly.

To his sister's husband, Earl of Panago,
He wrote, desiring him most earnestly
To bring both children home to Saluzzo,
With an honourable escort, publicly.
But one thing was enjoined absolutely:
That he, no matter who came to enquire,
Was to tell no one whose the children were,

But say, the maiden was about to wed
The Marquis of Saluzzo very soon.
All that the earl was asked to do, he did,
And on the day fixed, he set out upon
The road to Saluzzo with a rich train
Of lords and nobles, to escort the maid
And her young brother riding at her side.

She was attired for the marriage,
This lovely girl, with many a glittering gem;
Her brother, who was seven years of age,
Dressed splendidly as well, in a like fashion;
And thus with magnificence and rejoicing
And shaping towards Saluzzo their journey,
Day after day they rode upon their way.

PART FIVE

Meanwhile, and with his usual ruthlessness,
This marquis, to assay her even more,
Set out to put his wife to the uttermost
Proof of her spirit, to be wholly sure
That she was still as steadfast as before;
And, at a public audience one day,
Roughly addressed these words to Griselda:

'Indeed, Griselda, it's been very pleasant
To have had you for wife—more for your goodness
Constancy, loyalty, and obedience
Than any ancestry of yours, or riches;
But I now realize how true it is
That—as reflection leads me to conclude—
A great position brings great servitude.

'I may not do as any ploughman may.
My people are compelling me to take
Another wife, and clamour day by day;
Also the Pope, their rancour to abate,
I do assure you, gives consent to it;
And to be frank with you, this much I'll say:
My new wife is already on her way.

'So brace yourself to quit at once her place.
As for the dowry that you brought to me,
I waive it as a favour; take it back.
Now go home to your father's house,' said he,
'No one can always have prosperity.
Take my advice, and bear the blows of chance
Or Fortune with a steadfast countenance.'

And yet she answered him with fortitude:
'I knew, and I have always known,' said she,
'There can be no comparison, my lord,
Between your splendour and my poverty;
For these are things nobody can deny.
I never thought I merited at all
To be your wife; nor yet your servant-girl.

'And in this house, where you have made me lady,
I call on God in heaven to witness,
As I hope for Him to comfort me and aid me,
I never played the chatelaine or mistress,
But was a humble servant to your lordship,
And will be always, while I've life and breath,
More than to any other soul on earth.

'That in your kindness you should have so long
Held me in honour, and exalted me
Here, where I was not worthy to belong,
I thank both God and you; to Him I pray
May He reward you! There's no more to say,
And to my father gladly I'll return;
Until I come to die, I'll live with him.

'And there, where I was brought up from a child,
I shall live out my life till I am dead,
A widow, soul and body undefiled.
For since I gave to you my maidenhead
And am your own true wife, may God forbid
The wife of such a prince should ever take
Another man as husband or as mate!

'And as for your new wife, God in His grace
Grant you good fortune and prosperity;
For I will gladly yield to her my place,
In which it was such happiness to be.
For, since it pleases you, my lord,' said she,
'Who once was all my heart's ease, that I go,
Whenever you desire it I shall go.

'As for your offer of such dowry I
First brought to you, I well recall to mind
It was my miserable rags; which I
Would be hard put to it today to find.
O blessed God! how noble and how kind
You seemed, in both your words and looks, to be,
When we were made one on our marriage-day!

'It's truly said—at least I find it true,
For it has proved to be the case with me—
Love grown old is not the same as when it's new;
Indeed, no matter what adversity
I suffer—even if I have to die—
I never shall repent, in word or act,
That once I gave to you all of my heart.

'My lord, you know that in my father's house
Out of my wretched rags you had me stripped,
And in your kindness had me richly dressed;
That to you I brought nothing, before God,
But faith, nakedness, and my maidenhead;
And here again your garments I restore,
Also your wedding ring, for evermore.

'You'll find your other gems quite readily
I can assure you, safe inside your room.
Naked out of my father's house', said she,
'I came, and naked there I must return.
All that you wish I gladly will perform.
And yet I hope it is not in your thought
I should go naked hence, without a smock.

'You could not do so dishonourable a thing
As to let the belly where your children lay
Be seen by all the people, at my going,
Uncovered and all bare; therefore I pray
Let me not walk upon the public way
Naked as a worm! Remember, at one time
I was your wife, though an unworthy one.

'So, in recompense for the maidenhead
I brought with me but cannot take from here,
Permit me to be granted, as reward,
Just such a smock as I was used to wear,
That with it I may hide the womb of her
Who was your wife. And here I say goodbye
To you, my own dear lord, lest I annoy.'

'That smock', said he, 'which you have on your back,
Keep it on; take it when you go away.'
But found this almost more than he could speak,
For pity of her; and left suddenly.
And there she strips herself before the folk,
And in her smock, and nothing else, she goes
Barefoot, bareheaded to her father's house.

The people followed, weeping all the way,
And ever cursing Fortune on the road;
She kept from weeping; both her eyes were dry,
And all this time she did not speak one word.
It was not long before her father heard
The news; and then he cursed the day and hour
That Nature fashioned him a living creature.

For there's no doubt but that the poor old man
Always looked on her marriage with distrust,
And had suspected from the beginning
That, when the prince had satisfied his lust,
He'd soon begin to feel he had disgraced
His rank by having stooped so low; and would
Get rid of her as soon as ever he could.

To meet his daughter out he hurries; for
The noise the people made gave him good warning.
In her old coat he tried to cover her
As best he could, all the while sadly weeping,
But could not get the coat around her, seeing
The cloth was poor, older by many a day
Than it had been upon her wedding-day.

Thus with her father for a certain space
She lived, this paragon of wifely patience,
And neither by her words nor by her face
In public or in private, gave a hint
Of any wrong done to her, or offence;
Nor did she, judging from her countenance,
Ever recall her former high estate.

No wonder: while she was a marchioness
Her soul displayed complete humility,
No pleasure-loving heart, no delicate tastes,
No love of pomp or royal ceremony,
For she was full of patience and of kindness,
Discreet, without pretension, honourable,
And to her husband ever amenable.

Job is remembered for his patience mostly,
A thing the learned love to expatiate on,
Especially as found in men—but really,
Though scholars give but little praise to women,
As far as patience is concerned, there's no man
Can behave as well as women can, or be
One half so true—if so, it's news to me.

PART SIX

At last the Earl of Panago is come
From Bologna. The news spread far and wide,
And all and sundry heard he'd brought with him
A new marchioness, a second bride;
And with such pomp and splendour, that they said
There never had been seen by human eye
A finer sight in all West Lombardy.

The marquis, who had planned all this before
The earl's arrival, sent his messengers
To fetch that poor innocent Griselda;
And she, with humble heart and happy face,
And with no swelling hope within her breast,
Came at his bidding, knelt before his feet,
Greeted him soberly, and with respect.

'Griselda,' said he, 'I'm quite determined
This girl who is about to marry me
Tomorrow must be as royally welcomed
As may be in this house of mine,' said he.
'And all who come are to be entertained,
Seated and served according to degree,
As honourably as I can arrange.

'Of course I have no women capable
Of ordering the rooms as I would like,
And so I would be glad if you were able
To take on all the management of it.
Besides, you are familiar with my tastes.
And never mind your mean and wretched dress,
You'll do your duty at the very least.'

'Not only am I glad, my lord,' said she,
'To do what you desire, it is also
My wish to serve and please as best I may
Until I drop; this will be always so;
No, never, not for either weal or woe,
No, never shall the spirit in my breast
Swerve from its aim, or cease to love you best.'

And saying this, she went about to set
The house in order; there were beds to make,
Tables to lay; she did not spare herself,
Bidding the chambermaids for heaven's sake
Get on with it, and sweep, and scrub, and shake,
While she, the most hardworking of them all,
Prepared the bedrooms and banqueting-hall.

With the two princely children in his train,
The earl, arriving early in the day,
Set people running for a sight of them,
So rich the spectacle and pageantry;
And for the first time folk began to say
That Walter was no fool, and if he wished
To change his wife, it was all for the best.

She was the lovelier, so they all agreed,
And besides, nowhere near Griselda's age;
And fairer fruit might issue from their seed,
More acceptable for their high lineage;
Her brother, too, had such a handsome face
That people were delighted just to look,
And now approved their overlord's conduct.

'O turbulent mob, unstable and always
Faithless and swinging like a weather-vane!
Continually delighting in rumours,
Waxing and waning, changing like the moon,
And always full of clack not worth a damn!
False in your judgement, always to be doubted,
Whoever trusts in you must be an idiot.'

That's what the graver folk of the city
Were saying while the crowd gaped up and down,
For they were pleased, just for the novelty,
To have a new marchioness for their town.
No more, enough! I won't pursue this theme,
But turn to Griselda, and bear witness
To her constancy and industriousness.

She'd her hands full, busy with everything
That to the wedding-feast was relevant.
Not in the least put out by her clothing,
Coarse though it was, and somewhat torn and rent,
To the main gate with cheerful face she went
With other folk to greet the marchioness,
And after that continued with her duties.

And she received his guests with cheerfulness,
So efficiently, each in his degree,
That, far from finding any fault or blemish,
Folk wondered all the more who she might be
Whose wretched rags proclaimed her poverty,
Yet was so accomplished and so polite;
And they all paid due tribute to her tact.

And all this while Griselda never ceased
To praise the young girl, and her brother too,
With all her heart, with sincere kindliness,
So well, that no one might her praise outdo;
But when at last the noble guests withdrew
To sit at table, he began to call
Griselda, who was busy in the hall.

'Griselda,' said he, in a joking way,
'How do you like my new wife and her beauty?'
'Very much indeed, my lord; for, truth to say,
I never saw a lovelier girl than she.
God grant all happiness to her, I pray,'
Said Griselda, 'and I hope He allows
Delight enough to last you all your days.

'But one request I make—a warning too—
That you will never goad with tormenting
This gentle girl, as I have seen you do
With others; for I'd say in her upbringing
She's been more tenderly nursed; and to my thinking
Could not sustain the same adversity
As one both born and bred in poverty.'

And now, when Walter saw her happy face,
Her patience, with no rancour there at all,
However often he had done her mischief,
She stood as firm and steadfast as a wall,
Continuing in innocence through all,
His obdurate heart inclined to take pity
Upon Griselda's wifely constancy.

'My own Griselda, this will do,' said he,
'So be no more afraid, no more distressed;
Your kindness, goodness, and your constancy,
I have put as searchingly to the test
In wealth and want, as woman's ever was.
Dear wife, I'm sure now of your steadfastness.'
With which, he took her in his arms to kiss.

And she, in pure surprise, took no notice;
She did not seem to hear what Walter said,
Till out of her bewilderment she broke,
As if suddenly startled out of sleep.
'You are my wife,' said he, 'by Christ Who died
For us! The only wife I have, or had,
Or ever mean to have, so help me God!

'This is your daughter, whom you had imagined
To be my wife; this boy will certainly
Become my heir, as I have always planned;
He is indeed the child of your body.
I kept them at Bologna secretly;
So take them back; for now you cannot say
Your children have been lost or put away.

'And as for those who've spoken against me,
Let them take note that I have done this deed
Neither from malice nor from cruelty,
But to put to the proof your womanhood,
And not to kill my children—God forbid!
But keep them hid away in secret till
I knew your constancy and strength of will.'

At hearing this, she falls down in a swoon,
Heart-broken in her joy; then, recovering,
She calls both her young children to her bosom
And in her arms, most pitifully weeping,
Enfolds the two of them; tenderly kissing
Like any mother; and, in her embraces,
Her salt tears falling bathe their hair and faces.

What a heart-breaking thing it was to see
Her faint away, and hear her humble voice!
'A thousand thanks to you, my lord,' said she,
'For you have saved for me my children's lives!
Now I don't care if here and now I die;
Since I am loved by you and have your heart,
What matters death, or when my soul departs?

'O my dear children, O my tender young!
Your sorrowing mother always thought that surely
Some horrible animal or cruel hound
Had eaten you; but God in His mercy
And your kind father, have so tenderly
Kept you both safe'—and at that moment she
All suddenly slid senseless to the ground.

And as she fainted she held on so tightly
To the two children still in her embrace,
That it was only with great difficulty
And skill that they at length could extricate
The children. Tears on many a pitying face
Ran down; and the bystanders who were there
Could scarcely bring themselves to stay with her.

Walter comforts her, and her grief abates,
And she gets up, half shamefaced, from her trance;
They all make much of her, until at last
She has regained her poise and countenance.
And Walter tries with so much diligence
To please her, you'd delight to see the pleasure
Between the two, now that they were together.

Then the court ladies, when they saw their chance,
Swept her away with them into a bedroom,
And, stripping off all her rough ragged garments,
They clad her in a glittering golden gown,
Set on her head a richly jewelled crown,
And led her into the banqueting-hall
Where due homage was paid to her by all.

So this unhappy day ends happily,
For every man and woman does his best
To spend the day in feast and revelry,
Till stars begin to sparkle in the east;
And in the eyes of all, it was a feast
More magnificent, costly, and lavish
Than was the celebration of their marriage.

For many a year, in great prosperity,
These two lived on in harmony and peace,
Having seen their daughter marry splendidly
With a rich lord, one of the worthiest
In all of Italy; and Walter kept
Griselda's father with them at his court
In ease and quiet, till his soul departed.

His son succeeded to his heritage
In tranquil peace, after his father's day;
And he was lucky too in his marriage,
Although it's true he did not seek to try
His wife so hard; the world, one can't deny,
Is not so tough now as it used to be;
So listen to what Petrarch has to say:

'This tale has not been told so that wives should
Imitate Griselda in humility;
They'd find it intolerable if they did!
But that everyone, whatever his degree,
Should be as steadfast in adversity
As Griselda.' That's why Petrarch tells
This tale, and in the loftiest of styles.

For if a woman was so patient
To a mere mortal, how much more ought we
Accept what God sends us without complaint,
For it is reasonable, sirs, that He
Should test what He has made; He will not tempt
Those whom He has redeemed, as St James says
In his epistle;* never fear, He tries

His people all the time; and He allows
The biting lashes of adversity
To scourge us for our good, in various ways,
Not just to test the will, for surely He
From the beginning knew our frailty;
Then let us, since His rule is for our good,
Live in virtue and in patient fortitude.

Just one word, gentlemen, before I go:
It would be pretty hard to find, these days,
In any town three Griseldas, or two;
Because, should they be put to such assays,
Their gold's so poor now, made with such alloys
That, though the coin looks good enough to you,
Instead of bending, it will break in two.

So for the sake of the goodwife from Bath—
Whose great authority may the Lord maintain
And that of all her sex; too bad if not!
I'll cheer you up by singing you a song,
For I feel fresh, and in excellent form;
We've had enough of being serious.
Now listen to my song; it goes like this:

Chaucer's Epilogue

Griselda's dead, so is her patience,
And both are deader than a coffin nail;
I warn all husbands in the audience
Not to be too precipitate to assail
The patience of their wives, in hope to find
Griselda's; it is certain they will fail.

You high-born wives, so famous for prudence,
Should you permit humility to nail
Your tongues, or give the scholars evidence
For an even more unimaginable tale
Than Griselda's, so patient and so kind,
Beware lest Chichevache* devour you all!

Take after Echo; she keeps no silence,
Her disposition is antiphonal;
Don't be made fools of by your innocence,
Be on your toes instead, and take control,
And fix this lesson firmly in your mind;
The general good of all shall then prevail.

Superwives, stand up in your own defence!
Each is as huge and strong as a camel.
Then why permit a man to give offence?
You smaller wives, though feeble in battle,
Be fiercer than a tiger or a fiend,
Clack on and on like windmills, I counsel.

Why should you fear, or pay them reverence?
For if your husband armed himself in mail
The cutting arrows of your eloquence
Would pierce his breastplate and his tough ventail.
Take my tip too, and see you make him blind
With jealousy—he'll cower like a quail!

If you be fair, when others are present
Show off your beauty and your apparel!
If you be ugly, use extravagance,
For this will win you friends so you prevail.
Be light and gay as a leaf in the wind,
Leave him to weep and worry, whine and wail!

THE PROLOGUE OF THE MERCHANT'S TALE

'Of weeping, wailing, worrying, and mourning,
I've had more than my share, noon, night, and morning,'
The merchant said, 'like other married folk.
That's how it is, I think; for, no mistake,
I know too well that's how it goes with me.
I have a wife, the worst that there can be,
For even if the fiend were yoked to her,
My wife would be a match for him, I swear.
What use to rehearse each particular
Of her huge malice? She's a thorough tartar.
And there's a very wide, deep difference
Between Griselda's measureless patience
And my own wife's inordinate cruelty.
Were I a free man now, I'm damned if I
Would ever walk into that trap again!
Life's grief and trouble for us married men.
Just try it if you want to, you'll discover
I speak the truth, by St Thomas of India,
For most of us—I don't say all, mind you;
God forbid that it ever should be so!

  'Ah well, good Mister Host, two months, no more,
Have I been married; and yet I could swear,
Even if you cut his heart out with a knife,
No man who's been a lifelong bachelor
Could recount half as much unhappiness
As I could here and now tell of my wife,
And of her diabolic shrewishness.'

  'God bless you, Mister Merchant,' said our host,
'Seeing you're such an expert on the subject,
I beg you earnestly, tell us about it.'

  'Gladly,' he answered, 'but my heart's too sore
To speak of my own sorrow any more.'

THE MERCHANT'S TALE

Once on a time there lived in Lombardy
A noble knight, a native of Pavia,
And he lived there in great felicity

For sixty years a happy bachelor,
And used to take his sexual pleasure in
Whatever women pleased his appetite,
As is the habit of these fools of laymen.
And when this knight had passed his sixtieth year,
Either from senescence or piety
I can't tell which—but such a great desire
Came over him to be a married man,
That night and morning he does all he can
To spy out some young woman he might marry;
Praying to heaven to vouchsafe that he
Might have but one taste of that blissful life
Ever obtaining between man and wife,
And live thereafter in that sacred bond
In which the sexes were by God first joined.
'No other life is worth a bean, be sure:
For marriage is so pleasant and so pure,
Truly, it is an earthly paradise.'
Or so this old knight in his wisdom says.

    And certainly, as sure as God is king,
To take a wife is an excellent thing,
Especially when a man is old and grey;
Then she's the best part of his property.
That's when to take a wife who's young and fair,
On whom he may beget a son and heir,
And live a life of ease and happiness,
While bachelors can only sigh, 'Alas!'
When they, in love, meet with adversity;
For love is nothing more than childish folly.
Indeed, it's fitting that it should be so,
That bachelors should suffer pain and woe:
On shifting sands they build, and they will find
What they think stable to be shifting sand.
They live like any bird or animal
At liberty, and under no control;
Whereas a man who's married to a wife
Must lead a happy and well-ordered life
Under the marriage yoke, securely bound.
Well may his heart with happiness abound,
For who can be more biddable than a wife?

And who's more faithful and more attentive
Than his own mate, to tend him, ill or well?
Come weal or woe, she'll never let him down,
Or tire of loving and of tending him,
Though he lies bedrid till his latest breath.
And yet some learned men say it is not thus,
Of whom the chief is one Theophrastus*—
But what's the odds, should Theophrastus lie?
Said he, 'Don't marry for economy,
Thinking to cut down on the housekeeping:
A faithful servant is more painstaking
When caring for your goods, than your own wife.
For she will claim a half-share during life.
As heaven is my hope, if you fall ill
Your real friends, or some honest servant, will
Take better care of you than she who bides
Her time to lay her hands upon your goods.
And if you take a wife into your household,
You're very likely to end up a cuckold.'
These are the notions, and a hundred worse,
That this man writes—God lay on him a curse!
Pay no attention to such foolery;
A fig for Theophrastus! Now hear me.
    Undoubtedly a wife's the gift of God,
For every other kind of gift, indeed,
—Arable land, rents, commonage, pasture,
Movable property or furniture—
These are the gifts of Fortune, one and all,
And fleeting as a shadow on a wall:
But never fear—for let me tell you plain,
A wife will last, and in your house remain
A good deal longer than you bargained for.
    Marriage is a cardinal sacrament:
I hold him lost, the wifeless bachelor,
Who has to live unhelped and solitary—
Of course I'm not referring to the clergy,
I merely speak of the lay element.
Hear why—it's not for nothing I say this—
Woman is fashioned to be man's helpmeet.
When God almighty had created Adam,

And saw him belly-naked and alone,
Out of His boundless goodness He said then:
'Let us now make a helpmeet for this man,
A creature like himself.' Then He made Eve.
It's evident from this, proof positive,
That woman is for man's help and delight,
His comfort and his earthly paradise.
So biddable and so angelic is she,
How can they help but live in unity?
One flesh they are; and one flesh, so I'd guess,
Has but one heart, come grief or happiness.

A wife! Ah! Save and bless us, St Mary!
How can a man meet with adversity
Who has a wife? I'm sure I couldn't say.
No tongue can tell, no heart can imagine
The happiness that is between the twain!
If he is poor, she helps him in his work,
Cares for his gear, and never wastes a scrap;
And all that pleases him is her delight—
She never once says 'No' when he says 'Yes'.
'Do this,' he says. 'At once, sir,' she replies.
O wedlock, happy state, so dearly loved!
It is so pleasant and so virtuous,
And also so commended and approved!
So if you are a man and not a mouse
It's on your knees you ought to spend your life,
In thanking God for sending you a wife;
Or otherwise pray to the Lord instead
To send a wife to last you till you're dead.
Thenceforth your life is on a secure basis:
You can't go wrong, according to my guess,
If you will only do as your wife says.
Then you can hold your head up unafraid,
So faithful are they, and with that so wise;
And so, if you would imitate the wise,
See that you always do as they advise.

Think of Jacob who, as learned scholars tell,
Followed his mother Rebecca's counsel,
And tied the kid's skin round about his neck,
And won his father's blessing by that trick.

And think of Judith—history relates
That her wise counsel saved the chosen race,
When she killed Holofernes as he slept.

And there's Abigail whose good advice kept
Her husband Nabal from his death when he
Was to be killed; and there's Esther as well,
Who saved the chosen race with wise counsel,
And who saw to it that Mordecai was
Given advancement by Ahasuerus.

There's nothing in existence that ranks higher
Than an obliging wife, says Seneca.

So bear with your wife's tongue, as Cato bids;
She must command; you must put up with it;
Yet, as a favour, sometimes she'll obey.

She'll guard your domestic economy;
And it's no use for you to wail and weep,
If you've no wife to keep house when you're sick.
And here's a word of warning to the wise:
Cherish your wife, even as Christ His church.
For if you love yourself, you love your wife;
No man hates his own flesh; while he's alive
He cossets it; and so here's my advice:
Cherish your wife, or you will never thrive.
Never mind the jokes about them, man and wife
Have chosen the safest and the surest path
—That is to say, for ordinary folk—
Being so united, so knit together,
It's certain that no harm can befall either,
Especially the wife. And therefore he,
This January, the knight of whom I told,
Began to contemplate, as he grew old,
The life of happiness and virtuous quiet
That makes the state of marriage honey-sweet;
Until one day he sent out for his friends
To tell them what it was he had in mind.

He told them, with a grave and serious air,
'My friends, you know that I am old and hoar,
And near the grave—I'm almost at its brink—
God knows, it's of my soul that I must think.
My body I have foolishly expended;

Blessed be God, all that shall be amended!
I mean to make myself a married man
—My mind's made up—with all the speed I can.
I'm asking you to fix me up in marriage
With some young pretty girl of tender age
And quickly too, because I cannot wait;
I'll try to keep a look-out, for my part,
For someone I can wed without delay.
But—seeing that I'm one, while you are many—
You're likelier to find, sooner than I,
Just where it would be best for me to marry.
    'But let me sound a note of warning, friends:
No old wife for me, not by any means!
Not more than twenty years of age, that's flat!
I like my fish mature; not so my meat.
A pike's better', said he, 'than a pikelet;
But tender veal is better than old beef.
I want no woman thirty years of age;
For that's just fodder—bean-straw—winter forage!
And these old widows, as God knows, are up
To as many tricks and dodges as Wade's boat,*
Can stir up so much trouble when they please,
That I could never live with one in peace.
It's different schools that make the expert scholar;
Life's many schools make woman near as clever.
But you can guide a young thing, so I've found,
Just as warm wax is moulded in the hand.
Therefore I tell you plainly, and in brief,
That for that reason I'll have no old wife.
And just suppose it should be my misfortune
Not to take any pleasure in the woman?
I'd have to live a life of adultery
And go straight to the devil when I die.
And not one child on her would I beget:
I'd as soon be eaten up by dogs, as let
A stranger lay hands on my heritage.
Now listen, you: I'm not in my dotage,
I know why one should marry; furthermore,
I know that most who talk of marriage
Know less about it than my servant-boy

About the reasons one should take a wife.
First, if one can't live a continent life,
Then one may, with reverent devotion,
Take on a wife for lawful procreation
Of children, to the glory of God above,
And not for concupiscence or for love.
It's to avoid fornication also,
Each giving satisfaction when it's due;
Or so that each of them may help the other
In trouble, like a sister and a brother,
And live a life of saintly chastity.
But sirs, if you don't mind, that's not for me.
Because, thank God, I think that I can boast
My limbs are capable and vigorous,
Able to do all that a man should do;
And I myself know best what I can do.
Hoar though I am, it's like a tree I feel,
That blooms before the fruit begins to swell;
A blossoming tree is neither dry nor dead.
Nowhere do I feel hoar, save on my head;
My heart and every limb is evergreen
As laurel round the year. Now you have seen
Into my mind, and know what I propose,
I ask for your acquiescence to my wish.'
    Then various folk came out with various
Old tales and anecdotes concerning marriage.
Some condemned it, of course; some gave it praise;
But to sum up: at last, as happens always
With friends in altercation, there arose
A dispute between his brothers. He had two,
Of whom the first was known as Placebo;
If I'm not wrong, Justinus was the other.
    Placebo said, 'Dear January, brother,
You've not the slightest need, my dearest sir,
To seek advice from anybody here,
If it wasn't that you are so sapient
And so informed with consummate prudence,
As to be disinclined to depart from
That proverb handed down by Solomon,
Which is applicable to everyone:

"Do nothing without advice"—that was it—
"And then you will have nothing to regret."
But though for this we have Solomon's word,
My own dear brother, and my dearest lord,
As sure as God's my hope for my soul's peace,
I'd say your own opinion is the best.
For you can take it from me, dearest brother,
As all my life I've been a courtier,
And—though unworthy of it, heaven knows—
High in the estimation of great lords,
I've never had an argument with one.
In fact, I never contradicted them:
I kept in mind, a lord knows more than I.
Whatever he says goes, that's what I say;
So I say what he says, or something like it.
A counsellor would be a perfect idiot
Were he, while serving some great lord of rank,
Ever to dare presume, or even think,
That his ideas were better than his lord's.
No, they're no fools, I promise you, these lords!
And you yourself have shown us here today
Such solid judgement and such piety,
I entirely confirm and ratify
Your judgement, everything that you've been saying.
There's not a man, by God, in the whole town,
Nor in all Italy, could put it better!
And Christ Himself is well pleased with this plan.
Really and truly, sir, it shows great spirit,
In a man who's getting on, this getting married
To a young wife. Upon my soul, it shows
Your heart's in the right place—my word, it does!
Now in this matter act just as you wish,
For when all's said and done, I think that's best.'
    Justinus sat and listened quietly
To Placebo. Then he made this reply:
'Now, my dear brother, as you've had your say,
I ask you to be patient and hear mine.
Among his other maxims, Seneca
Observes one ought to take the greatest care
To whom one gives up property or land.

And if I ought carefully to consider
To whom I give away my goods and gear,
How much the more, then, should I not beware
To whom I yield my body up for ever?
I warn you seriously, it's no child's play,
Picking a wife without due consideration.
One ought to find out first, in my opinion,
If she's discreet, temperate or a drunk,
Or prideful, or in any way a tartar,
A scold, or else a spendthrift; rich or poor;
If she's a virago or termagant.
True, in this world one never does set eyes on
A horse with absolutely flawless action
—The ideal's never found in beast or man—
But it should satisfy us, when all's said,
For a wife to have more good in her than bad;
But finding out all this requires time.
And heaven knows, many's the tear I've shed
In private since I got myself a wife.
Though people may extol the married life
All I have found in it is cost and care
And obligations, of all blessings bare.
And yet, Lord knows, the neighbours round about,
And in particular the womenfolk,
—Droves of them—say I've the most constant wife,
And the most biddable that ever breathed;
But I know best where my shoe pinches me.
Do what you like; for it's all one to me;
You're getting on in years—think seriously
Before you venture upon married life,
Especially with a young and pretty wife.
By the Lord Who made water, earth, and air,
Even the youngest man among us here
Has found that he has quite enough to do
To keep his wife all for himself. Be sure
In less than three years you'll no longer please her,
That is to say, completely satisfy her.
Wives want so much attention paid in bed.
But pray take no offence at what I've said.'
　　'Now then,' said January, 'have you done?

Stuff your Seneca, and stuff your maxims!
I wouldn't give a basketful of greens
For your learned jargon. Wiser folk than you
Commend my plan—what say you, Placebo?'
  'I say', said he, 'that he's a villain
Who hinders matrimony, that's for certain.'
At which, and with no more delay, they rose,
Fully agreed that January should
Be married when he liked, to whom he would.

  Busy conjectures and extravagant fancies
About his marriage blew through January's
Imagination day by day like wind.
Night after night there flitted through his mind
Many a ravishing face and lovely figure.
As one who takes a brightly polished mirror
And sets it in a public market-place
To watch the many figures in that glass
As they go walking past, in the same way
January let his thoughts and inward eye
Rove over the young girls who lived near by.
He didn't know which he would settle for.
For if one of them had a lovely face,
Another would stand high in people's favour
For her benevolence and steadiness,
And so would have secured the people's voice.
And some were well-off, but had a bad name.
None the less, half in earnest, half in game,
He settled upon one of them at last,
And dismissed all the others from his heart,
And chose her on his own authority,
For love is ever blind, and cannot see.
And every night, when he had gone to bed,
He pictured in his heart, and in his head,
Her fresh loveliness, her youth so tender,
Her dainty waist, her arms so long and slender,
Her good breeding, sensible behaviour,
Her woman's ways and dependable nature.
And when he'd made his mind up that he'd get her,
He thought his choice impossible to better.
Having reached this resolution on his own,

He lost all faith in others' acumen.
There was, he felt, no possible objection
Against his choice—such was his delusion.
He sent out for his friends, and urgently
Begged for the pleasure of their company,
To visit him as soon as they could come;
Let them relax—the job, he said, was done,
And he had no more need to gad about:
His choice was fixed upon, his mind made up.

Placebo came, and his friends too, soon after;
And first of all he asked them as a favour
Not to offer arguments of any sort
Against the course he proposed to adopt,
Which course was pleasing to the Lord, said he,
True foundation for his felicity.

There was, he said, a young girl in the town
Whose loveliness had brought her great renown;
Although her station was a humble one,
Her youth and beauty were enough for him.
This girl, he said, he meant to make his wife,
And live in virtuous comfort all his life.
And he thanked God that he might have her wholly,
And no man share in his felicity.
Next, he begged them to help him in his need,
And so shape matters that he would succeed;
For then, said he, his heart would be at ease.
'Then,' said he, 'nothing can go wrong, but for
One thing, which I shall mention now you're here,
A thing that rather sticks in my conscience.

'It's something', said he, 'that I heard long since:
That none are twice permitted perfect rapture—
On earth as well as heaven, that's to say.
For even if you manage to keep away
From all the seven deadly sins, and free
From all the ramifications of that tree,*
Yet there's such absolute felicity,
So much delight and comfort in marriage,
I'm always frightened lest in my old age
I should be leading such a happy life
So comfortable and free from grief and strife,

That I'll have had my heaven here on earth.
Because if the true paradise is bought
With suffering and penance infinite,
How then can I, living in the delight
That all these married men find in their wives,
Enter our Lord's eternal paradise?
That is my fear, and so I ask you both,
Settle the question for me, if you please.'
    At this, disgusted with his foolishness,
Justinus made a derisive reply,
But, not to make too long a tale of it,
Refrained from citing his authorities.
He said, 'If that's the only obstacle,
It may be God will work a miracle
Before you're given the last sacrament,
And in His mercy see that you repent
Of marriage, and of the married life,
In which you say there's neither grief nor strife.
The Lord forbid that He should not have sent
Grace to a married man, that he repent
A good deal oftener than a single man!
And therefore sir—I think it's the best plan—
Never despair: but bear in mind that she
For all you know, may prove your purgatory!
For she may be God's instrument, His whip,
And then, you'll see, your soul is bound to skip
Up swifter than an arrow from a bow
To heaven: where I hope to God you'll know
That there is not, and that there'll never be
In marriage half enough felicity
Ever to stand in your salvation's way
If, as is reasonable, you enjoy
The delights of your wife in moderation,
And don't give too much sexual satisfaction,
And keep, of course, from other kinds of sin.
That's all I have to say; my wit is thin.
Don't worry any more about it, brother,
But let's dismiss the subject, and pass on.
That lady from Bath, if you've followed her,
Has dealt well and succinctly with this matter

Of marriage, and the problems that you face.
And now farewell: God save you through His grace.'

     And saying this, Justinus and his brother
Took leave of January and each other;
And, having seen there was no help for it,
They then, by dint of astute and discreet
Bargaining, ordered matters so that May
(Such was her name) should marry January
With all dispatch, as soon as ever she could.
But it would only waste your time if I
Recounted every document and bond
By which she was enfeoffed of his land,
Or told you all about her rich array;
But in the end the day came when they went
To church to take the holy sacrament.

     Out comes the priest, about his neck the stole,
Bids her to be wise as Rebecca, faithful
As Sara in observing marriage vows;
The customary prayers he recites,
Signs with the cross, and bids God bless their house,
And so makes all secure with holy rites.

     Thus they were married with due ceremony,
And at the banquet May and January
Sat on the dais with the notables,
The palace filled with merriment and joy,
With music and delicious eatables,
The choicest viands of all Italy;
Before them instruments of sweeter tone
Than any music that was ever made
By Orpheus or Theban Amphion;
And, heralding each course, the music played
Louder than Joab's trumpet-blast, more clear
Than Theodamus' horn at Thebes, when
The city was besieged, its crisis near.*
Bacchus poured out the wine on every side;
On every man the goddess Venus smiled,
For January had become her man,
And was about to test his mettle in
A marriage, as he had before while free;
And so, a flaming torch in hand, danced she

Before the bride and all the company.
Believe me, I'd go so far as to say
Hymen, the god of weddings, never saw
In all his life a bridegroom half so gay.
Now hold your tongue, you poet Martian!*
You who wrote about that very merry
Wedding—Philology and Mercury—
And of the songs that all the Muses sang!
Inadequate your pen, also your tongue,
Even to try to tell of such a marriage!
When tender youth is wed to stooping age
The joke's so rich, it's past description—
Just have a go, and see if I am wrong!

    And May—she sat with so charming an air,
She seemed like an enchantment to look on.
Queen Esther never looked with so demure
An eye on Ahasuerus,* I'll be sworn.
I can't describe the half of her beauty
And loveliness, but this much I can say,
Like a clear morning in the month of May,
Brimming with beauty and delight was she.

    Whenever he looked upon her countenance
Old January fell into a trance
Of ravishment, and in his heart began
To bode ill to her and anticipate
How he would hug her in his arms that night
Closer than Paris ever clasped Helen;
And yet he felt compunction when he thought
How he must fall on her that very night.
'Alas for her!' thought he, 'the tender creature!
God grant that you'll be able to endure
My lust for you—it is so sharp and keen!
And more than you'll be able to sustain—
Lord forbid I should do all that I might!
I only wish to God that it were night,
That night would last for ever and a day,
And all these people here had gone away.'
And in the end he did all he felt able,
Short of his own dishonour as an host,
To steer them slyly from the dining-table.

When the right moment came, and they arose,
Then all began to dance and to carouse,
While some ran scattering spices through the house;
All filled with joy and happiness save one,
A squire of the name of Damian,
Who carved at the knight's table every day.
So smitten was he with his lady May,
He was half-demented with the pain of it;
He all but swooned and perished on the spot,
For he was one who had been badly burned
By Venus, dancing past with torch in hand,
And so he took to his bed there and then.
Of him I'll say no more for the time being,
But there I'll leave him, weeping and lamenting,
Till lovely May takes pity on his pain.

O perilous fire, breeding in the bedding!
O household foe, at hand to do one's bidding,
O sneaking servant, smooth domestic hireling,
Snake in the bosom, perilous and sly!
God shield us, one and all, from your acquaintance!
O January, drunken with the joy
Of matrimony, look how Damian,
Damian, your squire and your liegeman born,
Means to bring shame on you, and infamy;
God grant that you perceive your enemy!
For in this world there's no worse plague to bear
Than the enemy at home, who's always there.

Now, having accomplished his daily arc,
No longer in that latitude could the sun
Stay lingering above the horizon.
Night covered with its mantle, coarse and dark,
From end to end the hemisphere of sky.
The merry crowd take leave of January,
Showering delighted thanks on every side,
And back home to their houses gaily ride,
Where they attend to business as they wish,
Or, when they feel it's time, go take their rest.

Soon afterwards, impatient January
Wanted to go to bed; he wouldn't dally.
He swallows clarry, hippocras, vernage,*

And hot spiced wine to fortify his courage;
He'd many an aphrodisiac medicine
Which that damned monk, the wretched Constantine,
Writes about in his book *On Copulation*;*
He drinks the lot up without hesitation.
Then, turning to his bosom friends, says he:
'As soon as you can, for the love of God
Clear all the house—but do it tactfully.'
And they have done this, just as they were bid.
Then a last toast was drunk, the curtains drawn,
The bride was brought to bed, dumb as a stone;
And when the priest had blessed the bridal bed,
Everyone went away and left the room;
And January clasped into his arms
His paradise, his mate, his lovely May,
Petting and soothing her with many a kiss,
Rubbing the bristles of his gritty beard
(Which was like sharkskin, and as sharp as briars;
After his fashion he was freshly shaved)
Against her tender delicate soft face:
'Now I must take some liberties', he says,
'With you, my wife—and upset you perhaps,
Before the time comes when I shall descend.
None the less, consider this,' says he,
'There is no workman of whatever kind
Can do a job both well and in a hurry.
We'll take our time, and do it properly.
It doesn't matter how long we make merry,
We two are linked in holy matrimony:
And blessed be the yoke that we are in,
For nothing that we do can be a sin.
A man can't sin if it's with his own wife,
He cannot hurt himself with his own knife;
For we're permitted by the law to frolic.'
He laboured on till day began to break,
And then he took a sop of bread in wine,
Then sat up straight in bed; and then he sang
Both loud and clear; began to play the goat,
Kissing his wife, as randy as a colt,
As full of chatter as a magpie is.

The slack skin round his neck, O how it shakes
As January sings—or rather, croaks!
God knows what lovely May thought in her heart,
Seeing him sit bolt upright in his shirt
And nightcap, with a neck so shrunk and lean;
She didn't think his antics worth a bean.
At length he said, 'I think I'll go to sleep,
Now day has come, I cannot stay awake.'
And down he laid his head, and slept till nine.
In due course he got up; but lovely May
Kept to her chamber until the fourth day
As bridal custom is—it's for the best,
For every labourer must sometimes rest,
Or otherwise he cannot long endure,
And that is true of every living creature,
Whether of fish or bird or beast or man.

Now I'll return to wretched Damian,
Pining away for love, as you shall hear;
And this is what I'd like to say to him:
I'd say, 'Alas, poor silly Damian,
Now answer me this question if you can:
How will you tell your lady of your woe?
For lovely May is bound to answer No,
And will, if you should speak, give you away.
God help you then! That's all that I can say.'

The lovesick Damian burned with Venus' fire
Until he almost perished with desire.
At last, no longer able to endure
Living like this, he staked all on a venture:
And, secretly borrowing a pencase, wrote
A letter. In it Damian poured out
His grief in form of a complaint or lay,
A poem to his lovely lady May,
And in a silk purse, hung inside his shirt,
He's placed it so that it lies next his heart.

The moon which was, at noon upon the day
That January married lovely May,
Standing in Taurus, had slid to the sign
Of Cancer—May had kept her room so long:*
For among gentlefolk it's customary.

A bride should never dine in company
Until four days—three at the very least—
Have passed; and then she may attend the feast.
On the fourth day—counting from noon to noon—
There in the hall, when the High Mass was done,
Sat January and his lovely May
Who looked as fresh as a bright summer's day.
And it so happened that the good old man
Was prompted to remember Damian,
And exclaimed, 'By the saints! How can it be
Damian's not in attendance upon me?
Is he still sick? How has this come about?'
The squires who were standing at his back
Made his excuses, saying it was illness
Prevented him attending to his duties;
No other cause could have kept him away.

   'I'm sorry to hear that,' said January,
'For he's a first-rate squire, on my word!
It would be a great pity if he died.
He's as capable, discreet, and trustworthy
As any man of his rank known to me,
At that a manly fellow, and a useful,
And just the type that's likely to do well.
But after dinner, as soon as I may,
I'll visit him myself, and so will May,
To give him all the comfort that I can.'
And this speech won applause from everyone
For January's courtesy and kindness
In comforting his squire in his sickness;
It was, they felt, a gentlemanly deed.
'Madam,' said January, 'take good heed
That after dinner, when you've left the hall
To retire with your ladies, that you all
Go up to take a look at Damian
And cheer him up—he is a gentleman—
And tell him I'll be paying him a visit
As soon as I have rested for a bit;
Now don't be long, for here I mean to bide
Till you are back, and sleeping by my side.'
And, having said this, he began to call

A squire, the major-domo of his hall,
To discuss certain things he wanted done.

Attended by her women, lovely May
Held her course straight to where poor Damian lay,
And there beside his bed she sat her down,
To cheer him up as well as she was able.
And so, when Damian saw a favourable
Moment for it, he put, with none the wiser,
And no more sign than a long heavy sigh,
Into her hand the purse that held the letter
In which he had set down all his desire.
And this is what he whispered in her ear:
'Take pity on me—don't give me away!
Should this be known, I am as good as dead.'
This purse within her bosom she has hid,
And off she goes—you'll get no more from me.
But now she has come back to January,
Who was sitting comfortably on his bed.
He took her, kissed and kissed her; laid his head
Against the pillow and was soon asleep.
Then she made pretence that she had to go
Where everybody has to, as you know;
And when she'd read Damian's letter through,
Finally tore it all up into shreds,
And threw it quietly into the jakes.

Whose thoughts were busier than lovely May's?
Down by old January's side she lies,
Until his coughing wakes him from his sleep;
Whereupon he beseeches her to strip
Stark naked, for her clothes got in the way,
And he was looking for a bit of fun,
So, willy-nilly, she had to obey.
But, lest the prudish should be vexed with me,
Just what they did, I do not dare to tell,
Or whether she thought it paradise or hell.
And so I'll leave them to it, till the bell
Rings out for evensong and they must rise.

Now whether it was chance or destiny,
Or nature, or the influence of the stars,
Whether the constellations in the sky

Stood at that moment favourably disposed
For anyone then putting in a plea
To any woman to play Venus' game
(It's said that there's a time for everything)
And win her love, I really cannot say;
Let God, Who knows that all things have a cause,
Be the sole judge, for I will hold my peace.
But the fact is that young and lovely May
Took such a fancy to the sick Damian,
It was impossible to drive away
The thought that she might somehow comfort him.
She thought, 'I shan't care who's upset by this,
That's certain! Here I give him my promise
That of all living things I'll love him best,
Although he should own nothing but a shirt.'
How quickly pity flows in noble hearts!

    Here you may see how great generosity
Moves women when they weigh things carefully.
Some of them are—there are enough of them—
Tyrants with hearts as hard as any stone,
Who would have let him perish there and then
Far sooner than have granted any favour;
Who'd have rejoiced in their cruel pride,
And have cared nothing for the homicide.

    Soft-hearted May, with pity overcome,
With her own hand has written Damian
A letter yielding him her entire heart.
Nothing was lacking but the time and place
Where lovely May might satisfy his lust,
Which will be just as he arranges it.
And when she saw her chance, the lovely May,
Visiting Damian in his room one day,
Under his pillow dexterously thrust
This letter—he can read it if he likes!
She takes his hand and gives it a good squeeze
So secretly that no one notices;
Bids him recover. Then January sent
For May to come to him; and off she went.

    Up rises Damian from his bed next day,
His sickness and despair quite gone away;

He combs and trims and prinks, and all to please
And look attractive in his lady's eyes;
And he attends January as well,
As humble as a hound that's called to heel;
He makes himself so pleasant to them all
(If you've the gift, the thing to have is guile)
That of him they have only good to say,
And in his lady's favour he stands high.
So I'll leave Damian to get on with it,
And for my part I'll go on with my tale.
    Some say that happiness is in delight,
That true felicity is sensual;
So January tried with all his might
To live in such style as befits a knight,
And lead a life of utmost luxury:
His house and all his gear and furnishings
As suited to his rank as are a king's.
Among other of his fine possessions, he
Had built a garden walled about with stone;
There was no prettier garden to be seen:
Beyond a doubt, I honestly suppose
That he who wrote *The Romance of the Rose**
Would find it difficult to depict its charms;
And even—god of gardens though he be—
Priapus might not be competent to tell
The beauty of the garden and its well
That stood under a laurel always green.
Many a time would Pluto and his queen
Proserpina, and all their magic band,
Come and make music, dancing hand in hand
About that well; so people used to say.
    This noble knight—that is, old January—
Took such delight in walking in this garden
He wouldn't trust the key to anyone
Except himself; he carried in his pocket
A silver latchkey to unlock the wicket
—The little garden-gate—at his good pleasure.
And when he wished to pay his wife her due,
He would go thither in the summer weather
With May his wife, and no one but they two.

And all those things which were not done in bed,
He in the garden with advantage did.
And in this manner many a happy day
Old January passed with lovely May.
But earthly happiness comes to an end,
As January found, like other men.
    O sudden Chance! O unstable Fortune!
Full of deceit, like the deceiving scorpion,
Whose head fascinates what it means to sting;
Whose tail is death, and death by poisoning.
O brittle joy! Sweet and cunning venom!
How subtly you can paint, O monstrous Fortune,
Your gifts with all the hues of permanence,
Deluding one and all with that pretence!
Why have you so deceived old January,
After you had befriended him so fully?
For now you have torn from him both his eyes;
Such is his grief, he only wants to die.
    Noble and openhanded January
Amid his pleasure and felicity
Has been struck blind, alas! quite suddenly.
And now he weeps and wails pitifully,
While, to cap all, the fires of jealousy,
The fear his wife might fall in some folly,
So burnt his heart, he felt he'd just as soon
Have someone come and kill the pair of them.
Alive or dead, he couldn't bear the thought
That she might be another's wife, or love;
She ought to live a widow, clothed in black
For ever, solitary as the dove
That lives alone when it has lost its mate.
But, true enough, after a month or so,
His grief began at long last to abate;
Realizing that there was no remedy,
He put up patiently with his mishap,
Except for this: he couldn't help but be
Jealous, with a continual jealousy,
Which jealousy was so outrageous
He wouldn't let his wife go anywhere,
Not in his hall, nor in another's house,

Unless he kept a hand on her always.
And lovely May, because of this, wept often,
For she so dearly loved her Damian
That either she must have her way with him
Or die at once. What could she do but wait
In expectation that her heart would break?

    Upon the other hand, poor Damian
Became the saddest, sorrowfullest man
You ever saw; for neither night nor day
Could he exchange a word with lovely May
About his plans, or hint at them to her,
Without January being there to hear,
For he kept his hand upon her all the time.
Nevertheless, what with writing back and forth,
And secret signals, he knew what she thought,
While she herself knew what he had in mind.

    O January, what would it avail
If you could see as far as ships can sail?
What difference, to be beguiled and blind,
Or be beguiled, and yet have eyes to see?
Just think of Argus with his hundred eyes;
For he, no matter how he peers and pries,
Gets hoodwinked just the same; like, the Lord knows,
So many who are sure it's otherwise.
Best drop this subject; I shall say no more.

    The lovely May, of whom I spoke before,
Took in warm wax an imprint of the key
To the little wicket-gate that January
So often used when entering his garden.
And, knowing what she had in mind, Damian
Secretly forged a copy of that key.
There's no more to be said; but presently
A miracle, connected with that key,
Will come about; you'll hear it if you wait.

    O noble Ovid, what you say is true:
There's no trick, though it cost time and sweat,
That Love won't find and put to use somehow,
As the story of Pyramus goes to show!
Thisbe and he, though watched and guarded well
On every side, came to an understanding

By whispering to each other through a wall—
Now who could have imagined such a thing?
   But to my tale: in the first week of June,
Being egged on by his wife, old January
Took a great fancy to make holiday
With no one but their two selves in the garden.
And so one morning to his wife says he,
'Rise up, my wife, my lady, and my love;
The turtle's voice is heard, O my sweet dove,
Winter is over and gone, with all its rain,
Come forth with thy dove's eyes, O lady mine,
Thou art all fair; thy breasts fairer than wine!
The garden is enclosèd all about;
Come forth, my snow-white bride! do you come out;
Truly, sweet wife, I'm stricken to the heart,
There is no spot in thee that I have found.
Come out, let us make love to one another,
You whom I chose for wife and for my pleasure.'
   Such old and wanton verses he would quote.
She made a sign to Damian that he
Should go in front, with his counterfeit key.
So Damian unlocked the wicket-gate
And quickly slipped inside, in such a way
That nobody could either see or hear it,
And in a bush he crouched down quietly.
   Then January, as blind as a stone,
Took up May's hand in his, and went alone
With her and none but her into the garden.
Smartly he clapped the little wicket to.
   'There's no one here', said he, 'but me and you,
Dear wife, who of all beings I most love;
For by the Lord Who reigns in heaven above,
I'd sooner cut my own throat with a knife
Than do you any hurt, my own true wife!
For the Lord's sake remember how it was
That I chose you—not out of avarice,
But out of love for you, and for love only.
And although I am blind and cannot see,
Be faithful to me, and I'll tell you why.
There are three things that you will gain thereby:

First, love of Christ; secondly, your honour;
Next, my whole estate, castle, town, and tower,
I give to you—draw conveyances up
Just as you please; and, as I hope for bliss,
It shall be done before tomorrow's sunset.
But first let's seal our covenant with a kiss;
And though I may be jealous, blame me not.
I am so bound up with you in my heart,
That when I contemplate your loveliness
And my old age, its unsuitableness,
I cannot bear, though I should die for it,
To be out of your company for a minute,
I love you so; of that you need not doubt.
Now kiss me, my dear wife; let's stroll about.'

    When lovely May had listened to these words
Of January's, gently she answered,
But first of all burst into tears: 'I have
As well as you', said she, 'a soul to save;
Also my honour, and that delicate bud
Of wifely loyalty, the womanhood
Entrusted to your hands when the priest bound
My body to your body; on which ground,
My dearest lord, this shall be my reply
If you don't mind: May the day never dawn
—Or let me die the worst of deaths, I pray—
When I shall do my family so much shame,
Or otherwise bring dishonour on my name,
As to be faithless: for a deed so black,
Have me stripped naked and put into a sack,
And in the nearest river have me drowned.
I am a gentlewoman, and no whore.
Why say such things? but men are evermore
Faithless, and never stop reproaching women.
The only constancy shown by you men
I do believe, is in distrusting us.'

    While speaking, she caught sight of Damian
Crouching behind the bush, and gave a cough;
She signed him with her finger to be off
And climb a tree near by, laden with fruit,
And up he went; indeed, he understood

Her thoughts, and any gesture she might make,
Better than her husband January could;
For she'd explained the whole thing in a letter,
And how he was to go about the matter.
So here I'll leave him sitting in a pear-tree,
And, in the garden, May and January.

Bright was the day, and blue the firmament,
Phoebus was sending down his golden rays
Cheering each bud with his incalescence,
Being at that time in Gemini, I'd say,
And not far from his northern declination
In Cancer, which is Jupiter's exaltation.*
Now it so happened that, this fine bright morning,
There were, upon the far side of the garden,
Pluto, who is king of faery land,
And many a lady with him in the train
Following Proserpina, his wife and queen,
Whom he had ravished from Sicilian
Etna, where in a field she gathered flowers;
You can read the whole tale in Claudian,*
How Pluto fetched her in his grisly car.
As I was saying, this king of faery land
Upon a bench of fresh green turves sat down,
And when he'd done so, thus addressed his queen:

'Dear wife,' said he, 'what no one can gainsay,
And what experience teaches every day,
Are the trickeries women practise upon men.
I could provide a million instances
Of your dishonesty and fickleness.
Richest of the rich, O wisest Solomon,
Most consummate in knowledge and renown,
For anyone with brains and mother-wit,
Your words are worth remembering by heart!
And this is what he says of human goodness:
"One man among a thousand have I found:
A woman among all those have I not found."

'Thus says the king who knows your wickedness.
And I believe the son of Sirach, Jesus,*
Almost never mentions women with respect.
Plague and brimstone light upon your bodies!

Do you not see that honourable knight
Whom his own servant is about to cuckold,
Because he's blind, alas! as well as old?
Look at that lecher perching in the tree!
Now I shall grant a royal boon: that he,
This old, and blind, and honourable knight,
Receive again the faculty of sight
Just when his wife begins her devilry:
Then he'll know all about her harlotry,
To the reproof of her and others too.'

   'You will,' said Proserpina, 'will you now?
Then by my grandsire Saturn's soul I swear
I shall provide her with a perfect answer,
And for her sake, all women ever after,
That, if caught out in any misdemeanour,
With a straight face they'll trot out an explanation,
And bear down those who make the accusation.
For lack of answer none of them shall die.
Though taken in broad daylight, we'll reply,
Put a bold face on it, and vow, and cry,
Recriminate and upbraid cunningly,
And leave you men as ignorant as geese.

   'What do I care for your authorities?
I'm well aware this Jew, this Solomon,
Found fools among us, many more than one,
But although he found no good woman, yet
Plenty of other men there are who've met
Women who're faithful, virtuous, and good.
Witness all those who dwell in Christ's abode,
Who proved with martyrdom their constancy.
You'll find record, in Roman history,
Of many a true and faithful wife also.
Now, sir, don't lose your temper; even though
Solomon said that he found no good woman,
Grasp if you can the meaning of the man:
He meant, no creature can be truly good,
Not man nor woman either, only God.

   'Well then! why in the name of God, the one
True God, make so much of this Solomon?
What if he built a temple, the Lord's house?

What if he were both rich and glorious?
He built a temple to the false gods too.
What more forbidden thing could a man do?
Whitewash him as you will, it is no matter:
He was a lecher and an idolater
Who, in old age, the one true God forsook.
If God had not (as it says in His book)
Spared Solomon for his father's sake, he should
Have lost his kingdom sooner than he would.
For I don't care a rap for what you men
Write about women, vilifying them!
I am a woman, I must speak or burst.
As he has called us spitfires, no good manners
Will stop me speaking ill of one who slanders,
No, I had rather cut my hair off first!'

  'Madam,' said Pluto, 'calm down, I give up!
But as I've sworn an oath to give him back
His sight, my word must stand, I warn you plainly.
As I'm a king, it doesn't do to lie.'

  'And I', said she, 'am Queen of Faerie.
She'll have her answer, that I guarantee!
Let's bandy no more words about the matter,
And I won't contradict you any longer.'

  Now let us turn again to January,
Who's in the garden with his lovely May,
And singing merrier than a popinjay
'I love you best, I love you best of all!'
He wanders up the garden paths until
He's reached that pear-tree where young Damian
Is happily perching overhead among
The branches and the leaves so fresh and green.

  The lovely May, all glowing and bright-eyed,
Began to sigh, and said, 'Oh, my poor side!
No matter what,' said she, 'and come what may,
I must have one of those pears that I see
High up there, or I really think I'll die,
I've such a craving for those small green pears.
Do something, for the love of heaven, sir!
I tell you that a woman in my state
May feel so great a hankering for fruit

That if she doesn't get it, she may die.'
   'Alas!' he cried, 'if only I'd a boy
Who could climb up! Alas! alas!' cried he,
'I am so blind.' 'What matters that?' said she,
'For heaven's sake, if only you'd agree
To clasp both of your arms about that tree
—For I know too well how little you trust me—
I'd easily be able to climb up
If I might set my foot upon your back.'
   'Of course you may,' said he, 'do what you like:
If it would help, you could have my heart's blood.'
So he bent down, and on his back she stood,
And caught hold of a branch, and up she goes!
Now don't be angry with me, ladies, please;
I'm not the sort to beat about the bush,
I'm a rough chap—anyway, Damian
At once yanked up her smock, and in he thrust.
   When Pluto saw this mischief being done,
He gave the old man his sight back again,
And he could see once more as well as ever.
When he could see again, what man was gladder
Than January? but his thoughts were still
Fixed on his wife. He raised his eyes, until
He saw how Damian was dealing with her
Up in the pear-tree, and in such a manner
As may not be expressed, at least politely.
And thereupon he raised a roar and cry
Like a mother when her child is like to die:
'Help! Murder! Stop thief!' he began to cry,
'What are you up to, you big brazen strumpet?'
   'Now, sir, what's wrong with you?' his wife retorted,
'Be reasonable, have a little patience!
I've just been helping you to cure your blindness.
Upon my soul, I'm telling you no lies,
They said the only way to heal your eyes,
The best thing I could do to make you see
Was to tussle with a man up in a tree—
Lord knows I only meant it for the best.'
   'Tussle!' he cried, 'it went in, anyway!
God grant that you both die a shameful death!

He plugged you, as I saw with my own eyes—
Hanged if I didn't.'
                              Said she, 'In that case
The remedy's not working; certainly,
If you could see, you'd never talk like that.
You have some glimmerings, no perfect sight.'

   'I can see', said he, 'as well as ever I could
Out of both eyes, thanks to almighty God:
And, on my word, that's what I thought he did.'

   'You're mazed and dazed, my good sir,' said she.
'This thanks I get for helping you to see!
Alas!' cried she, 'that ever I was so kind!'

   'There, there, my dearest, put it out of mind.
Come down, my life, and if I spoke amiss,
God help me, I am very sorry for it.
But by my father's grave, I really thought
That I'd seen Damian take you, and your smock
Right up against his chest,' said January.

   'Well, sir, you can think what you like,' said she.
'But, sir, a man that wakes up from his sleep
Can't take in everything at once, or see
Things rightly till he's properly awake.
A man who's long been blind, in the same way,
When he recovers sight, won't see as well
At first, as one whose eyesight has been back
A day or two—so, for a little while,
Until your vision's settled, many a sight
May delude or mislead; and so, be careful,
I beg of you; because, by heaven's King,
There's many a man who thinks he's seen a thing
And it's quite different from what he thinks it.
Misunderstand a thing, and you'll misjudge it.'
And saying this, she jumped down from the tree.

   Who is so happy as old January?
He kisses and embraces her again,
And very, very gently strokes her womb,
And leads her home with him into the palace.
Now, gentlemen, I bid you all rejoice:
Thus ends my story of old January;
God bless us, and His mother, virgin Mary!

EPILOGUE TO THE MERCHANT'S TALE

'Now God have mercy on us!' cried our host,
May the Lord keep me from a wife like that!
Just look what stratagems and subtleties
There are in women! Busier than bees
To diddle us poor fellows. On my oath,
They never miss a chance to twist the truth,
That's clear enough from this good merchant's tale.
But I've a wife—I'm sure she's true as steel,
Though in all other respects she's a poor one;
For she's a rattling spitfire with her tongue,
And she has heaps of other faults beside;
Never mind that! Forget it! You know what?
Between ourselves alone let it be said,
I only wish to God I wasn't tied
To her—and I would be a damn fool if
I were to reckon up her every fault,
And because why? It would get back to her,
Told her by someone in this company,
By whom, there really is no need to say,
Since women know the market for such ware!
I've not brains enough, either, to begin
To tell it all; and so my tale is done.'

Fragment V (Group F)

'Squire, come over here, if you don't mind.
Tell us some tale of love—for I'll bound
You know as much of it as any man.'
    'No, sir,' said he, 'but I'll do what I can
With all my heart; I'm not one to rebel
Against your wishes; so I'll tell a tale.
But please excuse me if I tell it badly.
I'll do my best. Now listen to my story.'

THE SQUIRE'S TALE

At Sarai,* in the land of Tartary,
There lived a king who warred continually
With Russia; thus died many a valiant man.
This noble king was known as Cambuscan,*
And in his day was of so great renown
That there was nowhere found, by sea or land,
So excellent a lord in everything.
He lacked no quality that makes a king.
As for the faith in which he had been bred,
He kept, as he had vowed, its laws and creed;
Moreover, he was brave, and rich, and wise,
Lenient, just, equitable always;
True to his word, gentle and honourable,
In character as steadfast as the pole;
Young, strong, and lively; in arms as mettlesome
As any knight bachelor at his court;
Handsome in person, favoured, fortunate,
And always keeping up such regal state
That nowhere was there such another man.
    Now this great king, this Tartar Cambuscan,
Had two sons by Elpheta his wife,
Of whom the eldest was named Algarsyf,

The other son was known as Cambalo.
Cambuscan had a younger daughter too,
The youngest of them all, called Canace.
I can't convey the half of her beauty,
For I have neither tongue nor skill to tell,
Nor would I dare attempt so high a task.
Besides, my English is not equal to it;
You'd need to have a master of rhetoric,
Versed in the art of figurative speech,
To give an idea of her loveliness;
Not being one, I do the best I can.

    And it so happened that when Cambuscan
Had worn for twenty years his diadem,
He had the feast of his nativity,
As had become, I think, his annual custom,
Proclaimed throughout his city of Sarai
The last day of the ides of March that year.*
Phoebus the sun was radiant and clear,
Because he was close to his exaltation
In the face of Mars, and entering its mansion
In Aries, the hot and fiery sign.
Most pleasant was the weather, and benign,
So that the birds, what with the season and
The fresh young greenery and bright sunshine
Sang loudly of their loves; it seemed to them
They'd found a shelter and protection
Against the sword of winter, sharp and cold.

    Now this King Cambuscan of whom I told
Sat in his royal robes, high on his dais,
Crowned with his diadem, in his great palace,
Holding high festival in such splendour
As you'd not see the like of anywhere;
Were I to tell of all there was to see
It would take up all of a summer's day;
But there's no need to detail every course,
Or note the order in which each was served;
Of their exotic soups I'll make no mention,
Their dishes of young heron or roast swan,
For in that country, so old knights tell us,
There are some dishes thought delicious,

Which in this country are thought little of;
But there's no one man who can list the lot.
I won't keep you, the morning's wearing on,
For it leads nowhere, and is waste of time;
I'll go back to the point where I began.

  Now it so happened, after the third course,
And while the king was seated royally
At table, listening to his minstrels play
Before him, singing their melodious songs,
In at the hall door suddenly there burst
A knight astride upon a horse of bronze,
In one hand bearing a great looking-glass,
And wearing on his thumb a golden ring,
While at his side a naked sword was hung;
And up to the high table the knight rode.
In the whole hall not one man spoke a word
For wonder at this knight; but old and young
Are watching him intently, all agog.

  The strange knight who came in so suddenly
And was, but for his head, armed cap-à-pie
In rich accoutrements, now greets them all
In order of their seating in the hall,
King, queen, and lords; and with such deference
In words, in bearing, and in countenance,
That Gawain with his antique courtesy,
Were he to have come back from Faerie,*
Could hardly have improved upon a word.
And then, at the high table, he delivered
In ringing tones the substance of his message
According to the form used in his language,
And not a word or syllable was flawed;
The better to emphasize his story,
He fitted look and gesture to each word,
As is taught those who study oratory.
And though I cannot imitate his style
(No, never could I climb so high a stile!)
I can say what follows is the general gist.
The main points that he made amount to this
—So far as I remember, that's to say:
  'The King of India and Arabia

Salutes you, sir, upon this festive day
With every possible good wish,' said he.
'And he sends you, in honour of your feast,
By me—who stand here wholly at your service—
This horse of bronze, which in a complete day
—In four-and-twenty hours, that's to say—
Can take you where you wish, in wet or dry,
Carry you bodily to any spot
You have a mind to visit, and without
Hurt to yourself at all, through thick and thin;
Or should you wish to fly up in the air
High as an eagle when it wants to soar,
This horse you see will always take you there,
In safety to whatever place you like,
Even if you fall asleep upon its back;
And, at the twisting of this pin, return.
He who made it was up to every trick;
Before completing this experiment
He waited long for the right combination
Of planets, for the luckiest constellation;
He knew all magic seals, and spells that bind.

'This mirror here, which I hold in my hand,
Is of such power, that in it you can see
When any danger or adversity
Is coming to your kingdom, or to you,
And plainly tell who is your friend or foe.

'And furthermore, should any pretty lady
Have set her heart on any kind of man,
If he should cheat, she'll see his treachery,
And his new love, all his duplicity,
So plain and clear that nothing will be hidden.
So, with the start of the sweet summer season,
This mirror here, and this ring that you see,
He has sent to my lady Canace,
Your excellent daughter who is sitting there.

'The power of the ring—if you desire
To know—is this: If she would please to wear
The ring upon her thumb, or place it in
The purse she carries, there's no bird that flies,
But she shall plainly understand its song,

And comprehend its meaning whole and clear,
And answer it again in its own tongue;
And she'll have knowledge of each herb that grows,
And whom it benefits by its properties,
Although his wounds be never so deep and wide.
   'This naked sword, that hangs here at my side,
Is of such power that it will cut and bite
Right through the armour of what man you strike,
Were it as thick as any branching oak;
And anyone who's wounded by the stroke
Shall never heal, until for pity's sake
You rub him with the flat on the same place
Where his hurt is; and then the wound will close.
All this is absolute truth, and no pretence;
Nor will it fail while it is in your hands.'
   Having in this manner ended his account,
Out of the hall the knight rides, and dismounts.
His horse, that gleams as brightly as the sun,
Stands in the courtyard, stockstill as a stone.
Without delay, the knight is shown his room,
And is unarmed, and seated at the feast.
   And then with royal pomp they fetched the gifts,
That is to say, the sword and the mirror,
Which in due course were borne to the high tower
By officers appointed for the purpose;
To Canace herself the ring was brought
With due ceremony where she sat at table.
As for the brazen horse—this is no fable—
It was not to be shifted, as they found,
But stood as if cemented to the ground.
There was no man could budge it from the spot,
Even with the aid of pulley or windlass,
And why? They had no notion how it worked.
And so they had to leave it where it was
Till the knight showed them how the horse was moved,
As, later you shall hear.
                              Great was the crowd
That swarmed about to stare upon this horse
As it stood there, so still and motionless;
It stood as tall, was of such length and breadth,

As well proportioned with regard to strength,
As any horse that's bred in Lombardy;
And yet it was all that a horse should be,
So quick of eye, that one could take it for
A thoroughbred courser from Apulia.
No question but it was, from tail to ear,
Unimprovable by nature or by art
In any way at all; or so they thought.
But all the same, the greatest wonder was
How it could go, when it was made of brass;
It must be fairy magic, they supposed.
But different folk had different ideas:
There were as many theories as heads.
They made a murmur like a swarm of bees,
Making up fanciful hypotheses,
Quoting old poems; and they said it was
Like the winged flying horse called Pegasus,
Or else the horse of treacherous Sinon,
The Greek who brought Troy to destruction,
As you can read in the old romances.
'Fear keeps on nibbling at my heart,' said one,
'I'm certain that it's packed with armed men
Who plan to take and overthrow this city.
Not to look into it would be a pity.'
Another whispered quietly to a friend,
'He's talking through his hat! It's much more like
An illusion of the kind that's worked by magic,
Done by these conjurers at some big feast.'
Thus they talk and squabble, voicing various doubts,
A thing that all ignorant folk are apt
To do, when faced with matters more complex
Than they, in their ignorance, comprehend;
They're always willing to suppose the worst.

   Some of them marvelled at the magic mirror
That had been carried up to the main tower:
How could such things be seen in it? said they.

   Another answered, that it might well be
That there was some quite natural explanation,
That the whole thing was done by combinations
Of angles, cunningly contrived reflections;

And said that there was one like it in Rome.
Vitello, Alhazen, and Aristotle
Were mentioned, for they wrote in their own day
Of curious mirrors and of optical
Perspective glasses, as all know who've heard
Their books read out.*

                        Some wondered at the sword
That could cut and pierce through everything,
And fell to talking of the Mysian King
Telephus, and Achilles' marvellous spear,*
For with it he could either wound or cure,
In the same way as you could with that sword
Of which, and of whose powers, you've just heard.
They spoke of ways of tempering metals,
Which can be done, they said, with chemicals,
And how and when the tempering should be done:
Matters which are unknown to me, for one.

    And then they spoke about Canace's ring:
Of such a miraculous specimen
Of the ringmaker's craft they'd never heard,
Excepting Moses and King Solomon,
Who were reputed masters in that art.*
They talked like this in small groups drawn apart.
But none the less some said how odd it was
To use the ash of ferns for making glass,
When glass does not look like the ash of ferns;
But it's a thing that has been known so long
That it's no cause for argument or wonder.
Some speculate as much on what makes thunder,
The ebb and flood of tides, mist, gossamer,
And everything, until they've found the answer.
And so they gossiped, argued, theorized,
Till from the table King Cambuscan rose.

    Phoebus had left the tenth mansion at noon:
That royal king of beasts, the noble Lion,
With the star Aldiran between his paws
Was still ascending, making it two hours
Past the meridian,* when the Tartar king
Rose from his table on the dais, and
Before him went the minstrels, loudly playing

Till he came to the royal presence-chamber,
Sounding upon their various instruments
What seemed to be a heavenly harmony.
Children of Venus, joyful lovers, dance,
For in Pisces their goddess is set high,
And looks upon them with a friendly eye.

    The noble king is seated on his throne;
Presently the strange knight is brought to him,
And he joins in the dance with Canace.
High spirits of this kind, frolic and fun,
No dull dog can describe; it needs a man
Well versed in love, and practised in love's play,
Some merry party-goer, fresh as May,
Such fun and festivity to portray.

    Now who could tell of the exotic dances,
The lovely faces and the secret glances,
And coverings-up for fear they should be seen
By other eyes, the eyes of jealous men?
No man but Lancelot, and he is dead!
So all this merriment I'll disregard,
And say no more, but leave them to their fun
Till supper, when they all prepare to dine.

    The steward bids them hurry with the wine
And spices; all the while there's music playing.
The ushers and the squires disappear,
And soon the spices and the wine appear.
They eat and drink; and at the end of it
Go to the temple, as is meet and right.
They sup, the service over, by daylight:
No need to tell of everything they ate!
All of us know that at a royal feast
There's lots for everybody, high and low,
Besides more dainties than I'll ever know.
Then after supper the King Cambuscan
His lords and ladies all attending him,
Went out to look upon the brazen horse.

    Never was there such wonder at a horse
Since the great siege of Troy, where there was
Another kind of horse to wonder at!
But in the end Cambuscan asked the knight

What were its magic powers, what could it do?
And begged to be taught how to manage it.

The horse began to frisk and curvet when
The knight laid hand upon its bridle rein.
And he made answer: 'Sir, there's nothing to it.
But, when you want to ride him anywhere,
Just twist this pin that's fixed inside his ear,
Which I will show you when we are alone.
Then you must tell him where you want to go,
Or name the country where you'd like to ride.
And when you reach the place you want to stay,
Bid him descend, and twist another pin,
For this is what controls the whole machine,
And then he will obey you and descend,
And stop there quietly; there's not a man
On earth can drag or carry him from thence.
Or if you wish to bid him go away,
Then twist this pin; he'll vanish in a trice,
Completely disappear from human sight,
But return when you want him, day or night,
Whenever you wish to call him back again;
The moment we're alone, I'll tell you how.
Ride when you like; that's all you have to do.'

When he had been instructed by the knight,
And fully grasped the principle of the thing,
That noble valiant king, filled with delight,
Returned home to make merry as before.
The bridle was borne up into the tower
With his most precious jewels for safekeeping.
As for the horse, it vanished out of sight;
Don't ask me how; anyway, I'm not telling.
And so I'll leave, in happiness and joy,
Cambuscan and his nobles to their feasting
Almost until the dawning of the day.

PART TWO

Nurse and conducer of digestion, Sleep
Came with a wink and warning: drinking deep,
Together with hard work, demands repose;

And so he kissed them with a yawning mouth,
Saying that it was time that they lay down:
Blood dominates from midnight until dawn.*
'Look after blood, it's nature's friend,' said he.
Yawning, they gave him thanks in twos and threes,
And all began retiring to their beds
As Sleep commanded, for they thought it best.

    Their dreams will not be told, at least by me;
Their heads were full of fumes that stupefy
And bring dreams of no consequence or weight.
And so they all, for the most part, slept late
Till nine next morning: all but Canace.
Leading, as women do, a temperate life,
She took leave of her father very early,
And went to bed soon after fall of night.
She didn't want to appear pale and drawn
And out-of-sorts and jaded in the dawn,
And so took her first sleep, and then awoke.
Because her heart had taken such delight
In both the magic ring and magic mirror,
A dozen times Canace changed colour,
And in her sleep, so deep the impression
The mirror made, she saw it in a dream.
Therefore, before the sun began to rise,
Her governess was summoned to her side;
She said she wanted to get up and dress.

    Old crones are nosy: so the governess
Answered at once, and this is what she said:
'Where in the world will you go, madam mistress,
So early, when all people are asleep?'

    'I must get up, I can no longer sleep,'
Said Canace, 'I want to walk about.'

    Her governess summons a great retinue
Of women—up they get, some ten or twelve;
Up rises lovely Canace herself,
Rosy and bright as the new-risen sun
When it has climbed four degrees in the Ram,
And it was just past six when she was dressed.
She set out walking at an easy pace,
Clad lightly, as was consonant with freedom

In walking, and the sweet and pleasant season;
With only half a dozen in her train,
She wanders down an alley in the park.

    Though from the ground a vapoury mist emerged
Making the sun seem roseate and huge,
Nevertheless so lovely was the scene
It delighted all their hearts; what with the spring,
And the fine weather and the early dawn,
And all the little birds that she heard sing.
For in a flash she understood their meaning,
Just from their song, and all that they were thinking.

    The nub of any tale—the why it's told—
If delayed until the interest has cooled
After one's listened a long while for it,
Savours the less, the longer it's spun out,
In ratio to the tale's prolixity;
And for that reason, so it seems to me,
It's high time I myself came to the point,
So I'll cut short this walk of Canace's.

    Within a withered tree, as white as chalk,
As Canace was delighting in her walk,
There perched a falcon, which began to cry,
Until the whole wood echoed her sad cry.
And she had beat herself so pitilessly
With both her wings, that the red blood ran down
The whole length of the tree; and ever again
She would cry out and shriek, and with her beak
Stab at herself; and so loud was her shriek,
That there's no tiger, nor no cruel beast,
No animal that lives in wood or forest,
But would have wept, supposing it could weep.
If I were able properly to picture
A falcon, then no man alive would ever
Hear of another half so beautiful
In plumage or nobility of form,
And in all other attributes as well!
A peregrine falcon she appeared to be,
From some far land; and every now and then
As she perched there, for loss of blood she'd swoon,
Till she had all but fallen from the tree.

As the king's lovely daughter, Canace,
Had on her finger the magical ring
By which she could understand everything
That any bird might say in its own tongue,
And answer it in its own tongue again,
She understood all that the falcon said;
And for pity of it almost dropped down dead.
Fast as she can she hastens to the tree,
And looks up at the falcon, filled with pity;
And then held out her lap, for she could tell
That from its branch the bird was bound to fall
When next it swooned away for loss of blood.
Watching a long while there, Canace stood,
But in the end made up her mind to speak,
As you will hear. Thus she addressed the hawk:
   'What is the cause, if you're allowed to tell,
That racks you so with the fierce pangs of hell?'
Thus Canace, to the hawk overhead.
'Is it for grief at death, or loss of love?
For these are the two things, as I believe,
Most apt to cause a noble heart to grieve,
Since other griefs are not worth speaking of.
For you are taking vengeance on yourself,
And that's clear proof that either fear or fury
Must be the cause of your self-cruelty;
No one is hunting you, that I can see.
For the love of God, take pity on yourself.
Or what can be your help? Never before
Have I seen a bird or animal anywhere
Misuse and bruise itself so pitifully.
It kills me to look on such agony,
I feel for you so great a compassion!
Come down from that tree, for God's love come down,
And, as I am true daughter of a king,
If I find out the real cause of your sorrow,
I will, if it should lie within my power,
Put matters right before the day is over,
I swear to you by the great God of nature!
And I'll be able to find herbs in plenty
With which to cure your wounds, and heal them quickly.'

The falcon shrieked more piteously than ever
And, falling suddenly to earth, lay there
Swooning in a dead faint, still as a stone.
And so Canace laid her in her lap
Until the bird recovered from her swoon,
When, having wakened from her fainting-fit,
In her hawk-language she began to speak:
'That pity soon repairs to noble hearts
Which feel the sharp pangs of another's smart
As if they were their own, is daily proved
As much in one's experience as in books,
As anyone can see; for noble hearts
Display in noble deeds their nobleness.
My lovely Canace, you feel compassion
As I can plainly tell, for my affliction,
Because of the true womanly kindliness
That Nature has implanted in your heart.
And with no hope of any betterment,
But only to obey your kind request,
That others may take warning by my case
Just as a beaten dog will teach a lion,*
To that end only, for no other reason,
And while I have the time and breathing-space,
Before I go, I'll pour out all my sorrow.'
    And ever, while the one told of her grief,
The other wept as if she'd turn to water,
Till in the end the falcon bade her cease,
And with a sigh began her story thus:
    'Black was the day that I was born! Brought up,
Fostered and fed in a grey marble rock,
So tenderly that nothing troubled me,
I had no notion what adversity
Might mean, till I was able to take wing
And soar into the sky, high under heaven.
There was a tercelet falcon lived near by,
Who seemed a well-spring of nobility;
Though full of perfidious treachery,
It was so cloaked in quiet modesty,
With such a show of truth and honesty,
Such wish to please, such dancing attendance,

Who could have guessed that it was all pretence,
So deep in grain he dyed his false colours!
Just as a snake hides itself under flowers
To bide its opportunity to sting,
Just so this hypocrite, love's paragon,
Proffers homage and gallant courtesies,
Keeping up an appearance of devotion
Such as accords with honourable love.
As with a tomb, all's perfection above,
But under is a corpse, as we all know;
Such was this hypocrite, in sun or snow;
And in this way he pursued his intent,
—Only the devil understood what he meant—
He wept so long, so long he lamented,
Year after year pretending to pay court,
Till my too tender and too foolish heart,
All innocent of his consummate guile,
And fearing he might die—or so I thought—
Believing all his oaths and promises,
Granted him love, upon this condition:
That come what might, my honour and good name
Should always be preserved inviolate
Both in the public eye, and in private;
That's to say, as to one deserving them,
I gave to him my soul, and all my heart,
But God knows, and he knows, not otherwise!
And I took his for mine, and for all time.
But there's a saying, very old and true,
That honest men and thieves don't think alike:
So when he saw that things had gone so far,
And that I'd granted him my entire love
Upon such terms as I have told you of,
And yielded him my faithful heart as freely
As he swore he had given his to me—
Why then, this tiger, full of double-dealing,
With humble devotion and deep reverence kneeling,
So like a noble lover in his seeming,
So ravished—as it would appear—for joy,
Not even Jason, nor Paris of Troy,
—Jason? Not he, nor any other man

Since Lamech, who was the first man of all
To love two women, as old authors tell,
Not any man since the first man was born,
Could imitate a twenty thousandth part
Of his cunning in sophistry and deceit,
Nor have been worthy to unlatch his shoe
When it came to double-talk and outward show,
Or so give thanks as he gave thanks to me!
His manner and his ways were heaven to see,
What woman could resist! So exquisitely
Turned out, and so well groomed and combed was he,
As polished in his talk as in appearance!
I so loved him for his obligingness,
And for the truth I thought was in his heart,
Were anything to cause him the least hurt,
However little, and I knew of it,
I seemed to feel death tearing at my heart.
And in short, matters went as far as this:
My will became the instrument of his.
That is to say, my will obeyed his will
In all things, as far as is reasonable
Within the bounds of decorum and honour.
No, never had I one so dear, or dearer,
Than he, God knows! nor ever shall again.

   'So it went on a year or two, or longer,
When I supposed nothing of him but good,
But in the event this is how things stood:
He had to go away, as fate decreed,
And leave the country I was living in.
That it was grief to me, you need not question:
It cannot be described; but I will say
The pain of death was thus made known to me,
I felt such grief that he could not remain.
And so the day came when he said goodbye,
And with such sadness that I really thought
He felt as much unhappiness as I,
When I heard him speak and saw his change of hue.
But none the less I thought him to be true,
And that he would indeed come back again
Within a little while. As happens often,

Reasons of honour made it necessary
That he should go; and since it had to be,
I made a virtue of necessity,
And took it well. I hid my grief from him
As best I might, and took him by the hand,
And said this to him, swearing by St John:
"See, I am wholly yours; be you to me
As I to you have been, and aye shall be."
What he replied, there's no need to rehearse.
Who could speak better than he, or act worse?
All that fine talk—and look at what he did!
"If you dine with the devil, then you'll need
A good long spoon"—or so I have heard said.
At last he had to set out on his way,
And when it suited his purpose to halt,
He had this saying well in mind, I'm sure:
"All things, returning to their own true nature
Rejoice"—I think that that's what people say.
Men have a natural love of novelty
Like birds that are kept in captivity:
You care for them, and feed them night and day,
And line the cage with straw as soft as silk,
And give them sugar, honey, bread, and milk,
But just as soon as the cage-door is up,
Their feet will kick and overturn the cup;
Off to the woods they go, to feed on worms,
A change of diet has for them such charms!
They've such an inborn love of something new
As neither birth nor breeding may subdue.
     'So was it with this tercelet, alas!
Though nobly born, lively and debonair,
Handsome to look on, modest, generous,
He saw a vulgar kite upon the wing,
And of a sudden felt a love so strong,
Clean gone was all the love he had for me;
And that is how my lover broke his faith.
So now he is the lover of this kite,
And I'm forsaken, with no remedy.'
And saying this, the falcon gave a shriek,
And straightway fainted in Canace's breast.

Great was the sorrow for the hawk's misfortune
Felt by Canace, and by all her women;
They could not think how they might cheer her up.
But Canace took the bird home in her lap,
And gently bandaged up the places where
She'd hurt herself in tearing with her beak.
Now all that Canace can do is dig
Herbs from the ground to make fresh salves from rare
Delicately coloured plants, with which to cure
The hawk. She busied herself day and night,
Did all she could for it with all her might,
And built a cage to place beside her bed,
And covered it with cloth of blue velvet
—Blue standing for the faith that's found in women.
The outside of the cage was painted green,
With pictures of unfaithful birds, such as
Owls and tercelet falcons and titmice;
And beside these were painted, in derision,
Scolding magpies all crying shame upon them.

　　Nursing her hawk, I'll leave Canace there,
And for the moment I shall say no more
About her ring, till I come to explain
Just how the falcon won her love again,
Repentant—for the story tells us so—
Through intercession of that Cambalo,
Son of King Cambuscan, of whom I spoke.
But from now on I'll proceed to relate
Adventures, perils, and desperate battles,
And marvels and unheard-of miracles.

　　First I shall tell you of King Cambuscan
Who took so many cities in his time,
And after that I'll speak of Algarsyf,
And how he won Theodora for his wife,
The hazards he endured, from which he was
Delivered by the magic horse of brass;
Then of the other Cambalo I'll speak,
Who fought with the two brothers in the lists
For Canace, whom in the end he won.
And where I left off, there I shall begin.

PART THREE

Apollo whirls his chariot so high,
Till in the house of cunning Mercury—*

Cetera desunt

*Here follows what the Franklin said to the Squire, and what
the Host said to the Franklin*

'My word, Squire, you've come well out of it,
Most nobly too! And I commend your wit,'
The franklin said, 'considering your youth.
You speak so feelingly, I've only praise!
If you ask me, there's nobody present
Likely to be your match in eloquence,
That's if you live! God send you best of luck,
More power to your elbow from henceforth!
It gives me great delight to hear you talk.
I have a son, and by the living God,
Even though you were to hand me on the spot
An acreage worth twenty pounds a year,
I tell you that I'd rather that he were
A man of sense like you! For what's the good
Of property if you don't use your head?
I've ticked him off before, and shall again,
For he's got no inclination to learn;
All he does is dice, and lose all he has.
He'd rather talk with some low serving-lad
Than with a gentleman from whom he could
Learn true good breeding, how to be polite—'
    'A fig for your good breeding!' cried our host.
'What's all this, Franklin? Sir, for heaven's sake,
You know quite well that each of you has got
To tell at least a tale or two, or break
His promise—'
                    'I am quite aware of that,'
The franklin said. 'Don't take offence, I beg,
If I've got just a word or two to say
To this young man.'

                              '—Now get on with your story,
And not another word!'
                              'I shall, and gladly.
Mister Host,' said he, 'I promise to obey
Just as you wish. Now hear what I've to say.
I'll not be crossing you in any way,
So far as my wit serves! Pray heaven above
That my tale gives you pleasure! Then I'll know
For certain sure that it is good enough.'

THE PROLOGUE OF THE FRANKLIN'S TALE

In their own day those noble old Bretons
Made ballads of all kinds of happenings,
Rhymed in the original Breton tongue;
Ballads, romances, which were either sung
Accompanied by musical instruments,
Or read for pleasure. I have in remembrance
One I'll be pleased to tell, as best I can.
    But, gentlemen, as I'm a plain, blunt man,
Before beginning I must first beseech
That you excuse my homely style and speech.
I never studied rhetoric, that's certain;
And so the things I say are bare and plain.
I never made of Parnassus my pillow,
Or studied Marcus Tullius Cicero.
Colours of rhetoric*—I pass them by;
The colours that are used for paint and dye,
Or grow in fields, those colours I can see.
Colours of speech are too far-fetched for me;
They're something I've no feeling for at all.
But if you like, then you shall hear my tale.

THE FRANKLIN'S TALE

In Armorica—that is, Brittany—
There was a knight who loved and served a lady
And did his absolute best in her service;
Many a labour and great enterprise

He undertook before she could be won.
For none more lovely walked beneath the sun,
And yet so noble was her ancestry
He barely mustered the temerity
To tell her of his longing and distress.
But she at last, for his deservingness,
And most of all his mild subservience,
Felt such compassion for his sufferings
That in the end she secretly agreed
To take him for her husband and her lord,
The kind of lordship men have over wives.
And that they both might lead happier lives,
He swore upon his honour as a knight
That never in his life, by day or night,
Was he to exercise his authority
Against her wish, or to show jealousy,
But follow her in all things, and obey,
As any lover ought to with his lady;
Though for appearance' sake, master in name,
Lest, as a husband, he be put to shame.

She thanked him, and with all humility
Answered: 'Sir, since in your magnanimity
You offer me so free and loose a rein,
God forbid that through any fault of mine
We should be parted by discord or strife;
Sir, I will be your humble, faithful wife,
I promise you, until my breath shall cease.'
Thus they both lived in harmony and peace.

For, sirs, there's one thing I can safely say:
Friend has to yield to friend, lover to lover,
If they would long keep company together:
Love won't be shackled by authority.
Enter authority—what happens then?
Love claps his wings, and farewell! he is gone.
Love is a thing as any spirit free.
Women, by nature, wish for liberty,
Not to be treated like some underling;
And so do men, unless I'm much mistaken.
In love, whoever's the most patient lover
Is bound to have advantage of the other.

A sovereign virtue, patience surely is,
For, as the scholars say, it vanquishes
Where harshness cannot win. You cannot chide
Or take umbrage at every hasty word.
Learn to put up with it, for otherwise
You'll have to, whether you want to or no.
There's nobody on earth who doesn't do
Or say the wrong thing sometimes, that's for sure.
Anger, sickness, influence of the stars,
Drink, grief, a change of mood, so often cause
A man to do or say what he'll regret.
You can't retaliate for every slight,
Those with self-control must use moderation
According to circumstance and occasion.
And so that they might live in harmony,
That good and sensible knight has promised her
Forbearance, and she's promised faithfully
That he shall find no lack of it in her.

Here is a modest, sensible accord:
Thus she accepts her servant and her lord,
Servant in love, and lord in marriage,
From thenceforth both a master and a slave.
A slave? No, set in mastery above,
Since he has both his lady and his love,
His lady indeed, but his wife also,
According to the law of love. And so,
Having attained to this felicity,
He takes his wife home to her own country,
Not far from Penmarch,* where his dwelling is,
And there he lives in perfect happiness.

Who but a married man could tell the ease,
The joy, the comfort and the happiness
That is between a husband and his wife?
A year or more they led this pleasant life,
Until the knight that I am speaking of—
Arveragus of Caerrud was his name—
Began to make preparations to live
In England, which was also called Britain,
A year or two, and seek renown in arms,
For his whole heart was set upon such things;

And there he lived two years, so the book says.
  Now I'll stop talking of Arveragus,
And speak instead of Dorigen his wife,
Who loved her husband more than her own life.
For his absence she weeps; she weeps and sighs,
As noble ladies do, when they so please.
She mourns and loses sleep; wails, fasts, and cries;
And longing for his presence so torments her
The whole wide world seems meaningless to her.
Then all her friends, who saw her heavy mood,
Comforted her in every way they could.
They exhort her, they tell her night and day
She's on the way to kill herself, alas!
If she goes on; and all for no real cause.
All possible consolations in this case
They give, and busy themselves diligently
To free her from her heavy melancholy.

  You all know that in the due course of time
If you continue scratching on a stone,
Little by little some image thereon
Will be engraven. Thus her friends went on
Comforting her so long, till in the end
She, with the help of hope and common sense,
Received the impress of their consolation,
Which loosened at long last her heavy sorrow:
She could not have endured such grief for ever.

  Moreover, during this unhappiness,
Letters came to her from Arveragus,
To say that he was well, would soon return;
For otherwise her heart must have been broken.

  When her companions saw her grief abate,
They begged her on their knees, for heaven's sake
To come and walk with them and drive away
Her dark imaginings and melancholy.
And finally she granted that request,
For she could plainly see it would be best.

  Now as her castle stood hard by the sea,
She'd often walk there in the company
Of friends, upon a cliff high up, and spy
The many ships and barges sailing by

Upon their courses, going where they pleased;
But this was part and parcel of her grief,
For to herself she would so often say,
'Will no ship of the many that I see
Bring home to me my husband? Then my heart
Would heal, delivered from this bitter hurt.'

    At other times she would sit there and think,
And cast her glances downwards from its brink,
But when she saw the black forbidding rocks,
Terror would seize her heart until it shook
So she could scarcely keep upon her feet,
But would sit down upon the grass, and gaze
With sadness at the sea; and then she'd say,
Sorrowfully, with many a heavy sigh:

    'Eternal Lord! Thou Who foreknowest all,
And guidest thus the world with sure control,
Thou makest nothing, so men say, in vain.
But, Lord, these rocks, so hostile, black, and grim,
Which rather seem the work of a foul chaos
Than any creation of a God so perfect,
So omniscient, so unchangeable;
Why hast Thou created so irrational
A work, which neither south, north, west, nor east
Benefits either man or bird or beast;
Good for nothing that I know of but confusion.
Seest Thou not, Lord, how they are men's destruction?
The bodies of a hundred thousand men
These rocks have killed, though none remember them.
Of Thy work, mankind is so fair a part,
That in Thine Own image Thou madest it;
Then it seemed that Thou hadst great charity
Towards mankind—but how, then, can it be
That Thou hast made means to destroy it—things
That do no good, but are injurious?
The scholars will say what they like, I know,
And prove, in logic, all is for the best
By means of arguments I cannot follow.
But may the same God Who made winds to blow
Preserve my husband! Such is my conclusion,
For to the learned I leave all disputation.

Yet would to God above that all those black
Rocks had been sunk in Hades for his sake!
Those rocks are murdering my heart with fear.'
Thus would she speak, with her eyes full of tears.

Her friends realized that roaming by the sea
Was not a source of pleasure, but dismay,
So looked for her amusement somewhere else,
Escorting her by rivers, pools, and wells,
Likewise in other delectable places;
They danced, they played at backgammon and chess.

And so one fine day, early in the morning,
It chanced they all went to a nearby garden,
Where they had made provision for supplies
Of food and drink and other necessaries,
There to amuse themselves the livelong day.
It was the morning of the sixth of May,
And May had painted with her gentle showers
The garden, filling it with leaves and flowers;
All by the art of man so skilfully
Laid out, that in very truth this garden
Was unmatched in its marvellous beauty
Unless by Paradise itself, or Eden.
The fragrance of its flowers, their fresh sight,
Would lighten any heart that ever was
Unless too great a sickness, grief too harsh,
Were to weigh down and hold it in distress,
So filled was it with beauty and delight.
And after dinner, they began to dance,
Also to sing—save only Dorigen,
Who never ceased to mourn and to lament
Because she could not see him at the dance,
Who was her husband and her lover too.
None the less there was nothing she could do,
So for a little time she had to stay,
And hope to let her sorrow pass away.

Now at this dance, in front of Dorigen
Among the other men there danced a squire:
Handsomer he, gayer in his array,
So I would judge, than is the month of May.
He sang and danced better than any man

Who ever lived on earth since time began.
Were I to try to tell what he was like,
I'd say he was the handsomest man alive,
Young, strong, and talented, and rich and wise,
And popular and well-thought-of besides.
To cut it short, the truth is that he'd been
Two years and more in love with Dorigen
Without her knowing it. This gallant squire
Servant to Venus (Aurelius was his name)
Had loved her more than any living creature,
But never dared to tell her of his pain.
He suffered inward torment without measure,
Was in despair; not one word dared he say;
But sometimes in his songs he would betray
His passion in a general lamentation:
He'd sing, 'I love, and am not loved again'.
Around this theme he composed many lays,
Songs, lyrics, roundels, complaints, virelays,
Saying his grief was more than he dared tell,
How he pined as a Fury pines in Hell,
How he must die (he sang) as Echo did,
Who feared to tell Narcissus of her grief.
He didn't have the hardihood to betray
His love for her in any other way,
Except perhaps, that sometimes, at a dance
Where young folk meet for courting and romance,
It may well be he looked upon her face
Entreatingly, as if beseeching kindness;
But she was unaware of what he meant.
But none the less, before they parted thence,
As Aurelius was Dorigen's neighbour,
A man of reputation and of honour,
And she had known him a long time before,
It chanced they fell in talk. Aurelius
Nearer and nearer drew to his purpose,
Then, when he judged the time was ripe, spoke thus:
    'Madam, by God Who made the world,' said he,
'If I'd but known that it would make you happy,
Would that the day that your Arveragus
Went over the sea, that I, Aurelius,

Had gone where I'd not ever again return:
For I know too well that my devotion's vain,
That my one reward is a breaking heart.
Madam, have pity on my cruel hurt,
With one word you can either kill or cure.
Would to God that I were buried at your feet!
I have no time now to say any more.
Have pity on me, or I die, my sweet!'

    She turned and looked upon Aurelius:
'What are you saying? Is this what you want?
I never before suspected what you meant.
But now, Aurelius, I know your intent,
By that same God Who gave me breath and life,
I shall never ever be a faithless wife
Either in word or deed, if I can help it!
I shall be his to whom I have been knit.
Take that for final answer, as from me.'
And then, a moment later, jokingly:

    'Aurelius,' she went on, 'by God above!
Even yet I might consent to be your love,
Since I see you lament so pitifully.
The day you clear the length of Brittany
Of all the rocks upon it, stone by stone,
So that no ship that sails upon the sea
Can be obstructed on its way by them,
I say, when you have swept the coast so clean
Of rocks that not a stone is to be seen,
Then I will love you more than any man.
Here's my word on it, so far as in me lies.'

    'Have you no hope to offer otherwise?'

    'No, by the Lord that made me!' she replies,
'For I know that it can never come to pass.
Let all such follies slip out of your heart.
What pleasure can a man get out of life
From making love to someone else's wife,
Who can possess her body when he likes?'

    At this Aurelius was filled with grief.
With heavy heart, and many heavy sighs,
'An impossibility, madam!' he replies,
'I must die a horrible, unlooked-for death.'

Without another word he turned from her.
Then all her other friends came crowding in,
And they began to wander up and down
The garden walks; and being unaware
Of what had passed, soon started to renew
Their revels till the bright sun lost its hue,
The horizon having reft away its light
(This is as much to say that it was night),
When they went joyful and contented home:
All but poor Aurelius, he alone.
To his own house he went with heavy heart.
He sees there's nothing for him now but death.
It seemed to him he felt his heart grow cold.
On his bare knees he fell, with hands upheld
To heaven above, and in his frenzy made
A prayer; half out of his wits with grief,
And without knowing what it was he said,
He prayed with breaking heart, and thus began
His lament to the gods; first to the sun:
  'Phoebus Apollo, Lord and governor
Of every plant and tree and herb and flower,
Who gives, according to your declination
And lodging in the zodiac, low or high,
To each of them its time and its due season,
Cast a compassionate, merciful eye
On poor Aurelius, who is all but lost.
See, Lord, innocent as I am, my lady
Decrees my death, unless you should take pity
Upon my dying heart, in your goodness.
I know, Lord Phoebus, that if you so wish,
Next to my lady you can help me best.
Now I pray you allow me to explain
What help I need, and how it may be given.
  'Your blessed sister, radiant Lucina,*
Queen and paramount goddess of the sea,
(Though Neptune has the godship of ocean,
Yet Lucina is empress over him)
—Lord Phoebus, as you know that her desire
Is to be lit and lightened at your fire,
Wherefore she follows you with eagerness,

Just so the sea is drawn by its nature
To follow her, because she is goddess
Of sea, of every river, every brook;
And so, Lord Phoebus, this is what I ask
—Perform this miracle, or break my heart!—
When you, the sun, are next in opposition
(Which will be the sign of Leo, the Lion)
Will you pray her so great a tide to bring
That by at least five fathoms it must drown
Armorican Brittany's highest rock;
And for two years let this great flood remain.
Then to my lady I can safely say,
"Now keep your promise; for the rocks are gone."
'Lord Phoebus, work this miracle for me.
Beg her to go no faster than you do;
I say, beseech your sister not to go
Faster, for two years, on her course than you.
And then she will be always at the full,
So that the spring-tide is continual.*
But if she will not vouchsafe to grant me
My dearest sovereign lady in this way,
Beseech her to sink every rock deep down
Into her own dark region underground
Where Pluto has his home; or never I
Shall have my lady. Barefoot I will go
To Delphi, Lord, your temple there to seek.
Lord Phoebus, see the tears upon my cheek!
Take pity, have compassion on my pain!'
And saying this, he fell down in a swoon,
And for a long time lay there as if dead.

  His brother, who knew of his sufferings,
Picked him up and carried him to his bed.
In torment and despair, distress of mind,
There I shall let that wretched creature lie,
And choose, for all I care, to live or die.

  Arveragus, that flower of chivalry,
Is come home safe and sound and crowned with glory,
And many another noble knight with him.
Ah, you are happy now, O Dorigen!
You have your lusty husband in your arms,

Your gallant knight and valiant man-at-arms,
Who loves you as the very breath of life.
Nor is he given to imagining
That any spoke of love to her, his wife,
While he was gone; of that he had no fear.
But, paying no attention to such things,
He dances, jousts, and makes life gay for her;
And so I leave them in their happiness:
Now I will tell of sick Aurelius.

    Two years and more in torment and distress
He lay, this miserable Aurelius,
Before he could set foot upon the ground;
And all this while no other comfort found
Save in his brother, a savant who knew
The whole affair, and all his sufferings too;
He dared not breathe, you can be very sure,
A word of it to any other creature.
He hid it in his breast more secretly
Than Pamphilus his love for Galatea.*
Seen from without, his breast appeared unscarred,
Yet ever in his heart lodged the sharp barb;
And surgeons know it's hazardous to treat
A wound that's only healed on the surface,
If you can't reach the barb, or get at it.
But for him, secretly, his brother wept;
Until at last it came to his remembrance
That while he was at Orleans in France
Where the young students, who are all on fire
To read about the occult arts, will pry
In every nook and cranny there to learn
Recondite skills and sciences if they can;
He recollected that it chanced one day
While studying at Orleans, that he saw
A book about white magic, that his comrade
(Though there to learn a very different trade,
And at that time a bachelor of law)
Left hid inside his desk; this volume had
Much to say about magical operations
Touching the eight-and-twenty different mansions
Belonging to the moon,* and such nonsense

As isn't worth a fly, not in our times;
For Holy Church will not allow chimeras
Like these, which are against our creed, to harm us.
And when this book came to his remembrance,
Such joy was his, his heart began to dance;
And to himself under his breath he said,
'My brother very shortly will be cured,
For I am sure that there are sciences
By which phantasmas and appearances
Can be produced, like those created by
Expert conjurers; often I've heard say
That they, at feasts, have made the sea come in
With a boat on it rowing up and down
Inside a hall. Sometimes there seems to come
The semblance of a grim and grisly lion,
Sometimes blossoming flowers on a mead,
Sometimes a vine, with grapes both white and red,
Sometimes a castle built of mortared stone;
And when they please, suddenly like a dream
They vanish, as it seems, from all men's sight.

   'So I conclude that if I only might
Find at Orleans some old companion
Who knows about these mansions of the moon,
Or of some other higher magic, then
My brother might possess his love through him.
By phantasmas a magician could make
It seem to all men's eyes that every rock
That blackens Brittany were swept away,
And ships were sailing up and down the sea
Along the coast; and then, if this endured
A week or two, my brother would be cured;
For Dorigen would have to keep her word,
Or otherwise be put to shame at least.'

   Why should I make a longer tale of this?
To his brother lying in his bed he came,
And so encouraged and exhorted him
To go to Orleans, that without delay
He got up and set off upon his way,
Hoping to be released from misery.

   When they had almost come to the city,

Not more than half a mile from it they met
A youthful scholar strolling by himself.
He greeted them politely in Latin,
And then he said a most surprising thing:
'I know', said he, 'the reason for your coming.'
And then, before they'd gone another step,
He told them all that they had in their minds.

    The Breton scholar asked after the friends
That he had known there in the days of old;
But all of them were dead now, he was told,
And when he heard this, he broke down and wept.

    Aurelius now alighted from his horse
And went with the magician to his house,
Where they were made comfortable and at home.
No lack of delicacies to delight them!
In all his life, he thought, he'd never seen
A home as well appointed as this one.

    Before they supped, the magician made appear
Forests and parklands full of running deer,
Among them harts with antlers towering high,
The biggest ever seen with human eye;
Aurelius saw a hundred killed by hounds,
While others bled from cruel arrow-wounds.
After the deer had vanished, next he saw
Falconers by the banks of a fine river
With hawks, and with the heron they had killed.

    Next, he saw knights at joust upon a field,
And after that the magus, to enhance
His pleasure, showed his lady in a dance
In which it seemed that he was dancing too.
When the deviser of this magic show
Thought it was time, he clapped his hands together,
And farewell! all our entertainment's over.
And yet they never stirred from out the house
While they were watching the whole marvellous
Display, but sat together quietly
In the workroom that was his library,
With not another soul there but those three.

    And now the magician called for his squire
And said, 'Is supper ready? I declare

It's an hour since I told you to prepare
Our supper, when these gentlemen and I
Came to the study where my books are kept.'

   Answered the squire, 'Sir, just when you like.
It's ready, even should you want it now.'
'Then let us go and eat, that would be best.
For sometimes even lovers need a rest.'

   Supper over, and they fell to bargaining
What the magician's reward should be
For removing every rock in Brittany,
And from the Gironde to the mouth of Seine.

   First he held off, and swore by God above
Less than a thousand pounds he wouldn't have,
Nor was he keen to do it for that sum.

   But Aurelius cheerfully answered him,
'A fig for that! For what's a thousand pounds?
It's the whole wide world, which they say is round,
I'd give to you, if I were lord of it.
And so, as we're agreed, the bargain's struck,
And you'll be paid in full, upon my oath.
But see that no forgetfulness or sloth
On your part keeps us here beyond tomorrow.'

   'No,' he replied, 'I give my word of honour.'

   Then in good time Aurelius went to bed
And spent almost the entire night in sleep,
His sad heart finding respite from distress
After his tiring day and hope of bliss.

   Next morning, just so soon as it was day,
They took the nearest road to Brittany.
Aurelius, and with him the magician,
Alighted safely at their destination.
And this was, say the books, as I remember,
The cold and frosty season of December.

   The ageing sun, dull copper in colour,
That in the heat of summer earlier
Had gleamed with glittering rays of burnished gold,
Is now descended into Capricorn,*
And there, I think, his beams but palely shine.
How have the bitter frosts, with sleet and rain,
Destroyed the green in every garden yard!

Janus sits by the fire with double beard,
He's drinking wine out of his great ox-horn,
And set before him is the tusked boar's head.
'Sing Noel!' is the cry of every man.

    Aurelius, in every way he can,
Welcomes the magus as an honoured guest,
And then beseeches him to do his best
To free him from his cruel pain; or he'd
Cut his own heart to pieces with a sword.

    That cunning magus pitied him so much,
He made, as far as possible, all haste.
Diligently he watches for the right
And favourable hour, day and night,
For the commencement of the operation—
That is, the setting up of a deception,
Some magic trick or some hallucination
—I'm not much versed in astrologic jargon—
Till she, and everyone, would think and say
That not one rock was left in Brittany,
Or else that they had all sunk under ground.
At length the favourable hour was found
For the performance of his wretched tricks
And heathen, diabolic wickedness.
His Toledan tables were set up,
Newly corrected and brought up to date,*
With tables to calculate planetary
Anni collecti, anni expansi;
Nothing was lacking: tables of data,
His astrolabes and arcs and other gear,
Centres and tables of proportions
By which he calculated his equations.
By the eighth sphere, and its precession,
He knew exactly how far Alnath moved
From the head of the fixed Aries above,
Which is in the ninth sphere, as we suppose;
And how expertly he'd worked out all this!

    When he had found the moon's first position
He computed the rest by proportion,
And could predict the rising of the moon,
And in which planetary face or term

Of the zodiac, and all the rest of it;
He was then sure of the appropriate
Lunar position for his enterprise;
He also knew the other ceremonies
Needed for such phantasmas and wickedness
As heathens used to practise in those days.
Therefore the magus made no more delays
But through his magic, for a week or two,
Made it seem all the rocks had gone away.

Aurelius, who was still in suspense
Whether he'd win his love or miss his chance,
Was waiting for this miracle night and day.
When he realized all obstacles had gone,
That all the rocks had vanished, every one,
At once he fell down at the magus' feet
Saying, 'I, poor sorrowful Aurelius,
Give thanks to you and to my lady Venus
Who rescued me from misery and grief.'
And then he set off to the temple where
He knew he would be sure of seeing her,
His lady Dorigen. When his chance came,
He with a tremulous heart and humble air
Greeted his sovereign lady then and there:
'My own true love!'—thus the unhappy man—
'Whom I most fear and love, and whom alone
Of all the world I least wish to displease,
Were it not that I suffer such distress
For you that I must perish at your feet
This minute, nothing would make me repeat
How miserable and forlorn I am!
But indeed I must either die or speak—
You kill me, for no fault, with keenest pain.
But though you have no pity for my death,
Reflect before you go back on your oath—
Think better of it, by the Lord above;
Relent, before you kill me for my love.
Madam, you know you gave your troth and plight
—Not that I would claim anything as of right
Of you, my sovereign lady; rather ask
A favour—yet in that garden, in that place

Remember what the promise was you made
When in my hand you pledged to me your word
To love me best—God knows that's what you said,
Even if I be unworthy of your love.
Madam, all that I say is more to save
Your honour here and now, than my own life.
For I have done as you commanded me,
If you would but vouchsafe to go and see.
Do as you like; remember what you said;
For you will find me here, alive or dead;
It's up to you whether I live or die,
But this I know, the rocks have gone away.'

     He took his leave; and dumbstruck there she stood,
Her whole face drained of every drop of blood.
She'd never thought to fall in such a trap.
'Alas that this should ever be!' she said,
'I never dreamt the possibility
That such a monstrous thing could ever be.
It is against the processes of nature.'
And home she goes, a sorrowful creature,
So full of dismay she can scarcely move.
All the next day or two she weeps and grieves,
And often swoons; it's pitiful to see.
But she would not tell anybody why,
For Arveragus was gone out of town.
With pale and downcast countenance she began
To commune with herself and make her moan:

     'Fortune,' she cried, 'against you I complain,
Who have trapped me, all unknowing, in your chain,
From which there's nothing able to succour
Or help me to escape, except dishonour
Or death—one of these two I'll have to choose.
But none the less I would far rather lose
My life than give my body up to shame,
Know myself faithless, or lose my good name,
And surely by my death I would be freed.
And have not many a noble wife and maid
Cut short their own lives before now, alas!
Chosen to die rather than to transgress?
     'Indeed they have—these stories bear witness.

'When the Thirty Tyrants, full of viciousness,
Had Phidon killed in Athens at a feast,
They had his daughters placed under arrest
And brought stark naked in front of them, to feed
Their filthy pleasure; and they made them dance
Upon the pavement in their father's blood—
God rain on them misfortune and mischance!
And so these wretched virgins, filled with dread,
Rather than surrender their maidenhood
Ran off and threw themselves into a well.
And there they drowned themselves, as old books tell.

'Also those people in Messenia brought
From Sparta fifty virgins for their lust:
There was not one of the whole company
That was not killed; they willingly chose to die
Rather than give up their virginity;
Which being so, why should I fear to die?
Think of the tyrant Aristoclides
That lusted for the virgin Stymphalis,
Who, when her father had been killed one night,
Ran to Diana's temple, and clasped tight
The image of the goddess with both hands,
And would not leave it; none could part her hands,
Or wrest them from the image of the goddess,
Till she was killed there in that very place.

'It seems to me, if virgins scorn so much
To be polluted by men's filthy lust,
A wife ought rather kill herself than be
Defiled. And what about Hasdrubal's wife
Doing away, at Carthage, with her life?
For when she saw the Romans win the town,
She picked up all her children and jumped down
Into the fire, and rather chose to die
Than be dishonoured by the enemy.
Did not poor Lucrece kill herself in Rome
Soon after she'd been ravished by Tarquin,
Only because she thought it would be shame
To live on after losing her good name?
The seven virgins of Miletus all
Killed themselves in despair, rather than be

Raped, violated by those men from Gaul.
There are a thousand stories I could tell
As I suppose, all touching on this theme.
For example, when Abradates was slain,
His loved wife killed herself; let her blood run
In Abradates' gaping wounds, and said:
"If I can help it, no man will pollute
My body at least!"

        'And now why should I add
More instances, seeing so many have
Killed themselves rather than be violated?
For me, all things considered, it were best
To kill myself, than to be thus defiled.
I shall be faithful to Arveragus,
Or kill myself in one way or another,
As did Demotion's beloved daughter,
Rather than be defiled.

          'How piteous
And sad it is to read, O Scedacus,
How your two daughters died, who killed themselves
For a like reason! As pitiful, or more,
As when, rather than yield to Nicanor,
That Theban virgin chose to kill herself.
Another Theban virgin did the same:
Violated by a Macedonian,
Her death redeemed the maidenhood she lost.
What shall I say of Niceratus' wife,
Who, being in like case, took her own life?
How true was Alcibiades' love, who died
Rather than leave his body unburied!
Think what a wife Alcestis was,' said she.
'And what says Homer of Penelope?
For all Greece knows about her chastity.
It is recorded of Laodamia
That when Protesilaus fell at Troy,
After his death she would no longer live.
The same is true of noble Portia:
Without Brutus she could no longer breathe,
She'd given him the heart from out her breast.
Artemisia's perfect fidelity

Is honoured everywhere in heathendom.
Queen Teuta! O your wifely chastity
Serves as a mirror for all married women.
And I can say the same of Bilia,
Of Rhodogune, and of Valeria.'*

Thus Dorigen lamented day by day,
All the while making up her mind to die.
But none the less, on the third evening
That noble knight, Arveragus, came home.
And when he asked what she was weeping for
So bitterly, she only wept the more.
She cried, 'I wish I never had been born!
'I've said this— this I've promised—' she began,
And told him everything, just as you've heard;
There's no need to go over it again.
The husband then in friendly tones answered
As I'll relate, with a good-humoured face:
'Is there anything else, Dorigen, but this?'

'No!' cried she, 'No! God help me if there is!
This is too much, even if it be God's will!'

'Now, wife,' said he, 'let sleeping dogs lie still,
For perhaps all may yet be well today.
But you shall keep your word, I swear you shall!
As I pray God have mercy upon me,
The love that I bear to you is so great
I'd rather stick a dagger through my heart
Than have you fail your promise or break faith.
Honour's the dearest thing in a man's keeping.'
But when he had said this, he burst out weeping,
And said, 'I forbid you, on pain of death,
Ever at all, while you have life and breath,
To speak to anyone of this affair.
My grief, as best I can, I will endure;
I shall not go about with a long face,
Lest any suspect you, or even guess.'

And then he called a squire and a maid.
'Go at once with Dorigen,' he said,
'Take her with you to such-and-such a place.'
They took their leave and left; but as it was,
They'd no idea why she was going there,

For he'd no wish to tell of the affair.

    Perhaps a lot of you will think that he's
A fool to put his wife in pawn like this.
But hear the tale before you cry out on her.
She may have better luck than you suppose:
First hear the tale, then sit in judgement on her.

    Now the young squire—Aurelius I mean—
Who was so much in love with Dorigen,
Happened by accident to come upon
His lady in the middle of the town
Right in the very busiest street, and bound
Towards the garden, as her promise was;
And he was going to the garden too,
For he kept close watch when he saw her go
Out of her house to any kind of place.
However it came about, thus they met.
He greeted her, with joy in his face,
And asked where she was going. As if half mad,
'Straight to the garden, as my husband bade,
To keep my promise there, alas, alas!'

    Then he began to ponder upon this,
And in his heart he felt great compassion
For Dorigen, and for her affliction,
And for that noble knight Arveragus,
Who had commanded her to keep her promise,
So loath was he his wife should break her faith;
And all of this so touched his heart with ruth
That, looking at the thing from every side,
He thought it better to deny himself
His pleasure, than perform so mean a deed
In the face of so much generous nobleness;
And so he turned to her and briefly said,

    'Madam, say to your lord Arveragus
That as I perceive his great courtesy
To you, and also see your great distress,
And that he'd choose being shamed (a thing too sad)
Rather than to allow you break your word
To me, I'd sooner bear unending sorrow
Than part the love that is between you two.
Madam, I now remit into your hand

As cancelled, every pledge and every bond
That you have ever made me up to now,
That you have ever made since you were born.
My word on it, I never shall reprove
Or reproach you for any promise made
Or given me; and here I take my leave,
As of the very truest and best wife
That ever yet I knew in my whole life.'
But let all wives beware of promises,
At least let them remember Dorigen!
Thus there's no doubt but that a squire can
Behave as courteously as any knight.

On her bare knees she thanked him, then went back
Home to her husband; and she told him all
That you have heard me say; be sure of this,
He was more pleased at it than I can tell.
And now why should I linger out the tale?

Arveragus and Dorigen his wife
Lived all their days in perfect happiness;
No discord came between them ever again.
He cherished her as if she were a queen,
And she for ever after remained true.
That's all you'll get from me about those two!

Aurelius, who had spent his all, began
To curse the day and hour he was born.
'Alas!' he said. 'Alas that I should owe
A thousand pounds' weight of the purest gold
To this astrologer! What shall I do?
Turn beggar, for my heritage must be sold?
So far as I can see I'm ruined now.
I can't stay here and disgrace all my kin,
Unless I can get better terms from him.
I'll try him out, however: I shall say
I'll pay him every year, on a set day,
And I'll thank him for his obligingness,
And see to it that I don't fail my promise.'

With heavy heart he visited his coffer,
And brought his gold to the astrologer
To the value of five hundred pounds, I'd guess,
Entreating him to have the graciousness

To give him time enough to pay the rest.
'Master,' he said, 'I think that I can boast
I've never failed to keep my word as yet.
And I will guarantee to quit my debt
Come what may, even if it means I must
Go begging, and in nothing but my shirt.
But if you'd grant—upon security—
A respite of two years, or even three,
I'd be all right; otherwise I must sell
My heritage and what I have, that's all.'

The astrologer, when he had heard him out,
Answered him gravely thus: 'Have I not kept
My word to you, the bargain that we made?'
    'Yes, well and truly,' said he, 'yes, indeed.'
    'Have you not had the lady you desired?'
    'No,' he answered, 'no.' And sadly sighed.
    'Why so? Tell me the reason if you can.'
At which Aurelius at once began
To tell him all: I don't see any need
To repeat here what you've already heard.
    'So noble-hearted is Arveragus,
He'd sooner die in sorrow and distress
Than that his wife should ever break her word.'
He also told him of Dorigen's grief,
How loath she was to be a faithless wife,
And how, that day, she'd have far rather died.
She'd made her promise in all innocence;
She'd never heard tell of hallucinations.
'This made me feel for her so great a pity:
As freely, then, as he sent her to me,
As freely did I send her back to him.
That's all about it, there's no more to say.'
    'My dear friend,' answered the astrologer,
'Each behaved like a gentleman to the other.
You are a squire, and he is a knight:
But God forbid, with all His blessed might,
A scholar should not act the gentleman
As well as any of you—that's for certain!
    'Sir, I remit you of your thousand pounds
As much as if you'd just sprung from the ground

And never had set eyes on me before.
I will not take a penny from you, sir;
Not for my labour, nor for all my skill.
You've paid my keep, generously and well.
It is enough: so goodbye, and good day!'
He mounted on his horse, and went his way.
Gentlemen, I'll ask a question now:
Which of them was most generous, think you?
Now tell me before you go any further.
I have no more to tell: my tale is over.

Fragment VI (Group C)

THE DOCTOR OF MEDICINE'S TALE

Once on a time, says Titus Livius,*
There lived a knight known as Virginius,
A man of much distinction and more worth,
As rich in friends as he was great in wealth.
  Now this knight had a daughter by his wife;
He had no other children all his life.
A lovely girl, excelling in beauty,
There was no woman lovelier than she;
For Nature had, with sovereign diligence,
So moulded her surpassing excellence
As if she were to say, 'Thus I, Nature,
Can, when I want to, fashion and colour
A living being—who can match my work?
Not Pygmalion, were he to carve and cut,
Hammer and forge and paint away for ever!
Apelles and Zeuxis would lose their labour*
Whether they carve, or forge, or paint, or hammer,
Did they presume to imitate what I make.
For He, the prime Creator of all,
Appointed me His vicar-general
To fashion and to colour every creature
Exactly as I please; each living thing
Under the waxing or the waning moon
Is my concern, and I will ask nothing
For all my work: we are in full accord;
I made her for the honour of my Lord,
Just as I do with all my other creatures,
Whatever be their form or their colours.'
I think that that's what Nature meant to say.
  And only fourteen years of age was she,
This girl in whom Nature took such delight.
For just as she can paint the lily white,
Or roses red, she painted hues like these

Upon the fine limbs of this noble creature
Before her birth, and just where they should be;
To her thick tresses Phoebus gave a dye
Like to the colour of his burnished rays.
If she was perfect in her loveliness,
She was a thousand times more virtuous.
In her no quality at all was lacking
That merits praise, at least by the discerning.
She was as chaste in soul as in body:
Therefore she blossomed in virginity
With perfect modesty and temperance,
With perfect self-denial and patience,
With sobriety of manner and of dress.
Discreet she was, when called on to reply;
Although she was, I dare say, wise as Pallas,
Her talk was simple, plain, and womanly,
Because she used no grandiloquent phrases
To appear learned; for, when speaking, she
Put on no airs; all that she said declaring
With every word her virtue and good breeding.
Modest she was, with a maid's modesty,
Steadfast in heart; and she was ever busy
To keep herself from idleness and sloth.
Bacchus was never master of her mouth,
For venery is fired by wine and youth,
Like oil or fat when cast upon the flames.
Moved by her native virtue, unconstrained,
She'd often pretend illness to avoid
All company where there was likelihood
Of indecorum, as there is in places
Where people go to flirt: feasts, dances, parties.
Such things make children brazen and mature
Too early on, which is the great danger,
As we all know; and so it's always been.
For she can learn assurance later on,
And all too soon, when she's a woman grown.
   Now all you duennas of mature age,
In charge of daughters of the gentlefolk,
Pray hear me out, and do not take umbrage.
Remember how you came to get the job—

It's one of two things: either you have kept
Your chastity, or else were frail and fell,
And, as you know the old game pretty well,
Have given up such naughtiness for good;
See to it therefore that you never slacken,
For Jesus' sake, in teaching virtue to them.

A deerstealer who has forsworn his taste
For his old trade, can keep a forest best,
Makes the best gamekeeper of any man.
Now guard them well, for if you will, you can.
See to it that you never wink at vice,
Lest you be damned for wicked connivance;
All those who do are traitors to their trust.
Now mark what I shall tell you, and note this:
Of all betrayals, the most pestilent
Is the betrayal of an innocence.

You who are fathers, and you mothers too,
If you have children, whether one or more,
Do not forget, while they are in your care,
That you must answer for their supervision;
Take care you do not lead them to destruction
By the example of your way of living,
Or else because you do not punish them;
For if it should so happen that they perish,
I dare say you will pay most dearly for it.
Watched by a lazy shepherd and a careless,
Many's the lamb the wolf has torn to pieces.
But for the nonce one parable is enough;
I must resume my tale where I left off.

The maid I'm speaking of governed herself
So well, she'd no need of a governess;
Her life was like a book where girls might read
Every good word and every virtuous deed
Becoming to a maid; so warm-hearted
And prudent, that her fame spread far and wide
Both for her beauty and her kindly heart;
Throughout the land all lovers of the good
Would sing her praises, save the envious
Who always grieve at others' happiness,
And always joy at others' misfortune

(This point is noted by St Augustine).
    Well, one day this girl chanced to go to town,
Visiting the temple with her mother
As young girls do; it was the custom there.
Now there was then a justice in that town,
The judge and governor of the whole region.
It happened that his glance fell on this maid
As she came by the spot where the judge stood;
So struck by her was he, his heart and mood
Changed in a moment, captured by her beauty;
And to himself he muttered quietly,
'I'm going to have that girl, no matter what!'
    At this the devil slipped into his heart,
And in a trice had shown to him a ruse
By which she might be won to his purpose.
Not bribery, he felt, nor violence
Would work for him, since she was rich in friends,
Her virtue so established. It was clear
He never could win her to his desire,
Nor ever force her into carnal sin.
And so he, after much deliberation,
Sent for a hanger-on of his in town,
A bold and crafty rascal known to him.
And the judge told this ruffian everything
In utmost secrecy; and made him swear
Not to reveal it to a living creature,
For if he did, it would cost him his head.
When the villainous plot had been agreed,
The judge, delighted, made a fuss of him,
And gave him presents, rich and precious.
    And when they had worked out, from first to last,
Their cunning scheme to gratify his lust
(You will hear all about it soon enough),
Off home he goes, this ruffian Claudius.
The infamous judge, who was called Apius—
Such was his name, for this is a notable
Historical fact and by no means a fable,
But in the main true, there's no doubt of that—
This crooked judge, I say, now sets to work
To speed the fulfilment of his desire.

And it so happened, that one day soon after,
That this base judge, according to the tale,
Seated as usual in his judgement-hall,
Was passing judgement upon various cases,
When in this lying blackguard Claudius rushes:
'Sir, if it please you, do me justice in
This my most pitiable petition,
Which is my suit against Virginius.
And should he try to say it is not thus,
I'll prove it, and provide good evidence
That what my bill of complaint says is truth.'

The judge replied: 'On this, in his absence,
I am not able to pass final judgement.
But have him summoned, and I'll gladly hear
The case; I'll see you get full justice here.'

Virginius came to learn the judge's will;
And there and then they read the wicked bill,
The purport of which was as you shall hear:

'Sir Apius, dear my lord, it would appear
On showing of your servant Claudius,
That there's a knight, namely Virginius,
Who holds a bondslave that belongs to me,
Against all law, against all equity,
Against my express wish; one mine by right,
One who was stolen from my house at night
When she was very young: which I shall prove
So please you, with the evidence I have.
She's not his child, whatever he may say.
And therefore of you, my lord judge, I pray
Deliver me my bondslave, if you will.'
And that was the whole substance of his bill.
Virginius stared at the fellow—but
Before he could get so much as one word out,
Or prove upon his honour as a knight,
With many witnesses to bear him out,
That all his adversary said was false,
This evil judge—who would by no means wait
Or hear a word more from Virginius—
Gave judgement, and pronounced his verdict thus:

'I rule this man must have his slave forthwith;

She may be kept no longer in your house.
Go fetch her now, to be placed in our keeping.
The man shall have his bondslave; that's my ruling.'
    And so that noble knight, Virginius,
Thus forced, by verdict of this Apius,
To give his dearest daughter up to him
To live in lechery and filthy sin,
Makes his way home, and sits down in his hall,
And sends for her whom he loves more than all.
Then with a face as dead and cold as ash,
He gazed upon her meek and humble face;
A father's pity pierced him through the heart,
Yet could not change his mind; it was made up.
    'Daughter,' said he, 'Virginia is your name:
There are two choices, either death or shame,
For you to make—alas that I was born!
What have you ever done to merit death,
To die beneath the sword's edge, or the knife?
O my dear daughter, ender of my life,
Whose bringing-up has brought me such delight
That you were never once out of my thought!
O daughter, you who are the latest sorrow
Of my whole life, its latest joy also,
O gem of chastity, accept your death
With patience, for I am resolved on it,
And it is love, not hate, will have you dead,
My pitying hand that must strike off your head.
Alas that Apius ever looked on you!
This is his unjust judgement passed today'—
And he explained the circumstance to her
As you've heard tell: need I say any more?
    'O mercy, dearest father,' said the maid,
And saying this, both of her arms she laid
About his neck, as she was used to do.
The tears burst from her eyes. 'And must I die,
Is there no pardon then, no remedy?'
    'No, none, my dearest daughter,' he replied.
    'Then give me time, dear father,' answered she.
'Let me lament my death a little space,
For even Jephthah gave his daughter grace

Before he struck her dead, in which to mourn.
And God knows that she had done nothing wrong,
Except to run to be the first to see
And welcome him with fitting ceremony.'*
With these words she fell fainting to the ground,
And when she had recovered from her swoon
She raised herself, and to her father said,
'Blessed be God that I shall die a maid!
Give me my death before I can be shamed.
Do your will with your child, and in God's name!'
And over and again the girl implored
That he should strike but gently with his sword,
And as she spoke these words, fainted and fell.
Her father, with a sorrowful heart and will
Struck off her head, and seized it by the hair
And went to offer it to Apius, where
He was still passing sentence in the court.
According to the tale, when the judge saw it
He bade them take and hang him on the spot;
But right then, in a thousand people burst
To save him, out of pity and compassion,
Because the villainy had been made known.
For folk had a suspicion of the thing:
The way the rogue had presented his claim
Showed it was by consent of Apius,
For they all knew that he was lecherous.
And so they went for Apius there and then;
Without delay they threw him into prison,
And there he killed himself; and Claudius,
Who was the servant of this Apius,
Was sentenced to be hanged upon a tree;
And if Virginius had not, out of pity,
Pleaded for him, so that he was exiled,
Most certainly the man would have been killed.
Without distinction they hanged all the rest
Who had been party to this wickedness.

　　Here you may see how sin reaps its reward.
Beware then! for no man knows whom the Lord
Will smite, nor how the worm of conscience
May wince at a man's wicked life and sins,

However hid and secret they may be,
And known to no one except God and he;
And, whether lay or learned, he cannot tell
In what way or how soon dread death shall call.
So this is the advice I'd have you take:
Give sin up now, before it is too late.

What the Host said to the Doctor and the Pardoner

Our host then broke out swearing, and cried: 'God!
Lord save us! By Christ Jesus' nails and blood,
A lying rascal, and a crooked judge!
The worst death you can think of is too good
For judges and for lawyers of their sort!
And anyway, the poor young girl is dead.
Alas, her beauty was too dearly bought!
And, as I always say, it's very plain
That all such gifts of Nature, or Fortune,
Have fatal consequences, very often.
Her beauty was her death, as one might say.
Ah, what a miserable end she had!
From both those gifts that I spoke of just now,
We usually derive more harm than good.
But truly, my good sir, it was indeed
A most distressing tale to listen to.
But none the less it can't be helped—and so
Let's say no more. And now, God save and keep
Your noble self, and all your urinals,
Chamberpots, medicaments, cordials,
And every box of linctus that you've got—
May heaven and Our Lady bless the lot!
But as I live and breathe, you're a real man,
And you might be a bishop, by St Ronyan!
Didn't I manage all the hard words right?
Though I can't talk in your technical jargon,
You really touched my heart, I know—in fact
I almost had a cardinal* attack.
By corpus bones! Unless I take a tonic,
Or else a draught of fresh and malty ale,
Or hear at once some really cheerful tale,

My heart will give out, pitying that girl!
You there, friend Pardoner,' our host went on,
'Look sharp, crack a few jokes, let's have some fun!'
    'I'll do just that,' said he, 'by St Ronyan!
But first,' said he, 'as here's an alehouse sign,
I'll have a drink and snack, and then begin.'
    But forthwith all the gentlefolk protested:
'Don't let him give us any of his filth!
Tell us some moral tale, so we can learn
Wisdom by it, and then we'll gladly listen.'
    'Agreed,' said he, 'but first I've got to think
Up something decent while I have a drink.'

THE PROLOGUE OF THE PARDONER'S TALE

Radix malorum est cupiditas: Ad Thimotheus, sexto

'Gentlemen,' said he, 'I take pains to preach
In churches with a lofty, resonant voice,
Regular as a bell I ring it out,
For everything I say I have by heart:
My text's the same one as it always was—
Radix malorum est cupiditas *

love of $ is the Root of all evil

    'To start with, I declare where I've come from,
And then produce my certificates, one by one;
My licence with the seal of our lord bishop
Which I show first—that's to protect myself
So that nobody, whether priest or cleric,
Dares interdict me from Christ's holy work.
It's only after that I say my piece:
Documents, certificates, mandates, bulls
From popes, patriarchs, bishops, cardinals,
I show; and say a few words in Latin
—That's to give spice and colour to my sermon—
It also helps to stir them to devotion.
Then I bring out long boxes made of glass,
Chockful of rags and bones, each one a relic,
Or so they think; and I've got, set in brass,
The shoulderbone of one of Jacob's sheep.

cheating poor people

"Dearly beloved brethren," I begin,
"Now listen carefully. Just dip this bone
Into a well; and then if calf or cow,
Or sheep or ox, chance to swell up and sicken,
From eating worms, or else from being stung
By serpents, here's all that you have to do:
Take water from that pool, and wash its tongue,
At once it will be cured. And furthermore,
Of pox, of scab, and any kind of sore,
The sheep that drinks its water from this well
Shall be quite healed. Remember this as well:
If once a week the owner of the stock
Should drink, before the crowing of the cock,
A draught of water from this well while fasting,
According to that saintly Jacob's teaching
His cattle and his stock shall multiply.*

                                } cattle & livestock multiply

  "Also, gentlemen, it cures jealousy
Should any man fall in a jealous rage,
Make his broth with this water; I'll engage
He never will mistrust his wife again,
Though he may know the truth about her sin,
And she'd had priests for lovers by the dozen!
  "And here's a mitten too, as you can see.
Whoever puts his hand inside this mitten
Shall find the grain he sows will multiply,
Whether it's wheat or oats, so long as he
Makes a copper or a silver offering.
Good people, I must warn you of one thing:
If in this church there should be any person
Who has committed sin so horrifying
That he dare not confess to it for shame;
Or if there's any woman, young or old,
Who's turned her husband into a cuckold,
Such persons shall have neither grace nor power
To make an offering to my relics here.
But all who are clear of that kind of sin,
May come and make an offering in God's name
And be absolved, by the authority
This papal mandate here has given me."
  'And by this dodge I've gained, year after year,

A hundred marks since I was pardoner.*
I stand up in my pulpit like a priest;
When the bumpkins have all settled in their seats
I preach just as you've heard me say; and tell
A hundred taradiddles more as well.
And then I do my best to stretch my neck
And bob my head in every direction
Over the folk, now this way, and now that,
Just like a pigeon sitting on a barn.
Both hands and tongue are busy, and so quick
That it's a joy to watch me at my work.
I only preach of avarice and the like,
And in this way induce them to be free   LOL
In giving cash—especially to me.
Because my only interest is in gain;
I've none whatever in rebuking sin.
No, none! When they are pushing up the daisies,
Their souls, for all I care, can go to blazes.
No doubt about it, many a good sermon
Is mostly prompted by a bad intention;
Some curry favour and use flattery
To gain advancement through hypocrisy;
Some spring from hate, and some from vanity.
If there's no other way I dare attack,
I can sting with my tongue; and when I preach
I sting so hard, the fellow can't escape
Slander and defamation, if so be
He's wronged my fellow-pardoners, or me.
Even if I don't give his actual name,
Yet everybody knows that he's the one
From hints, and other circumstantialities—
That's how I deal with people who annoy us;
That's how I spit out venom, under guise
Of piety, and seem sincerely pious.
    'I'll tell you in a word what I'm about:
I preach for money, and for nothing else.
And so my text is what it always was:
Radix malorum est cupiditas.
Thus I know how to preach against the vice
Which masters me—and that is avarice.

Though I myself am guilty of the sin,
I know how to make other people turn
From avarice, and bitterly repent.
But that is not my principal intent.
I only preach for the emolument
But for the present, that's enough of that.
    'Next, I tell many parables and fables
Of long ago; these bumpkins love old tales,
They're easy to remember and repeat.
What do you take me for? While I can preach
And earn good money for the things I teach,
Am I to choose to live in poverty?
It's never crossed my mind—not bloody likely!
I mean to preach and beg, and live thereby
Wherever I go, in whatever lands.
You'll never catch me working with my hands
At begging I can make a better living
Than St Paul ever did at basket-making;
He's an apostle I won't imitate.
For I'll have money, wool, and cheese, and wheat,
Though given by the poorest serving-lad,
Or by the poorest widow in the place,
Were all her children dying of famine.
No, no! I'll drink the ichor of the vine,
And have a pretty girl in every town.
But hear me out now, gentlemen: in sum,
Your pleasure is that I should tell a tale.
Now that I've had a jar of malty ale,
By God on high, I hope to tell you something
Bound to be reasonably to your liking.
For although I'm a pretty vicious chap,
I can tell a story with a moral to it:
Here's one I preach to bring the money in.
Now if you'll all be quiet, I'll begin.'

THE PARDONER'S TALE

In Flanders there was once a company
Of youngsters wedded to such sin and folly
As gaming, dicing, brothels, and taverns,
Where, night and day, with harps, lutes, and citherns,
They spend their time in dicing and in dancing,
Eating and drinking more than they can carry;
And with these abominable excesses
They offer up the vilest sacrifices
To the devil in these temples of the devil.
Their oaths so blasphemous and terrible,
It makes your flesh creep just to hear them swear.
The body of our blessed Saviour
They shred to pieces with their oaths, as if
They think the Jews have not rent Him enough.
They laugh at one another's wickedness.
And in there come the dainty dancing girls,
Graceful and slim; harpers and procurers,
The young fruit-sellers and confectioners,
Who are in fact the devil's officers,
Who light and blow the fire of lechery,
Which is so close conjoined with gluttony.
I take Holy Writ to be my witness,
Lechery springs from wine and drunkenness.
    Think how the drunken Lot, against all nature,
Slept, without knowing it, with both his daughters,
So drunk he did not know what he was doing.
    When Herod (as all know who've read the tale)
Was gorged with wine as he was banqueting,
He gave the order, there at his own table,
To have the guiltless John the Baptist slain.
    And Seneca is doubtless right in saying
There is no difference that he can find
Between a man who's gone out of his mind
And one who's drunk; except it be that madness
Lasts longer, when it comes, than drunkenness.
O accursed Greed, first cause of our undoing!
Origin of our damnation and ruin,
Till Christ redeemed us with His precious blood!

In short, how dearly indeed we've all paid
For that abominable first transgression—
The world corrupted for the sake of Greed!
　　Be sure, our father Adam and his wife
For that same sin were driven from Paradise
To labour and to woe. While Adam fasted
He was in Paradise, as I have read;
But when he ate of the forbidden fruit
Upon the tree, he was at once cast out
Into the world of trouble, pain, and sadness.
We've cause to cry out against Gluttony!
O if men knew how many a malady
Proceeds from gluttony and from excess,
They'd be so much more moderate and frugal
With what they eat when they sit down at table.
O how the short throat and fastidious mouth
Cause men to labour east, west, north, and south
In earth, and air, and water, just to get
A glutton all the choicest food and drink!
St Paul, you treat the subject best, I think:
'Meat for the belly, and the belly for meats,
But God shall destroy both'—thus St Paul says.*
The Lord knows it's a filthy thing, alas!
To speak its name—yet filthier is the deed,
When a man drinks the white wine and the red
Until he turns his throat into a jakes
Through that accursed and damnable excess!
　　For the Apostle, with tears in his eyes,
Sadly remarks: 'Many walk, of whom I
Have told you often, and now tell you weeping,
That they are enemies of the cross of Christ,
Their end is death, their belly is their god.'*
O paunch! O belly! O you stinking bag!
Filled full of dung and rotten corruption,
Making a filthy noise at either end,
What an enormous labour and expense
To keep you going! These cooks, how they pound
And strain and grind, and transform and transmute
One thing into another, to placate
Your greedy gluttonous lustful appetite!

Out of the very toughest bones they beat
The marrow, since they will throw nothing out
That may slip down the gullet sweet and smooth.
And to give a still better appetite,
With spices culled from leaf and bark and root,
They make delicious sauces. None the less
Be sure that those indulging such delights
Are dead while they are living in that vice!

    Wine stirs up lechery and drunkenness,
Is full of quarrelling and wickedness.
You sot, how blotched and altered is your face,
How sour your breath, how beastly your embrace;
And through your drunken nose there seems to come
A noise like 'Samson, Samson, Samson, Samson'
—Though Samson never touched a drop of wine!
You fall down like a stuck pig; your tongue's gone;
So has your self-respect; drink is the tomb
Of a man's wit and judgement and discretion.
For no one under the domination
Of drink can keep a secret in his head.
Keep clear of wine then, whether white or red,
Especially from the white wine of Lepe
They have on sale in Fish Street, or Eastcheap.*
Because this Spanish wine, in some strange way,
Creeps into other wines that grow near by;
Such vapours rise from it, the man who thinks
He's in Eastcheap at home, after three drinks
Finds he's in Spain, right in the town of Lepe,
And not in Rochelle or in Bordeaux town;
And that's when he starts snorting, 'Samson! Samson!'

    But listen, sirs, one word more, if you please!
Let me point out that all the victories,
All the great deeds in the Old Testament
Through grace of God, Who is omnipotent,
Were won by means of abstinence and prayer;
Look in the Bible, and you'll find it there.

    Look at Attila, that great conqueror,
Think how he died in shame and dishonour,
And bleeding at the nose in drunken slumber.
I need not say a captain should keep sober.

Give serious consideration, above all,
To that commandment given to Lemuel—
Not Samuel, but Lemuel, I say—
For if you read the Bible you will see
What it lays down on serving wine to those
Who are administrators of justice.*
Enough of this; that will, I think, suffice.

   Now that I've said my piece concerning Greed,
Your gambling is the next thing I'll forbid.
Mother of lies! That's what gambling is,
True mother of deceits, damned perjuries,
Manslaughter, abominable blasphemies,
And waste of time and money. Furthermore,
It's a reproach, a matter of dishonour,
To be reputed for a common gambler.
The higher a man's rank may be, the lower
He's thought to sink. And if he be a prince
Who gambles, then the general opinion,
In all that has to do with governing
And politics, holds him in less esteem.

   Stilbon, who was a shrewd ambassador,
Was sent to Corinth with great pomp and splendour
From Sparta, to conclude an alliance;
And on arriving there, he chanced to find
All of the leading citizens of the land
Playing at dice. And so, soon as might be,
He slipped away, back to his own country:
'I will not lose my good name here,' said he,
'Nor will I do myself such dishonour
As to ally you with a set of gamblers.
Send other competent ambassadors:
For on my honour I prefer to die
Than to become the instrument whereby
Spartans ally themselves to dice-players!
I will not be the agent of a treaty
Between them and you, so glorious in honour!'
That's what he said, that wise philosopher.

   Look at the way the King of Parthia,
As told in *Polycraticus*,* sent a pair
Of golden dice to King Demetrius

condems
gambling

In scorn, because he gambled; and for this
He held Demetrius' glory and renown
To be of no account, not worth a pin!
Kings can find better ways of killing time.

  A word or two on oaths and perjuries,
As treated by the old authorities;
Swearing and blasphemy are abominable;
Perjury is still more reprehensible.
Almighty God forbade swearing at all—
See what St Matthew says; and above all,
This saying of the holy Jeremiah:
Speaking of oaths, he laid down: 'Thou shalt swear
In truth, in judgement, and in righteousness'*
But idle swearing's sinful wickedness.
See the first part of the Table of the Law,
The hallowed commands of the Lord in heaven,
What commandment the second* lays down there:
'Thou shalt not take the Name of God in vain.'
And see how He forbids us all to swear
Before forbidding killing, or worse sin;
This, I say, is the order in which they stand;
As all who comprehend them understand,
It is the second of the Ten Commandments.
And furthermore, I tell you flat that vengeance
Is never going to depart the house
Of him who offers up outrageous oaths:*
'By God's own precious blood!' and 'By God's nails!'
And 'By the blood of Jesus Christ at Hailes!*
My throw's a seven, yours a five and three!'
'By God's two arms, if you try cheating me,
I'll run this dagger through your heart and side!'
Such is their fruit, those two damned bits of bone:*
Perjury, anger, cheating, homicide.
Now for the love of Christ, Who died upon
The cross for us, and for our redemption,
Leave off all swearing, use no oaths at all!
But, gentlemen, I'll now begin my tale.

  The three loose-livers of whom I'm to tell,
A long while before the first matin bell
Had seated themselves in a tavern, drinking,

And, as they sat, they heard a handbell clinking—
A corpse was being carried to its grave.
At this one of them called his serving-lad:
'Ask who it is,' said he, 'and look alive!
Run and find out whose corpse is passing by:
And see you get his name.' 'Sir,' said the boy,
'There is no need at all for me to go;
I was told before you came, two hours ago.
And he, indeed, was an old friend of yours.
He was killed last night, all of a sudden, as
He sat up on his bench, blind drunk. There came
A softly treading thief, Death is his name,
Who's killing everybody everywhere,
And cut his heart in pieces with a spear,
And thereupon made off without a word.
Thousands he's killed, in the plague raging here.
If I were you, sir, I'd be on my guard
Before I went near such an adversary!
Always be ready to meet him anywhere—
My mother taught me that; I can't say more.'
    The innkeeper broke in, 'By St Mary!
What the child says is true; he's killed this year
In a big village over a mile from here
Every man, woman, child, workman, and boy.
That's where he's living now, I'm pretty sure.
The wisest thing's to keep a good look-out,
Or else he's like to do a fellow dirt.'
    'God's arms!' exclaimed one of these debauchees,
'Is the fellow then so dangerous to meet?
In highways and in byways, street by street,
I'll seek him out, I vow it on God's bones.
Now listen, fellows: let us three be one,
Each of us hold his hand up to the other,
And each of us become the other's brother,
And we will kill this black betrayer, Death.
And kill the killer, by God's holy breath,
And that before the sun goes down on us!'
    They pledged their word, the three of them together,
That they would live and die for one another,
As though each were the other's own born brother.

And up they jumped in frenzied drunken rage,
Set off in the direction of that village
The innkeeper had spoken of before.
Many and gruesome were the oaths they swore,
Tearing Christ's blessed body limb from limb,
Death shall be dead, if only they can catch him!
    When they'd not gone as much as half a mile,
Just as they were about to cross a stile
They met a poor old man, who greeted them
Humbly—'God save and keep you, gentlemen!'
    But the most insolent of these three rakes
Answered him back: 'Be damned to you, you wretch!
Why so wrapped up, and muffled to the eyes?
And why live on so long in such dotage?'
    The old man looked at him hard in the face,
And said, 'It is because I cannot find
Anyone, though I walked to the world's end,
In any city or in any village,
Who would exchange his youth for my old age.
And therefore I must stay an old man still
For just so long as it is heaven's will.
Not even Death, alas, will take my life!
So like a restless prisoner I pace,
And on the earth, which is my mother's gate,
Go knocking with my staff early and late,
Saying, "My dearest mother, let me in!
See how I wither, flesh, and blood, and skin!
Alas, when will my poor bones be at rest?
Dear mother, I would barter my strongbox
That's stood so long a time within my room,
Just for a haircloth shroud to wrap me in!"
But she will not do me that favour yet,
And so I bear a pale and withered face.
    'But, sirs, it is not courteous of you
To speak so roughly to an old man, who
Has not offended you by word or deed.
It's there in Holy Writ for you to read:
"Thou shalt rise up before the hoary head
Of an old man"*—and therefore do no harm,
I warn you, to an old man while you're young,

Any more than you'd like to have it done
To you in old age, should you live so long.
Now God be with you! I go where I must go.'
    'By God you shall not! Not so fast, old fellow,'
The second of the gamblers answered him:
'You shan't get off so easily, by St John!
You spoke just now about that ruffian Death
Who's killing all our friends the country round.
My word on it, as sure as you're his spy,
You'd best tell where he is, or else you'll pay,
By God and by His holy sacrament!
It's clear that you and he are in agreement
To kill young folk like us, you bloody cheat.'
    'Well, gentlemen,' said he, 'if you're so keen
To find out Death, turn up this winding road,
For on my word I left him in that grove
Under a tree, and there he will abide.
For all your braggadocio he'll not hide.
See that oak there? Right underneath you'll find
Death. God be with you, Who redeemed mankind,
And save you and amend!' said the old man.
And thereupon all three began to run
Until they reached the tree, and there they found
Gold florins, newly minted, fine and round,
And near eight bushels of them, so they thought.
Thenceforth it was no longer Death they sought,
Each of them was so happy at the sight,
Those florins looked so beautiful and bright.
They set themselves down by the precious hoard.
It was the worst of them spoke the first word:
    'Brothers,' he said, 'mark what I've got to say:
Although I play the fool, I'm pretty fly.
Upon us Fortune has bestowed this treasure
So we can live in luxury for ever.
We'll spend it—easy come, and easy go!
Whew! Holy God, but who could guess or know
That we'd have such a slice of luck today?
If only we could get this gold away,
And carry it to my house, or to yours,
—I needn't say that all this gold is ours—

We'd be in clover, happy as can be!
But obviously it can't be done by day.
People would say that we were downright thieves,
And for our rightful treasure, have us hung!
It is at night this treasure must be moved,
With every care and cunning, if we can.
And therefore this is my advice—let's all
Draw lots, and then see where the lot shall fall;
And he who draws the shortest straw shall run
Fast as he can, rejoicing, to the town,
And on the quiet buy us bread and wine.
The other two must keep a sharp look-out
And guard the gold; and if no time be lost,
We'll carry off the treasure when it's dark,
Take it wherever we decide is best.'
The speaker held the straws in his closed fist,
Told them to draw, and see where the luck fell;
And it fell to the youngest of them all,
And he set off at once towards the town.
And thereupon, so soon as he was gone,
One of the two who stayed said to the other:
'You know, of course, that you are my sworn brother.
I'll tell you something that you won't lose by.
As you can see, our friend has gone away,
And here is gold, and that in greatest plenty,
All waiting to be split between us three.
How would it be, if I can work it so
That it is only shared between us two,
Wouldn't I be doing you a friendly turn?'

   'But', said the other, 'how can it be done?
He knows quite well the gold is with us here.
What shall we do? What shall we say to him?'

   Said the first villain: 'Now, can you keep mum?
I'll tell you in a word what's to be done,
All we need do to bring it safely off.'

   'I'm on,' returned the other. 'My word on it,
Never you worry, I won't let you down.'

   'Now,' said the first, 'you know that we are two,
And two of us are stronger than just one.
Wait till he's settled, and when he sits down

Jump up, as if to grapple him in joke,
And I will skewer him right through the back
While you are scuffling with him as in fun—
And with your dagger see you do the same.
And when it's over, all this gold shall be
Shared out, dear fellow, between you and me.
Then each of us can follow his own bent,
Gaming and dicing to his heart's content.'
And thus it was this precious pair agreed,
As you've just heard me tell, to kill the third.

The youngest—the one going to the town—
Keeps turning over and over in his mind
Those lovely shining florins, new and bright.
'O Lord!' exclaimed he, 'if I only might
Keep all that treasure for myself alone,
There's none alive beneath the heavenly throne
Of God, who'd live as happily as I!'
And then at last the Fiend, our enemy,
Put it into his head to go and buy
Poison with which to murder both his friends.
You see, such was the life he led, the Fiend
Had leave to bring him to an evil end.
Because it plainly was his fixed intent
To kill them both, and never to repent.
So off he goes with no more loss of time
To find an apothecary in the town.
He asked the man if he would sell him poison,
He wanted it for putting his rats down;
Also there was a polecat in his yard
That had killed all his chickens, so he said;
For if he could he'd like to get back at
The vermin that despoiled him day and night.

The apothecary told him: 'You shall have
A thing so strong that, as my soul's to save,
In the whole world there is no living creature
Which, if it swallows any of this mixture,
No bigger amount than a grain of wheat,
But must then lose its life upon the spot;
Yes, it must die, and that in a less while,
Believe me, than it takes to walk a mile:

This poison is so strong and virulent.'

    The wretch reached out his hand for it and went,
Taking the poison with him in a box.
He hurried to a man in the next street,
From whom he borrowed three large bottles. Then
He poured the poison into two of them,
And for his own drink kept the third one clean,
Because he had made up his mind to work
Throughout the night at carrying off the gold.
And when—the devil fetch him!—he had filled
His three great bottles to the brim with wine,
He made his way back to his friends again.

    What need is there for sermonizing further?
Just as they'd planned his murder earlier,
They killed him on the spot; when this was done,
The first said to the other, 'Let's sit down
And drink and celebrate; and after that
We'll bury him.' By chance, as he said this,
He took the bottle where the poison was,
And drank, and gave it to his friend to drink,
And thereupon they both died on the spot.

    Avicenna himself has not set down
In any section of his book, *The Canon
Of Medicine*—or so I would suppose—
Symptoms of poisoning more dire than those
The wretched pair endured in their last hours.
Such was the end of the two murderers,
And of the treacherous poisoner as well.

    Most accursed sin! Iniquitous evil!
Treacherous homicide! O wickedness!
O gambling, greed, and lechery and lust!
You villainous blasphemer against Christ,
With great oaths born of habit and of pride!
Alas, mankind! How does it come about
That to your Maker, by Whom you were made,
And by Whose precious heart's blood you were bought,
You are so cruel and so false, alas!

    Dear brethren, God forgive you your trespass,
And keep you from the sin of avarice;
My holy pardon here can save you all,

And will, so long as you make offerings
Of gold and silver coin, spoons, brooches, rings—
Bow down your heads before this holy bull!
Come, ladies, make an offering of your wool!
I'll put your name down on my prayer-roll,
And you shall enter to the bliss of heaven
I shall absolve you, by my holy power,
You who make offerings, as clean and pure
As you were born!
               —There you are, gentlemen!
That's how I preach. And may Jesus Christ
Healer of souls, grant that you may receive
His pardon, for, believe me, that is best.

   But, sirs, there's one thing I forgot to add:
I've got relics and pardons in my bag
As good as anybody's in England,
All given to me by the Pope's own hand.
If any here should wish, out of devotion,
To make an offering, and have absolution,
Let them come forward now, and kneeling down
Humbly receive my blessing and pardon.
Or take my pardon as we go along,
Take it at every milestone, fresh and new,
Only renew, and yet again renew,
Your offerings in sound gold and silver coin.
It's a great thing for everybody here
To have with you a competent pardoner
As you ride through the land, should occasion
Arise, and anyone need absolution.
Who knows? For one or two of you might fall
Down from his horse and break his neck, that's all.
Think what a safeguard it must be for you
That I, who can absolve both high and low
When soul from body is about to go,
Should chance to fall in with your company!
Let me suggest that our host here begin,
Since he's the one who's most wrapped up in sin.
Step forward, Mister Host—your offering first,
And you can kiss the relics, every one!
All for a penny! Out now with your purse!

'No, not a hope! I'd sooner have Christ's curse!
Lay off!' said he. 'Not on your life I won't.
You'd only make me kiss your dirty drawers,
And swear they were the relic of some saint,
Though they were stained all over by your arse!
By the True Cross, that St Helena found,
I'd rather have your ballocks in my hand,
Than any relic in a reliquary.
Let's cut them off, and I'll help you carry
Your balls and have them set in a pig's turd!'

But the pardoner answered not a word;
He was so angered that he wouldn't speak.

'Well,' said our host, 'no use to try and joke
With folk like you, who can't keep their hair on.'
But at this point the worthy knight cut in,
For he saw the others had begun to laugh.
'Let's have no more of this; that's quite enough!
Now, Mister Pardoner, smile and cheer up!
As for you, Mister Host, come, my dear chap,
I beg you, shake hands with the pardoner.
And you, come over here, Pardoner, pray,
And let's all laugh and have fun as before.'
At this they shook hands, and rode on their way.

Fragment VIII (Group G)

THE PROLOGUE OF THE SECOND NUN'S TALE

That servant to and nourisher of vice,
She who is called in English Idleness,
That portress at the gate of sin's delights,
We ought to counter with her opposite—
That is, with innocent industriousness,
While doing all we can to keep our distance,
Lest the fiend seize us through our indolence.

For he, that with his thousand subtle snares
Is ever watching, ready to entrap
Any indolent idler that he sees,
Can easily and quickly spring the trap,
So you won't know he has you in his grip
Till he has fairly caught you by the lapel:
So work hard as you can, and don't be idle.

And even if we had no fear of death,
It plainly stands to reason, none the less,
That Idleness is arrant slothfulness,
From which comes neither profit nor goodness.
Because Sloth holds Idleness on a leash
Only to sleep and eat, drink, and devour
What other people have to labour for,

To put away from us such idleness,
Which causes ruin and calamity,
I have here tried to do my faithful best
To translate from *Legenda Aurea**
Thy glorious life and suffering and death,
Thou with thy garland wrought of rose and lily,
Thee I mean, maid and martyr, St Cecilia!

INVOCATION TO THE VIRGIN MARY

And thou that art the flower of virgins all,
Of whom St Bernard loved so well to write,
On thee, at my beginning, first I call:
Comfort of sinners, help me to relate
Thy maiden's death, who won through her merit
Eternal life, and overcame the fiend,
As, later, men may read in her legend.

Thou maid and mother, daughter of thy Son,
Thou fount of mercy, and of souls the cure,
In whom God chose to dwell and make His home,
Meek, yet exalted over every creature;
Thou who didst so so ennoble our nature
That He did not disdain to clothe and bind
His Son in blood and flesh of humankind.

Within the blessed cloister of thy side
Man's form was taken by the love and peace
That of the threefold world is Lord and guide,
Whom earth and sea and heaven without cease
Praise evermore; and thou, unspotted maid,
Bore of thy body—yet stayed virgin pure—
The Creator of every creature.

United in thee is magnificence
With mercy, goodness, and so much of pity
That thou, which art the sun of excellence,
Not only helpest those who pray to thee,
But oftentimes, in thy benignity,
Before they even make their petition
Dost go before, and art their lives' physician.

And now, fair virgin, meek and blessed, aid
Me, banished in this wilderness of gall;
Think of the woman of Canaan, who said
'And yet the dogs eat of the crumbs that fall
From their lord's table', and was blessed withal;
And though I, an unworthy son of Eve,*
Be sinful, yet do thou accept my faith.

And because faith is dead if deeds are lacking,
That I may be delivered from that darkness
Grant unto me the wit and scope for working!
O thou that art so fair and full of grace,
Be thou my advocate in that high place
Where without end the angels sing Hosanna,
Mother of Christ, dear daughter of St Anna!

My prisoned soul illumine with thy light,
For it is troubled by the contagion
Of this my flesh, and also by the weight
Of earthly lust, and of false affection;
O haven of refuge, O salvation
Of those who are in sorrow and in pain,
I shall turn to my task: do thou sustain.

Yet I beg you who may read what I write,
Please to forgive if I make no pretence
To ornament the story I narrate,
For I am offering the words and sense
Of one who held the saint in reverence ,
And wrote the tale; I follow her legend;
What is amiss, I pray you to amend.

INTERPRETATION OF THE NAME OF CECILIA AS
PROPOUNDED BY JACOBUS JANUENSIS IN
THE LEGENDA AUREA

First I'll expound the name Cecilia,
Seen in the light of the saint's history:
It signifies, in English, 'heaven's lily'*
For her pure chasteness and virginity;
Or, for the whiteness of her purity
And freshness of conscience, and of good fame
So sweet an odour, 'lily' was her name.

Or Cecilia may mean 'path for the blind'*
For the example set by her good teaching;
Or—as in the authorities I find—
Cecilia is made up by conjoining

'Heaven' with 'Leah', thereby signifying
By 'heaven' contemplation of the holy,
By 'Leah' her unceasing activity.*

Cecilia may be also said to mean
'Lacking in blindness' because of the light*
Shed by her shining virtues and wisdom;
Or look—perhaps this radiant virgin's name
Is 'heaven' with 'leos'—it could well be right,
Her good and wise works setting the example,
That she should be called 'heaven of the people'.*

For 'leos', 'people' is the English word,
And just as in the heavens one can see
The sun and moon and stars on every side,
So in this noble maiden, spiritually
One sees the courage and magnanimity
Of faith, and also wisdom's perfect radiance,
And various works brilliant with excellence.

And just as those astronomers describe
Heaven's spheres as swift, and round, as well as burning,
Even so Cecilia, beautiful and white,
Was swift and diligent in all her doings,
Round and perfect in her persevering,
And ever burning with the radiant flame
Of charity. Now I've explained her name.

THE SECOND NUN'S TALE

Here the Second Nun's Tale of the Life of Saint Cecilia begins

This lovely maid Cecilia, her Life says,
Was Roman born, and of a noble line,
And from her cradle fostered in the faith
Of Christ, Whose gospel never left her mind.
Of her it is recorded, as I find,
She never ceased to pray, fear and love God,
Beseeching Him to guard her maidenhood.

And when for this young girl the time had come
To give her hand in marriage to a man,
—This was a youth known as Valerian—
She, when the day fixed for the wedding came,
In humble piety of heart put on
Under the golden robe that so became her,
Next to her tender flesh, a shirt of hair.

And while the organ played its melody
She would sing in her heart to God alone,
'O Lord, keep Thou my soul and my body
Pure and unspotted, lest they be undone.'
And, for His love who died upon a tree,
She fasted every third or second day,
Was ever busy at her orisons.

The night came, when she had to go to bed,
Taking, as custom is, her husband with her;
But the moment that they were alone, she said,
'O sweet and most beloved husband dear,
There is a secret you may wish to hear;
Most willingly and gladly I will tell it
So long as you swear never to reveal it.'

On this Valerian swore a solemn oath
That in no circumstances, come what may,
Would he betray her secret; then at last
She said, 'There is an angel that loves me;
This angel loves me with a love so great,
Wherever I am, sleeping or awake,
He is at hand, to safeguard my body.

'And were he to perceive you—have no doubt—
Touching or making carnal love to me,
Why, then and there he'll kill you in the act,
And in the flower of your youth you'll die;
But if it's with a pure heart you love me,
Then he will love you for your purity,
And show to you his radiance and joy.'

Valerian, by God's will thus reproved,
Answered, 'If I'm to trust you, let me see
With my own eyes this angel; should it prove
To be an angel in all reality,
Then I shall do as you have asked of me;
Be sure, if it's another man you love,
Right there, and with this sword, I'll kill you both.'

To which Cecilia at once replied,
'You'll see the angel if you wish,' said she.
'If you'll believe in Christ, and be baptized.
Now go,' she told him, 'to the Appian Way,
Three miles and no more out of the city,
And speak to the poor folk who live near by,
And I shall tell you what you are to say.

'Tell them that I, Cecilia, sent you to them
For secret needs, and for a holy purpose,
That they might show you old and saintly Urban.
And when you've seen St Urban, say the words
That I have told you. And, when he has purged
All sin and guilt and wickedness from you,
You'll see that angel then, before you go.'

Valerian set off to find the spot,
And, as he'd been directed, there he found
The saintly old man, Urban, lying hid
In the catacombs, in the saints' burial ground,
And without more delaying he announced
What he had come for; and when Urban heard,
He raised his hands for joy and praised the Lord,

And from his eyes he let the salt tears fall.
'Almighty Lord, O Christ Jesus!' said he,
'Sower of pure counsel, Shepherd of us all,
The fruit of this pure seed of chastity
That Thou hast sown in Cecilia, take to Thee!
How like a bee, busy and innocent,
Cecilia serveth Thee, Thine own servant!

'That husband, very like a rampant lion,
Whom she has just now married, she sends here
To Thee, as meek and gentle as a lamb!'
As he was speaking, an old man appeared*
Clad in white raiment, radiant and pure,
A book with golden letters in his hand,
And suddenly stood before Valerian.

And he fell down in terror, like one dead,
On seeing him; the other thereupon
Lifted him up, and then began to read:
'One Lord, one Faith, one God, one Christendom,
One Father omnipotent and supreme,
And Father of all creatures everywhere.'
These words were written in gold letters there.

When these words had been read, said the old man:
'Do you believe this? Answer yes or no.'
'All this I do believe,' said Valerian,
'Indeed I would maintain no living man
Could ever imagine a thing more true.'
The old man vanished then—he knew not where—
And the Pope Urban christened him right there.

   Valerian goes home to find Cecilia
Standing beside her angel in his room.
Two garlands made of roses and of lilies
This angel carried; one in either hand.
It was to Cecilia, I understand,
He gave the first; and afterwards he took
The other to Valerian, her helpmate.

'With clean unspotted thoughts and pure bodies
Cherish these garlands all your lives,' said he.
'I have brought them to you from Paradise;
I promise you they never will decay,
Nor ever lose their sweet smell; that no eye
Shall look on them, unless the owner be
One who is chaste and loathes all lechery.

'And because you, Valerian, so soon
Took the right path, when it was shown to you,
Ask what you wish, and you shall have your boon.'
'I have a brother', said Valerian,
'Whom I love more than any living man.
I pray you that he may be granted grace
To know the truth, as I do, in this place.'

'Most pleasing to the Lord is your request:
Both of you, bearing the palms of martyrdom,
Shall be invited to His blessed feast.'
And, as he spoke, his brother Tiburce came.
When he perceived the fragrance in the room
That from the roses and the lilies spread,
He greatly wondered in his heart, and said:

'I wonder that, at this time of the year,
Whence that sweet odorous perfume can come,
The roses and the lilies I smell here,
For even if my hands were full of them,
I shouldn't think their scent could be more strong.
And in my heart the fragrance that I feel
Has changed me; I am not the same at all.'

Valerian said, 'Two coronals we have,
One snow-white, one rose-red, that brightly shine,
Which your eyes have no power to perceive,
But, as it's through my prayer you can divine
Them by their smell, so, dearest brother, you
Shall see them, if you hasten to believe
As you should, and acknowledge what is true.'

Tiburce replied, 'Is it in reality
You speak, or do I hear you in a dream?'
Returned Valerian, 'In a dream, surely,
Up to this moment you and I have been.
But now we live in truth for the first time.'
'How do you know?' asked Tiburce. 'In what way?'
Valerian said, 'Listen to what I'll say.

'It was God's angel who taught me the truth,
Which you shall see, if only you'll deny
The idols and be pure—otherwise not.'
(And of the miracle of the two wreaths,
In his preface, St Ambrose chose to speak.*
That loved and noble teacher solemnly
Commends it, and he puts it in this way:

'St Cecilia, in order to receive
The palm of martyrdom, filled with God's grace
Gave up the world, gave up the marriage-bed;
Witness Valerian's and Tiburce's
Conversion, to whom God in His goodness
Chose to assign two fragrant coronals
Of flowers, brought to them by His angel.

'This virgin brought these men to bliss above;
The world has come to know the worth, for certain,
Of dedicated chastity in love.')
And then Cecilia made it clear and plain
To him all idols are futile and vain,
Not only are they dumb, they're also deaf;
And she enjoined Tiburce to cast them off.

'Who does not believe this, is a brute beast,'
So Tiburce answered her, 'and that's no lie.'
And, hearing this, she kissed him on the breast,
Filled with delight that he could see the truth.
'I count you as my kinsman from today,'
This blessed virgin, lovely and beloved,
Told him; and after that went on to say:

'Just as the love of Jesus Christ', she said,
'Made me your brother's wife, just so do I
Accept you here and now as my comrade,
Because you've made your mind up to deny
Your idols. Go now with your brother, be
Cleansed and baptized, so that you may behold
That angel's face, of which your brother told.'

To this Tiburce replied, 'First tell me where
I am to go, dear brother, and to whom?'
'To whom?' Valerian said, 'be of good cheer,
For I am taking you to Pope Urban.'
'To Urban, brother? Dear Valerian,'
Cried Tiburce, 'you're not taking me to him?
It seems to me that would be a strange thing.

'Do you not mean that Urban', he went on,
'Who has so often been condemned to die,
And lives in holes and corners, on the run,
And dares not stick his head out—he would be
Burned at the stake in the red fiery flames
If he were found or seen—and so would we;
They'd burn us too, to keep him company.

'And while we're looking for that deity
Hidden so secretly away in heaven,
On earth, at any rate, it's burned we'll be!'
Vehemently Cecilia answered him:
'Folk may well be afraid, and with good reason,
To lose this life of ours, my own sweet brother,
If there were only this life, and no other.

'A better life is in another place,
One never to be lost—no fear of that—
Of which God's Son has told us through His grace.
And by that Father's Son all things were made;
All beings that are capable of thought
He has entrusted, through the Holy Ghost,
With souls—the truth of this is not in doubt.

'God's heavenly Son, by word and miracle
When He was on this earth, showed to us here
There was another world where we may dwell.'
To this Tiburce replied, 'O sister dear,
Were you not saying to us earlier
Something like this—"There's but one God, and He
Is Lord in truth"—and now you speak of three?'

'I'll explain that', said she, 'before I go.
'Just as a man has got three faculties,
Imagination, memory, reason too,
Just so three Persons easily may be
In the one Being of the Deity.'
Eagerly Cecilia began to preach
To Tiburce of Christ's coming, and to teach

All the particulars of His Passion,
And how God's Son had been constrained to dwell
On earth, to bring about man's redemption,
Fettered in sin, and deadly cares as well;
All these things she explained to him until
Tiburce soon after with Valerian
Went with his mind made up to Pope Urban,

Who, thanking God with glad and joyful heart,
Baptized Tiburce, and there perfected his
Instruction, and confirmed him as God's knight.
And after that Tiburce achieved such grace
That every day he saw, with his own eyes,
The angel sent from God; whatever boon
He asked of heaven, was bestowed on him.

It would be hard to tell in order all
The many miracles that Jesus wrought
For them—but not to make too long a tale,
The Roman legal officers sought them out
And haled them up before the magistrate,
One Almachius, who questioned them and learnt
What they believed. And then he had them sent

To the image of Jupiter, and said,
'If either of you will not sacrifice
To him, my sentence is, strike off his head.'
These martyrs I am speaking of were seized
By Maximus, clerk to the magistrate,
Who felt such compassion he wept for pity
When the time came to lead them to the city.

And when this Maximus had heard their teaching
He got the executioners to give him leave
To take them to his house; and before evening
Their preaching stripped away the false beliefs
Of the executioners, and erroneous creed
Of Maximus and his people, every one,
And taught them to believe in God alone.

   Cecilia came when it was growing dark,
With priests who baptized all of them together;
And later, when it drew towards daybreak,
Spoke to them with a grave and resolute air:
'Christ's own dear beloved knights, be without fear,
And cast away from you all works of darkness,
Go arm yourselves, put on the arms of brightness.

'You have indeed fought a good fight: your course
Is finished, and your faith you have preserved.
Take the unfading crown of righteousness;
The Lord, the righteous Judge whom you have served
Shall give it to you as you have deserved.'
And when Cecilia had spoken thus,
They led them out to make their sacrifice.

But when they had been taken to the place,
To waste no words in telling you what happened,
They would not burn incense, nor sacrifice,
But on their knees the two of them fell down
With humble hearts and resolute devotion;
And both their heads were struck off on the spot,
And to the King of Heaven their souls went up.

Thereupon Maximus, who saw this happen,
Bore witness, weeping with heart fit to break,
That he had seen their souls soar up to heaven
Along with angels, radiant with light;
His words converted many, and for that
Almachius had him scourged with whips of lead,
And mercilessly flogged till he was dead.

Cecilia took him up and buried him
Gently by Tiburce and Valerian
In the same grave, and under the same stone;
And after this Almachius lost no time
But ordered his law-officers to bring
Cecilia, that she might in his presence
Make sacrifice to the god and burn incense.

But they, converted by her wise teaching,
Wept bitterly, and then, believing all
Her words, began continually crying,
'Christ, the Son of God, His Co-Equal,
Is true God; we believe this heart and soul.
He has so good a servant in His service!
This we maintain with one voice, though we perish.'

Almachius, having heard about this business,
Bade Cecilia be fetched, that he might see
What she was like; here's what he asked her first:
'What kind of woman, now, are you?' said he.
'I am a noblewoman born,' said she.
'I ask you, though it may be to your harm,
What is your faith, and your religion?'

'You've begun your inquisition foolishly,'
Said she, 'you want one query to include
Two answers; so you questioned stupidly.'
Almachius to that argument replied:
'How comes it that your answers are so rude?'
When this was asked, she answered: 'How comes it?
Out of a pure conscience and true belief.'

Almachius went on, 'Have you no respect
For my authority?' Cecilia replied,
'There's very little need to fear your might:
The power of all mortal men is like
A bladder filled with wind; when it's blown up
You can, with no more than a needle-prick,
Let all the wind out and deflate its pride.'

'You have begun by being wrong,' said he,
'And still you persevere in being wrong.
Have you not heard the edict and decree
Our noble mighty princes have ordained?
All Christian folk must pay the penalty
If they do not renounce Christianity;
But all those who abjure it may go free.'

'Your princes err, just as your nobles do,'
Said she, 'by an idiotic law
You make us guilty, and it is not true.
Because, although you know our innocence,
Seeing we hold Christ's name in reverence,
And seeing that we bear the name of Christian,
You'd lay a crime on us, as well as odium.

'But we, who know the virtue of that name
May not and cannot renounce it,' said she.
Almachius answered, 'Of these two, choose one:
Sacrifice, or repudiate Christendom;
So that you can escape death in that way.'
And thereupon the lovely blessed maid
Began to laugh, and to the judge she said:

'O judge, you stand convicted in your folly!
Would you have me repudiate innocence
To be an evildoer?' said Cecilia.
'See how he lies in open audience!
He stares, he rages, he has lost all sense!'
At this Almachius cried, 'Unhappy wretch,
Do you not know how far my arm can stretch?

'Have not our mighty princes let me have
Both power, yes, and the authority
To have folk executed or let live?
Why do you speak so proudly, then, to me?'
'I only speak with steadfastness,' said she,
'Not proudly; let me tell you, on our side
We've deadly hatred for that sin of pride.

'And if you're not afraid to hear the truth,
I'll openly and clearly demonstrate
That you have uttered a great falsehood here
In saying that your princes gave you power
To put a man to death, or make him live—
You, who can only take away a life!
That's all the power or licence that you have!

'But you can say your princes made you servant
To death; and if you lay claim to be more
You lie, so weak and feeble is your power.'
'Enough', cried Almachius, 'of your impudence!
Now sacrifice to the gods, before you go!
Insult me as you please; for I don't care,
I can bear it like a philosopher;

'But there's one thing that I will not endure:
What you've been saying of our gods,' said he.
Replied Cecilia: 'O stupid creature!
You've said no word since you first spoke to me
That did not proclaim your stupidity,
And show you up in all ways as a crass
Ignorant official, and worthless judge.

'You might as well be blind, for all the good
Your eyes are to you. When a thing is stone
And seen to be a stone by everyone,
Why, that same stone you want to call a god!
Take my advice, and touch it with your hand,
Feel it all over; stone is what you'll find;
Since you can't see, because your eyes are blind.

'How shaming is it that the people should
So mock at you, and laugh at your folly!
It's common knowledge that almighty God
Is in His heavenly dwelling in the sky,
And that these idols, as is plain to see,
Are of no use to you or themselves either,
And are in actual fact not worth a feather.'

These words and words like these she spoke to him
Till he grew furious, and ordered them
To take her to her house. 'In her own home
Burn her', he bade them, 'in a bath of flame.'
And as he had commanded, it was done;
They shut and sealed her up inside a bath,
And day and night fed a huge fire beneath.

All the long night, and the next day as well,
Despite the fire, and despite the heat,
She sat there, cool, and felt no pain at all,
Nor did it draw from her one drop of sweat.
But it was in that bath she had to meet
Her death: Almachius, evil in his heart,
Sent his agent to kill her in the bath.

Then he struck her three blows upon the neck,
This executioner; but by no means
Could cut it quite in two. Now in those times
It was by law forbidden to inflict
On anyone the pain of a fourth stroke,
Whether a light or heavy blow; therefore
This executioner dared do no more,

But half dead, with neck cut open, there
He left her lying, and away he went.
The Christian people who had been with her
Took sheets to catch her blood till it was staunched.
For three days she lived on in this torment.
The Christian faith she never ceased to teach
Those whom she had converted; or to preach.

To them she gave her goods and furnishings,
And to Pope Urban she committed them,
And said, 'I have asked this of Heaven's King,
To have respite for three days, and no more,
To recommend to you, before I go,
These souls; and also that I might endeavour
To turn my house into a church for ever.'

Saint Urban, with his deacons, secretly
Bore off the corpse, and buried it by night
Among the other saints, most honourably.
Today her house is Saint Cecilia's church,
Consecrated by Saint Urban, as was right;
And there Christ, and His saint, are fittingly
Honoured and worshipped to this very day.

THE PROLOGUE OF
THE CANON'S ASSISTANT'S TALE

After the life of St Cecilia
Was ended, we had scarcely ridden more
Than five miles when, at Broughton-under-Blean,
Our company was caught up by a man
Clad in black clothes; he had on underneath
A white surplice. His hack was dapple-grey,
In such a sweat as you would not believe;
It seemed that he'd spurred hard, three miles at least.
The horse his servant rode was sweating too,
In such a lather, he could barely go.
The foam frothed round his breastplate, spotting him
All over like a magpie with the foam.
He carried little: just a doubled-over
Bag made of leather, lying on his crupper:
This worthy travelled light, for it was summer.
And I began to wonder in my heart
What he could be, until I noticed that
His hood was sewn together with his cloak;
Then, having turned it over in my mind,
I judged he was a canon of some kind.
His hat hung down behind him by a cord,
For it was at no ambling pace he rode;
He had in fact been galloping like mad.
He'd placed a burdock-leaf beneath his hood
To ward off sweat and keep his forehead cool.
And it was something, just to see him sweat!
His forehead dripped as if it were a still
Brimful of plantain leaves, or pellitory.

As he came up with us, he gave a cry,
'God save and bless this merry company!
'You've given me', said he, 'a good hard gallop
Because I was so keen to catch you up
And join', he said, 'this happy company.'
His assistant was as full of courtesy,
And said, 'I saw you riding, gentlemen,
Very early in the morning from your inn,
So gave my lord and master here the tip,
For he's so eager to join in the fun
And ride with you; he loves to have a gossip.'

   'Good luck to you for telling him, my friend,'
Our host replied; 'it certainly looks as if
Your master were both wise and erudite
If I can judge—and a wag too, I'll bet!
Can he not tell a tale by any chance,
A tale or two to cheer our party up?'

   'Who, sir? My master? You've come to the right shop!
Of fun and games he knows more than enough:
Trust me, if you knew him as well as I
You'd be amazed at his ingenuity
And competence in skills of every sort.
He's undertaken many a great project
You gentlemen would find right difficult
To carry out, unless he showed you how!
He may not look much, riding here with you,
But he's a man it pays to get to know!
Not for a tidy sum would you forgo
His acquaintance—I'll wager all I own!
He is a man of very great acumen,
Mark my words well: a most superior man.'

   'Then will you tell me please,' replied our host,
'Is he a priest or isn't he? Or what?'

   'No, he's good deal better than a priest,'
Replied the man, 'and in a word or two
Host, if you wish, I'll sketch his trade for you.

   'I tell you that he knows such hidden arts
—But it is not from me you'll learn his tricks,
Though I do help him in his work a bit—
That all this ground that we are riding over

From here as far as Canterbury town,
He could turn all of it clean upside down,
And pave the whole of it with gold and silver!'
　　Our host exclaimed—when he'd been told all this—
'Bless us! It seems most wonderful to me,
If your master has so great an intellect,
And therefore merits everyone's respect,
He thinks so little of his dignity.
In fact his cassock isn't worth a groat,
I'd bet my life—and on a man like that!
All torn and tattered—and it's filthy too.
Why is he such a sloven, may I ask,
When he can well afford much better cloth,
—Supposing he can do all that you say?
Now will you kindly tell me that? Please do.'
　　'Why ask me?' he replied. 'So help me God,
I know he'll never come to any good!
—But I shan't ever own to saying that,
So please to keep it underneath your hat—
For he's too sharp by half, that's my belief.
And as they say, "Enough's good as a feast":
Too much is a mistake. That's why in this
I count him for an idiot and an ass.
For when a man has too much intellect
It often happens he misuses it.
That's what my master does: sore grief to me!
God mend it! And that's all I have to say.'
　　'Never mind that, my good man,' said our host,
'But since you understand your master's arts,
Let me press you to tell us what he does,
Since he's so clever and ingenious.
Where do you live—that is, if I may ask?'
　　He answered, 'In the suburbs of a town,
Skulking in dead-end lanes, in holes and corners
Where thieves and robbers naturally forgather,
Living in fear and hiding, clandestinely
Like all who do not want their presence known.
That's how it is with us, I tell you straight.'
　　'Now,' said our host, 'let me ask something else.
What's happened to the colour of your face?'

'Bad luck to it, by Peter!' said the man.
'I am so used to blowing up the fire
That I suppose it's gone and changed its colour.
I've got no time for peering in a glass,
But work to death, and study alchemy
To make gold out of copper, lead, or brass.
We mill around and gawp into the fire,
But for all that we fail of our desire,
For every single time things turn out wrong.
But there are lots of folk that we take in,
And borrow gold from—say a pound or two,
Or ten, or twelve, or many times that sum,
And make them think the very least we'll do
Is double the amount: make one pound, two.
Yet up to now it's failed, though we keep hoping
To bring it off; and so we keep on groping.
But in that science we're so far behind
We can't catch up, whatever we may say
Or swear we'll do; it slips so fast away.
Yes, it will make us beggars in the end.'

Now, while his man was talking in this vein,
The canon drew near, and heard everything
That his assistant said: for this canon
Always suspected folk whom he heard talking.
Truly, as Cato says, a guilty man
Thinks everybody only talks of him.
And that's why he edged closer to his man
So that he could hear all the conversation.
And then he shouted at him: 'Hold your tongue.
Don't say another word! For if you do,
You'll pay for it, and it will cost you dear.
You're slandering me in front of all these folk,
What's more, you're telling things you should keep dark.'

'Tell away,' cried our host, 'no matter what!
Don't give a fig for any threat of his!'

'My faith, no more I will,' the other said.

When the canon saw there was no help for it,
That all his secrets were to be betrayed,
For shame and vexation he turned and fled.

'Ah,' his assistant cried, 'now for some fun.

Now I can tell you, seeing that he's gone,
The devil choke him! everything I know.
I'll have no more to do with him henceforth,
Whether for pence or pounds, I promise you.
May shame and sorrow dog him to his death,
That fellow who first brought me to this game!
It is no game for me, I tell you straight!
That's what I feel, whatever you may say.
And yet, for all my misery and toil,
For all my worry, drudgery, and hard luck,
I couldn't ever leave it anyway.
Now would to God in heaven I'd the wit
To tell all that's to do with alchemy!
But none the less I can tell you a bit.
My master's gone, so I'll hold nothing back;
All that I know about it, I'll reveal.'

THE CANON'S ASSISTANT'S TALE

For seven years I've lived with this canon,
And I am none the better for his learning.
All that I ever had by it I've lost,
And so have many more than I, God knows.
And where I used to be so well turned out
In bright new clothes, with other gear as smart,
Now I must wear an old sock on my head.
And where my colour was once fresh and red,
Now it is wan, and of a leaden hue—
Whoever takes it up is bound to rue!
As for my eyes, they water from the wool
Pulled over them—the earnings of my toil!
Try making gold, and see how well you fare!
For that elusive science stripped me bare,
I've nothing left, whichever way I turn;
And I'm so deep in debt, into the bargain,
For all the gold I've borrowed, that in fact
Long as I live, I'll never pay it back.
Let everyone be warned by me for ever!
Whoever tries his hand at it is done for

From that time on, if he goes on with it.
Because, so help me God, all that he'll get
Will be an empty purse and addled head.
And when, thanks to his folly and madness,
He's gambled on it and lost all he has,
He eggs on other folks to do the same,
And, like himself, lose everything they own.
For rascals it's a comfort and a joy
To have companions in their misery.
An educated man once told me that.
No matter! Now I'll speak about our work.

When we are in the place where we practise
Our mystic science, we look wondrous wise,
Our jargon is so technical and abstruse!
I blow the fire till my heart gives out.
What need for me to specify the exact
Proportions of the ingredients we use,
The ounces—five or six, as it may be—
Of silver, or some other quantity;
Or busy myself naming all the things,
Orpiment,* burned bones, and iron filings,
Or tell how these ingredients are put,
Ground to fine powder, in an earthen pot,
And paper is put in, and also salt,
Before the powders I have spoken of—
And covered tightly with a sheet of glass,
And so on and so forth, besides much else;
And how the pot and glass is sealed with clay
So that no air whatever can escape;
And how we make the fire slow or brisk,
And the worry and the trouble that we have
With our materials in their vaporizing,
And in amalgamating and calcining*
Of quicksilver—crude mercury it's called.
In spite of all our skill we've always failed.
For nothing's any use, whether it be
Orpiment, sublimated mercury,
Ground litharge,* ground on sheets of porphyry,
So many ounces each—our work's in vain.
And neither is the solid matter sticking

To the bottom of the pot, nor vapours rising
Therefrom, of any help in what we're doing:
But all our labour, all our work and worry,
And also, devil take it! all the money
That we've put in, is lost and thrown away.

There are many other things pertaining to
This science of ours, but as I'm no scholar
I cannot name them in their proper order,
Still, let me list them as they come to mind,
Though I can't classify them or align—
Armenian clay,* borax, verdigris;
And sundry vessels, earthenware or glass;
Alembics, flasks, phials, crucibles,
Vaporizers, gourd-retorts, and urinals,
Stuff like that, dear enough at any price.
But there's no need to catalogue them all,
Rubeficated water,* and bull's gall,
Arsenic, sal ammoniac, and brimstone;
And I could, if it weren't a waste of time,
Reel off a list of herbs like agrimony,
Valerian, and moonwort, and so on;
Tell of our lamps kept burning, night and day,
To bring off, if we can, our enterprise;
Tell of our furnace for calcification
Of water, also its albification;*
Of chalk, unslaked lime, white of egg, ashes,
Of different powders, dung, and clay, and piss;
Waxed receptacles, saltpetre, vitriol,
And different fires made of wood and coal;
Salt of tartar, common salt, alkali,
Our combusts and coagulates; and clay
That's mixed with horse and human hair; and oil
Of tartar, yeast, rock alum, wort, argol,
And realgar; and also our absorbing
And incorporating processes; citronizing*
Of silver; our cementing and fermenting;
Our moulds, assaying vessels, and much more.

And I shall tell you, in their proper order,
As I heard them named so often by my master,
Of the four spirits and the seven bodies

Just as he taught me. The first spirit is
Quicksilver, and the second orpiment,
The third, sal ammoniac; the fourth, brimstone.
Now for the seven bodies: here they are:
Gold for the sun, and silver for the moon,
And Mars is iron; Mercury, quicksilver;
Saturn is lead, and Jupiter is tin;
Venus is copper, and that makes up seven!

    Whoever practises this damned vocation
Will never make enough by it to live on,
And every penny he lays out on it
He's bound to lose: of that I have no doubt.
Would you make parade of idiocy?
Come on then, go and take up alchemy!
And if you've got a penny to invest,
Roll up, you too can be an alchemist!
Maybe it is an easy trade to learn?
No, by the Lord no! Be you priest or canon,
Or monk or friar, or no matter what,
Though you sit at your book both day and night
Trying to learn this weird and wonderful art,
It's all in vain, by God! And worse than that!
As for teaching it to an unlettered man—
Bah! Don't talk of it, for it can't be done.
And whether he has booklearning, or none,
No matter! In the end it is all one.
For in either case, by my soul's salvation,
If they go in for alchemy, when all's done
They'll find it makes no difference at all;
Which is to say, that both are bound to fail.

    But I've forgotten to make rehearsal
Of acids, filings, fusible metal,
Of softening and hardening material,
Of oils, ablutions—to tell all would surpass
In length the length of any book there is;
So I imagine it would be as well
For all of us if I were to lay off
Reciting names, for I have named enough
To raise the very grimmest fiend from hell.

    Ah, well, forget it! The Philosopher's Stone

Or elixir, is what we're all pursuing;
And if we had it we'd be home and dry.
But as it is, I swear to God on high
For all our skill and ingenuity,
Having tried everything, it still won't come.
It's made us squander everything we own,
Which drives us almost insane with regret
But for the hope that creeps into our hearts,
Making us think, however hard we're hit,
That we'll be rescued by it in the end.
How sharp and hard, hopes and imaginings
Like these! Take it from me, it won't be found;
I warn you all the quest is never-ending.
It's trusting to the future that has led
These folk to part with all they ever had.
For them alchemy is a bitter sweet
For which they never lose their appetite
Or so it seems—for if they'd but a sheet
In which to wrap themselves up in at night,
And an old clout for walking in by day,
They'd sell them both to waste on alchemy.
They can't desist, till everything has gone.
And all the time, no matter where they be,
You can tell them by smell—the smell of brimstone.
For all the world they stink like a he-goat;
Believe you me, the reek's so rank and hot
That it would knock you down half a mile off.
So if you want to, you can tell these folk
By the pong that they give off, and threadbare clothes.
Take one of them aside and ask him why
He's down at heels and dressed so shabbily,
He'll whisper in your ear, under his breath,
That were he spotted, he'd be put to death
Because of what he knows about this science.
That's how these folk take in the innocent!
    Enough of that—I'll get on with my story.
Before the pot is put upon the fire,
My master heats the metals up together
With other things in the right quantity,
A job my master does, and none but he

—I can speak openly, now he is gone
For, all admit, he can work skilfully.
At any rate he has that reputation,
And yet he's always running into trouble.
You ask me how? It happens all the time:
Bang goes the pot, and bang goes everything!
These metals are so very combustible,
Unless they're stone and lime, our walls aren't able
To stand up to them—they'll pierce anything.
Straight through the wall they go; some burying
Themselves in earth; we've lost pounds like that—
And some gets scattered all around the floor,
Some shoots up to the roof. I have no doubt,
Though the devil never shows himself to us,
He's in there with us, the old jackanapes!
For, down in hell where he is lord and master,
There couldn't be more wrath and woe and rancour.
For when the pot explodes, then we're in trouble,
We feel ill done by and begin to squabble.

    Some say the way the fire was laid was wrong,
And others no, it was not properly blown
(At which, because it is my job, I'm scared).
'Stuff! You ignorant blockhead!' says a third,
'It wasn't tempered as it ought to be.'
'No,' says a fourth, 'now shut up, and hear me.
It was because the firing wasn't beech.
As I'm alive, that's all there is to it!'
I can't tell why it happened; all I know
Is that we're in the middle of a row.

    'Well,' says the boss, 'there's nothing to be done.
I won't be caught like that another time.
And I am pretty sure the pot was cracked.
But be that as it may, no need to panic:
So sweep the floor as usual, and be quick.
Don't lose heart, put a smile on, and cheer up!'

    Then the debris is swept into a heap
And the floor covered with a canvas sheet,
And all the rubbish thrown into a sieve
And sifted and picked over many a time.

    'By God,' says one, 'here's some of our metal,

Although it seems we haven't got it all.
And if on this occasion things went wrong,
It may be they'll come right another time.
We've got to risk our money—Lord save us,
No merchant is for ever prosperous,
And that's a fact! For at one time the sea
Drowns all his goods, and at another they
Come safe to land—'
                                'Quiet there, you fool!'
My master shouts, 'next time I'll find a way
To bring our ship home in a different style.
And if I don't, sirs, let me answer for it.
Something went wrong somewhere, I'm sure of that.'

   Another says the furnace was too hot,
But be it hot or cold, I'll say again
That every single time it turns out wrong.
We fail to win what we would have, and yet
Rave in our madness to the crack of doom.
And when we're all together in a room,
Then every man jack seems a Solomon!
If I remember right, I was once told
That everything that glisters is not gold;
Not every apple that is good to see
Is good to eat, whatever folk may say.
And look, that's just the way it is with us:
The one who seems the wisest is, by Jesus!
The biggest fool when it comes to the proof,
And the most honest-looking is a thief.
That's something I shall make you all believe
Before my tale is ended, and I leave.

PART TWO

Amongst us there's a canon regular
Who'd poison a whole city, though it were
Big as Nineveh, Alexandria, Rome,
Troy and three other cities put together.
I don't think you'd be able to set down
His bottomless deceit, his trickeries,

Not if you were to live a thousand years!
There's nobody in the whole world can touch him
At double-dealing; and, when he converses,
He'll talk in such a convoluted jargon
Spoken so craftily, that in no time
He'll make a fool of anyone, unless
He is another devil, like that canon.
He's diddled many people before this,
And will again, so long as he has breath;
Yet folk go miles, on horseback and on foot
To seek him out and make his acquaintance,
Without a notion of his fraudulence.
And if you like I'll tell you all about it.

    You honourable canons regular,
Don't imagine I'm slandering your order,
Even if my story is about a canon.
You'll find, in every order, some bad hat,
But God forbid a whole fraternity
Should pay for just one man's depravity!
To slander you is no part of my purpose,
I only want to put right what's amiss.
This tale is not directed just at you,
But lots of other people. As you know,
Among the twelve apostles called by Jesus
None of them was a traitor except Judas.
Why, then, should the others be to blame
When they were innocent? I say the same
Applies to all of you, except for this:
If in your convent there is any Judas,
Just take my tip, remove him in good time
Unless you don't mind losing your good name.
Now, gentlemen, take no offence, I pray:
I mean no harm; so hear what I've to say.

    In London there was once an annueller,*
A chantry priest who'd lived a long time there,
And made himself so useful and agreeable
To the woman in whose house he ate at table,
She wouldn't let him pay a penny for
His food or clothes, however fine they were;
So he was never short of ready money.

But never mind; I'll get on with my story,
And tell you everything about the canon
Who brought this chantry priest to rack and ruin.

   One day this rascal of a canon came
To the lodging-house where this priest had his room,
Entreating him to lend a certain sum
Of gold, which he would pay him back again.
'I'll pay you back upon the day agreed.
And if you find I'm playing you a trick,
Why, have me hung next time, hung by the neck!'

   The priest gave him a gold mark there and then;
The canon thanked him over and again,
And took his leave and went upon his way,
Then brought the money back on the third day,
And handed the gold over to the priest,
To his extreme delight and happiness.

   'Really,' he said, 'I don't mind in the least
Lending a man a pound or two, or three,
Whatever it is that I may have on me,
If he's the honest sort who'll always pay
No matter what, on the appointed day;
I never can say No to such a man.'

   'What!' the canon cried. 'Me let you down?
Now that's a new one, an unheard-of thing.
My word is something that I'll always keep
Until the day I crawl into my grave.
God forbid that it should be otherwise!
You can be as sure of that as of your Creed.
I thank God—luckily I can say this—
No man alive has ever been the worse
For lending me his gold, or money either.
In my make-up there's no deceit whatever.
And now, sir, as you've been so good to me,
And treated me with so much courtesy,
To pay you back a little for your kindness
I'll show you something: if you'd like to learn,
I'll mount for you a simple demonstration
To show my expertise in alchemy.
Now just watch, and with your own eyes you'll see me
Perform a miracle before I leave.'

'Indeed, sir?' the priest answered. 'Will you now?
Then, by St Mary! by all means do so.'
Returned the canon, 'I'm at your command, sir,
And God forbid it should be otherwise!'
How well that shark knew how to advertise
His services and his abilities!
How very true it is, such 'proffered service
Stinks'—it's an adage of the old and wise.
And very soon I'll prove it in the case
Of this canon,—fountain of all trickeries,
Who always takes most pleasure and delight
(For his heart's brimful of such fiendish plots)
In leading to destruction Christian folk.
God keep us all from his humbuggeries!
He didn't know the man with whom he dealt,
And felt no premonition of his fate,
Poor simple innocent, poor silly priest!
Soon to be blinded by covetousness,
Your understanding clouded, out of luck,
With no idea at all of the deceit
Prepared and plotted for you by that fox!
You'll never manage to elude his tricks.
Therefore, to hasten to the conclusion,
Which is about your ruin and undoing,
Unhappy man! I'll press on with the story
That tells of your thick-wittedness and folly,
And of the deceit of that other wretch,
As far as my ability will stretch.
So you suppose this canon was my boss?
No, by queen of heaven, Mister Host,
It wasn't him, it was another canon,
Who was about a hundred times as cunning.
He's taken people in, time after time—
I'm sick of rehearsing his fraud in rhyme!
And every time I talk about about his fraud
For very shame of him my cheeks grow red.
At any rate, both cheeks begin to glow,
For I've no colour, as I ought to know,
Left in my face; because the different fumes
Given off by all those metals I have named

Have wasted and consumed my complexion.
Now mark the iniquity of this canon!

'Sir,' said he to the priest, 'send your man out
To fetch some mercury, and fetch it quick;
Two or three ounces ought to be enough.
And I'll show you, as soon as he is back,
A marvel such as you have never seen.'

Replied the priest, 'No sooner said than done.'
He told his man to go and bring the stuff,
Who, ready at his bidding, soon set off
And came back with the mercury—in brief,
He brought three ounces of it to the canon,
Who very carefully put the mercury down,
Then told the man to bring some charcoal in
So he could set to work without delay.

The man brought in the charcoal right away,
And then the canon took from out his breast
A crucible, and showed it to the priest.
'See this receptacle?' said the canon,
'Now take it in your hand, and place therein
An ounce of this mercury, and begin
In Christ's name, training as an alchemist!
Very few there are I'd be prepared to show
This much of my science. For you'll see now
The experiment done right before your eyes.
And I'll transmute this metal in a trice
And make—no lie—silver as good and fine
As any that is in your purse or mine,
Or anywhere, and make it malleable;
Or else count me a liar who's unable
To show his face in public anywhere!
I've got a powder here to do the trick—
My skill depends on it; it cost me dear.
I'll show you—but first send your servant out,
And shut the door, while we two go about
Our secret business, so that none can spy
While we are working at our alchemy.'

All he commanded to be done was done.
Soon as this servant of the priest's had gone
His master saw to it the door was shut,

And without waste of time they set to work.
    The priest, as he was told by this cursed canon,
Hastened to place the crucible upon
The fire, which he diligently blew.
Into the crucible the canon threw
A powder meant to hoodwink the poor priest.
I haven't got a notion what it was,
But whether it was made of chalk, or glass
Or what have you, it wasn't worth a curse.
He bade the priest look sharp and pile the charcoal
Till it was well above the crucible.
'In token of my friendship,' said the canon,
'Your own two hands will do what must be done.'
    'A thousand thanks!' the priest, delighted, cried,
And piled the charcoal as the canon bade.
While he was hard at it, this fiendlike wretch,
That scoundrel canon, whom the devil fetch,
Out of his bosom took a seeming charcoal,
A bit of beech wherein he'd bored a hole
In which he'd placed an ounce of silver filings,
All tightly sealed with wax to keep them in.
Understand that this charcoal counterfeit
Was not, of course, prepared upon the spot,
But made beforehand, like some other stuff
He brought with him, and which I'll tell about.
Before he came, he'd planned to trick the priest,
And so he did before they went their ways;
He couldn't lay off till he'd bled him white.
Just to speak of him sets my teeth on edge.
I'd like to pay him out if I knew how,
But he is here today, and gone tomorrow,
So shifty, now you see him, now you don't.
    Now mark this, gentlemen, for the love of God!
Taking that bit of charcoal I spoke of
The canon palmed it in his hand, well hid,
And while the priest busily made a bed
Of coal, as I've described, the canon said,
'My friend, that's the wrong way of doing it.
That is not bedded as it ought to be,
But I'll soon put it right again,' said he.

'Just let me fiddle with it for a while,
I'm feeling sorry for you, by St Giles!
You're hot enough: I can see how you sweat!
Here, take a cloth and wipe away the wet!'
And while the priest was mopping at his face
The canon, damn him, took his counterfeit
Coal and placed it carefully in the middle
Of the charcoal that was on the crucible,
And blew till it began to glow and burn.

    'And now let's have a drink,' said the canon,
'Don't worry, everything will turn out right,
Take it from me. Sit down, and let's relax.'
And when at length the canon's beechwood coal
Was burned, the filings fell out of the hole
Into the crucible, as you'd expect,
Since they'd been placed exactly over it;
But the poor priest was unaware of this,
Believing that the coals were all alike,
So he'd no notion of the canon's trick.
And when the time was ripe, the alchemist
Said to the other, 'Get up, Mister Priest,
And stand beside me. As I'm fairly certain
You've got no mould, I must ask you to step
Outside and bring us back a piece of chalkstone;
And with luck I'll cut it into shape
And make a mould out of it if I can.
While you're about it, bring a bowl or pan
Filled to the brim with water, and you'll see
How successful our work will prove to be.
And, lest you ever nurse a wrong suspicion
Or doubt about my doings while you've gone,
I'll keep in sight, go with you and return.'
They first unlocked, then locked the door; in short
They took the key with them when they went out,
And came straight back again without delay—
But why should my tale take the whole long day?
He took the chalk and cut it into shape,
And made a mould of it, as I'll relate.

    Now listen: he took out of his own sleeve
—Hanging's too good for him—a small thin sheet

Of silver, not more than an ounce in weight.
Now watch him work his diabolic trick!
    He cut the mould to fit this silver bar,
Doing the job so slyly that the priest
Saw nothing; hid it up his sleeve once more,
And then picked up the stuff from off the fire
And poured it in the mould, with a pleased look,
Then threw it in the vessel filled with water,
While at the same time ordering the priest:
'Look what's in there, put your hand in and grope;
And you will find some silver there, I hope.'
—And what the devil else would you expect?
A silver sliver's silver, isn't it?
The priest plunged his hand in and fished out
A bar of purest silver. Filled with glee
In every vein, when he saw what he'd got,
He cried, 'God's blessing, and His mother's too,
The blessing of all saints be upon you,
Good Mister Canon! And their curse on me,
If I am not your man for evermore
If you will undertake instructing me
In this admirable art and secret lore.'
    'But none the less I'll have a second try,'
Said the canon, 'it's so that you can pay
Closer attention, and become expert.
And then, if need be, on another day
You can try your hand yourself in my absence
At this ingenious and subtle science.
Go, get another ounce of mercury,'
The canon went on, 'do the same with it
—Don't argue now—as with the other one
Which is now silver.'
                         And so here's the priest
Busying himself, doing the best he can
To perform all that this accursed canon
Tells him to do—how hard he blows the fire
Hoping that it will win his heart's desire!
As for the canon, he was all this while
Holding himself in readiness to beguile
The priest a second time; and as a blind,

What do you think he carried in his hand?
A hollow stick—now, gentlemen, watch out!—
The end of which held one ounce, and no more
Of silver filings, placed there as before
In the case of the charcoal counterfeit;
The filings tightly stoppered up with wax
So that he wouldn't lose the smallest scrap.
Now, while the priest was busying himself,
The canon went up to him with his stick
And, as before, he threw the powder in—
And may the foul fiend flay the hide off him
For his deceit! His every thought and act
A lie! With his ingenious loaded stick
The canon began stirring the charcoal
That had been placed above the crucible
Until the heat began to melt the wax
(As any but a blockhead knows it must)
And all that was within the stick ran out
And fell at once into the crucible.

    It couldn't have been bettered, gentlemen!
When he'd been fooled like this a second time,
The priest, suspecting nothing, was so glad
I cannot find the words that would describe
His joy and jubilation and delight!
And once again he offered all he had,
Body and soul alike, to the canon.
Who said, 'Well, sir, I may seem poor to you,
But, as you'll find, I know a thing or two.
I'm telling you that there's still more to come.'
He went on: 'Is there any copper here?'

    And the priest answered him, 'I think so, sir.'
    'If not, go and buy some without delay.
Now off with you, dear sir; don't take all day.'

    Away he went, and brought the copper back;
The canon took the copper and weighed out
An exact measure: no more than an ounce.

    My tongue's too inadequate an instrument
To utter what I think, or to pronounce
Words worthy of that double-dealing cheat,
That canon, of all wickedness the fount!

He seemed a friend to those who knew him not,
But he was fiendish, both in deed and thought.
I'm sick of telling of his knavery,
And yet I must declare it none the less,
That other people may be warned thereby,
And for no other reason, truth to tell.

He placed the copper in the crucible,
Then hastily transferred it to the fire;
Sprinkled the powder, got the priest to blow
Bent double at the bellows as before,
And all of it was nothing but a hoax,
That's how he made a monkey of the priest!
Next thing, he poured the copper in the mould,
And after that he placed it in the pan
Of water, into which he plunged his hand,
While up his sleeve, as I've already told,
He had a bar of silver tucked away.
He deftly shook it out—God damn the wretch!
—The priest knew nothing of his crafty tricks—
And left it in the bottom of the pan,
Then fumbled in the bottom till he found
And with a wonderful adroitness palmed
The bar of copper—unseen by the priest—
Hid it, then tapped the other on the chest
And said, as if in joke, 'Lord, this won't do!
Bend down and help me now, as I helped you,
Plunge in your hand and see what we've got there!'

And when the priest picked up the silver bar,
The canon said to him, 'Now let's be off
With these three metal bars that we have made,
To some goldsmith and find out what they're worth,
For on my word they're silver—if they're not
Pure solid silver, why, I'll eat my hat!
But that's a thing we'll soon put to the proof.'

So they took these three bars to be assayed,
Tested with fire and hammer by the smith;
That they were all they should be, none denied.

Was that besotted priest not overjoyed?
No bird was gladder at the break of day,
No nightingale more apt to sing in May,

No lady readier to dance and sing,
Or talk of love and matters feminine,
Nor yet no knight-at-arms more keen to win
His lady's favour with a doughty deed,
Than was that priest to learn this sorry trade!
And, turning to the canon, the priest said,
'Now tell me, for the love of Him Who died,
And if you think that I deserve it of you,
What will the formula cost me? Tell me now.'

'I warn you, by Our Lady, that it's dear,'
Said the canon. 'Except me and one friar,
There's nobody in England who can make
This powder.'
         'Never mind, but for God's sake
What must I pay for it? Do please tell me.'

'It's dear, I tell you; that's for sure,' said he.
'Sir, if you really want it—in a word
It'll cost you forty pounds,* so help me God!
Had you not shown me friendship earlier,
You would have had to pay a great deal more.'

Then the priest fetched the sum of forty pounds
In gold, and handed it to the canon
For this same formula. Everything he did
Was fraud, dissimulation, and deceit!

'Mister Priest,' said he, 'as regards my art,
I want no fame; I'd rather keep it dark;
So if you want to show me your regard,
Keep quiet on the matter—if folk heard
What I can do, they'd be so filled with envy
At me, because I practise alchemy,
It could well cost my life—by God it would!
No two ways about that.'
         'Now God forbid!
You don't say!' cried the priest. 'I'd rather spend
All that I have, though it cost me my wits,
Rather than see you suffer such a fate!'

'For your good wishes, sir, the best of luck,
Goodbye, a thousand thanks!' said the canon.
He went off, never to be seen again
After that day. When in his own good time

The priest tries out the formula—heigh-ho!
It doesn't work—he's diddled and he's done!
And that is how he baits his hook, this canon,
To lure folk on, and bring them to their ruin.

Think, gentlemen, how in all ranks of life
Men fight for gold, till hardly any's left.
So many are taken in by alchemy
I really do believe, in all good faith,
It's the chief reason for that scarcity.
And alchemists all talk so cloudily
Folk can't make head or tail of what they say,
If, indeed, nowadays they have the wit.
They can jabber on like jackdaws, polish up
The gibberish in which they take delight,
But what they're trying for, they'll never get.
If you've the cash, you'll have no trouble learning
How to transmute your money into nothing!

Here's the reward of this tomfoolery:
It transmutes happiness to misery,
Empties the biggest and heaviest purses;
And alchemy makes people earn the curses
Of those who've lent their money for the purpose.
They ought to be ashamed—can't people learn
To flee from fire when they know it burns?
To those who use alchemy, here's my tip:
Unless you want to lose all, give it up!
And better late than never; better late
—Never to prosper is too long a wait.
You can search for ever and you'll never find
The secret. Bold as Bayard,* who is blind
And blunders on and doesn't give a damn,
And will as boldly bump against a stone
As step aside—that's what you alchemists are.
I tell you, if you can't see straight, take care
Your brains aren't blinded too. Search where you like
With eyes wide open, you won't win a trick,
Not at this game, but rather squander all
That you can grab, or borrow, beg, or steal.
Damp down the fire lest it burn too fast—
Don't meddle any more with that black art

Is what I mean—or else your luck's clean out.
And if you like I'll tell you right away
What the real alchemists have got to say.
    Arnold of Villanova,* or New Town,
In his *Rosarium Philosophorum*
Says truly, 'Nobody can mortify,
That is, transmute, the metal mercury
Without the knowledge of its brother, brimstone.'
Trismegistus was first to lay it down
—That father of alchemists—and he says
'Be sure the dragon will not die unless
Killed by its brother'—meaning by the dragon
Mercury or quicksilver, and none other;
Brimstone, or sulphur, is the dragon's brother,
One taken from the sun, one from the moon.*
'Therefore,' says he—now mark what I am saying—
'Let no man trouble to explore this art
If he can't understand the aims and jargon
Of alchemists—and if he does, why then,
He is a pretty foolish sort of man.
Because this art and science is', said he,
'Indeed a mystery in a mystery.'
    And there was that disciple of Plato:
One day he asked a question of his master
(See his *Senioris Zadith Tabula
Chemica*).* This is what he wished to know:
'Tell me the name of the Philosopher's Stone.'
And Plato answered, 'It is called Titan.'
'And what is that?' 'The same as Magnesia,'
Said Plato. 'Is that the case, dear master?
This is *ignotium per ignotius*.*
What's Magnesia, if I may be so curious?'
'Let's say that it's a liquid that is made
Out of the four elements,' Plato said.
'Tell me its principle, and the basis
Of that liquid, good master, if you please.'
'No,' answered Plato, 'absolutely not!
Without exception, alchemists have sworn
Never to discover it to anyone,
Or even write about it in a book.

That secret is so very dear to Christ,
He does not wish for it to be revealed
Save only when it pleases His godhead
To enlighten humankind with such knowledge,
And also to deny it—as He wills.
And that is all; there's no more to be said.'
    And so I thus conclude: since God in heaven
Will not permit alchemists to explain
How anyone may discover this stone,
My best advice is this—let it alone.
For he who makes of God his adversary
By doing anything that is contrary
To His will, certainly he'll never thrive
Though he works at alchemy all his days.
And here I stop, for ended is my tale,
And may God grant all good men balm for bale!

Fragment IX (Group H)

THE MANCIPLE'S PROLOGUE

Don't you know where there stands a little town,
A place that people call Bob-up-and-down,
Under Blean wood, on Canterbury road?*
It's there our host began to crack his jokes:
'Well, gentlemen! It looks as if we're stuck.
Dun's in the mire! Who's to pull him out?*
Will nobody, for love or money, wake
Our friend back there? For he's a sitting duck,
Some thief might easily rob and tie him up!
Look at him nodding off—Cock's bones, look how
He'll tumble off his horse before you know!
Isn't it that confounded London cook?
Make him come forward; I'll bring him to book.
He's got to tell us all a tale, I say,
Although it won't be worth a bunch of hay.
Wake up, you cook, God damn you!' cried our host,
'What ails you to be sleeping in the morning?
Fleas in the night perhaps? Or were you drinking,
Or maybe toiling all night with some slut,
Till you can't even hold your noddle up?'
    The cook, who was all pale and colourless,
Answered, 'God bless my soul! For there has fallen
On me, I don't know why, such heaviness
I'd rather have a sleep than have a gallon
Of the best wine they sell in all Cheapside.'
    'Well, Mister Cook,' the manciple replied,
'If it's of any help, and won't displease
Anyone here who's riding in our party,
And if our host is good enough to let me,
I will for now excuse you of your tale,
For, on my word, your face is pretty pale,
Also your eyes are a bit glazed, I think;
As I should know, your breath's a rancid stink:

It's evident you must be feeling poorly.
From me, for one, you'll get no flattery!
Look at him yawning there, the drunken lout,
As if he'd swallow us upon the spot
Just keep your mouth shut, man, for heaven's sake!
May the devil stick his dirty foot in it!
Your putrid breath is poisoning us all.
For shame, you pig, you stinking animal!
Take a good look at this fine fellow here:
Would you like a crack at quintain, my sweet sir?*
I'd say you were in splendid shape for it!
I take it that you're drunker than an ape,
And that's when people start to play the fool.'
This speech enraged the cook, and made him boil:
He shook his head like mad at the manciple,
But couldn't speak; then his horse threw him off,
And there he lay, until they picked him up—
That's pretty fair horsemanship for a cook!
Too bad he ever let go of his ladle!
Before they got him back into the saddle
There was a mort of heaving to and fro
To lift him up, no end of trouble too,
So unwieldy was he—though he looked a ghost!

Then, turning to the manciple, our host
Remarked 'As I hope to be saved, I think
This fellow is so overcome with drink
He'll only botch the telling of his tale.
Whether it's wine, or old or fresh-brewed ale
That he's been drinking, he talks through his nose
And snorts and wheezes as if he'd a cold.
Also he's got more than enough to do
To keep himself and that horse of his too
Out of the mud; if he again falls off,
We'll all have our work cut out lifting up
That heavy drunken carcass—so begin
Your story, sir; I've had enough of him.

'All the same, Manciple, I'd say you were
A fool to twit him for his failings here:
Maybe some other day he'll lay a trap,
Trump up some charge and so get his own back:

I mean, he'll touch on one or two small things,
Pick holes in your accounts and reckonings
As not above-board, if put to the proof.'

'No,' said the manciple, 'that would never do!
For he could easily trip me up like that.
I'd sooner buy the mare he's riding on,
Such as it is, than start to brawl with him.
I wouldn't want to make him angry, no,
All that I said was only for a joke.
And now guess what? I have here in a flask
A sup of wine—yes, a good vintage too—
Now wait: you'll see me have a little game.
I'll get that cook to drink some, if I can;
I'll stake my life on it, he won't say no!'

And to be sure, as it turned out, the cook
Drank deep (and more's the pity) from the flask
—What was the need? He'd drunk enough already—
And, having played a tune upon the bottle,
Handed the flask back to the manciple.
No end delighted with that drink, the cook
Gave the manciple the best thanks he could.

At this our host said, laughing fit to burst,
'Now I can plainly see it's necessary
To carry plenty of good drink with us,
For it will turn rancour and acrimony
To harmony and love, and pacify
So many wrongs. O blessed be thy name,
Thou who canst thus turn earnest into game,
Honour and thanks to thy divinity,
O Bacchus!—but you'll hear no more from me
Upon that theme. Manciple, please begin
Your tale.'

                    'All right, sir,' he replied. 'Now listen.'

THE MANCIPLE'S TALE

Here the Manciple's Tale of the Crow begins

When Phoebus lived with us on earth below
As old books tell, there was no gallanter
Young knight than he in all the world; also
He was beyond a doubt its best archer;
He slew the serpent Python as it lay
Asleep and basking in the sun one day;
And many another great and famous deed
He brought off with his bow: it's there to read.

　　And he could play on any instrument:
Music it was to hear him when he sang,
To hear his voice, so pure and clear in tone.
Surely the King of Thebes, Amphion,
Whose singing raised the stones that walled his city,
Could not have sung one half so well as he!
Moreover he was the handsomest man
That is, or has been, since the world began.
What need is there to tell what he looked like?
There was no better-looking man alive;
Also he was, to cap it all, a model
Of flawless worth: noble and honourable.

　　Flower and paragon of youth was he
In liberal and chivalrous conduct,
This Phoebus; and, according to the story
He always carried, on the chance of sport,
—In token, also, of his victory
Over the serpent Python—a great bow.

　　Now in his house this Phoebus had a crow
Which he'd kept in a cage for many a day,
And taught to speak, as people teach a jay.
And this white crow, white as a snow-white swan,
Could imitate the speech of anyone,
When he'd a mind to speak, or tell a tale.
In all the world was never nightingale
Could sing a hundred thousandth part as well!

　　Now in his house this Phoebus had a wife,

Dearer by far to him than his own life;
And night and day he did his very best
To content her and treat her with respect,
Bar this: so jealous was he, truth to tell,
He would have gladly kept her in a gaol.
He'd no wish to be fooled, no more than does
Any in a like case—but what's the use?
There isn't anything that one can do.
A good wife—pure in mind and body too—
Ought never to be watched; and that's for certain;
In any case, it's labour spent in vain
To guard a bad one—it just can't be done!
Absolute folly, to my way of thinking,
To waste time keeping watch upon a woman—
The ancient writers said so in their time.

 To get back to the story I began:
I left good Phoebus doing all he can
To please her, thinking if he gave her pleasure,
Combined with manly, masterful behaviour,
No other man could oust him from her favour.
But, God knows, there's nobody can coerce
Or change in any way a thing which nature
Has naturally implanted in a creature.

 Take any bird, and put it in a cage,
And heart and soul endeavour to engage
In gently tending it with food and drink
And all the dainties of which one can think,
And keeping it as clean as ever you can;
Although its cage be of the finest gold,
Yet it would rather twenty thousand times
Fly to the forest, where it's rough and cold,
And go and feed on horrible things like worms.
Not for a moment will it cease to try
Escaping from its cage, if that may be;
The bird wants nothing but its liberty.

 Or take a cat, and feed it up with milk,
And tender meat, and make its bed of silk;
But let it see a mouse run by the wall,
It will abandon milk and meat and all,
And every dainty that is in the house,

Such is its appetite for eating mouse.
It's here you see desire dominate,
And judgement overcome by appetite.

A she-wolf's nature is of this low kind:
She'll take the roughest wolf that she can find,
Or least reputable, if she's on heat,
And it's the time when she must have a mate.

But all these instances refer to men
Who are untrue, and by no means to women.
Men have a concupiscent appetite;
The lowest things will serve for their delight,
However beautiful their wives may be.
Worse luck, this flesh of ours loves novelty
So much, it seems we cannot long take pleasure
In anything that's consonant with virtue.

Thus Phoebus, who suspected no deceit,
Was, despite all his excellent qualities
Deceived: she had another man in tow,
A man worth nothing in comparison;
For, more's the pity, it is often so,
And cause of much unhappiness and harm.

It so fell out, while Phoebus was away,
His wife sent for her fancy-man one day.
Her fancy-man? That's a coarse term indeed!
I beg your pardon: overlook it, please!

But as wise Plato says—it's there to read—
The word must be in keeping with the deed.
To give the right impression of a fact,
The word must be related to the act.
Now, I'm a plain blunt man; here's what I say:
There isn't any difference, actually,
Between a woman who's a high-born lady,
If it should happen she's unchaste in body,
And any poor girl—none apart from this—
(Supposing both of them behave amiss):
Because the gentlewoman ranks the higher,
People call her the 'lady' of her lover;
As for the other woman, as she's poor,
They label her his doxy or his whore.
God knows, when you come down to it, dear brother,

The one's laid on her back just like the other!
   Likewise I say that there's no difference
Between an usurper and a thief for instance,
Or an outlaw—I say they are the same.
To Alexander it was once explained
That as it's obvious that a dictator
Having an army, has the greater power,
Being able with its aid to massacre,
Raze all flat, burn down house and home and all,
Behold! Folk call him a great general;
The outlaw who, with his small company,
Can never do half as much harm as he,
Or bring such terrible ruin to the land,
Is called a thief or outlaw or brigand.
But, as I'm not erudite in the least,
I won't quote cartloads of authorities,
But go on with my tale as I began.
   As soon as Phoebus' wife sent for her lover,
They had it off together, then and there:
Hanging as always in its cage, the crow
Saw them at work, and never said a word.
But when its master came back home, the bird
Began to sing 'Cuckoo! Cuckoo! Cuckoo!'
Said Phoebus, 'Bird, what are you singing now?
It was another song you used to sing,
So gay it filled my heart with rejoicing
To hear your voice! What kind of song is this?'
   Replied the crow, 'A fitting song, Phoebus!
By God,' it said, 'in spite of your great worth,
Your handsome figure and your noble birth,
Despite your singing and your music-making,
You've been hoodwinked, for all your vigilance,
By one of no account set in the balance
With you! And what's more, as I live and breathe,
He isn't worth the cost price of a gnat!
In your own bed I saw him hump your wife.'
   Need I say more? Not mincing words, the crow
Gave him sure proof of her adultery,
And of his own ignominy and shame,
Which, it kept saying, its own eyes had seen.

Phoebus at length began to turn away;
He felt his heart must break in two for sorrow.
Bending his bow, he strung to it an arrow
And, raging, killed his wife; what more to say?
That's how it ended; in remorse for it
He broke up all his instruments of music,
His psaltery and harp, guitar and lute;
And then he broke his arrows and his bow,
And after that he spoke thus to the crow:

'Betrayer!' Phoebus said, 'your scorpion tongue
Brought me to ruin and confusion!
Alas that I was born! Would I had died!
O my dear wife, O jewel of delight,
Who was to me so constant and so true,
Now you lie dead, no colour in your face,
Innocent, I'll be sworn, and quite guiltless!
O reckless hand, so vile a deed to do!
O clouded mind, O fury all too heedless,
Recklessly smiting the innocent down,
Mistrustful, full of false suspicion,
Where was your sense, where did your judgement go?
O let all men beware of being rash!
Never believe without absolute proof.
Strike not too soon, before you're certain why,
Consider, think it over carefully
Before you act from anger or vexation
On no more warrant than a mere suspicion.
Thousands have perished and been brought to dust
Through reckless rage! I'll kill myself for grief.'
Then to the crow: 'O you villainous wretch!
I'll pay you back now for your lying tale.
You used to sing just like a nightingale,
But now, you wretch, you are to lose your song,
And those white feathers, every single one,
And never in your whole life speak again.
For thus men are revenged upon a traitor:
You and your offspring shall be black for ever,
Never again to make a pleasing sound,
Ever to cry against the storm and rain,
To show it was through you my wife was slain!'

He leapt upon the white crow there and then,
And tore out all its feathers, every one,
And made it black, and took away its song,
And speech as well, and slung the crow out at
The door to the devil, bad luck go with it!
And that's the reason why all crows are black.

  Take warning by this fable, sirs, I pray:
Watch out, and be most mindful what you say
Nor ever tell a man—not on your life!
That somebody's been pleasuring his wife;
Or he'll hate you like poison—that's for certain.
Learned scholars say that the great Solomon
Teaches a man to keep guard on his tongue.
But, as I say, I'm not a bookish man,
Still, this is what my mother once told me:
'For heaven's sake think on the crow,' said she,
'Watch your tongue well, my son, and keep your friend,
A wicked tongue is worse than any fiend;
Against the devil you can cross yourself.
The Lord, my son, in His unending goodness
Has walled the tongue about with lips and teeth,
So that a man should think before he speaks.
My son, so many folk—as scholars teach—
Have been undone because they talked too much;
And if there should be, speaking generally,
No harm in a few words picked carefully,
You ought at all times to restrain your tongue,
Except when speaking of the Lord, my son,
When taking pains to honour Him in prayer.
Son, the first virtue that you should learn here
Is to restrain and keep watch on your tongue;
It's what all children learn when they are young.
My son, great evil springs from ill-advised
Loquacity, when few words will suffice.
There, that's what I was always told and taught.
For sinfulness abounds in too much talk:
Do you know what a reckless tongue can do?
Just as a sword will hack an arm in half,
A tongue can cut a friendship right in two.
A windbag is to God abominable:

Read Solomon, so wise and honourable,
Read Seneca, and read the psalms of David.
Don't speak, my son, when you can nod your head.
Let everyone believe that you are deaf
If you should hear a windbag talking mischief.
The Flemings have—you may find it of use—
A saying: "The less chatter, the more peace."
No need for worry, son, if you have said
Nothing malicious; you can't be betrayed.
But once a man has spoken out of malice,
In no way can he unsay what he's said.
Whatever's said is said, and off it flies
However you repent it or regret.
He is in that man's power, to whom he's said
Words that he's disposed later to regret.
Watch out, my son, and never be a source
For gossip, whether it be true or false.
Among all folk, wherever you may go,
Keep watch upon your tongue: think of the crow.'

Fragment X (Group I)

THE PARSON'S PROLOGUE

By the time that the manciple's tale had ended,
The sun from the meridian had descended
So low that it was not, I'd estimate,
Much more than twenty-nine degrees in height.
It was then four o'clock, as I could guess:
Eleven foot, a little more or less,
My shadow lay at that time, as against
My height—11/6 was the proportion.
And furthermore, the moon's exaltation,
I mean Libra,* continued to ascend
As we were entering a village-end;
And thereupon our host—as usual, he
Gave the lead to our happy company
In matters of this kind—spoke up like this:
'Now, gentlemen and ladies,' he began,
'We're short of only one more tale—just one.
You've carried out my wishes and ideas;
We've heard, I think, from every rank and class
A tale; we've almost accomplished my plan.
God send the best of luck to him who tells
This last and liveliest of all the tales!

    'Now, what are you—a curate, Mister Priest?
Or else a full-fledged parson? Out with it!
Let's have the truth! Whichever you may be,
See you don't go and spoil our fun,' said he.
'For everyone but you has told his tale.
Shows us what's in your bag: come on, unbuckle!
For from the look of you it seems to me
You're capable of spinning us a yarn
That's worth the hearing, on some weighty theme.
Tell us a tale this minute, by cock's bones!'
    To this the parson made a tart response:
'You won't get any stories out of me.

For St Paul, when he wrote to Timothy,
Reproves all those who turn away from truth,
And tell romances, fables and like trash.
Why should my hand sow chaff, when if I wish
I can sow wheat? So I say, if you care
For moral and more edifying matter,
And if you're willing to give me an audience,
Then I will gladly, for Christ's reverence,
Give you such lawful pleasure as I can.
But I'm a Southron, don't forget; not one
For "rum, ram, ruf"—I can't alliterate,
Not that I think rhyme better, the Lord knows;
So if you like—I'll not equivocate—
I shall tell you a pleasing thing in prose,
And so wind up the game and make an end.
And now may Jesus in His mercy send
To me the wit that I may be your guide
Upon that perfect, glorious pilgrimage
Men call the heavenly Jerusalem.
If you agree, I shall begin my tale
Without delay—so tell me what you feel
About the idea—what more can I say?

    'But all the same I place this homily
Under correction of the learned; I am
Unversed in texts, and so I'll give you nothing,
Trust me, beyond the bare essential meaning.
Therefore I make this solemn protestation,
That what I say is subject to correction.'

    These words we very soon assented to,
It was the right thing, so we thought, to do,
That is, to end with something edifying,
And to afford the parson a fair hearing;
And so we told our host that he should say
That we all wanted him to tell his tale.

    Our host became the spokesman for us all,
'Good Mister Priest, good luck to you,' said he,
'Deliver us your dissertation,
But hurry up: the sun's about to set.
Bring forth your harvest, and don't take all day.
God grant that you make a good job of it!

' Say what you please, and we will gladly listen.'
And upon this, the priest began his sermon.

THE PARSON'S TALE

THIS is the longest of the tales, and it is not a tale at all but a
sermon. Like the *Tale of Melibeus* it is written in prose, and I
have also omitted it as being unlikely to interest the general
reader. Briefly, the *Parson's Tale* is a sermon on Penitence in
which is embodied a long treatise on the Seven Deadly Sins. It
begins by defining (as the Parson had promised in his *Prologue*)
'the right way to Jerusalem the Celestial'—i.e., penitence. It is
probable that the *Parson's Tale* was written in Chaucer's old age
when he realized he would be unable to complete *The Canterbury
Tales* as he had planned, and was a way of winding them up in
conformity with the 'Retraction' which follows.

THE AUTHOR'S VALEDICTION

Now I pray all those who hear or read this little treatise, if there be anything in it which pleases them, to thank Our Lord Jesus Christ from Whom proceeds all wisdom and all goodness; and if there be anything that displeases them, then I pray them to ascribe the fault to my incompetence and not my will, for I would gladly have spoken better had I the ability. As the Bible says, 'All that is written is written for our instruction' and that has been my aim.

And so I meekly beseech you, for God's mercy, that you pray for me, that Christ have mercy upon me and forgive me my trespasses, in particular my translations and my authorship of works of worldly vanity, the which I revoke in this retraction: *Troilus and Cressida, The House of Fame, The Legend of Good Women, The Book of the Duchess, The Parliament of Fowls,* those of the Canterbury Tales that tend towards sin, *The Book of the Lion,* and many other books could I remember them; and many a song and lascivious lay; that Christ in His great mercy forgive me the sin.

But for the translations of the *Consolation* of Boethius, and other books of legends of the saints, and works of morality and devotion, for these I thank Our Lord Jesus Christ and His Blessed Mother and all the saints of heaven, entreating them that they should send me grace to lament my sins and study my soul's salvation from henceforth till the day I die; and grant me the grace of true penitence, confession, and penance in this present life, through the merciful grace of Him Who is King of Kings and Priest over all Priests, Who redeemed us with the precious blood of His heart; that I may be one of those who shall be saved on the day of doom. *Qui cum patre et Spiritu Sancto vivit et regnat Deus per omnia secula. Amen.*

Here ends the Book of the Canterbury Tales compiled by Geoffrey Chaucer, on whose soul Jesus Christ have mercy.

EXPLANATORY NOTES

General Prologue

1 *Aries, the Ram*: the first sign of the zodiac, in Chaucer's time it was supposed to govern from 12 March to 11 April.

palmers: pilgrims, so called because they carried palms to show that they had been to Jerusalem.

The holy blessed martyr: St Thomas à Becket, murdered in Canterbury Cathedral in 1170.

2 *almost beyond price was his prestige*: of the Canterbury pilgrims the Knight is highest in rank. He is generally taken to represent Chaucer's ideal of knighthood, but a brilliant recent study, *Chaucer's Knight: the portrait of a medieval mercenary* by Terry Jones (Eyre Methuen, 1980) sees his portrait of the Knight as a blistering satire on contemporary professional mercenaries like the condottiere Sir John Hawkwood (d. 1394) who fought only for pay and plunder and ignored the rules of chivalry. One of his main points is that the Knight seems to have taken no part in the great patriotic battles of the Hundred Years War, such as Crécy or Poitiers, but instead attended such dubious exploits as the sack of Alexandria, and even to have fought for the Saracen Bey of Palatia 'against another heathen in Turkey'.

However, it has been pointed out by Maurice Keen in his essay 'Chaucer's Knight' (*English Court Culture in the Later Middle Ages*, ed. V. J. Scattergood and J. W. Sherborne, Duckworth, 1983) that a military record like the Knight's was neither uncommon nor necessarily disreputable, and that if some of his campaigns offered good prospects of plunder, others certainly did not; for instance, his crusading in Lithuania. Also it seems to me unlikely on artistic grounds that in describing the Canterbury pilgrims Chaucer would have led off with such an out-and-out villain as the Knight seems to be in Terry Jones's interpretation of the text.

THE KNIGHT'S CAMPAIGNS

Alexandria: besieged and sacked by King Peter de Lusignan of Cyprus in 1365. (In 1363 King Peter had visited England to obtain recruits for his crusade.) See also the *Monk's Tale*: 'Of Peter King of Cyprus'.

Prussia and Lithuania: the Knight would have crusaded (like Chaucer's friends the Le Scropes of Yorkshire) with the Teutonic Knights against the pagans of Lithuania. At the beginning or end of a campaign a great feast would be held for visiting contingents, and a place of honour would be reserved at the high table for knights who performed the most notable feats.

Algeciras: near Gibraltar, in Granada, Spain; captured from the Arabs in 1344.

Benmarin: now present-day Morocco, and part of Algeria.

Ayas and Adalia: King Peter of Cyprus captured Adalia in Turkey in 1361, and Ayas, chief port of Armenia, in 1367.

Tramassene: present-day Tlemcen in Algeria.

Palatia: on the coast of Turkey. Its Bey was expelled in 1390 by the Ottoman Turk Bajazet.

4 *She kept ... on milk and fine white bread*: nuns were forbidden by church law to keep dogs.

5 *gauds*: large beads that divided smaller prayer-beads into groups of ten.

   Amor vincit omnia: 'Love conquers all.'

   cell: a small subordinate monastery.

6 *Limiter*: friars licensed to beg were limited to certain areas, and so called 'limiters'.

   And many was the marriage ... even pay for: because he had seduced them himself.

   licentiate: licensed to hear confession.

7 *In principio*: 'In the beginning'—the first words of the Gospel of St John, used by friars as a greeting.

   cloisterer: a monk or friar confined to the monastery.

9 *fee-simple, without entail*: property owned absolutely, without conditions or limitations.

11 *a Dartmouth man, for all I know*: Dartmouth was notorious for its pirates.

   And where it came from, and from which humour: all matter, including the human body, was thought to be made of the four elements: air, water, earth, and fire. The human constitution was composed of four humours or vital fluids corresponding to these elements: blood (hot and wet: element, air); phlegm (cold and wet: element, water); black bile or melancholy (cold and dry:

element, earth); yellow bile or choler (hot and dry: element, fire). Diseases were due to an imbalance or disturbance of these 'humours'. People's characters were often defined by them— 'sanguine', 'choleric', and so on.

12 *Well-read was he in Aesculapius ... and Gaddesden*: these medical authorities are (1) the ancient Greeks: Aesculapius (god of medicine), Dioscorides (*c*. AD 50), Rufus (early second century AD), Hippocrates (founder of Greek medicine, b. 460 BC); (2) Arabian authorities: Hali (d. 994), Galen (second century AD), Avicenna (eleventh century), Rhazes (ninth century), Serapion (twelfth century), Averroës (1126–98), Damascenus (*c*. 777–857), Constantine (1015–87); (3) contemporary European authorities: Bernard (fourteenth century), Gilbertus (late thirteenth century), and Gaddesden (? 1280–1361).

13 *For she was gap-toothed, if you take my meaning*: teeth set wide apart were a sign of a lascivious nature, and also that the owner would travel.

14 *To seek some chantry ... as chaplain by a guild*: a chantry was an endowment to sing mass daily for the repose of a soul. Guilds maintained chapels in London churches; to become chaplain of one was likewise a profitable sinecure.

15 *A worthy manciple*: a manciple is an officer or employee who is responsible for buying provisions for a college or other institution.

16 *a reeve*: a steward or estate-manager appointed by a landowner to superintend his farms and workmen.

a summoner: an officer employed to summon delinquents to appear before the ecclesiastical courts and also to enforce payment of tithes and church dues. He also had power to punish adultery, fornication, and other sins not punishable by common law. The *Friar's Tale* is a satire on the abuses practised by summoners.

17 *'Questio quid juris'*: 'What is the law on this point?'

'Significavit': the opening word of a writ remanding excommunicants to prison.

18 *a garland ... outside a pub*: garlands on poles advertised a house as a tavern.

a peerless pardon-seller: pardoners or pardon-sellers sold papal indulgences, that is, commutation of penances imposed for sins. The profits were supposed to go to religious organizations or to be used for some pious purpose. Pardoners from Charing Cross had a bad reputation.

veronica: a copy of the handkerchief of St Veronica in Rome, which she lent to Christ while carrying the Cross. The imprint of His face was left on the handkerchief.

The Knight's Tale

55 *Tars*: probably Tarsia, in Turkestan.

59 *threefold deity*: Diana is known as Luna in heaven, Proserpina in hell, and Diana or Lucina on earth.

70 *for the expelling . . . neither vomit nor excrete*: in medieval medicine, three 'virtues' or powers were supposed to control the body —the 'natural' (in the liver), 'vital' (in the heart), and 'animal' (in the brain, which governed the muscles). Chaucer is saying that Arcita's injured brain could not activate the muscles to expel the poison from his liver.

   Alas, my bride!: Chaucer based the *Knight's Tale* on Boccaccio's *Teseide*, in which Arcita marries Emily on his deathbed.

77 *his cousin and his wife*: see note to p. 70 above.

The Miller's Prologue and Tale

79 *ranting like a Pilate on the stage*: that is, like the Pilate in the medieval mystery plays.

81 *Almagest*: an astronomical treatise by the great second-century astronomer, Claudius Ptolemy of Alexandria.

86 *he proffers cash*: coin was scarce in medieval times, so cash would be a useful and acceptable present, especially in a town, where there would be things to buy.

The Reeve's Prologue and Tale

100 *It seems her father was the village parson*: as priests could not marry, Simkin's wife must have been illegitimate, and consequently her father would have to give a large dowry with her.

   his freeman status and degree: as a freeman the miller could not be called upon to perform services by the lord of the manor; so he would be anxious not to damage his status.

101 *the Solar Hall at Cambridge*: Solar Hall, or King's Hall, later merged in Trinity College. It was so called because of its 'sunchambers' or bay-windowed living-rooms.

102 *Watcheer, Simon! . . . how's yor canny lass?*: both Alan and John are made to speak in a Northumbrian dialect. The place where they came from, Strother, does not now exist but may have been

near Castle Strother, near Wooler in Northumberland. John swears by 'St Cuthbert', a Northumbrian saint; he was bishop of Lindisfarne (d. 669).

103 *As the mare told the wolf, once on a time*: this refers to an old fable in which the mare tells the wolf, who wants to buy her foal, that the price is written on her hind foot. When the wolf tries to read it, she kicks him.

108 *'Help, holy cross of Bromeholme! . . . to Thee I call!'*: a piece of the True Cross was preserved in the priory of Bromeholm in Norfolk. *'In manus tuas!'* 'Into Thy hands (I commend my spirit)', Luke 22:46.

The Cook's Tale

111 *sometimes hauled with fanfares to Newgate*: 'When disorderly persons were carried to prison, they were preceded by minstrels, in order to call public attention to their disgrace' (Skeat).

The Sergeant-at-Law's Introduction, Prologue, Tale, and Epilogue

114 *In youth he wrote of Ceix and Halcyon . . . neither will I*: the story of Ceix and Halcyon is in Chaucer's first long poem, *The Book of the Duchess*. His *Legend of Good Women*—the lawyer calls it *The Legend of the Saints of Cupid*—is unfinished, and eight of the ladies whom the lawyer lists are not to be found in the poem as we have it. The two incest stories which so horrify the lawyer are told in John Gower's *Confessio Amantis*; it is likely that Chaucer was pulling Gower's leg for him.

115 *the 'Metamorphoses' of Ovid*: in the *Metamorphoses* Ovid tells the story of the nine daughters of Pierus, King of Emathia, who challenged the Muses to a contest of song. They lost and were turned into magpies.

116 *no losing double aces . . . the best chance*: in the dice game of Hazard double aces are a losing throw, and six and five a winning one.

121–2 *O Primum Mobile . . . the auspicious to the malign!*: according to medieval astronomy, the Primum Mobile was the outermost of nine spheres revolving round the earth, which was central and stationary. Each of the seven innermost spheres carried one of the seven planets, of which the Moon was one. The eighth sphere bore the fixed stars and moved slowly from west to east, while the ninth, or Primum Mobile, revolved daily from east to west, carrying everything with it. In this passage Chaucer is saying that the movement of the Primum Mobile placed the planets, especially Mars, in an unfavourable position for Constance's marriage.

127 *Egyptian Mary*: St Mary of Egypt, a repentant prostitute, lived in the desert for forty-seven years on three loaves of bread.

146 *I think I smell a Lollard in the wind*: Lollards were heretic followers of John Wyclif (1320–84), first translator of the Bible into English and church reformer. The name is thought to derive from the verb 'lollen' or 'lullen'—'to sing softly'.

147 *phisoboly*: in the original text, this was 'phislyas', a word whose origin and meaning is unknown. Probably a nonsense word: the uneducated Sea-Captain was having a shot at some technical term and muffing it.

The Sea-Captain's Tale and Epilogue

148 *It's for the sake of . . . we revel merrily!*: this tale was probably meant to be told by the Wife of Bath. When Chaucer changed his mind and assigned it to the Sea-Captain, he overlooked these lines.

152 *Ganelon of France*: Ganelon betrayed Charlemagne's army at Roncesvalles. His punishment was to be torn apart by wild horses. The story is told in the twelfth-century *Chanson de Roland*.

159 *corpus dominus*: it ought to be 'corpus domini', 'the Lord's body', but the host is no scholar.

The Prioress's Tale

161 *'Alma redemptoris'*: 'O Alma redemptoris mater' ('loving mother of our Redeemer')—the anthem sung at Advent.

164 *this second Rachel*: 'In Rama was there a voice heard, lamentation, and weeping, and great mourning, Rachel weeping for her children, and would not be comforted, for they are not.' (Matthew 2:18)

166 *Young Hugh of Lincoln*: a young boy supposed to have been killed by Jews in 1255, and commemorated in the old *Ballad of Sir Hugh*, or *The Jew's Daughter*.

The Monk's Prologue and Tale

175 *by St Madrian's holy bones*: St Madrian is an unidentified saint —probably one of the Host's malapropisms.

176 *a cellarer*: an official in charge of provisions.

182 *Tropheus*: said to be a prophet of the Chaldees, but no one knows anything about him.

185 *Zenobia*: Septima Bathzabbia, Queen of Palmyra and one of the heroines of antiquity. She extended her empire as far as Chalcedon opposite Byzantium (Istanbul) and occupied Egypt. She was defeated by the Roman Emperor Aurelian in 272. He exhibited her at his triumph but spared her life, and she ended her days in Rome.

187 *my master Petrarch*: Chaucer found the story of Zenobia in Boccaccio's *De Mulieribus Claribus*, but attributes it to Petrarch, either through ignorance or by mistake. It is an odd fact that Chaucer never mentions Boccaccio in any of his writings.

189 *Pedro, King of Spain*: Pedro the Cruel, 1334–69. By all accounts he deserved his nickname. He was stabbed to death by his brother Enrique after a long civil war. The Black Prince fought on his side at the battle of Najera (1365) and John of Gaunt, Chaucer's patron, married Pedro's daughter Constance in 1371.

It was a black eagle . . . lured the king into a trap: The 'black eagle on a field of snow' refers to the arms of Bertrand du Guesclin, who lured Pedro to his death; the 'nest of evil' was Sir Oliver Mauny (*mau ni*=wicked nest) who assisted him. This Breton knight, says the Monk, was not like Charlemagne's Oliver, the loyal friend of Roland, but like the traitor Ganelon who betrayed Charlemagne's army at Roncesvalles.

Peter, King of Cyprus: Pierre de Lusignan (d. 1369), under whom the Knight fought at the siege of Alexandria in 1365.

190 *Bernardo of Lombardy*: Bernabo Visconti, Duke of Milan, deposed and died in prison—probably poisoned—in 1385. Skeat notes 'The date of Dec. 18, 1385 is that of the latest circumstance incidentally referred to in the *Canterbury Tales*.' Chaucer probably met him when he went on an embassy to Milan in 1378. The stanza must have been written almost as soon as the news of Bernabo's death reached England: 'And you were killed, I don't know how or why.'

191 *Whoever would hear more . . . he won't let you down*: Chaucer's account of Ugolino is taken from Dante's *Inferno* (Canto xxxiii) but differs in some details.

194 *Holofernes*: see the Book of Judith in the Apocrypha.

195 *King Antiochus*: see the Book of Maccabees, chapter 9, in the Apocrypha.

197 *And Fortune turned your six-spot to an ace*: six was the highest, ace the lowest, throw at dice.

198 *your father-in-law, great Pompey*: a mistake: Pompey (Gnaeus Pompeius) was Caesar's son-in-law. His father-in-law was Pompeius Rufus.

Brutus Cassius: like other medieval writers, Chaucer made one person of Caesar's assassins Brutus and Cassius.

The Nun's Priest's Tale

203 *the equinoctial circle . . . all his power*: the equinoctial circle was an imaginary circle in the heavens round the equator, which made a complete revolution every 24 hours: therefore an hour equals fifteen degrees on the equinoctial.

205 *One of the body humours is excessive*: see *General Prologue*, note to p. 11.

209 *St Kenelm . . . King of Mercia*: Cenhelm, son of Cenwulf, King of Mercia. He succeeded his father at the age of seven in 821 and was later murdered by his aunt, Cwenthryth.

210 *the King of Egypt . . . no effect*: see Genesis 37, 40, and 41.

211 "*In principio/Mulier est hominis confusio*": 'In the beginning. woman is man's ruin.'

Now when the month . . . had passed also: in other words it was 3 May—the same day as the fight between Palamon and Arcita in the *Knight's Tale*.

212 *new Ganelon . . . utter grief to Troy!*: Ganelon betrayed Charlemagne's army at Roncesvalles in the *Chanson de Roland*. Sinon devised the wooden horse that brought about the fall of Troy (*Aeneid* II, 259 ff.).

213 *St Augustine . . . 'conditional' necessity*: St Augustine of Hippo, 345–420, Thomas Bradwardine, Archbishop of Canterbury (d. 1349), and Boethius, *c.* 470–525, who wrote the *De Consolatione Philosophiae* which Chaucer translated, were recognized authorities in the debate about free will and predestination. 'Conditional' necessity allowed for some exercise of free will; 'simple' necessity did not.

214 *that book called 'Brunel's Ass' . . . he lost his benefice*: Brunellus, or *Speculum Stultorum* ('Mirror of Fools') by Nigel Wireker (*c.* 1280) was a satirical poem in Latin. The story to which the fox refers is about a priest's son who accidentally breaks a chicken's leg. Five years later, when he was to be ordained by a visiting

bishop so that he could succeed to his father's benefice, the chicken—by then a grown-up rooster—refused to crow at the usual time in the morning, which made him too late for his ordination, and he was ruined for life.

215 *O Geoffrey de Vinsauf . . . elegized so movingly his death*: Geoffrey de Vinsauf wrote *Poetria Nova*, a treatise on poetry and the art of rhetoric, once regarded as authoritative. Chaucer was much influenced by it as a young man, but in the following verses he parodies its precepts.

216 *Not even Jack Straw . . . to lynch and kill*: one of the few references to contemporary events in *The Canterbury Tales*. Jack Straw was a colleague of Wat Tyler, and one of the leaders of the Peasants' Revolt of 1381. When the rebels entered London, the London apprentices and workmen took the opportunity of massacring the Fleming woollen manufacturers, merchants and artisans, who had been brought in and encouraged by Edward III, and whose success and prosperity made them unpopular.

The Wife of Bath's Prologue and Tale

223 *His 'trouble in the flesh' . . . I've 'power of his body' and not he*: see Corinthians 7:4 and 28.

These are the very words . . . you'll find it there: the great astronomer Claudius Ptolemy, an Alexandrian Greek of the second century. None of the proverbs that the Wife of Bath quotes come from his *Almagest*, but from a collection of sayings attributed to him.

224 *No flitch of bacon . . . Essex at Dunmow*: at Dunmow in Essex a side or flitch of bacon was customarily awarded the couple who could show they had not quarrelled or regretted their marriage over the past twelve months.

227 *the Almagest*: see note to p. 223.

231 *the rood beam*: a beam with a crucifix, spanning the arch dividing the chancel from the nave.

234 *I wore St Venus' birthmark and her seal*: everyone was supposed to bear some mark representing the planet under whose influence he or she was born.

235 *summer-game*: Midsummer-Eve revels.

Valerius and Theophrastus: two related anti-feminist works: 'Letter of Valerius to Rufus about Not Marrying' by a twelfth-century writer, Walter Map; and 'The Golden Book of Marriage' by Theophrastus.

236 *Tertullian, Chrysippus, Trotula, and Heloise*: Tertullian (third century AD) wrote 'An Exhortation to Chastity' and similar works. Chrysippus is mentioned by St Jerome. Trotula was supposed to be a woman doctor who wrote a treatise on the diseases of women. Heloise (d. 1164) was the wife of Abelard, who was castrated for marrying her.

    Who drew the picture of the lion? Who?: one of Aesop's fables, in which a lion sees a picture of a man killing a lion and remarks that if the painter had been a lion the picture would have been different.

240 *limiters*: see *General Prologue*, note to p. 6.

247 *It's rarely man climbs . . . nobility*: these three lines are a quotation from Dante's *Divina Commedia* (*Purgatorio*, VII, 121 ff.).

248 *Tullius Hostilius . . . highest rank of all*: Tullius Hostilius, 673–42 BC, began life as a shepherd.

The Friar's Tale

254 *I live far in the north country*: hell was supposed to be in the north.

259 *Twelve pence will do*: worth perhaps as much as £25 in modern money.

The Summoner's Tale

262 *limiter*: a begging friar. See note to p. 6, in the *General Prologue*.

263 *'qui cum patre'*: 'who with the Father'—the first three words of the formula with which sermons and prayers were concluded.

264 *'Deus hic'*: 'God be here'—the usual benediction on entering a house.

266 *And now may walk alone*: after serving fifty years, a friar would be granted the privilege of walking alone instead of accompanied.

    We live as the Apostle has advised: see 1 Timothy 6:8.

268 *Jovinian*: a heretic against whom St Jerome wrote his treatise *Ad Iovinianum*.

    "cor meum eructavit": 'My heart is inditing a good matter'—the opening words of Psalm 44 in the Vulgate. The verbe *eructare* also means 'to belch'.

269 *"Do not be as a lion . . . flee from thee"*: see Ecclesiasticus 4:35.

270 *As luck would have it (says Seneca)*: the three anecdotes that follow are all found in Seneca's *De Ira*.

271 *"Placebo"*: 'I will please'—the first word of Psalm 114 in the Vulgate.

272 *"Make no friendship . . . lest it repent thee'*: see Proverbs 22:24–5.

from the time of Elijah . . . thank the Lord: the Carmelites claimed that their order was founded by Elijah on Mt Carmel.

273 *letter of fraternity*: Skeat notes that friars granted letters of fraternity under the conventual seal to laymen who had given them benefactions or were likely to leave them money in their wills. In return the benefactors received a brotherly participation in such spiritual benefits as friars could confer.

274 *the Schools have done me that honour*: the university had conferred on him his degree of Master of Divinity.

The Oxford Scholar's Prologue and Tale

278 *Petrarch*: Francesco Petrarch, 1304–74. He found the story of Griselda in Boccaccio's *Decameron*, and translated it into Latin. Chaucer based his story of Griselda on Petrarch's version. These lines have been taken to mean that Chaucer met Petrarch in Padua, but there is no firm evidence.

279 *Lignano*: Giovanni de Lignano, *c.* 1310–83, professor of canon law at the university of Bologna. As Chaucer mentions his death, the *Oxford Scholar's Prologue* must have been written later than 1383.

311 *as St James says/In his epistle*: see 1 James 1:13–14.

312 *Chichevache*: 'lean cow'—the name of a monstrous cow which, according to an old French fable, fed only on patient wives—hence its emaciation.

The Merchant's Prologue and Tale

315 *Theophrastus*: author of the 'Liber Aureolus de Nuptiis' quoted by St Jerome in his *Contra Iovinianum*.

318 *Wade's boat*: Wade was a famous Germanic hero and is mentioned in the Anglo-Saxon poem of *Widsith*; but nothing is known about him or his magic boat Wingelock or Guingelot. But as Skeat remarks, 'Old widows, says Chaucer in effect, know too much of the craft of Wade's boat; they can fly from place to place in a minute, and if charged with any misdemeanour, will swear they were a mile away from the place at the time alleged. Mr Pickwick, on the other hand, being only a man, failed to set up the plea of an alibi, and suffered accordingly.'

323 *the seven deadly sins ... ramifications of that tree*: the seven
    deadly sins and their subdivisions were often likened to a tree
    with its numerous twigs and branches.

325 *Theban Amphion ... its crisis near*: Amphion, a son of Zeus,
    played on the lyre with such effect that the stones moved of their
    own accord to build the wall round Thebes. Joab the Israelite was
    one of David's generals ('Joab blew the trumpet'—2 Samuel 2:28).
    Theodamas seems to be the Thiodamus in the *Thebiad* of Statius.
    He was not a trumpeter but an augur, and his invocation to attack
    Thebes was succeeded by a sound of trumpets.

326 *Martian*: Martianus Capella, the fifth-century author of *De
    Nuptiis Philologiae et Mercurii*.

    Queen Esther ... eye on Ahasuerus: see the Book of Esther 5:2, in
    the Apocrypha.

327 *clarry, hippocras, vernage*: these are all spiced wines, said to be
    aphrodisiac.

328 *the wretched Constantine*: Constantinum After (mentioned in the
    General Prologue) was a twelfth-century Carthaginian monk.

329 *The moon ... May had kept her room so long*: Chaucer's way of
    saying that four days had passed.

333 *he who wrote The Romance of the Rose*: Chaucer is referring to
    Guillaume de Lorris, author of the first part of the *Roman de la
    Rose*.

338 *Phoebus ... Jupiter's exaltation*: in other words it was the twelfth
    of June.

    Claudian: Claudius Claudianus, a fourth-century poet, author of
    De Raptu Proserpine, an epic poem in four books.

    the son of Sirach, Jesus: the author of Ecclesiasticus in the
    Apocrypha.

The Squire's Tale

344 *Sarai*: the ancient Tartar capital, now Tzarev, near Stalingrad.

    Cambuscan: either Genghis Khan (1162–1227), or his grandson,
    Kublai Khan. But it was another grandson, Batu Khan, who made
    war on Russia.

345 *Ides of March*: 15 March.

346 *Faerie*: fairy land, where, according to tradition, King Arthur was
    taken after the battle of Camlan.

350 *Vitello, Alhazen ... Their books*: Alhazen, or Ibn Al-Huitham,
c. 956–1039, an Arab physicist and astronomer, author of a work
on optics translated by Vitello, or Witelow, a thirteenth-century
Polish mathematician. Virgil, in medieval times, was reputed to
be an enchanter and to have set up a magic mirror in Rome in
which an approaching enemy could be detected thirty miles
away.

Telephus, and Achilles' marvellous spear: Telephus was married
to one of Priam's daughters. Achilles wounded him, then healed
him with the rust from his spear.

Excepting Moses and King Solomon ... masters in that art: in
medieval times Moses and Solomon were reputed to be magicians,
like Virgil.

Aldiran ... past the meridian: Skeat identifies Aldiran with the
star Hydrae, near the forepaws of the constellation Leo. These
lines are Chaucer's elaborate way of saying it was 2 p.m. on
15 March.

353 *Blood dominates from midnight until dawn*: blood was supposed
to be the chief power at night, dominant from 12 a.m. till 6 a.m.
It was one of the four 'humours' (see *General Prologue*, note to
p. 11).

356 *Just as a beaten dog will teach a lion*: this is a reference to the
proverb, 'beat the dog before the lion'—i.e., punish a weak
creature in front of a powerful one, and the latter will take warn-
ing by it. See *Othello*, II. iii. 272: 'even so one would beat his
offenceless dog to affright an imperious lion'.

361 *Apollo ... cunning Mercury*: in other words, two months later.
The *Squire's Tale* breaks off here.

The Franklin's Prologue and Tale

362 *Colours of rhetoric*: rhetorical ornaments, devices, or figures of
speech. It was a term much used by Geoffrey de Vinsauf in his
Poetria Nova (see *Nun's Priest's Tale*, note to p. 215).

364 *Penmarch*: on the coast of Brittany, near Finisterre.

370 *Lucina*: the moon.

371 *the spring-tide is continual*: spring-tides occur when the sun and
moon are in opposition. Aurelius is asking that when the sun is
next in Leo, and the moon in opposition, that the moon may keep
pace with the sun for two years, so that the tide remains high for
that time.

372 *He hid it . . . his love for Galatea*: Pamphilus Maurilianus was a thirteenth-century poet whose *Liber de Amore* relates his love for a lady called Galatea. A manuscript of the poem exists (MS Bodley 3703).

magical operations . . . Belonging to the moon: according to medieval astrology, the twenty-eight stations of the moon correspond to the twenty-eight days of a lunar month.

375 *the ageing sun . . . Capricorn*: i.e., it was after 13 December, when the sun had entered the winter solstice.

376 *His Toledan tables . . . up to date*: here Chaucer plunges into a plethora of the latest astrological technicalities, to make the Orleans magician more impressive. Few of his audience can have understood them all; his translator certainly doesn't. But here are some gleanings from Skeat's notes to his edition of *The Canterbury Tales*:

Toledan tables: medieval astronomical tables were calculated from the latitude of Toledo.

Anni collecti, anni expansi: when calculating the movement of a planet periods of 1 to 20 years are '*anni expansi*' and from 20 to 3000 years '*anni collecti*'.

An astrolabe was an early form of sextant used for measuring the altitude of the sun and stars.

Centres: Skeats says 'centre' was 'the technical term for the end of the small brass projection on the "rete" of an astrolabe which denoted the position of a fixed star'.

Tables of proportions: a table 'by which fractional parts of a year can be taken into consideration in calculating the motions of the planets'.

The eighth sphere and its precession: see the *Sergeant-at-Law's Tale*, note to pp. 121–2.

Alnath: The eighth sphere was that of the fixed stars, supposed to move slowly from west to east about the poles of the zodiac, to account for the precession of the equinoxes, whose exact amount could be ascertained by observing the distance between the fixed star Alnath in the head of Aries and the true equinoctial point situated in the ninth sphere, or Primum Mobile. Alnath was also the moon's first mansion.

Planetary face: The signs of the zodiac were divided into thirds, or 'faces', and each face was assigned to a planet.

381 *Artemisia's perfect fidelity ... Valeria*: Artemisia was the wife of King Mausoleus, who built the Mausoleum.

Tueta was an Illyrian queen.

Bilia was the wife of Duillius, who in 260 BC defeated the Carthaginians at sea.

Rhodogune, a daughter of Darius, killed the nurse who tried to persuade her to marry again.

Valeria, the wife of Servius, also refused to marry twice.

The Doctor of Medicine's Tale

386 *Titus Livius*: the historian Livy (59 BC–AD 17). However, Chaucer probably took the story from the *Roman de la Rose*.

Apelles and Zeuxis would lose their labour: Apelles and Zeuxis (fourth century BC) were the greatest painters of ancient Greece.

392 *'Let me lament ... fitting ceremony'*: see Judges 9:29–40. Jeptha promised to sacrifice the first thing that came out of his house if God granted him victory over the Ammonites. It was his daughter who ran out; Jeptha fulfilled his vow, but first granted her two months' grace.

393 *cardinal*: another of the Host's malapropisms; he should have said 'cardiacal' or 'cardiac'.

The Pardoner's Prologue and Tale

394 *Radix malorum est cupiditas*: 'Love of money is the root of all evil' (1 Timothy 6:10).

395 *His cattle and his stock shall multiply*: see Genesis 39:37–9.

396 *A hundred marks since I was pardoner*: a hundred marks was a considerable sum: perhaps £2000 or so in today's money.

399 *'Meat for the belly ...'—thus St Paul says*: see 1 Corinthians 6:13.

'Many walk ... their belly is their god': see Philippians 3:18–19.

400 *white wine of Lepe ... Eastcheap*: Lepe was a town in Spain near Cadiz which exported cheap white wine. Spanish wines were cheaper than French, then as now. Fish Street ran into Thames Street, where Chaucer's father was a vintner.

401 *For if you read the Bible ... justice*: see Proverbs 31:4–50.

Polycraticus: a book by John of Salisbury, secretary to St Thomas à Becket, the source of this and the preceding anecdote.

402 *'Thou shalt swear . . . in righteousness'*: see Matthew 5:33–4, and
    Jeremiah 4:2.

    See the first part . . . What commandment the second: i.e. the
    third commandment, according to the Authorized Version.

    vengeance . . . outrageous oaths: see Ecclesiasticus 23:12.

    'By the blood of Jesus Christ at Hailes!': Hailes Abbey in
    Gloucestershire, now a ruin, where a phial of Christ's blood was
    once preserved.

    bits of bone: dice.

404 *"Thou shalt rise . . . an old man"*: see Leviticus 19:32.

408 *Avicenna . . . The Canon of Medicine*: Avicenna was the Western
    name for the great Arabian philosopher and scientist, Ibn Sina
    (980–1037). He features in the Doctor of Medicine's list of
    authorities in the *General Prologue*.

The Second Nun's Prologue and Tale

411 *I have here . . . Legenda Aurea*: the *Second Nun's Tale* is mostly
    an almost literal translation from the *Legenda Aurea* of Jacobus
    de Voragine.

412 *son of Eve*: this slip—for it is a nun that is supposed to be speak-
    ing—is, like the one at the beginning of the last stanza of the
    'Invocation', an indication that the *Second Nun's Tale* is an early
    work that Chaucer incorporated into the *Canterbury Tales*. It is
    almost certainly *The life of St Cecilia* that he mentions in his
    Legend of Good Women among his other works

413 *'Heaven's lily'*: Cecilia=*coeli lilia*=heaven's lily.

    'path for the blind': Cecilia=*caceis via*=path for the blind.

414 *Leah*: see Genesis 29:32–5. Leah was a symbol of the active life.

    'Lacking in blindness': from *'quam caecitate carens'*, 'as if lacking
    in blindness'.

    'heaven' with *'leos'*: Cecilia=*coelum*+*leos* (Anglo-Eaxon 'leod',
    Greek *laos*=people).

417 *an old man appeared*: obviously St Paul.

419 *In his preface, St Ambrose chose to speak*: i.e., the preface to the
    mass for St Cecilia's Day in the Ambrosian liturgy.

The Canon's Assistant's Tale

432 *Orpiment*: arsenic trisulphide. In the following lines Chaucer is
    displaying an extremely accurate acquaintance with alchemical
    terms and techniques.

432 *almagamating and calcining*: almagamating: mixing or compounding metals; calcining: oxidizing.

litharge: lead monoxide.

433 *Armenian clay*: a fine red clay.

Rubeficated water: 'reddened' water used for making gold. 'Albificated' or 'whitened' water was for making silver.

albification: clarifying or whitening: see note above.

argol . . . citronizing: argol and realgar: crude cream of tartar, and red orpiment, or arsenic disulphide. Citronizing: turning yellow or citron colour, supposed to be a necessary step in forming the Philosopher's Stone.

438 *annueller*: a priest who sings annual masses for the souls of the dead.

447 *forty pounds*: a considerable sum, about £4000 today.

448 *Bayard*: a proverbial horse.

449 *Arnold of Villanova*: The French alchemist, Arnodus de Villanova (*c.* 1235–1314), author of a treatise on alchemy from which Chaucer quotes.

Trismegistus . . . the moon: Trismegistus: Hermes Trismegistus, supposed author of many books on magic and alchemy. The sun and moon were symbols of gold and silver respectively.

Senioris Zadith Tabula Chemica: though Chaucer attributes it to Plato, this book was in fact the work of a tenth-century Arab alchemist, Muhammid ibn Umail.

ignotium per ignotius: 'explaining the unknown by the more unknown'.

The Manciple's Prologue and Tale

451 *a little town . . . on Canterbury road*: Bob-up-and-down was probably Harbledown, in Blean Forest, between Boughton and Canterbury.

Dun's in the mire! Who's to pull him out?: Skeat notes that this is an old party game. 'Dun', like 'Dobbin', is the name for a horse. 'In this game, a log of wood was brought into the room, and the cry raised, "Dun's in the mire"—i.e., the horse is stuck in the mud—and two of the company try to drag it along; if they fail, another comes to help, and so on.' What the Host means is 'Let's get a move on!'

452 *a crack at quintain, my sweet sir?*: quintain was a form of joust-
ing. The quintain was a crossbar turning on a pivot, with a shield
at one end and a sandbag at the other. The jouster had to hit the
shield with his lance and at the same time escape being hit by the
swinging bag.

The Parson's Prologue

461 *The sun from the meridian had descended ... Libra*: Skeat notes
that in Chaucer's treatise on the Astrolabe, part II, sections 41–3,
the poet explains the method of taking altitudes. 'He here says
that the sun was 29° high, and in 11. 6–9 he says that his height
was to his shadow in the proportion of 6 to 11. This comes to the
same thing, since the angle whose tangent is 6/11 is very nearly
29°.' Skeat also points out that 'the moon's exaltation' is certainly
a mistake, made either by Chaucer or his scribes, for 'Saturn's
exaltation'.

The Oxford World's Classics Website

www.worldsclassics.co.uk

- Information about new titles
- Explore the full range of Oxford World's Classics
- Links to other literary sites and the main OUP webpage
- Imaginative competitions, with bookish prizes
- Peruse the Oxford World's Classics Magazine
- Articles by editors
- Extracts from Introductions
- A forum for discussion and feedback on the series
- Special information for teachers and lecturers

www.worldsclassics.co.uk

American Literature

British and Irish Literature

Children's Literature

Classics and Ancient Literature

Colonial Literature

Eastern Literature

European Literature

History

Medieval Literature

Oxford English Drama

Poetry

Philosophy

Politics

Religion

The Oxford Shakespeare

A complete list of Oxford Paperbacks, including Oxford World's Classics, Oxford Shakespeare, Oxford Drama, and Oxford Paperback Reference, is available in the UK from the Academic Division Publicity Department, Oxford University Press, Great Clarendon Street, Oxford OX2 6DP.

In the USA, complete lists are available from the Paperbacks Marketing Manager, Oxford University Press, 198 Madison Avenue, New York, NY 10016.

Oxford Paperbacks are available from all good bookshops. In case of difficulty, customers in the UK can order direct from Oxford University Press Bookshop, Freepost, 116 High Street, Oxford OX1 4BR, enclosing full payment. Please add 10 per cent of published price for postage and packing.